JUDICIAL
Legal Limits of

AUSTRALIA AND NEW ZEALAND
The Law Book Company Ltd.
Sydney : Melbourne : Perth

CANADA AND U.S.A.
The Carswell Company Ltd.
Agincourt, Ontario

INDIA
N. M. Tripathi Private Ltd.
Bombay
and
Eastern Law House Private Ltd.
Calcutta and Delhi
M.P.P. House
Bangalore

ISRAEL
Steimatzky's Agency Ltd.
Jerusalem : Tel Aviv : Haifa

MALAYSIA : SINGAPORE : BRUNEI
Malayan Law Journal (Pte.) Ltd.
Singapore and Kuala Lumpur

PAKISTAN
Pakistan Law House
Karachi

JUDICIAL REVIEW:
Legal Limits of Official Power

by

C. T. EMERY
Lecturer in Law, Durham University and
Sometime Fellow of Emmanuel College,
Cambridge

and

B. SMYTHE
Professor of Law, Durham University

Foreword by

THE HON. SIR GORDON SLYNN
An Advocate-General of the Court of Justice
of the European Communities and
Visiting Professor of Law,
Durham University

©
Sweet & Maxwell
1986

Published in 1986 by
Sweet & Maxwell Limited of
11 New Fetter Lane, London,
Computerset by Promenade Graphics Limited, Cheltenham.
Printed in Scotland.

British Library Cataloguing in Publication Data

Emery, C. T.
Judicial review : legal limits of official power.
1. Judicial review of administrative acts
—Great Britain
I. Title II. Smythe, Bernard
344.102'66 KD4902

ISBN 0–421–34520–9
ISBN 0–421–34530–6 Pbk

To Lizzie and Jane

FOREWORD

It is not so very long ago that Lord Reid could say that we did not have a system of administrative law in the United Kingdom because until then we had not needed one. Yet, since the appearance of Wade's *Administrative Law* and De Smith's *Judicial Review of Administrative Action,* administrative law has been a serious and important part of law teaching in most if not all our universities and in many polytechnics. The vast increase in the number of cases coming before the courts, following the procedural changes introduced to allow a single form of application for judicial review, has made the subject one of even greater importance to the student as it is no doubt of greater interest to the non-lawyer member of the public. "GCHQ" was only the tip of the iceberg.

Because so much of that law is made by judges in the context of specific cases, principles are constantly developing, sometimes inconsistencies appearing and being ironed out.

This book sets out to recount the growth and to explain the techniques but, above all, to analyse the basic concepts underlying judicial review. It claims primarily to be, and is, a "teaching" book. It is not, however, as its authors claim, only an "elementary" book at any rate in the usual sense of that word. If it had been, it would be a "quick read." It is far from that. Every chapter shows the great care which has been taken in the research and the serious thinking which underlies what has been written.

The differences between appeal in the full sense, appeal on a point of law and supervisory review; the move away from error of law on the face of the record to a consideration of whether a body has acted within jurisdiction; the perennial problem of distinguishing between "law" and "fact" and between "void" and "voidable"; the real ambit of *Edwards* v. *Bairstow* and *Wednesbury*; the impact of *Anisminic*; the effectiveness of ouster and limitation clauses; teasing out "purpose" and "scope of powers" from statutory provisions; the flexibility of the court's approach to what is "unfair procedure"; the debate on *O'Reilly* v. *Mackman* are only examples of the many aspects of the subject which are discussed clearly and in depth.

There is a wealth of judicial citation and practical exercises (*e.g.* the *vires* of the acts of a bus company delivering parcels other than by bus) which are an essential part of the teaching material. But the authors go far beyond this. The inquiring approach of the teacher of jurisprudence goes along with that of the administrative lawyer in demanding answers to "how" and "why" concepts have developed and, equally important, as to why they have not. It is a challenging as well as a didactic book.

The authors, expressly, do not set out to rival Wade or De Smith; their purpose is different. This is a book not only to introduce the subject but to be used with one or other of those books. There is much material to provoke likely seminar discussion and to show both to students and to a wider readership that what the judges have done since 1945 (even if it can be subjected to critical academic analysis and even though there may be much room for further development) is such that the old feeling that our system of administrative law is wholly inferior to that of some civil law countries is now out of date. This book arrives at a time of considerable judicial activity and is a major contribution to the teaching and understanding of the subject.

European Court of Justice.

Gordon Slynn,
Advocate General.

PREFACE

Too many law undergraduates understand too little of the law of judicial review. They discover, perhaps, that notions such as "error of law," "natural justice" (or "fairness"), "reasonableness" and "public" and "private" law are central; but further progress is often impeded when they find that the notions are difficult to grasp and that it is easier to demonstrate uncertainties than to discern consistent principles in their application. The legal and constitutional role of the law of judicial review is, of course, hotly debated. We refer to this debate in Chapter 1, but it seems to us self-evident that some close acquaintance with the law itself is a prerequisite of any constructive contribution to the debate.

In writing this book we set out to provide an elementary introduction for undergraduates to a subject much treated in works of great depth and scholarship, but lacking a novice's guide. To write an "elementary" introduction, of course, requires an author to identify clearly the "elements," the principles, of the subject. As already intimated, there are those who will say that this subject has no discernible principles, and indeed the task of identifying principles has proved difficult. Some perhaps will judge that, even if the difficulties be surmountable, we have failed to surmount them. Still, with trepidation, we offer the book as our attempt in this direction. If the attempt be judged worthwhile, the book may be of interest to those other than undergraduates.

If we succeed even partially in our attempt to identify coherent principles in this branch of law we do so, of course, because the principles are there to be identified. If they are there, they are largely the creation of the judges; and among the judges of our time the late Lord Diplock was pre-eminent in this field. In recent years some of Lord Diplock's judgments may have given pause to those who prefer a judge to confine his remarks to what is strictly material to the case in hand. But with the passage of time it may appear that Lord Diplock has imparted to the law of judicial review a stimulus towards coherence comparable to that imparted 50 years ago by Lord Atkin to the law of negligence. We may recall too that Lord Diplock himself acknowledged the great contribution to the development of the law in this field of Professor de Smith whose *Judicial Review of Administrative Action* substantially identified "judicial review" as a subject capable of and requiring detailed exposition and close analysis.

In the making of this book we have enjoyed the support, and surely tried the patience, of many. We wish to thank especially our wives, to whom the book is dedicated; our secretary of secretaries, Mrs. Sheila Jobling; our colleagues and students at Durham; and our publishers to whom we delivered the manuscript, three months late, at Christmas 1985.

Salter's Gate, C.T.E.
December 1985 B.S.

We are grateful to the publishers for producing the tables of cases and statutes and for allowing us to incorporate at proof stage material which came to hand before May 1, 1986. Among later reported cases, we would have mentioned (in Chapter 2, page 60) *Shepherd & Co. Ltd.* v. *Jerrom* [1986] *The Times,* July 22 in which The Court of Appeal seems to us to have asserted an unwarrantably wide jurisdiction on questions of fact and degree arising before industrial tribunals; and (in Chapter 5, pages 183 *et seq.*) *Westminster City Council* v. *Greater London Council* [1986] 2 All E.R. 278, the controversial "forward-funding" case.

September 1986 C.T.E.
B.S.

CONTENTS

Foreword vii
Preface ix
Table of Cases xiii
Table of Statutes xxvi
Abbreviations xxxi

I. THE NATURE OF REVIEW

1. Introduction 3
2. Review Jurisdiction 29

II. GROUNDS FOR REVIEW

3. Error of Law 93
4. Law, Fact and Degree 129
5. Law and Policy 168
6. Irregular or Unfair Procedure 206

III. THE MACHINERY OF REVIEW

7. Supervisory Review: Its Place in the Legal System 247
8. Applications for Judicial Review 269
9. Choice of Machinery 311

Index 319

TABLE OF CASES

A. *v.* Liverpool City Council [1982] A.C. 363 .... 81, 317
ACT Construction Ltd. *v.* Customs & Excise Commissioners [1981] 1 W.L.R. 322 120
Agriculture, etc. Training Board *v.* Aylesbury Mushrooms Ltd. [1972] 1 W.L.R. 190 .... 209, 229
Ali *v.* Home Secretary [1984] 1 W.L.R. 663 151
An Bord Bainne Co-operative Ltd. (Irish Dairy Board) *v.* Milk Marketing Board [1984] 2 C.M.L.R. 584 .... 268, 304
Anisminic Ltd. *v.* Foreign Compensation Commission [1969] 2 A.C. 147 .... 49–52, 54–56, 59, 102–103, 137, 140–148, 152–161, 164, 166, 173, 240, 251, 300, 303, 307
Anns *v.* Merton London Borough Council [1978] A.C. 728 .... 87, 88, 89
Aristides *v.* Minister of Housing and Local Government [1970] 1 All E.R. 195 222
Arsenal Football Club Ltd. *v.* Ende [1979] A.C. 1 312
Ashbridge Investments Ltd. *v.* Minister of Housing and Local Government [1965] 1 W.L.R. 1320 .... 116, 150
Associated Picture Houses Ltd. *v.* Wednesbury Corporation [1948] 1 K.B. 223 .... 128, 131, 140, 148, 179–183, 186–188, 192, 194, 204–205, 221, 236, 317
Att.-Gen. *v.* Aspinall (1837) 2 M. & C. 613 .... 172, 267
—— *v.* Cockermouth Local Board (1874) L.R. 18 Eq. 172 248
—— *v.* Crayford Urban District Council [1962] Ch. 575 132
—— *v.* De Keyser's Royal Hotel Ltd. [1920] A.C. 508 .... 75, 81
—— *v.* Dyson [1911] 1 K.B. 410 260
—— *v.* Fulham Corporation [1921] 1 Ch. 440 132
—— *v.* Gt. Eastern Rly. Co. (1880) 5 App.Cas. 473 131
—— *v.* Manchester Corporation [1906] 1 Ch. 643 .... 24, 132
—— *v.* Oglender (1740) 1 Ves.Jun. 246 249
—— *v.* Prince Ernest Augustus of Hanover [1957] A.C. 436 300
—— *v.* Ryan [1980] A.C. 718 240
—— *v.* Smethwick Corporation [1932] 1 Ch. 562 132
Att.-Gen. *ex rel.* McWhirter *v.* I.B.A. [1973] Q.B. 629 249
Att.-Gen. (Hong Kong) *v.* Ng Yuen Shiu [1983] 2 A.C. 629 .... 198, 219, 220
Ayr Harbour Trustees *v.* Oswald (1883) 8 App.Cas. 623 .... 84, 197

Baker *v.* Willoughby [1970] A.C. 467 .... 111, 112
Baldwin & Francis Ltd. *v.* Patents Appeal Tribunal [1959] A.C. 663 164
Banaskiewicz *v.* Mulholland *The Times*, April 19, 1985, C.A. 235
Barber *v.* Manchester Regional Hospital Board [1958] 1 W.L.R. 181 224
Barnard *v.* National Dock Labour Board [1953] 2 Q.B. 18 .... 251, 307
Barnes *v.* Irwell Valley Water Board [1938] 1 K.B. 21 83
Barraclough *v.* Brown [1897] A.C. 615 313
Bates *v.* Lord Hailsham [1972] 1 W.L.R. 1373 229
Bean *v.* Doncaster Amalgamated Collieries Ltd. [1944] 2 All E.R. 279 ... 98, 100
Becker *v.* Home Office [1972] 2 Q.B. 407, C.A. 133
Bedfordshire County Council *v.* Central Electricity Generating Board [1985] J.P.L. 43 280
Berkhampstead Grammar School, *Re* [1908] 2 Ch. 25 222

Biddulph *v.* Vestry of St. George, Hanover Square (1863) 33 L.J. (Eq.) 411 ... 190
Birkdale District Electric Supply Co. *v.* Southport Corpn. [1926] A.C. 355 197
Blackburn *v.* Att.-Gen. [1971] 1 W.L.R. 1037 ... 76
Bone *v.* Mental Health Review Tribunal [1985] 3 All E.R. 330 ... 211, 317
Bourgoin S.A. *v.* Ministry of Agriculture, Fish and Food [1985] 3 All E.R. 585 ... 89, 304
Boyce *v.* Paddington Borough Council [1903] 1 Ch. 109 ... 250, 295, 301
Bracegirdle *v.* Oxley [1947] K.B. 349 ... 94, 97
Bradford Metropolitan City Council *v.* Brown, *The Times*, March 18, 1986 280
Bradbury *v.* Enfield L.B.C. [1967] 1 W.L.R. 1311 .... 207, 208, 210, 212, 250, 285, 315
Bradlaugh, *ex parte* (1878) 3 Q.B.D. 509 ... 49
Bradley & Sons *v.* Environment Secretary [1983] J.P.L. 43 ... 211
Brayhead Ltd. *v.* Berkshire County Council [1964] 2 Q.B. 303 .... 208, 210–212
British Airways Board *v.* Laker Airways Ltd. [1985] A.C. 58 ... 236
British Launderers' Research Association *v.* Hendon Rating Authority [1949] 1 K.B. 462 ... 109, 110, 111, 112, 113
British Oxygen Co. Ltd. *v.* Board of Trade [1971] A.C. 610 ... 195
Bromley London Borough Council *v.* Greater London Council [1983] 1 A.C. 768 ... 19, 85, 172, 184, 185
Brownsea Haven Properties *v.* Poole Corporation [1958] Ch. 574 ... 289
Brutus *v.* Cozens [1973] A.C. 854 ... 101, 103, 105, 107
Bunbury *v.* Fuller (1853) 156 E.R. 47 ... 31, 66, 138
Burmah Oil Co. Ltd. *v.* Bank of England [1980] A.C. 1090 ... 79, 81
—— *v.* Lord Advocate [1965] A.C. 75 ... 75
Bushell *v.* Secretary of State for the Environment [1981] A.C. 75 .. 218, 226, 234

Cababé *v.* Walton-on-Thames Urban District Council [1914] A.C. 102 ... 98
Calvin *v.* Carr [1980] A.C. 574 ... 64, 222, 241
Campbell *v.* Paddington Corporation [1911] 1 K.B. 869 ... 83
—— *v.* Rochdale General Commissioners [1975] 2 All E.R. 385 ... 241, 317
Cannock Chase District Council *v.* Kelly [1978] 1 W.L.R. 1 ... 192, 193
Capel *v.* Child (1832) 2 C. & J. 558 ... 217
Carltona Ltd. *v.* Commrs. of Works [1943] 2 All E.R. 560 ... 186, 194
Chandler *v.* Director of Public Prosecution [1964] A.C. 763 ... 76, 79, 81
Cheall *v.* A.P.E.X. [1983] 2 A.C. 180 ... 228
Cheney *v.* Conn [1968] 1 W.L.R. 242 ... 5
Cinnamond *v.* British Airports Authority [1980] 1 W.L.R. 582 ... 228
Cinzano (U.K.) Ltd. *v.* Customs & Excise Commissioners [1985] 1 W.L.R. 484 ... 101, 145
Clarke *v.* Chadburn [1985] 1 W.L.R. 78 ... 284
Cocks *v.* Thanet District Council [1983] 2 A.C. 286 .. 148, 255, 263, 268, 278, 300, 304
Cole Bros. Ltd. *v.* Phillips (Inspector of Taxes) [1982] 1 W.L.R. 1450, H.L. ... 120
Coleen Properties Ltd. *v.* Minister of Housing and Local Government [1971] 1 W.L.R. 433 ... 148, 149
Colonial Bank of Australia *v.* Willan (1874) L.R. 5 P.C. 417 ... 139
Coney *v.* Choyce [1975] 1 W.L.R. 422 ... 208, 210, 211
Congreve *v.* Home Office [1976] Q.B. 629 ... 176
Connelly *v.* Director of Public Prosecutions [1964] A.C. 1254 ... 243
Conway *v.* Rimmer [1968] A.C. 910 ... 79
Cooper *v.* Wandsworth Board of Works (1863) 14 C.B.(N.S.) 180 ...... 30, 66, 74, 83, 217, 240

Council of Civil Service Unions v. Minister for the Civil Service [1985] A.C. 374 .... 58, 74–78, 81, 91, 116, 181–182, 189, 190, 218
Cresswell v. Board of Inland Revenue [1984] 1 C.R. 508 122
Customs & Excise Commissioners v. Viva Gas Appliances [1983] 1 W.L.R. 1445, H.L. 121
Cutler v. Wandsworth Stadium [1949] A.C. 398 265

Daley, *Re* [1983] A.C. 347 135
Davies v. Gas Light & Coke Co. [1909] 1 Ch. 708 289
—— v. Presbyterian Church of Wales [1986] 1 All E.R. 705 .... 119, 125
Davis v. Carew-Pole [1956] 1 W.L.R. 833 231
Davy v. Spelthorne B.C. [1984] A.C. 262 .... 253, 268, 271, 297
Dawkins v. Antrobus (1881) 17 Ch. D. 615 214
Day v. Brownrigg (1878) 10 Ch. D. 294 270
De Verteuil v. Knaggs [1918] A.C. 557 .... 217, 231
Dimes v. Grand Junction Canal Proprietors (1852) 3 H.L.C. 759 .... 236, 238, 240
Din v. London Borough of Wandsworth [1983] 1 A.C. 657 .... 142, 145, 254
Director of Public Prosecutions v. Head [1959] A.C. 83 .... 63, 67, 68, 73, 74
Dobie v. Burns International Security Services (U.K.) Ltd. [1985] 1 W.L.R. 43 60
Doherty v. Allman (1878) 3 App.Cas. 709 290
Dowty Boulton Paul Ltd. v. Wolverhampton Corpn. [1971] 1 W.L.R. 204 197
—— v. —— (No. 2) [1976] Ch. 13 197
Dunkley v. Evans [1981] 1 W.L.R. 1522 199
Dunlop v. Woollhara Municipal Council [1981] 2 W.L.R. 693 89
Durayappah v. Fernando [1967] 2 A.C. 337 .... 224, 230, 240
Dutton v. Bognor Regis Urban District Council [1972] 1 Q.B. 373 87
Dyson v. Att.-Gen. [1911] 1 K.B. 410 .... 64, 251, 297, 299, 300
Dyson Holdings Ltd. v. Fox [1976] Q.B. 503 .... 25, 103, 104, 106

Eagil Trust Co. Ltd. v. Pigott-Brown [1985] 3 All E.R. 119 235
Eastleigh B.C. v. Betts [1983] 2 A.C. 613 .... 59, 196
Edwards v. Bairstow [1956] A.C. 14 .... 101, 112, 114, 116–117, 119–126, 128, 130–132, 147–149, 162, 165, 177, 181, 189, 314
Edwick v. Sunbury-on-Thames Urban District Council [1962] 1 Q.B. 229 .... 209, 210
Ellis v. Dubowski [1921] 3 K.B. 621 .... 194, 201
Ellis & Sons Fourth Amalgamated Properties v. Southern Rent Assessment Panel (1984) 14 H.L.R. 48 .... 313, 314
England v. Secretary of State (1981) 3 F.L.R. 222 109
Errington v. Minister of Health [1935] 1 K.B. 249 .... 225, 226
Estate & Trust Agencies (1927) Ltd. v. Singapore Improvement Trust [1937] A.C. 898 289
Ettridge v. Morrell, *The Times*, May 5, 1986 268
Everett v. Griffiths [1921] 1 A.C. 631 67
Evans v. Bartlam [1937] A.C. 473 204

F, *Re* [1977] Fam. 165 70
Fairmount Investments Ltd. v. Secretary of State for the Environment [1976] 1 W.L.R. 1255 232
Farmer v. Cotton's Trustees [1915] A.C. 922 116
Findlay, *Re* [1985] A.C. 318 .... 196, 220
Fraser v. Mudge [1975] 1 W.L.R. 1132 234

Freeman *v.* Wansbeck Borough Council [1984] 2 All E.R. 746 304
Fullbrook *v.* Berkshire Mags. Ct. Committee (1971) 69 L.G.R. 75 281
Furnell *v.* Whangarei High Schools Board [1973] A.C. 660 223
Furniss *v.* Dawson [1984] A.C. 474 121

G. *v.* G. [1985] 1 W.L.R. 647 204
Gammans *v.* Ekins [1950] 2 K.B. 328 106
Garden Cottage Foods Ltd. *v.* Milk Marketing Board [1984] A.C. 130 304
George *v.* Secretary of State for the Environment (1979) 38 P. & C.R. 609 309
Gillick *v.* West Norfolk Area Health Authority [1985] 3 All E.R. 402 .... 91, 182, 268, 301, 302
Givaudan *v.* Minister of Housing and Local Government [1967] 1 W.L.R. 250 .... 208, 211
Gouriet *v.* Union of Post Office Workers [1978] A.C. 435 . 22, 132, 248, 250, 266, 279, 301
Gowa *v.* Att.-Gen. [1985] 1 W.L.R. 1003 200
Greater London Council *v.* Secretary of State for the Environment [1985] J.P.L. 868 .... 55, 312
Green *v.* Minister of Housing and Local Government [1967] 2 Q.B. 606 60
Guaranty Trust Co. of New York *v.* Hannay & Co. [1915] 2 K.B. 536 .. 250, 299
Gunning *v.* Mirror Group Newspapers [1986] 1 W.L.R. 546 119

H.K., *Re* [1967] 2 Q.B. 617 218
Hadkinson *v.* Hadkinson [1952] P. 285 70
Hall & Co. Ltd. *v.* Shoreham Urban District Council [1964] 1 W.L.R. 240 .... 182, 183
Hamond *v.* Howell (1674) 86 E.R. 816 71
Hanson *v.* Radcliffe Urban District Council [1922] Ch. 490 .... 174, 193
Harrington, *Re* [1984] A.C. 743 .... 243, 284, 287
Harrogate B.C. *v.* Simpson (1985) 25 R.V.R. 10 106
Healey *v.* Minister of Health [1955] 1 Q.B. 221 315
Herbage, *Re*, *The Times*, Oct. 25, 1985 314
Herring *v.* Templeman [1973] 3 All E.R. 569 273
Hill *v.* Anderton [1983] A.C. 328 .... 134, 135
Hipperson *v.* Electoral Officer [1985] 3 W.L.R. 61 105
Hoffman-La Roche (F.) & Co. A.G. *v.* Secretary of State for Trade and Industry [1975] A.C. 295 .... 63, 64, 66, 229, 304
Hollier *v.* Plysu Ltd. [1983] I.R.L.R. 260, C.A. 100
Hopkins *v.* Smethwick Local Board of Health (1890) 24 Q.B.D. 712 216
Hoveringham Gravels *v.* Secretary of State for the Environment [1975] 1 Q.B. 754 112
Howard *v.* Bodington (1877) 2 P.D. 203 .... 207, 208, 209
—— *v.* Secretary of State for the Environment [1985] Q.B. 235 .... 210, 212
Hughes *v.* D.H.S.S. [1985] A.C. 776 220
—— *v.* Viner [1985] 3 All E.R. 40 211

I.R.C. *v.* Nat. Fed. of Self-Employed and Small Businesses Ltd. [1982] A.C. 617 .... 253, 270, 275, 276, 279, 282, 293, 297, 304, 307, 312
—— *v.* Scottish and Newcastle Breweries Ltd. [1982] 1 W.L.R. 322 120
Investors in Industry Commercial Properties Ltd. *v.* South Bedfordshire District Council [1986] 1 All E.R. 787 88
Investors in Industry Ltd. *v.* Norwich City Council [1986] 2 All E.R. 193, H.L. 45, 205
Isaacs *v.* Robertson [1984] 3 W.L.R. 705 70

Islam *v*. London Borough of Hillingdon [1983] 1 A.C. 688 .... 121, 145, 149

J (A Minor) (Wardship: Jurisdiction), *Re* [1984] 1 W.L.R. 81 81
James *v*. Minister of Housing and Local Government [1966] 1 W.L.R. 135 .. 208, 210
Jenkins *v*. Lombard North Central plc [1984] 1 W.L.R. 307 104
John *v*. Rees [1970] 1 Ch. 345 .... 214, 228
Jon Beauforte Ltd., *Re* [1953] Ch. 131 85

Kavanagh *v*. Chief Constable of Devon [1974] Q.B. 624 233
Khawaja *v*. Home Secretary [1984] A.C. 74 150
Kruse *v*. Johnson [1898] 2 Q.B. 91 .... 31, 66

Laker Airways Ltd. *v*. Department of Trade [1977] Q.B. 643 .... 8, 27, 74, 75, 173
Lambert *v*. Ealing London Borough Council [1982] 1 W.L.R. 550 254
Lassence *v*. Tierney (1849) 1 Mac. & G. 551 111
Lavender & Son Ltd. *v*. Minister of Housing and Local Government [1970] 1 W.L.R. 1231 .... 195, 196
Lawlor *v*. Union of Post Office Workers [1965] Ch. 712 214
Leary *v*. National Union of Vehicle Builders [1971] Ch. 34 222
Lee *v*. Enfield London Borough Council (1967) 66 L.G.R. 195 250
Leeds Corporation *v*. Jenkinson [1935] 1 K.B. 168 175
Legg *v*. Inner London Education Authority [1972] 1 W.L.R. 1245 250
Lees *v*. Secretary of State for the Environment [1985] 2 W.L.R. 805 105
Lennard *v*. International Institute for Medical Science, *The Times*, April 29, 1985, C.A. 235
Liversidge *v*. Anderson [1942] A.C. 206 186
Livingstone *v*. Westminster Corporation [1904] 2 K.B. 109 200
Local Government Board *v*. Arlidge [1915] A.C. 120 233
London & Clydeside Estates Ltd. *v*. Aberdeen District Council [1980] 1 W.L.R. 182 .... 64, 243
London Association of Shipowners & Brokers *v*. London & India Docks Joint Committee [1892] 3 Ch. D. 242 299
London Corpn. *v*. Cox (1867) L.R. 2 H.L. 239 281
London County Council *v*. Att.-Gen. [1902] A.C. 165 .... 132, 133
Luby *v*. Newcastle-under-Lyme Corporation [1964] 2 Q.B. 64 . 175, 176, 184, 187

M. (A Minor), *Re* [1985] 2 W.L.R. 811 81
M. (Minors), *Re* (1986) 130 S.J. 203 317
McC. (A Minor), *Re* [1985] A.C. 528 70–73
McDaid *v*. Clydebank District Council [1984] J.P.L. 579 51
McInnes *v*. Onslow Fane [1978] 1 W.L.R. 1520 217
Mahon *v*. Air New Zealand [1984] A.C. 808 .... 99, 100, 232
Malloch *v*. Aberdeen Corporation [1971] 1 W.L.R. 1578 .... 223, 224, 227, 228
Margate Pier Co. *v*. Hannam (1819) 3 B. & Ald. 266 212
Maritime Electric Co. *v*. General Dairies Ltd. [1937] A.C. 610 199
Marshalsea (Case of) (1612) 77 E.R. 1027 .... 67, 71
Martin *v*. Glynwed Distribution Ltd. [1983] I.C.R. 511, C.A. 100
Maynard *v*. Osmond [1977] Q.B. 240 234
Mead *v*. Haringey London Borough Council [1979] 1 W.L.R. 637 293
Melwood Units Pty. Ltd. *v*. Commissioner of Main Roads [1979] A.C. 426 205
Methodist Conference *v*. Parfitt [1984] Q.B. 368 119
Metropolitan Properties *v*. Lannon [1969] 1 Q.B. 577 239
Miles *v*. Wakefield Metropolitan District Council [1985] 1 W.L.R. 822 225

Mills *v.* L.C.C. [1925] 1 K.B. 213 .... 194, 195
Mohammed-Holgate *v.* Duke [1984] A.C. 437 180
Montreal Street Rly. Co. *v.* Normandin [1917] A.C. 170 .... 209, 210
Munks *v.* Munks (1985) 129 S.J. 65 70

Nakkuda Ali *v.* Jayaratne [1951] A.C. 66 216
Nancollas *v.* Insurance Officer [1985] 1 All E.R. 833, C.A. 117
Nethermere Ltd. *v.* Taverna [1984] I.R.L.R. 240 125
Newbury District Council *v.* Secretary of State for the Environment [1981] A.C. 578 .... 171, 176, 199
Norwich City Council *v.* Secretary of State for the Environment [1982] 1 All E.R. 737 .... 186, 188, 217
Nottinghamshire City Council *v.* Secretary of State for the Environment [1986] 1 All E.R. 199 .... 182, 195, 289
Nye (C.L.) Ltd., *Re* [1971] Ch. 442 53

O'Kelly *v.* Trusthouse Forte plc [1984] Q.B. 90 .... 94, 96, 118, 119, 125
O'Reilly *v.* Mackman [1983] 2 A.C. 237 ...... 140, 142, 148, 155, 157, 212, 219, 240, 254, 256, 261–263, 271, 293, 301, 304, 305, 308, 309, 310, 315
Osenton & Co. *v.* Johnston [1942] A.C. 130 204
Osgood *v.* Nelson (1872) 5 L.R.H.L. 636 234
Ottley *v.* Morris [1979] 1 All E.R. 65 .... 240, 242

Padfield *v.* Minister of Agriculture [1968] A.C. 997 .. 171–172, 178–180, 192, 196, 203, 236
Palmer *v.* Inverness Hospitals Board [1963] S.C. 311 224
Pasmore *v.* Oswaldtwistle Urban District Council [1898] A.C. 387 315
Patel *v.* University of Bradford Senate [1978] 1 W.L.R. 1488 273
Pawlett *v.* Att.-Gen. (1668) Hard. 465 .... 249, 251
Payne *v.* Lord Harris of Greenwich [1981] 1 W.L.R. 754 .... 235, 236
Peabody Fund *v.* Parkinson Ltd. [1985] A.C. 210 88
Pearlberg *v.* Varty [1972] 1 W.L.R. 534 .... 222, 223, 230
Pearlman *v.* Keepers of Harrow School [1979] Q.B. 56 .... 47, 156, 157, 166
Pepys *v.* London Transport Executive [1975] 1 W.L.R. 234 205
Pergamon Press Ltd., *Re* [1971] Ch. 388 .... 232, 233
Pickwell *v.* Camden London Borough Council [1983] Q.B. 962 ...... 185–186, 192
Poh, *Re* [1983] 1 W.L.R. 2 307
Pollway Nominees Ltd. *v.* Croydon London Borough Council [1985] 3 W.L.R. 564 52
Poyser and Mills Arbitration, *Re* [1964] Q.B. 467 211
Prescott *v.* Birmingham Corporation [1955] Ch. 310 .... 58, 172, 184, 203
Presho *v.* Department of Health and Social Security (Insurance Officer) [1984] A.C. 310 .... 103, 115
Priddle *v.* Fisher [1968] 1 W.L.R. 1478 205
Punton *v.* Minister of Pensions (No. 2) [1964] 1 W.L.R. 226 302
Pyx Granite Co. *v.* Minister of Housing and Local Government [1958] 1 Q.B. 554 .... 298, 313

R. *v.* Amber Valley D.C., *ex p.* Jackson [1985] 1 W.L.R. 298 .... 237, 238
—— *v.* Amendt [1915] 2 K.B. 276 248
—— *v.* Arundel Justices, *ex p.* Westminster Press Ltd. [1986] 1 W.L.R. 676 .. 70
—— *v.* Barker (1762) 3 Burr. 1265 283
—— *v.* Barnsley Licensing Justices, *ex p.* Barnsley, etc. Victuallers [1960] 2 Q.B. 167 .... 236, 238

R. *v.* Barnsley Metropolitan Borough Council, *ex p.* Hook [1976] 1 W.L.R. 1052 .... 176, 182, 203, 217
—— *v.* Birmingham Juvenile Court, *ex p.* N. (A Minor). *See* R. *v.* Birmingham Juvenile Court, *ex p.* S. (A Minor).
—— *v.* Birmingham Juvenile Court, *ex p.* S. (A Minor) [1984] 3 W.L.R. 387 109
—— *v.* Board of Visitors of Blundeston Prison, *ex p.* Fox-Taylor [1982] 1 All E.R. 646 232
—— *v.* Board of Visitors of Dartmoor Prison, *ex p.* Smith [1986] 2 All E.R. 651 136
—— *v.* Board of Visitors of Hull Prison, *ex p.* St. Germain [1979] Q.B. 425 219
—— *v.* Board of Visitors of Hull Prison, *ex p.* St. Germain (No. 2) [1979] 1 W.L.R. 1401 234
—— *v.* Board of Visitors of Swansea Prison, *ex p.* McGrath, *The Times*, November 21, 1984 234
—— *v.* Boundary Commission for England, *ex p.* Gateshead Borough Council; R. *v.* Boundary Commission for England, *ex p.* Foot [1983] Q.B. 600 .... 284, 289, 302
—— *v.* Bournemouth Crown Court, *ex p.* Weight [1984] 1 W.L.R. 980 243
—— *v.* Bradford [1908] 1 K.B. 365 .... 138, 139, 288
—— *v.* Brent Health Authority, *ex p.* Francis [1985] Q.B. 869 285
—— *v.* Brent London Borough Council, *ex p.* Gunning, *The Times*, April 30, 1985 219
—— *v.* Brighton Corporation, *ex p.* Shoosmith (1907) 96 L.T. 762 .... 190, 191
—— *v.* Bristol City Council, *ex p.* Pearce, *The Times*, December 7, 1984 233
—— *v.* British Broadcasting Corporation, *ex p.* Lavelle [1983] I.C.R. 99 225
—— *v.* Broadcasting Complaints Commission, *ex p.* Owen [1985] 2 W.L.R. 1025 .... 190, 191
—— *v.* Bromley London Borough Council, *ex p.* Lambeth London Borough Council, *The Times*, June 16, 1984, D.C. 271, 297
—— *v.* Burnham Committee, *ex p.* Professional Association of Teachers, *The Times*, March 30, 1985 204
—— *v.* Burton, *ex p.* Young [1897] 2 Q.B. 468 .... 238, 242
—— *v.* Camborne Justices, *ex p.* Pearce [1955] 1 Q.B. 41 .... 239, 240
—— *v.* Cardiff JJ., *ex p.* Salter [1986] F.L.R. 162 204
—— *v.* Cashiobury Hundred Justices (1823) 3 Dow. & Ry. 35 57
—— *v.* Central Criminal Court, *ex p.* Crook (1985) 82 L.S.Gaz. 1408, D.C. .. 70
—— *v.* Central Criminal Court Justices, *ex p.* L.C.C. [1925] 2 K.B. 43 153
—— *v.* Chancellor of Cambridge University (1723) 1 Str. 557 290
—— *v.* Cheshire Justices (1838) 8 Ad. & E. 398 99
—— *v.* Chichester Justices, *ex p.* Collins [1982] 1 W.L.R. 334 228
—— *v.* Chief Constable of Devon and Cornwall, *ex p.* Central Electricity Generating Board [1982] Q.B. 458 .... 284, 291
—— *v.* Chief Constable of Merseyside Police, *ex p.* Calveley [1986] 1 All E.R. 257 .... 313, 314, 316
—— *v.* Chief Constable of North Wales Police, *ex p.* Evans [1982] 1 W.L.R. 1155 .... 58, 224, 302
—— *v.* Chief Immigration Officer, *ex p.* Kharrazi [1980] 1 W.L.R. 1396 .... 146, 288
—— *v.* Chief National Insurance Commissioner, *ex p.* Connor [1918] Q.B. 758 281
—— *v.* Clerkenwell Green Metropolitan Stipendiary Magistrate, *ex p.* Ibrahim, *The Times*, December 7, 1983, D.C. 235

R. *v*. Commissioner Cripps, Q.C., *ex p*. Muldoon. *See* R. *v*. Cripps, *ex p*. Muldoon.
—— *v*. Commissioner of Metropolitan Police, *ex p*. Blackburn [1968] 2 Q.B. 118 .... 9, 179
—— *v*. —— (No. 3) [1973] 1 Q.B. 241 179
—— *v*. Commonwealth Public Service Commissioner, *ex p*. Killeen (1914) 18 C.L.R. 586 (Aust.) 282
—— *v*. Criminal Injuries Compensation Board, *ex p*. Clowes [1977] 1 W.L.R. 1353 290
—— *v*. Criminal Injuries Compensation Board, *ex p*. Ince [1973] 1 W.L.R. 1334 112
—— *v*. Criminal Injuries Compensation Board, *ex p*. Lain [1967] 2 Q.B. 864 .... 78, 273, 288
—— *v*. Cripps, *ex p*. Muldoon [1984] Q.B. 686 .... 153, 154
—— *v*. Croydon Crown Court, *ex p*. Smith (1983) 77 Cr.App.R. 277 291
—— *v*. Deputy Governor of Camphill Prison, *ex p*. King [1985] Q.B. 735 .... 147, 273
—— *v*. Derby JJ., *ex p*. Kooner [1971] 1 Q.B. 147 290
—— *v*. Diggines, *ex p*. Rahmani [1985] 2 W.L.R. 611, C.A. 232, 241
—— *v*. —— [1986] 1 All E.R. 912, H.L. 232
—— *v*. Dover Magistrates' Court, *ex p*. Kidner [1983] 1 All E.R. 475 317
—— *v*. Ealing London Borough Council, *ex p*. McBain [1986] 1 All E.R. 13 .. 145
—— *v*. East Berkshire Health Authority, *ex p*. Walsh [1985] Q.B. 152 .... 225, 262, 268, 289, 305, 309
—— *v*. Eastleigh Borough Council, *ex p*. Betts [1983] 2 A.C. 613, H.L. . 59, 196
—— *v*. Electricity Commissioners, *ex p*. London Electricity Joint Comm. Co. (1920) Ltd. [1924] 1 K.B. 171 287
—— *v*. Entry Clearance Officer, *ex p*. Amin [1983] 2 A.C. 818 .... 58, 202
—— *v*. Epping & Harlow General Commissioners, *ex p*. Goldstraw [1983] 3 All E.R. 257, C.A. 312
—— *v*. Fulham Rent Tribunal, *ex p*. Zerek [1951] 2 K.B. 1 135
—— *v*. Gaming Board, *ex p*. Benaim [1970] 2 Q.B. 417 .... 217, 230, 232
—— *v*. Garland (1870) L.R. 5 Q.B. 269 289
—— *v*. General Medical Council, *ex p*. Gee (1986) 83 L.S.Gaz. 125 273
—— *v*. Gillyard (1848) 12 Q.B. 527 151
—— *v*. Gloucestershire City Council, *ex p*. Miles (1985) 17 H.L.R. 292, C.A. 149
—— *v*. Governor of Brixton Prison, *ex p*. Walsh [1985] A.C. 154 133
—— *v*. Governor of Pentonville Prison *ex p*. Herbage, *The Times*, May 21, 1986 296
—— *v*. Greater London Council, *ex p*. Blackburn [1976] 1 W.L.R. 550 .... 194–195, 286, 288
—— *v*. Greater London Council, *ex p*. Westminster City Council, *The Times*, December 27, 1984 133
—— *v*. Greater Manchester Coroner, *ex p*. Tal [1985] Q.B. 67 .... 155, 157, 167
—— *v*. Greenwich London Borough Council, *ex p*. Cedar Transport Group [1983] R.A. 173, D.C. 308
—— *v*. Greenwich London Borough Council, *ex p*. Patel (1985) 129 S.J. 654, C.A. 51
—— *v*. Guildhall JJ., *ex p*. Prushinowski, *The Times*, December 14, 1985 314
—— *v*. H.M. Inspector of Taxes, *ex p*. Clarke [1974] Q.B. 220 211
—— *v*. H.M. Treasury, *ex p*. Smedley [1985] Q.B. 657 53
—— *v*. Hackney London Borough Council, *ex p*. Gamper [1985] 1 W.L.R. 1229 204

R. *v*. Hallstrom, *ex p*. W. [1985] 3 All E.R. 775 .... 67, 279, 296, 317
—— *v*. Hanley Revising Barrister [1912] 3 K.B. 518 292
—— *v*. Hendon Rural District Council, *ex p*. Chorley [1933] 2 K.B. 696 237
—— *v*. Hillingdon Health Authority, *ex p*. Goodwin [1984] I.C.R. 800 197
—— *v*. Hillingdon London Borough Council, *ex p*. Puhlhofer (1985) 17 H.L.R. 278 182
—— *v*. ——, *ex p*. Royco Ltd. [1974] Q.B. 720 .... 177, 202, 314
—— *v*. Home Secretary, *ex p*. Broom. *See* R. *v*. Secretary of State for Home Department, *ex p*. Broom.
—— *v*. Horseferry Road JJ., *ex p*. I.B.A., *The Times*, January 31, 1986 265–289
—— *v*. Huggins [1895] 1 Q.B. 563 239
—— *v*. Huntingdon District Council, *ex p*. Cowan [1984] 1 W.L.R. 501 .... 161, 217, 233, 316
—— *v*. Immigration Appeal Tribunal, *ex p*. Bastiampillai [1983] 2 All E.R. 844 179
—— *v*. Immigration Appeal Tribunal, *ex p*. Khan [1983] Q.B. 790 . 211, 212, 220
—— *v*. Immigration Appeal Tribunal, *ex p*. Mehmet [1977] 1 W.L.R. 795 233
—— *v*. Independent Broadcasting Authority, *ex p*. Rank Organisation plc, *The Times*, March 14, 1986 268
—— *v*. Independent Broadcasting Authority, *ex p*. Whitehouse, *The Times*, April 4, 1985, C.A. 195
—— *v*. Industrial Injuries Commissioner, *ex p*. A.E.U. (No. 2) [1966] 2 Q.B. 31 117
—— *v*. I.R.C., *ex p*. Preston [1985] A.C. 835 .... 198, 313
—— *v*. ——, *Re* Nathan (1884) 12 Q.B.D. 461 283
—— *v*. Inner London Education Authority, *ex p*. Westminster City Council [1986] 1 All E.R. 19 191
—— *v*. Insurance Cmr., *ex p*. Michael [1977] 1 W.L.R. 109 117
—— *v*. Ipswich Crown Court, *ex p*. Baldwin [1981] 1 All E.R. 596 .... 42, 314
—— *v*. Ipswich Justices, *ex p*. Edwards (1979) 143 J.P. 699 158
—— *v*. Jenner [1983] 1 W.L.R. 873 69
—— *v*. Judge Amphlett [1915] 2 K.B. 223 233
—— *v*. Kensington General Commissioners of Income Tax, *ex p*. Polignac [1917] 1 K.B. 486 281
—— *v*. Kent County Council, *ex p*. Bruce, *The Times*, February 8, 1986 .... 187, 283, 292, 294
—— *v*. Kent JJ., *ex p*. Smith [1928] W.N. 137 309
—— *v*. Kent Police Authority, *ex p*. Godden [1971] 2 Q.B. 662 232
—— *v*. Kingston upon Thames Justices, *ex p*. Khanna, *The Times*, November 21, 1985, D.C. 151
—— *v*. Knightsbridge Crown Court, *ex p*. Aspinall Curzon Ltd., The, *The Times*, December 16, 1982 165
—— *v*. Knightsbridge Crown Court, *ex p*. Goonatilleke [1985] 3 W.L.R. 553 .... 151, 232
—— *v*. Knightsbridge Crown Court, *ex p*. International Sporting Club (London) [1981] 3 W.L.R. 640 .... 165, 167, 235, 288
—— *v*. Knightsbridge Crown Court, *ex p*. Marcrest [1983] 1 W.L.R. 300 285
—— *v*. Lambeth London Borough Council, *ex p*. Sharp, *The Times*, December 28, 1984 208
—— *v*. Leyland Justices, *ex p*. Hawthorne [1979] Q.B. 283 232
—— *v*. Lincolnshire Justices, *ex p*. Brett [1926] 2 K.B. 192 .... 138, 139, 151
—— *v*. Liverpool Corporation, *ex p*. Liverpool Taxi etc. Association [1972] 2 Q.B. 299 .... 219, 237, 288

R. *v.* London Regional Passenger Committee, *ex p.* Brent London Borough Council, *The Times*, May 23, 1985 234
—— *v.* London Transport Executive, *ex p.* Greater London Council [1983] Q.B. 484 .... 19, 185, 202, 279
—— *v.* Lord Chancellor (Hailsham), *ex p.* Alexander, *The Times*, March 21, 22, 27, 1986 229
—— *v.* Macfarlane, *ex p.* O'Flanagan (1923) 32 C.L.R. 518 288
—— *v.* Mansfield Justices, *ex p.* Sharkey [1985] Q.B. 613 .... 196, 285
—— *v.* Medical Appeal Tribunal, *ex p.* Gilmore [1957] 1 Q.B. 574 . 48, 164, 165
—— *v.* Mental Health Review Tribunal, *ex p.* Clatworthy [1985] 3 All E.R. 699 317
—— *v.* ——, *ex p.* Pickering [1986] 1 All E.R. 99 .... 212, 316
—— *v.* Merseyside County Council, *ex p.* Gt. Universal Stores Ltd. (1982) 80 L.G.R. 639 185
—— *v.* Minister of Health, *ex p.* Davis [1929] 1 K.B. 619 272
—— *v.* ——, *ex p.* Yaffe [1930] 2 K.B. 98 272
—— *v.* Monopolies & Mergers Commission, *ex p.* Argyll Group plc [1986] 1 W.L.R. 763 .... 276, 286
—— *v.* Nat. Bell Liquors Ltd. [1922] 2 A.C. 128 .... 98, 99, 100, 150
—— *v.* National Coal Board, *ex p.* National Union of Mineworkers, *The Times*, March 8, 1986 268
—— *v.* National Insurance Commissioner, *ex p.* Hudson [1972] A.C. 944 47
—— *v.* National Insurance Commissioners, *ex p.* Secretary of State for Social Services [1974] 1 W.L.R. 1290 279
—— *v.* Newcastle JJ., *ex p.* Hindle [1984] 1 All E.R. 770 .... 288, 289
—— *v.* Newcastle-under-Lyme JJ., *ex p.* Whitehouse [1952] 2 All E.R. 531 .. 306
—— *v.* North Hertfordshire District Council, *ex p.* Cobbold [1985] 3 All E.R. 486 199
—— *v.* Northumberland Compensation Appeal Tribunal, *ex p.* Shaw [1952] 1 K.B. 338 .... 164, 165, 288
—— *v.* Nottingham County Court, *ex p.* Byers [1985] 1 W.L.R. 403 ...... 136, 291
—— *v.* Oxford, *ex p.* Levey, *The Times*, December 18, 1985 279
—— *v.* Oxford Regional Mental Health Review Tribunal, *ex p.* Secretary of State for the Home Department; R. *v.* Yorkshire Mental Health Review Tribunal (1986) 130 S.J. 505 288
—— *v.* Paddington Valuation Officer, *ex p.* Peachey Property Corpn. Ltd. [1966] 1 Q.B. 380 .... 274, 292
—— *v.* Police Complaints Board, *ex p.* Madden [1983] 1 W.L.R. 447 148
—— *v.* Postmaster General, *ex p.* Carmichael [1928] 1 K.B. 291 288
—— *v.* Rand (1866) L.R. 1 Q.B. 230 .... 238, 239
—— *v.* Raymond [1981] 3 W.L.R. 3 222
—— *v.* Registrar of Companies, *ex p.* Central Bank of India [1986] 1 All E.R. 105 .... 52, 53
—— *v.* Reigate and Banstead Borough Council, *ex p.* Paris (1984) 15 Fam. Law 28 145
—— *v.* Rochdale M.B.C., *ex p.* Cromer Ltd. [1982] 3 All E.R. 761 ..... 191, 202, 314
—— *v.* St. Edmundsbury Borough Council, *ex p.* Investors in Industry Commercial Properties [1985] 1 W.L.R. 1168 .... 237, 239
—— *v.* St. Lawrence's Hospital Statutory Visitors, *ex p.* Pritchard [1953] 1 W.L.R. 1158 288
—— *v.* Secretary of State for Education, *ex p.* Keating, *The Times*, December 3, 1985 267

R. *v.* Secretary of State for Education and Science, *ex p.* Birmingham District Council (1985) 83 L.G.R. 79 ... 281
—— *v.* Secretary of State for Trade, *ex p.* Anderson Strathclyde plc [1983] 2 All E.R. 233 ... 173
—— *v.* Secretary of State for Foreign Affairs, *ex p.* Trawnik, *The Times*, February 21, 1986 ... 54
—— *v.* Secretary of State for Social Services, *ex p.* Association of Metropolitan Authorities [1986] 1 All E.R. 164 ... 209, 210, 283, 289
—— *v.* ——, *ex p.* Child Poverty Action Group, *The Times*, August 8, 1985, C.A. ... 279, 280
—— *v.* ——, *ex p.* Connolly [1986] 1 All E.R. 998 ... 235
—— *v.* ——, *ex p.* Westhead, *The Times*, October 17, 1985 ... 91
—— *v.* Secretary of State for the Environment, *ex p.* Binney, *The Times*, October 8, 1983 ... 228
—— *v.* ——, *ex p.* Brent London Borough Council [1982] Q.B. 593 . 7, 196, 202, 217, 228, 288, 302
—— *v.* ——, *ex p.* Greater London Council [1985] J.P.L. 543 . 55, 227, 271, 288, 298
—— *v.* ——, *ex p.* Hillingdon London Borough Council [1986] 1 All E.R. 810 ... 194
—— *v.* ——, *ex p.* Hackney London Borough Council [1984] 1 W.L.R. 592 ... 200, 202, 228, 285, 303
—— *v.* ——, *ex p.* Leicester City Council (1985) R.V.R. 31 ... 211
—— *v.* ——, *ex p.* Norwich City Council [1982] Q.B. 808 ... 7, 19
—— *v.* ——, *ex p.* Ostler [1977] Q.B. 122 ... 56, 192
—— *v.* ——, *ex p.* Powis [1981] 1 W.L.R. 584 ... 150
—— *v.* ——, *ex p.* Ward [1984] 1 W.L.R. 834 ... 315
—— *v.* Secretary of State for the Home Department, *ex p.* Addo, *The Times*, April 18, 1985 ... 152
—— *v.* ——, *ex p.* Anderson [1984] 2 W.L.R. 725 ... 133
—— *v.* ——, *ex p.* Benwell [1985] Q.B. 554 ... 179, 182, 289
—— *v.* ——, *ex p.* Broom [1985] 3 W.L.R. 778 ... 179
—— *v.* ——, Bugdaycay [1986] 1 All E.R. 458 ... 151
—— *v.* ——, *ex p.* Gunnell [1985] Crim.L.R. 105 ... 216
—— *v.* ——, *ex p.* Khera; R. *v.* Secretary of State for the Home Department, *ex p.* Khawaja [1984] A.C. 74 ... 152
—— *v.* ——, *ex p.* McAvoy [1984] 1 W.L.R. 1408 ... 189
—— *v.* ——, *ex p.* Puttick [1981] 1 Q.B. 767 ... 281
—— *v.* ——, *ex p.* Swati [1986] 1 All E.R. 717 ... 211, 306, 313, 316
—— *v.* ——, *ex p.* Tarrant [1985] Q.B. 251 ... 233, 234
—— *v.* Secretary of State for Transport, *ex p.* Greater London Council [1985] 2 W.L.R. 574 ... 91, 199, 217
—— *v.* ——, *ex p.* Phillipine Airlines Inc. (1984) 81 L.S.Gaz. 3173, C.A. ... 232
—— *v.* Secretary of State for War [1891] 2 Q.B. 326 ... 293
—— *v.* Sevenoaks District Council, *ex p.* Terry [1985] 3 All E.R. 226 .. 237, 239
—— *v.* Sheffield Supplementary Benefits Appeal Tribunal, *ex p.* Shine [1975] 1 W.L.R. 624 ... 147, 286
—— *v.* Simpson (Calvin) [1983] 1 W.L.R. 1494 ... 104
—— *v.* Smith (Thomas George) (1984) 48 P.C.R. 392 ... 69
—— *v.* Special Commissioner, *ex p.* Stipplechoice Ltd. [1985] 2 All E.R. 465 ... 317
—— *v.* Speyer; R. *v.* Cassel [1916] 1 K.B. 595 ... 287
—— *v.* Stokesley Justices, *ex p.* Bartram [1956] 1 W.L.R. 254 ... 309

R. *v.* Stratford-on-Avon District Council, *ex p.* Jackson [1985] 1 W.L.R. 1319 ..... 279, 282, 308
—— *v.* Surrey Coroner, *ex p.* Campbell [1982] Q.B. 661 157
—— *v.* Sussex Justices, *ex p.* McCarthy [1924] 1 K.B. 256 ..... 239, 288
—— *v.* Thames Magistrates' Court, *ex p.* Polemis [1974] 1 W.L.R. 1371 231
—— *v.* Tottenham JJ., *ex p.* Joshi [1982] 1W.L.R. 631 180
—— *v.* Transport Secretary, *ex p.* Gwent County Council [1986] 2 All E.R. 18 226
—— *v.* Waltham Forest JJ., *ex p.* Solanke [1985] 3 W.L.R. 788 72
—— *v.* Wandsworth JJ., *ex p.* Read [1942] 1 K.B. 281 ..... 240, 314
—— *v.* Wear Valley District Council, *ex p.* Binks [1985] 2 All E.R. 699 ..... 217, 268
—— *v.* Wells St. Magistrates' Court, *ex p.* Albanese [1981] 3 W.L.R. 694 222
—— *v.* West Sussex Quarter Sessions, *ex p.* Albert and Maud Ltd. [1974] Q.B. 24 233
—— *v.* West Yorkshire Coroner, *ex p.* Smith [1982] 3 W.L.R. 920 ..... 135, 291
—— *v.* ——, *ex p.* Smith (No. 2) [1985] 2 W.L.R. 332 70
—— *v.* Yorkshire Mental Health Review Tribunal. *See* R. *v.* Oxford Regional Mental Health Review Tribunal.
Racal Communications Ltd., *Re* [1981] A.C. 374 ... 37, 94, 137, 140, 144, 147, 152, 154, 157
Raymond *v.* Honey [1983] A.C. 1 133
Redland Bricks Ltd. *v.* Morris [1970] A.C. 652 284
Reed *v.* Nova Securities Ltd., *The Times*, February 5, 1985 116
Rees, *ex p.*, *The Times*, May 7, 1986 153
Rhyl Urban District Council *v.* Rhyl Amusements Ltd. [1959] 1 W.L.R. 465 .. 84
Ridge *v.* Baldwin [1964] A.C. 40 ..... 62, 209, 215–218, 223–224, 227–228, 230–231, 240–241, 317
Roberts *v.* Hopwood [1925] A.C. 578 ..... 169, 171, 172, 185, 189, 192, 196, 203
Rogers *v.* Essex County Council [1985] 2 All E.R. 39 31
—— *v.* Home Secretary [1973] A.C. 388 79
Roncarelli *v.* Duplessis (1959) 16 D.L.R. (2d) 689 ..... 175, 193, 201, 203
Rooke *v.* Lord Kensington (1856) 2 K. & J. 753 299
Rootkin *v.* Kent County Council [1981] 1 W.L.R. 1186 ..... 199, 308
Rowing *v.* Minister of Pensions [1946] 1 All E.R. 664 100
Royal College of Nursing *v.* D.H.S.S. [1981] 1 All E.R. 545 ..... 300, 301
Russell *v.* Duke of Norfolk [1949] 1 All E.R. 109 230

Sagnata Investments Ltd. *v.* Norwich Corporation [1971] 2 Q.B. 614 205
Schmidt *v.* Home Secretary [1969] 2 Ch. 149 219
Secretary of State for Defence *v.* Guardian Newspapers Ltd. [1985] A.C. 339 79
Secretary of State for Education and Science *v.* Metropolitan Borough of Tameside [1977] A.C. 1014 ..... 7, 19, 186–188, 203
Shah *v.* Barnet London Borough Council [1983] 2 A.C. 309 ... 102–105, 107, 146, 288
Simpson *v.* Att.-Gen. [1955] N.Z.L.R. 271 ..... 210, 212
Sirros *v.* Moore [1975] Q.B. 118 ..... 71, 72, 73
Skinner *v.* Carter [1948] Ch. 387 ..... 66, 70
—— *v.* Northallerton County Court Judge [1899] A.C. 439 154
Smalley, *Re* [1985] A.C. 622 153
Smith *v.* Cardiff Corporation (No. 2) [1955] 1 Ch. 159 175
—— *v.* East Elloe Rural District Council [1956] A.C. 736 .. 55, 56, 62, 66, 69, 192
—— *v.* R. (1878) 3 App.Cas. 614 217

Smith *v.* Skinner (1986) 26 R.V.R. 45 .... 186, 193
Southend-on-Sea Corpn. *v.* Hodgson Ltd. [1962] 1 Q.B. 416 .... 198, 199
South East Asia Fire Bricks *v.* Non-Metallic etc. Union [1981] A.C. 363 .... 157, 166
South West Water Authority *v.* Rumbles [1985] 2 W.L.R. 405, H.L. 122
Stapley *v.* Gypsum Mines [1953] A.C. 663 112
Steeples *v.* Derbyshire County Council [1985] 1 W.L.R. 256 .... 55, 208, 237, 238
Stoke-on-Trent City Council *v.* B & Q (Retail) Ltd. and other appeals [1984] Ch. 1 .... 174, 193, 202, 280
Streames *v.* Copping [1985] 2 W.L.R. 993 317

T. (A.J.J.) (An Infant), *Re* [1970] Ch. 668 317
T. (A Minor), *Re* [1986] 1 All E.R. 817 209
Tehrani *v.* Rostron [1972] 1 Q.B. 182 47
Thomas *v.* University of Bradford [1986] 1 All E.R. 217 4
Town Investments Ltd. *v.* Department of the Environment [1978] A.C. 359 .. 272
Tsakiroglou *v.* Noblee Thorl [1962] A.C. 92 112
Uni-Ocean Lines *v.* C. Trade of Geneva S.A. [1984] 1 Lloyd's Rep. 244 121
Uppal *v.* Home Office, *The Times*, October 21, 1978 254

Victoria Square Pty. Co. Ltd. *v.* Southwark London Borough Council [1978] 1 W.L.R. 463 174
Vidyodaya University of Ceylon *v.* Silva [1965] 1 W.L.R. 77 224
Vine *v.* National Dock Labour Board [1957] A.C. 488 194

W. (A Minor), *Re* [1985] 2 W.L.R. 892 81
W. (A Minor), *Re* [1985] A.C. 791 317
Wandsworth London Borough Council *v.* Winder [1985] A.C. 461 .... 31, 66, 74, 260, 268
Watson *v.* Holland [1985] 1 All E.R. 290 111
West *v.* Buckinghamshire County Council (1984) 83 L.G.R. 449 89
Western Fish Products Ltd. *v.* Penwith District Council [1981] 2 All E.R. 204 200
Westminster City Council *v.* British Waterways Board [1985] A.C. 676 30
—— *v.* Great Portland Estates plc [1985] A.C. 661 .... 171, 176, 208, 211
Westminster Corporation *v.* L.N.W. Rly. [1905] A.C. 426 .... 190, 191
Westminster Renslade Ltd. *v.* Environment Secretary [1983] J.P.L. 454 177
Wheeler *v.* Leicester City Council [1985] 3 W.L.R. 335, H.L. 91, 176, 181
White and Collins *v.* Minister of Health [1939] 2 K.B. 838 .... 108, 116, 138–139
Wilford *v.* West Riding of Yorkshire County Council [1908] 1 K.B. 685 315
Williams *v.* Giddy [1911] A.C. 381 .... 181, 182
Wilson *v.* Colchester Justices [1985] 2 W.L.R. 694 228
Wiseman *v.* Borneman [1971] A.C. 297 .... 223, 229, 231, 237
Windsor Borough Council *v.* Brandrose Ltd. [1983] 1 W.L.R. 509 198
Woodling *v.* Secretary of State for the Environment [1984] 1 W.L.R. 348, H.L. 145
Woodward *v.* Sarsons (1875) 10 L.R.C.P. 733 212
Wootton *v.* Central Land Board [1957] 1 W.L.R. 424 205
Wrotham Park Estate *v.* Parkside Homes [1974] 1 W.L.R. 798 306

Zamir *v.* Home Secretary [1980] A.C. 930 .... 146, 151

TABLE OF STATUTES

1832 Uniformity of Process Act (2 & 3 Will. 4, c. 39) .. 249

1848 Indictable Offences Act (11 & 12 Vict., c. 42)—
- s. 17 158

1857 Crown Suits Act (20 & 21 Vict., c. 44) 81

1858 Chancery Amendment Act (21 & 22 Vict., c. 27) 263

1861 Offences against the Person Act (24 & 25 Vict., c. 100) 265

1869 Charitable Trusts Act (32 & 33 Vict. c. 110)—
- s. 7 220

1873 Supreme Court of Judicature Act (36 & 37 Vict., c. 66)—
- ss. 3–5 37

1875 Supreme Court of Judicature Act (38 & 39 Vict., c. 77)—
- Sched. 1 249

1876 Appellate Jurisdiction Act (39 & 40 Vict., c. 59)—
- s. 3 (1) 43

1887 Coroners Act (50 & 51 Vict., c. 71)—
- s. 6 157
- s. 35 157

1913 Mental Deficiency Act (3 & 4 Geo. 5, c. 28)—
- s. 56 (1) (*a*) 68

1925 Settled Land Act (15 & 16 Geo. 5, c. 18) 109

Law of Property Act (15 & 16 Geo. 5, c. 20)—
- s. 193 (4) 265

Supreme Court of Judicature (Consolidation) Act (15 & 16 Geo. 5, c. 49)—
- s. 31 (1) (*d*) 153

1933 Administration of Justice (Miscellaneous Provisions) Act (23 & 24 Geo. 5, c. 36)—
- s. 5 251

1934 Administration of Justice (Appeals) Act (24 & 25 Geo. 5, c. 40)—
- s. 1 (1) 43

1936 Public Health Act (26 Geo. 5 & 1 Edw. 8, c. 49)—
- s. 107 45

1938 Administration of Justice (Miscellaneous Provisions) Act (1 & 2 Geo. 6, c. 63) 38
- s. 9 286

1946 Statutory Instruments Act (9 & 10 Geo. 6, c. 36) 9, 13

1947 Crown Proceedings Act (10 & 11 Geo. 6, c. 44) 12
- s. 17 (3) 272, 297
- s. 21 81
  - (1) 296
  - (2) 295, 296
- s. 38 (2) 296
- s. 40 (2) (*b*) 54
  - (3) (*a*) 53, 54

1948 Companies Act (11 & 12 Geo. 6, c. 38)—
- s. 98 (2) 52
- s. 441 153

1950 Foreign Compensation Act (14 Geo. 6, c. 12) 49
- s. 1 141
- s. 4 (4) 50

1953 Prevention of Crime Act (1 & 2 Eliz. 2, c. 14)—
- s. 1 104

1956 Sexual Offences Act (4 & 5 Eliz. 2, c. 69)—
- s. 7 68

1957 Housing Act (5 & 6 Eliz. 2, c. 56)—
s. 17 (2) 174
s. 29 (3) 174
s. 37 (1) 52
s. 111 (1) 175
s. 113 (2) 175
1958 Tribunals and Inquiries Act (6 & 7 Eliz. 2, c. 66) 44
s. 9 44
s. 11 .... 49, 51, 164
(3) 51
Sched. 1 44
1959 County Courts Act (7 & 8 Eliz. 2, c. 22)—
s. 108 156
s. 109 156
1963 Betting, Gaming and Lotteries Act (11 Eliz. 2, c. 2)—
s. 28 (6) 126
1964 Licensing Act (c. 26) 45
s. 193 (6) 238
Police Act (c. 48) 20
Travel Concessions Act (c. 95)—
s. 1 184
1965 War Damage Act (c. 18) .. 18, 75
1967 General Rate Act (c. 9)—
s. 7 .... 45, 314
Criminal Justice Act (c. 80)—
s. 22 314
Leasehold Reform Act (c. 88) 156
1968 Criminal Appeal Act (c. 19)—
s. 2 (1) 242
Courts-Martial (Appeals) Act (c. 20)—
s. 1 (2) 153
Transport Act (c.73)—
s. 70 126
1969 Foreign Compensation Act (c. 20)—
s. 3 (1) 144
(2) 51, 144
(3) 52
(8) 51
(9) 52
Transport (London) Act (c. 35)—
s. 1 184
1969 Post Office Act (c. 48) 86
1970 Taxes Management Act (c. 9)—
s. 20 11
s. 31 10
s. 56 126
1971 Courts Act (c. 23)—
s. 4 (7) 153
Tribunals and Inquiries Act (c. 62)—
s. 12 (1) 165
(4) 165
s. 13 .... 42, 44
s. 14 .... 51, 54, 164
(3) 51
Sched. 1 44
Civil Aviation Act (c. 75)—
s. 3 (1) 173
Immigration Act (c. 77)—
s. 13 10
s. 20 126
Town and Country Planning Act (c. 78)—
s. 9 (5) 222
s. 12 (1) 207
(2) 207
(3) 207
(4) 207
(6) 207
s. 29 (1) 177
s. 35 59
s. 36 59
s. 53 59
s. 242 55
s. 243 (1) 51
s. 244 55
s. 245 .... 55, 211
s. 246 45
s. 247 .... 45, 59
1972 European Communities Act (c. 68) 85
s. 1 (1) 86
(3) 53
s. 9 85
Local Government Act (c. 70) 6
s. 82 238
s. 92 286
s. 94 238
s. 101 194
s. 102 194
s. 111 (1) 133
s. 161 186

1972 Local Government Act —*cont.*
s. 222 .... 280, 294
(1) 173
Criminal Justice Act (c. 71)—
s. 36 43
1973 Land Compensation Act (c. 26) 86
Fair Trading Act (c. 41)—
s. 73 (2) 173
1974 Consumer Credit Act (c. 39)—
s. 43 104
s. 44 104
s. 167 (2) 104
Housing Act (c. 44) 156
1975 Social Security Act (c. 14)—
s. 37A 105
s. 50 117
s. 93 45
s. 94 45
s. 101 126
Sex Discrimination Act (c. 65) 267
1976 Restrictive Practices Court Act (c. 33)—
s. 1 (1) 153
Bail Act (c. 63) 314
Supplementary Benefits Act (c. 71)—
s. 15 10
s. 15A 11, 125
1977 Rent Act (c. 42)—
Sched. 11 10
Housing (Homeless Persons) Act (c. 48) . 121, 160, 182, 266, 282, 300
s. 3 255
s. 4 (5) 255, 278, 291
s. 16 .... 145, 149
s. 18 196
National Health Service Act (c. 49) 77
s. 1 278
Unfair Contract Terms Act (c. 50) 265
1978 Employment Protection (Consolidation) Act (c. 44) 118
s. 67 11
s. 136 11
(1) 125
1978 Employment Protection (Consolidation) Act —*cont.*
s. 136—*cont.*
(4) 60
1979 Alcoholic Liquor Duties Act (c. 4)—
s. 54 101
Justices of the Peace Act (c. 55)—
s. 45 71
s. 52 72
s. 53 72
1980 Social Security Act (c. 30)—
s. 14 117
Magistrates' Courts Act (c. 43)—
s. 4 158
s. 111 (1) 42, 43, 155, 317
s. 127 (1) 134
s. 144 158
Housing Act (c. 51)—
Pt. 1 188
s. 23 188
Limitation Act (c. 58) 56
Local Government, Planning and Land Act (c. 65)—
s. 59 (11A) 195
1981 Contempt of Court Act (c. 49)—
s. 10 79
Supreme Court Act (c. 54)—
s. 8 (3) 153
s. 16 (1) 43, 155
s. 18 43
(1) (*c*) 153
s. 28 (1) 42
(2) 153
s. 29 38
(2) 47
(3) 70, 153
s. 30 286
s. 31 .... 38, 252, 269, 296, 297, 304
(1) 269, 310
(*a*) 38
(*c*) 287
(2) 253, 270, 272, 297
(*a*) 298
(*b*) 298
(3) 61

1981 Supreme Court Act—*cont.*
s. 31—*cont.*
(4) 304
(*b*) 304
(6) 308
s. 45 (1) 153
s. 60 47
s. 66 37
Acquisition of Land Act (c. 67)—
s. 25 55
1982 Social Security and Housing Benefits Act (c. 24)—
s. 28 176
Local Government (Miscellaneous Provisions) Act (c. 30)—
s. 1 .... 26, 45
s. 3 45
Sched. 1 45
para. 4 (4) 26, 173
Sched. 4 45
Local Government Finance Act (c. 32)—
s. 4 (1) 69, 314
(2) 314
s. 19 186
1983 Mental Health Act (c. 20)—
s. 139 .... 67, 279, 296
National Heritage Act (c. 47)—
s. 36 30
1984 Occupiers' Liability Act (c. 3) 265
Telecommunications Act (c. 12)—
s. 60 4
1984 County Courts Act (c. 28)—
s. 77 155
(1) 156
s. 81 35
s. 83 154
s. 84 154
Food Act (c. 30)—
s. 14 (2) 179
(6) 179
ss. 16–19 45
s. 19 (1) (*b*) 179
Rates Act (c. 33) 7
Finance Act (c. 43)—
s. 10 120
Sched. 6 120
Local Government (Interim Provisions) Act (c. 53) 227
1985 Companies Act (c. 6)—
s. 401 (2) 52
s. 721 153
London Regional Transport (Amendment) Act (c. 10) 217
Prosecution of Offences Act (c. 23) 9
s. 3 264
Local Government (Access to Information) Act (c. 43)—
s. 1 (1) 204
Local Government Act (c.-51) 6
Interception of Communications Act (c. 56)—
s. 7 (1) 51
(8) 51, 143

ABBREVIATIONS

De Smith J.R.A.A.	*Judicial Review of Administrative Action* by the late S. A. de Smith (4th ed., 1980) by J. M. Evans.
De Smith C. & A.	*Constitutional and Administrative Law* by S. A. de Smith (5th ed., 1985) by H. Street and R. Brazier.
Wade A. L.	*Administrative Law* by H. W. R. Wade (5th ed., 1982).
Craig	*Administrative Law* by P. P. Craig (1983).

Part I

The Nature of Review

Chapter 1
INTRODUCTION

This book is about the English Law of judicial review. We use the term "judicial review" to refer broadly to the jurisdiction of courts to keep public authorities within what we shall describe as their "remit."

We begin this introductory chapter with a sketch of the nature and scope of public authority—"official"—power (section A). In section B, by reference to the two notions of "liability" and "remit" we outline two distinct types of legal limit to official power. Next, under the heading "do we need judicial review?" we discuss briefly the constitutional place and function of judicial review (section C). In section D we show how the notion of remit, implying as it does the existence of fixed boundaries to official power, raises acute questions as to the respective roles of Parliament and the review courts in fixing those boundaries. Finally, in section E, we outline the scheme of the body of the book in which these questions, and others to which they give rise, are tackled.

A. Official Power

(1) What is a public authority?

There are in the United Kingdom, as elsewhere, numerous authorities created and adapted by the state to achieve ends conceived to be for the public good. Duties are imposed and powers conferred upon these state, or "public," authorities to enable them to achieve these ends. The sum total of the special legal authority thus created in the state we label "official power."[1] To give some substance to this notion we shall in this section sketch[2] the main types of public authority, their fields of competence and the sources of their power.

The term "public authority" includes the Crown, Parliament and the superior courts (all of non-statutory origin); and the multi-

[1] The term "administrative law" is used to describe (with varying emphasis) the legal regime governing public authorities. Judicial review is thus one part of administrative law.

[2] For substantial accounts reference should be made to works on constitutional law, *e.g.* de Smith C. & A. For accounts in the administrative law context, see Wade A.L., Part II; Garner's *Administrative Law* (6th ed., 1985); Craig, Part I. See too de Smith J.R.A.A., Chap. 1.

tude of other state authorities set up by or under the authority of Parliament and endowed with executive, legislative or adjudicative powers. The term "public authority" is not, however, capable of highly precise definition. Most of the authorities which we are about to notice in our sketch fall unarguably within the term. So, for example, government departments and local authorities fulfil all possible criteria: they are created by or under statute, endowed with statutory powers and funded by the public purse for the purpose of conferring what are conceived to be benefits upon the community or a section thereof.

However, there are many other authorities set up by or under statute and serving important public purposes. Some are endowed with statutory powers and some may even be funded partly by the public purse. Nevertheless, these bodies could not happily be termed "state" or "public" authorities because they lack one or more of the criteria mentioned. So, public limited companies are created under statutory authority but, unlike governmental authorities, exist primarily for the private benefit of their members (shareholders). Where government owns a large or majority shareholding in a commercial enterprise endowed with substantial statutory powers (*e.g.* British Telecom[3]) the line is more difficult to draw. Then take public, or charitable, trusts. These do indeed, like governmental authorities, exist solely for the benefit of the public. But in general they are only partly state-funded (via tax relief) and have been created by private individuals for purposes, within charity law, of their own choosing. Again, however, some charities look more like public authorities than others. The National Trust, for example, exists now under statute,[4] is endowed with wide statutory powers to acquire property for the nation and receives substantial sums from central and local government grants. Universities are educational charities commonly created by royal charter.[5] In many cases their title to property of institutions which they have superseded derives from statute and they are the recipients of large direct grants from the public purse. Nevertheless, they are subject to the legal regime of charitable trusts[6] rather than to judicial review as public authorities. Trade unions also,

[3] *i.e.* British Telecommunications plc, established under Telecommunications Act 1984, s.60.

[4] National Trust Acts 1907–1971.

[5] *i.e.* under Royal Prerogative power—see pp. 12–13.

[6] Including the jurisdiction of the university visitor (who has jurisdiction to settle disputes relating to the internal affairs of the university). On this jurisdiction and its relation to that of the courts, see *Thomas* v. *University of Bradford* [1986] 1 All E.R. 217; (1981) 97 L.Q.R. 610 (P.M. Smith).

despite their great power, public importance and legal immunities, are not public authorities. They are not creatures of statute, are self-funded and exist primarily for the benefit of their individual members.

This brief discussion of what is, and is not, a public authority is intended to indicate in the most general terms what legal entities are subject to the judicial review jurisdictions described in Chapter 2. We shall return to the issue of the boundaries between the public and private domains particularly in the context of remedies in Part III. We turn now to our sketch of official power.

(2) Parliament and the central government

Any account of the nature and extent of public authority power must begin with Parliament. Parliament (or, more accurately, the Queen in Parliament) as sovereign law-maker is the only public authority in the United Kingdom whose power may be said to have no legal limit. The nature and extent of the legislative sovereignty of Parliament is a matter which raises acute questions of constitutional law and theory.[7] But it suffices to say here that it is a rule of English Law that every Act of the Queen in Parliament must be accepted by the courts as a valid law-making act. "[I]t is not for [a] court to say that a parliamentary enactment, the highest law in this country, is illegal."[8] Moreover, Parliament, the only authority whose power knows no legal limit, is the very authority by which, or under whose auspices, the legally limited power of almost all other public authorities is created. And the power of those few public authorities whose origin is not statutory—the Crown and the superior courts—is subject to such legal limitations as Parliament may choose to impose.

As is well known, the government of the day, through its House of Commons majority largely controls the statutory output of Parliament. Since, as we said, official power is almost entirely statutory in origin it follows that the government effectively determines the scope of official power.

The central government operates principally through a number of departments of state headed by government ministers and staffed by permanent civil servants. A list of the most important domestic[9] departments and their chief concerns may serve as some reminder of the scope of the concerns of government in the contemporary welfare state. The Treasury is responsible for taxation

[7] De Smith C. & A., p. 75 *et seq.*
[8] *Cheney* v. *Conn* [1968] 1 W.L.R. 242 at 247, *per* Ungoed-Thomas J.
[9] *i.e.* excluding the Foreign and Commonwealth Office and Ministry of Defence.

policy and legislation administered largely through the Boards of Inland Revenue and Customs and Excise.[10] The Home Office has a wide range of responsibilities in the field of law and order; and, in particular, wields such power as the central government has over the police (see (4) below). The Department of the Environment was formed in 1970 by the amalgamation of the Ministries of Housing and Local Government, Transport (now once again a separate department) and Public Building and Works. Its responsibilities are indicated in part by the names of its constituent departments and include too responsibility at national level for town and country planning and kindred environmental matters such as new towns and urban development. The Department of Health and Social Security takes central government responsibility for the National Health Service and for the administration of the wide range of social security cash benefits both contributory (*e.g.* unemployment, sickness and industrial injury benefits and most state retirement pensions) and non-contributory (*e.g.* supplementary and child benefits). The areas of responsibility of the Departments of Trade and Industry, of Employment, Education and Science, and Agriculture, Fisheries and Food appear sufficiently from their names.

(3) Local government and public corporations

> "In general the central government departments in Britain do not directly provide or administer public services . . . . The normal pattern is for a department to formulate broad policy and for the execution of that policy to be primarily a matter for elected local authorities or semi-autonomous public corporations."[11]

Turning first briefly to the local authorities of elected councillors served by permanent officials. Today local authorities in England and Wales derive their powers chiefly from the Local Government Act 1972. Broadly, local authority functions are parcelled out between county and district councils.[12] County councils are the

[10] Which are in effect sub-departments (de Smith C & A, p. 201).
[11] De Smith J.R.A.A., p. 12.
[12] As from April 1, 1986 the Greater London and Metropolitan County Councils ceased to exist. Their functions were transferred to other existing local authorities and to certain newly-created authorities by the Local Government Act 1985.

local education authorities, and are responsible for local social services, major roads and the fire service. They share planning functions with the district councils, among whose most important exclusive responsibilities are council housing, public health, and many licensing functions.

The relationship between central and local government has never been entirely happy and at the present time is perhaps less so than ever: in 1984 the government for the first time took statutory power[13] to restrict directly the amount of rates which a local authority could levy. Although, as indicated, local authorities have extensive responsibility for the provision of a wide range of services to the public, the purse strings and the reins of policy are held firmly by the central government. Conflict between central and local government authorities as to what in law is the extent of their respective powers—in particular as to the extent of the multifarious statutory powers of central government to advise, to direct, to withold funds from and, ultimately, in some cases to act in default of local authorities—is now reflected, as we shall see,[14] in the case law of judicial review.

What of the semi-autonomous public corporations? These are bodies endowed with corporate status and powers by government-engineered statutes. Thus far they resemble government departments. But they differ in that their parent statutes make the corporations largely independent of government control in their day-to-day management and affairs. They are only "semi-autonomous," however, because the statute will commonly give a government minister powers to intervene at a policy-making level in the corporation's affairs; and, once again, the government has a strong grip on the purse strings.

Broadly one may distinguish two classes of public corporation, the operational and the regulatory. The distinction is between those corporations whose job is principally to do, and those whose job is principally to regulate the doings of others. Prime in the first class are, of course, the nationalised industries—*e.g.* coal, electricity, gas, steel, atomic energy, the railways and the post office. The supply of water is not commonly thought of as an "industry" but, since 1973, it (along with sewerage) has been the responsibility of public corporation water authorities and not, as previously, district councils. We may note here that the B.B.C. is the creature not of statute but of royal charter renewable from time to time under prerogative power exercised on ministerial advice (see

[13] Rates Act 1984.
[14] See, *e.g.* the *Tameside, Norwich* and *Brent* cases discussed in Chap. 5.

(6) below). Familiar examples of public corporations with both regulatory and operational features are the Milk Marketing Board and the Forestry Commission. More in the regulatory mould are the Civil Aviation Authority, the Countryside Commission and the Nature Conservancy Council.

Relationships between central government and public corporations are no doubt on the whole less strained than between central government and local authorities. The public corporations are, after all, the offspring of government: conceived in Whitehall and born at Westminster. Nevertheless, a certain tension is produced by the very fact that the corporations have been made semi-autonomous. Governments sometimes find themselves wishing that their, or their predecessors', offspring had less autonomy. And here too, as we shall see,[15] judicial review is sometimes utilised to resolve these tensions.

(4) The police

In this thumb-nail sketch of the extent of official power we turn next to the police. Some authorities such as the British Railways Board, the British Airports Authority and the Ministry of Defence, as well as the armed services, maintain police forces that have special and limited jurisdictions. These forces are an integral part of the authorities concerned and require no separate consideration here. Our concern is with the municipal police forces that exercise a general jurisdiction. Only the London Metropolitan Police are under direct central government (the Home Secretary's) control. The other forty or so forces are based broadly (since 1974) on local government county areas and are administered by statutory police committees composed of local councillors and magistrates in a ratio of two to one. However, while half of police finance is raised via local rates, the other half comes from central government which may withhold funds on the basis of an adverse report by its inspectors of constabulary. Because of this and because the Home Secretary has wide statutory powers as to general police organisation, central government control over organisation and manning levels is substantial. The day-to-day disposition of the police, however, falls to the Chief Constable of the force concerned. He is appointed by the police committee subject to the Home Secretary's approval. The powers of the police are mainly statutory but important among their non-statutory powers is the discretion whether or not to prosecute, a discretion which, as

[15] See, *e.g.* the *Laker Airways* (1977) case discussed in Chap. 5.

we shall see,[16] has been on occasion the subject of judicial review proceedings.

(5) Rules and adjudication

We have now glimpsed in barest outline some of the main areas of official power to act and to order. Commonly, the power to order is a statutory power to make rules or regulations with legal force and sanctions, *i.e.* power to make "delegated" or "subordinate" legislation. So, local authorities are empowered by statutes to make "byelaws." And almost all the statutory authorities mentioned elsewhere in this section have kindred power—commonly to make "statutory instruments" under the procedural regime of the Statutory Instruments Act 1946. In English Law rules and regulations differ radically from Acts of Parliament. For, as already observed, it may be said that the legislative power of Parliament is in law unlimited; but any power to make delegated legislation is limited by the terms of the empowering statute and may be the subject of judicial review if its limits are overstepped.

We have as yet made no reference to one hugely important and wide-ranging kind of official power—the power to adjudicate upon disputes. Indeed, this book is about the power of one kind of official adjudicatory authority, the courts, to decide one kind of dispute: disputes about the extent of official power. In as much as the courts themselves (whenever they act) exercise official power, they too (with one exception and one major qualification[17]) may be subject to judicial review. In this context, the hierarchical structure of the courts provides the framework for the scrutiny of the acts of lower courts by those above them, and explains the one exception. There is no court of law higher than the House of Lords acting in its judicial capacity, so there is no court of law to scrutinise its decisions. If the House of Lords goes wrong, only Parliament can correct it by legislation. We shall turn our attention to the courts shortly. Now, however, in our sketch of official power we must notice another type of adjudicatory authority—the statutory tribunal.

The individual's contact with public authorities often concerns the transfer of benefits of one sort or another from state to individual or vice versa. The benefit may be in cash, enuring either to the individual (as with social security benefits) or to the state (as with

[16] See, *e.g.* the *Blackburn* cases discussed in Chap. 5. As to the institution and conduct of criminal proceedings, see now the Prosecution of Offences Act 1985.

[17] The major qualification (the immunity of the superior courts from *supervisory* review—see Chap. 2, p. 37 is examined in Chap. 4, pp. 152–153. For the exception see immediately below.

taxation); or it may be in kind (as with the grant to an immigrant of leave to enter the country or the grant of a licence to a transport operator). Commonly an individual official will be empowered to make a decision in the first instance since it will be anticipated that most decisions of the sort concerned will not be contentious. So, for example, the benefit officer assesses entitlement to supplementary benefits; the inspector of taxes assesses income tax liability; and the immigration officer decides initially whether or not a would-be immigrant may enter the country. But although most such decisions may not be contentious, many will be, and disputes may arise.

Broadly, the disputes will be as to the application of known rules to the particular facts of a case. It has been the practice of governments since 1945 to legislate for the creation of independent statutory tribunals to decide disputes of these kinds. In all the fields mentioned and in many other areas Parliament has created statutory tribunals.[18] The supplementary benefit dispute will go to the supplementary benefit appeal tribunal[19]; the income tax dispute to the general or special commissioners of income tax[20]; the immigration question to an immigration adjudicator.[21] Again broadly, we may say that the issues assigned to statutory tribunals have two characteristics. First, they are the type of issue—the application of rules to particular facts—with which, classically, courts of law have dealt. Secondly, notwithstanding this, the issues are of a sort deemed inappropriate to be dealt with by courts in the ordinary way. In particular, the individual disputant may be unwilling and financially unable to take the issue to a court of law: the tribunal is a cheaper and less formal and so less forbidding forum. Furthermore, a tribunal whose whole work is in one particular field will build up an expertise in that field which can hardly be matched by a court of general jurisdiction.

We have mentioned so far only those statutory tribunals which, in broad terms, deal with disputes between individual and state about the disposition of benefits in the public domain. But there are many statutory tribunals (set up likewise for the reasons just referred to) whose chief concern is to deal with disputes arising in the field of private law. Particularly well-known examples are the rent assessment committees which hear appeals from rent officers' determinations of fair rents[22]; and the industrial tribunals which

[18] For a table of statutory tribunals see Wade A.L., pp. 824–828.
[19] Supplementary Benefits Act 1976, s.15.
[20] Taxes Management Act 1970, s.31.
[21] Immigration Act 1971, s.13.
[22] Rent Act 1977, Sched. 11.

deal with a wide range of issues arising from employment and redundancy.[23]

Statutory tribunals, then, have an important place in any survey of official power. They will figure prominently too in our account of judicial review of that power. Meanwhile, we should notice that it is not uncommon for there to be a hierarchy of statutory tribunals in a particular field. So, the second-tier tribunals in the supplementary benefit appeals system are the social security commissioners[24]; from the immigration adjudicators there is an appeal to the Immigration Appeal Tribunal[25]; and from industrial tribunals in some cases to the Employment Appeal Tribunal.[26] The membership of these second-tier tribunals invariably includes highly qualified lawyers[27] and the appeal may be confined to point of law only.[28]

Here too we should mention finally the statutory inquiry. As a preliminary to the exercise of official power in matters both great (such as the siting of a nuclear power station or nuclear waste disposal site) and small (such as the extension of a dwelling-house or the compulsory purchase of even a small area of land) Parliament has made provision for concerned parties to be heard at a public inquiry. Inquiries do not make decisions; but decisions are made on the basis of their findings. A fair procedure is thus all important, and we shall encounter statutory inquiries particularly when considering judicial review of irregular or unfair procedure.[29]

To summarise thus far. Official power may be the power of a central government department to formulate policy, allocate resources and make rules; or the power of a local authority to provide public services at local level but within the constraints of central government policy, powers and financial control. It may be the power of a public corporation to operate an industry or to regulate the provision of services or the disposition of resources in a particular field—again under more or less remote government control. Often the man in the street will meet official power first behind the counter in the social security or tax office or at the

[23] *e.g.* Employment Protection (Consolidation) Act 1978, s.67 (unfair dismissal).
[24] 1976 Act (above), s.15A; Appeals Rules (S.I. 1980 No. 1605).
[25] 1971 Act (above), s.20.
[26] 1978 Act (above), s.136.
[27] *e.g.* in the Employment Appeal Tribunal two industrial relations experts sit with a High Court judge.
[28] As in the cases in notes 24 and 26. For the meaning of "point of law," see Chap. 3.
[29] Chap. 6.

immigration control or licensing authority; and then, if he has a complaint, at a tribunal hearing or public inquiry.

(6) The Crown

As we said earlier, most official power is statutory in origin. But some is not. The sovereign legislative power of the Crown in Parliament derives from the constitutional settlement of the seventeenth century. What of the non-statutory ("prerogative") powers and legal capacity of the Crown outside Parliament? As to legal capacity: the Crown is in law a common law corporation sole—a non-statutory legal entity whose capacity to act (unlike that of a statutory authority) is in general no more circumscribed than that of a private individual. So, the Crown can, to the same extent as a private individual, own and dispose of property, make contracts and other agreements and commit torts.[30] In contrast, as we shall see, the terms in which a statutory authority is created impose certain limits on its legal capacity.[31]

As to prerogative powers: as Professor Wade reminds us,[32] legal power (as distinct from mere capacity in law to act) means "the ability to alter people's rights, duties or status under the laws of this country which the courts of this country enforce." Before the constitutional settlement of the seventeenth century Crown prerogative power was extensive. Now statute has so radically curtailed that power as to leave only a residue: but the residue which remains is of considerable importance. It is, in effect, a facet of central government power because, by convention, the monarch exercises prerogative powers on the advice of ministers.

Briefly surveying the surviving prerogative powers one may distinguish two broad types which, for convenience, we label "prerogatives of state" and "prerogatives of government." By "prerogatives of state" we mean such powers as those relating to the summoning and dissolution of Parliament and the power of assent to legislation; also state powers in the field of foreign affairs and the making of war and peace. By "prerogatives of government" we mean the powers whose exercise impinges upon particular groups or individuals within the state rather than upon the state at large. Foremost among these are certain powers relating to the

[30] The Crown Proceedings Act 1947 removed procedural bars to suing the Crown for breach of contract and in tort. The reigning monarch (*i.e.* the incumbent of the office as distinct from the office itself) remains totally immune from legal proceedings under the doctrine that "The King (or Queen Regnant) can do no wrong"—see de Smith C & A, p. 145.

[31] Chap. 2, pp. 84–85.

[32] *Constitutional Fundamentals* (1980), p. 46.

administration of justice: the power to discontinue criminal proceedings (*nolle prosequi*); the power, in effect, to authorise civil proceedings where, otherwise, a litigant would have insufficient standing to take a case to court (the Attorney-General's relator action)[33]; and the prerogative of mercy—the power to pardon and to commute sentences in criminal cases. Outside the administration of justice we may mention the Crown's power to confer honours and to create corporations by royal charter—chartered corporations include, as mentioned, the B.B.C. and most universities. And the Crown has residual prerogative power to appoint a visitor[34] to universities and certain other charitable corporations.

Finally we should mention the prerogative power to legislate by Order in Council. This is a power to make general rules in any sphere where the Crown's powers have not been curtailed by Parliamentary legislation. So, the Crown may still legislate by prerogative Order in Council for dependent territories. Domestically, the terms and conditions of employment of the civil service are still regulated by prerogative Order in Council. This is a form, albeit very limited in scope, of primary legislation and should not be confused with the statutory Order in Council, a form of secondary or delegated legislation substantially similar to the statutory instrument.[35]

Although important within their fields of operation, what we have labelled the royal prerogatives of government are clearly of very limited scope. More wide-ranging in their impact, however, are the government-controlled capacities of the Crown to contract and otherwise to order its affairs. If the government decides not to award government contracts to particular companies which are not following its guidelines on wage increases[36] it is exercising what one might describe as a power of negative patronage. Not strictly a legal power as above defined; but a powerful official slap on the wrist. Similar remarks might be made with regard to the Crown's discretion as to the issuing of passports[37] and the making of extra-

[33] See Chap. 7.

[34] See above, note 6.

[35] For statutory instruments, see above. Parliament adopts the nomenclature "order in council" for delegated legislation conferring powers on the Queen in Council. This is done either to enable any minister to exercise the powers or to impart a greater sense of formality in appropriate cases. See Wade and Bradley, *Constitutional and Administrative Law* (10th ed.), p. 615. Statutory orders in council are, like statutory instruments, subject to the provisions of the Statutory Instruments Act 1946.

[36] Wade, *Constitutional Fundamentals* (1980), p. 55.

[37] *Op cit*. p. 50.

statutory tax concessions.[38] We shall see later that the extent of judicial review jurisdiction in this whole field of Crown action other than under statutory powers is currently very much in question.[39]

B. Legal Limits of Official Power—"Liability" and "Remit"

It has been a feature of constitutional arrangements in the United Kingdom since the seventeenth century that public authorities are in general[40] subject to the ordinary law of the land administered in the ordinary courts of justice.

The phrase "the ordinary law of the land" refers to two distinct types of legal limit to which public authorities are subject. The first type of limit is familiar. We may label it "liability." Public authorities, like private individuals and many other legal entities, need to be able, as occasion arises, to make contracts and enter into other commercial arrangements. And, in general,[41] they are, like others, answerable for breaches of obligations thereby incurred. Likewise they are, in general, answerable for such breaches of the criminal law and such civil wrongs (*e.g.* torts, infringements of property rights) as they may commit, through their officers and employees, in the course of their activities.

Our second type of legal limit is perhaps less familiar. Unlike private individuals, some legal entities are regarded by the law as existing solely in order to achieve a purpose or purposes. A trustee as such exists only to manage property for his beneficiaries. He will be made to discharge his duties and prevented from going beyond his powers of dealing with the trust property. A limited company exists solely for the purposes contained in its memorandum of association and can be restrained from pursuing purposes beyond these. The law has taken broadly the same type of approach to public authorities. A public authority, like a trustee and like a limited company, is treated in English law as a vehicle for the attainment of certain purposes remitted to it. Public authorities are, as we have seen, the repositories of special statutory and com-

[38] *Op cit*. p. 57.
[39] See Chap. 2, pp. 74–81.
[40] The power of Parliament, as we have said, is subject to no legal limit; and, of course, it is a concomitant of the legislative sovereignty of Parliament that Parliament may widen or narrow such jurisdiction as the courts may have over any particular public authority or group of authorities. Furthermore, the jurisdiction of the courts with regard to the exercise of royal prerogative powers is subject to special considerations (see Chap. 2, pp. 74–81).
[41] For some qualifications to these general statements as to public authority liability, see Chap. 2, pp. 82–86.

mon law powers and duties. To the extent that an authority discharges its duties and exercises its powers so as to further the purpose for which it exists, it may be said to be acting within its "remit." To the extent that it acts so as to further extraneous purposes or fails to discharge its duties it goes outside its remit. Where on this account a court may intervene, we say that the public authority's action or inaction is subject to judicial review.

Certain aspects of the relationship between the two types of legal limit will be explored later in the book.[42] Here we may simply note that particular action or inaction of a particular public authority may be subject to either or both of the two types. For example, the question whether a public authority is guilty of a civil wrong may (or may not) turn on the question whether the authority has gone outside its remit. Throughout this book we use the label *remit issue* to refer to a question arising in litigation as to whether or not a public authority has gone outside its remit; and the label *liability issue* for a question as to whether an authority is liable in respect of a criminal offence or civil wrong.

We return to the notion of remit in part D of this chapter. First, however, we consider briefly the constitutional place and function of judicial review.

C. Do We Need Judicial Review?

Most public authorities, as we have seen, are the creatures of statute. They have been created by Parliament for specific purposes and endowed by the words of statute with powers deemed necessary and sufficient for the fulfilment of these purposes. Statutes are, of course, legal instruments conferring legal powers and imposing legal duties. Within the framework of our present constitutional arrangements it is of great significance that governments continue to implement their policies via numerous statutes conferring specific powers on particular authorities rather than via one or a few statutes conferring broad yet unspecific powers on "the government" in general.[43] This indicates, at least, an acknowledgement by the government that, if it wishes to change the law, it must

[42] See Chap. 2, pp. 29–32, 65–74, 82–90. Chap. 7, *passim*.

[43] In 1984 it emerged that the government was planning to replace some forty statutes relating to nationalised industries with a single statute giving ministers general powers to order the disposal of the industries' assets and to dismiss board members not complying with ministers' instructions. Following sustained pressure by the opposition and by nationalised industry chairmen, the plans were shelved—see *The Times* September 18 and 19, October 5, 1984.

invoke the authority of Parliament and procure the passing of a statute. It also identifies those instances in which the government considers that a change in the law is necessary to give effect to particular administrative intentions which might otherwise have been the subject of simple administrative instructions, such as ministerial circulars. Implicit here is the constitutional assumption that the government considers itself bound by the existing law, both statutory and judge-made. For part of the existing law is the jurisdiction of the ordinary courts to interpret statute and hence to determine the extent of the powers conferred and the duties imposed on public authorities by current statutory provisions. Such was the pattern of "government according to law" that emerged from the constitutional resettlement of the seventeenth century.

To the common lawyer, with a traditional suspicion of arbitrary power, and a traditional belief in the separation of powers and the independence of the judiciary, such a pattern requires no defence or justification. Today, however, many of these traditional views are being questioned, in a variety of ways and at a variety of levels. At the most fundamental level, it is asked whether law is still the most suitable mechanism for government, or at least whether it is still appropriate to allow the activities of a democratically elected government, seeking to act for the general good, to be subjected to review by non-elected judges with a traditional determination to safeguard individual rights. Since the agencies of the state do indeed enjoy special legal powers and have at their disposal the machinery of a ubiquitous and often impenetrable bureaucracy, is it still sensible to leave their control to the ordinary law of the land and to assert that their status in law is the same as that of any other litigant? Do not negotiation, arbitration and conciliation provide better means of regulating government than the polarising blunt instrument of adversarial litigation? Does the existence of that blunt instrument inhibit recognition of a need to accept reasonable compromises and, if litigation is inevitable, are the traditional common law courts the best forum that can be devised for the resolution of the problems of government?

It is not possible, in the compass of a work such as this, to do justice to the importance of the questions that are currently being asked,[44] nor is it possible to dismiss the questions by reference to

[44] For a well-documented account of theories as to the relationship between law and government, the nature of administrative law and the place within it of judicial review, see Carol Harlow and Richard Rawlings, *Law and Administration* (1984), to specific chapters of which reference is made below. For an analysis of administrative law as a process of power allocation, see Craig, Chap. 1.

those assumptions about the nature of the state that have justified the common law approach in centuries past. Ultimately, they are questions of political philosophy and a first step towards appreciating their significance is for the lawyer to concede that the traditional view of the law as something above and distinct from the business of government is itself part of a political philosophy.

The most fundamental of the current critiques of the relationship between law and government would require a constitutional resettlement in order to be implemented.[45] Less radical criticisms are levelled at the propriety of judicial review within the context of our present constitutional arrangements. In particular, it is often said that judicial review is intolerably uncertain and amounts to little more than a licence for judges to interfere arbitrarily with the machinery of government and administration.[46] Also, it is said that to the extent that any clear principles of judicial intervention do appear, they are constitutionally unacceptable because they represent either too wide or too narrow (according to the commentator's point of view) an encroachment into the field of government and administration.[47]

The aim of this work is to explain the principles of the law of judicial review within the context of current constitutional arrangements. That is not to suggest that those arrangements are considered correct and unchallengeable but, rather, it is to acknowledge the need for a clear and systematic analysis of the present position. It is hoped that such an exposition in addition to providing guidance to those who must understand the present position for practical purposes, will provide a sound basis from which one may begin to assess the critiques of the constitutional propriety of judicial review referred to above. A prerequisite of any accurate assessment must surely be a consciousness of the extent to which the law of judicial review does, or does not, display those principles of internal consistency and rationality upon which the common law ultimately relies to justify its authority.[48] It is thus hoped that some contribution may be made to the broader debate on the future of administrative law by presenting a concise and comprehensible picture of the optimum contribution that may be expected of the common law in this field.

[45] *e.g.* In *English Law—The New Dimension* (1974) Lord Scarman argued forcefully for constitutional and other changes which would enable the common law to play its traditional role in response to the challenges posed by major social and political developments of our time.

[46] See Harlow and Rawlings, *op cit*. Chaps. 9–11.

[47] *Op cit*. Chaps. 1–5.

[48] See, *e.g.* F.H. Lawson, *The Rational Strength of English Law* (1951).

To return to our theme of the need for judicial review, we have noted that the government of the day regards itself as bound by the existing law; regards it as necessary to change the existing law in order to implement many of its administrative intentions; regards it as necessary to invoke the authority of Parliament in order to effect those changes by legislation; and recognises that the courts regard themselves as having jurisdiction to determine the extent of public authority power and duty. Furthermore, it should be noted that, once legal powers have been conferred on some public authority, neither the government nor Parliament is recognised, under our present constitutional arrangements, as having jurisdiction to rule upon the extent of the powers granted. If it is considered that powers are being overstepped, or duties neglected, the government may have many ways of bringing pressure to bear upon the allegedly defaulting public authority,[49] but its view, or ruling, that the public authority is acting unlawfully, is of no legal force. For its part, Parliament can change the law so as to vary powers or duties and, as a remedy of last resort, can change the law retrospectively to make lawful that which may have been unlawful when done. However, while this possibility is implicit in the doctrine of parliamentary sovereignty, frequent resort to retrospective legislation would itself be regarded as calling for a constitutional resettlement.[50] It is obviously not a procedure suitable for use in the day-to-day business of administration.

Given these constraints and the restraints to which the government itself submits in relation to its own powers despite its ability to control Parliament, it would seem to be self-evident that, when the government, through Parliament, confers statutory powers upon some other public authority, it does not seek to confer upon that authority any status or position in law superior to that of the government itself. On this basis there is a need for some constitutional machinery capable of ensuring that the exercise of statutory powers conferred on other public authorities will be adequately controlled: of ensuring that those public authorities both do the job for which they were designed and do not, like Frankenstein's monster, acquire an autonomy which will make them masters rather than servants of their creator. This machinery should be designed to achieve as nearly as possible a balance between, on the one hand, the need for the public authority in

[49] See below, pp. 19, 20–21.

[50] An example of retrospective legislation widely regarded as unconstitutional is the War Damage Act 1965: see A.L. Goodhart in (1966) 82 L.Q.R. 97 at 110–114.

question to be given the full rein which Parliament intended it to have in the making and execution of policy; and, on the other, the need to prevent it from either exceeding or failing to fulfil the purpose for which it exists.

We have already observed that the question whether a public authority is guilty of a criminal offence or civil wrong may turn on the question whether the authority has gone outside its remit. The constitutional need which we have just identified may be served in such a case by (as appropriate) criminal prosecution or civil proceedings by a competent plaintiff. But what of a case where no criminal offence or civil wrong is alleged? The authority may nevertheless have exceeded its remit. Who, under present constitutional arrangements, is both likely to wish for a ruling to this effect and likely to be considered to have a sufficient interest in obtaining it?

Commonly the public authority in question will have derived its remit from a government-sponsored statute. May it happen that the government itself will wish to obtain a ruling on the extent of powers conferred upon such an authority? Certainly no litigant would seem to have a greater interest in doing so and on occasions a government will resort to the courts for this purpose.[51] Usually, however, when conferring powers, a government will ensure that it retains such control (*e.g.* financial or by way of express power to act in default[52] of the empowered authority) as will obviate the need for it to initiate review proceedings.

However, it is not uncommon for public authorities *inter se* to seek rulings upon the legality of each others' purported exercise of statutory powers.[53] Similarly, public authorities may need to seek rulings on the extent of their own statutory powers when the government exercises default powers where in its view the authority has failed to keep within its remit.[54]

[51] See, *e.g. Secretary of State for Education* v. *Tameside M.B.C.* [1977] A.C. 1014 (minister sued unsuccessfully to compel local education authority to go "comprehensive" as he had directed). For this case, and those cited in notes 53 and 54 below, see Chap. 5, pp. 183 *et seq*.

[52] For default powers, see Chap. 5, pp. 185–188.

[53] See, *e.g. Bromley L.B.C.* v. *Greater London Council* [1983] 1 A.C. 768 (borough councils established that G.L.C. exceeded its remit in imposing on them rate precept to pay for public transport fares reduction); *cf. R.* v. *London Transport Executive ex p. G.L.C.* [1983] Q.B. 484 (G.L.C. obtained declaration against transport executive that alternative G.L.C. fares reduction policy was not outside G.L.C. remit).

[54] See, *e.g. R.* v. *Environment Secretary ex p. Norwich City Council* [1982] Q.B. 808 (city council unsuccessfully challenged minister's use of default power to expedite sale of council houses).

Further, there may be circumstances in which no other public authorities are concerned but where it is of crucial importance to individuals or groups within society that a particular public authority should be kept within its remit. Let us take a graphic example relating to the arming of the police. Today, few in Britain would dispute that it is necessary on occasions for police officers to be armed. At the opposite extreme, perhaps even fewer would maintain that police officers should invariably be armed. Certainly an innovation of that magnitude would be a matter requiring the authority of Parliament. Local police authorities are given wide statutory powers and duties in relation to maintaining and equipping efficient police forces within their areas of responsibility.[55] However, it seems probable that most people would agree that an authority which refused to provide finance to allow any firearms to be purchased and stored against an emergency, and refused to finance any training whatsoever in the use of firearms by police officers in its area would be failing to discharge a duty remitted to it. Likewise an authority which adopted an opposite policy by earmarking in its estimates provision to enable all police officers in its area to be issued with personal firearms would appear to be exceeding its remit. Yet in neither of these extreme cases would any civil or criminal wrong necessarily be committed.

In such circumstances, there is little doubt that the government of the day, through its control of the purse strings or otherwise could bring both authorities into line.[56] Suppose however, the political sympathies of the government caused it to bring pressure to bear against only the authority whose actions were contrary to the government's own preferences in the matter. Suppose also that a proposal in favour of arming the police had recently been left to a free vote in Parliament and roundly defeated but the government, because of its own preferences, took no action against the authority which sought to ignore the obvious intention of Parliament. It is certainly arguable that an interested group or individual ought to be able to obtain a ruling on the legality or otherwise of the authorities' actions in these respects.

In less extreme terms, it could well be imagined that a government might not seek to ensure the obedience of a particular public

[55] Police Act 1964.

[56] For example, when during the 1984 miners' strike the South Yorkshire Police Authority resolved to sell the force's horses and dogs which had been used in the policing of picket lines, the Home Secretary indicated that he would use his powers under the 1964 Act to prevent the sale—see *The Times*, September 18 and 19, 1984. He later contemplated challenging the authority's resolution in the courts (*ibid.* October 11).

authority to statutory duties arising under legislation passed by its predecessor. Unless and until repealed by Parliament, that legislation remains law and to leave enforcement entirely in the hands of the government or another public authority would be to re-create a dispensing power of the sort long ago abolished.[57]

The preceeding paragraphs have given some indication of circumstances in which resort to the courts by way of judicial review might be thought to be the appropriate constitutional machinery to resolve issues as to the extent of a public authority's remit. As already observed, the broad theoretical question of the proper relationship between law and government is beyond the scope of this book. We may simply accept here that whether or not judicial review is indeed regarded as appropriate in the kinds of circumstances just referred to will depend in part upon both one's perception of what counts as (and is likely to encourage) "good administration" and one's general political philosophy.

Philosophical questions may bulk especially large when one considers the extent to which judicial review machinery should be available to the private individual. No doubt the principle that the individual should have some means of ensuring that the agencies of the state remain within their remit is an assumption which deserves to be examined. Our discussion, however, will focus on the extent of this right rather than on whether it should exist. We have seen that, broadly, English law treats a public authority like any other defendant if it is alleged by a private individual that the authority has infringed an established legal right. This may justify judicial review of the precise scope of the authority's remit when this is relevant to the question of whether or not the authority has committed a civil wrong. However, the right to a review arising in the course of litigation asserting interference with a recognised legal right is very different from arrangements which allow a private individual to require the courts to pronounce upon the extent of a public authority's power or duty when no civil liability is in issue.

We shall see later[58] that there will be cases when it will be difficult to tell whether or not a particular statute has conferred legal rights enforceable by private individuals in the event of a breach of a statutory duty. In such cases, some judicial proceedings will be necessary to resolve that question and it may well be that applications for review by individuals with very direct and real interests, perhaps falling just short of such rights, may be the most appropri-

[57] Bill of Rights 1688.
[58] Chap. 7.

ate, or only, means of ensuring that the statutory duty is properly performed.

In any event, if there is concern about the propriety of allowing private citizens to question the legality of administrative action intended to be for the general or public good, it could be argued that it would be better to re-examine the rules of standing,[59] which govern whether any individuals have a sufficient interest to entitle them to a ruling, rather than to dismantle the whole edifice of judicial review which, as has been demonstrated, serves other purposes, and often those of public authorities themselves.

In this section we have endeavoured to avoid asserting that the English law of judicial review is somehow canonised by traditional notions of the rule of law or government under law. We have attempted simply to indicate how judicial review may be regarded as an integral part of constitutional arrangements presently subsisting in this country. Amongst the criteria against which the constitutional propriety of judicial review will be judged is the consistency with which the courts identify principles which are capable of reasonably certain application. We should embark on our examination of the law of judicial review with this criterion particularly in mind.

Here, however, we should note that, however integral judicial review might be to our system of government, however consistent the courts might be in the identification and application of principles, there is and will remain an element of pure chance in the judicial policing of the limits of official power. We may recall the opening words of Professor de Smith's classic work: "Judicial review of administrative action is inevitably sporadic and peripheral."[60] Not only will many disputes arise in the administrative law field which are of a sort inappropriate to be decided by the courts, but also, as Lord Diplock once said:[61]

> "Courts of justice do not act of their own motion. In our legal system it is their function to stand idly by until their aid is invoked by someone recognised by law as entitled to claim the remedy in justice that he seeks."

The effectiveness of judicial review as a means of establishing the legal limits of official power is dependent on all the accidents and

[59] See Chap. 8.
[60] De Smith J.R.A.A., p. 3.
[61] *Gouriet* v. *Union of Post Office Workers* [1978] A.C. 435 at 496.

vagaries of litigation. Furthermore, administrative justice may be sought other than through the courts. We have referred already to statutory tribunals and public inquiries and may note here also what Professor de Smith referred to as "the enthusiasm for Ombudsmen"[62] as an indication that traditional legal and political mechanisms have been regarded as by themselves inadequate to secure administrative justice.

D. The Notion of Remit and the Boundaries of Official Power

We have described judicial review as the jurisdiction of courts to keep public authorities within their remit. "Remit" is not a term of legal art but, as we have indicated, it is used in this book to refer to the special legal competence (duties and powers) with which a public authority is invested in order to fulfil the purposes for which it exists. The notion of a public authority going outside its remit may seem to be clarified by the adoption of a familiar analogy. If we were to speak of keeping public authorities within the "boundaries" of their competence, the mental image might be created of a sports field with precise, clear and regular boundary-lines. In terms of this analogy an authority would go outside its remit (as a footballer puts the ball out of play) by crossing a boundary line. But if the analogy gives at first an impression of clarity and simplicity, closer inspection will show quickly that the impression is deceptive.

If the powers and duties of public authorities have neat white-line boundaries, who draws them? Why, Parliament, surely. Official power is almost entirely statutory in origin, so its boundaries will be fixed by the statutory words in which the power is conferred. In legislating, Parliament not only draws up the rules of the game but also acts as its own groundsman by marking the boundaries of the pitch upon which the game will be played. So, for example, a public authority charged solely with the provision of a public transport service would plainly overstep the mark if it branched out into the provision of houses for the homeless. In restraining it from so doing a review court would simply be acting as linesman on Parliament's touchline. But how far will this analogy of the courts as linesmen take us?

Suppose that a local authority is empowered by statute to provide a bus service and to supplement the passenger service by the carriage of parcels. The authority takes the view that it is not confined to allowing parcels to be handed to bus crews and carried to the bus termini for eventual collection by the consignees. Instead,

[62] J.R.A.A., p. 8.

it institutes a further service by which the parcels are collected from the termini by van and delivered to consignees' addresses. The authority may argue that it has power to use its buses for the "carriage of parcels" and that (accepting that it is impractical for buses to run to the very doorstep of every consignee), the use of the vans is incidental to the power as conferred, and in its view necessary to fulfil the purpose of the power. A contrary argument may be advanced by a public authority such as the Post Office with an interest in maintaining a grip on the parcels delivery market or by a dissentient ratepayer. The argument will be that the power conferred extends only to such "carriage" of parcels as may practicably be achieved by a bus service: *i.e.*, carriage to termini for collection by consignees. So there is doubt as to where the boundary line of this power is to be drawn. Parliament has not, it seems, drawn the line clearly.[63]

Now, it is tempting to say that "someone must decide" whether the doorstep service is within or outside the statutory power; and to argue that the "someone" should be (as in English law it is) a court of law. But if we say this, we must be clear how it affects our "courts as linesmen" analogy. The boundaries of official power, we said, are drawn by Parliament. But now we find that the boundaries may, in cases of uncertainty, be drawn not by Parliament but by the courts. It is as though play has begun on a pitch whose boundaries are revealed to the players only when the linesman's flag goes up to indicate that the line has been crossed. This may seem to have an "Alice in Wonderland" air about it. However, one must not exaggerate the extent of line-drawing power of this sort. If the groundsman has left a short stretch of boundary unmarked, the linesman may have to judge whether the players have crossed the boundary at that point. But this does not reduce the game to the level of Wonderland croquet.[64] Parliament has marked out the pitch with considerable, albeit not total, precision. The power is to provide a bus service for, inter alia, carriage of parcels. Very many activities quite clearly do, and very many quite clearly do not, fall within the power. But there are those activities also, such as the provision of the doorstep delivery service in our example, which arguably do, and arguably do not, fall within the limits of the power.

It may be thought that there are good reasons why this sort of

[63] Example suggested by *Att.-Gen.* v. *Manchester Corporation* [1906] 1 Ch. 643. See Chap. 4, p. 132.

[64] In which the Queen's soldiers bent double to act as hoops but kept moving from place to place, thus making play impossible.

statutory boundary dispute should be settled by the courts. In the first place, one might be inclined to say that the dispute is about "the kind of thing" that an authority can lawfully do, rather than about "the way in which" the authority may do that kind of thing. So, a ruling by the courts will not encroach upon what would commonly be regarded as the authority's own province of policy-making and execution.[65] Furthermore, such a ruling would ensure consistency of local authority understanding of the extent of the power in question. In a case such as this, then, it may seem not inappropriate that the courts should be in effect both groundsmen and linesmen. But there are cases of a different sort where the "courts as linesmen" analogy breaks down completely.

Suppose that a statute creates an authority to administer a particular kind of state benefit. The statute provides that the benefit is payable to persons in a defined class and to any "member of the family" of such persons. The authority decides that X is in the class but that Y who is said to have lived with X for ten years as his wife, although not married to him, is not a member of X's family for the purposes of the statute.[66] The authority's decision may have been based on any one or more of a large number of considerations relating, for example, to the authority's understanding of the word "family," its belief in X and Y's assertions of fact, its estimate of the significance of the period of their attachment, and so on. Our question is this: suppose that it could be shown that the refusal of Y's claim was wrong for any reason, would it follow that the authority could be said to have gone outside its remit: to have transgressed the boundaries of its power? In one sense the authority seems to be doing precisely "the kind of thing" for which it was created—*i.e.*, administering the state benefit in question. In this respect the case appears to differ from our parcel service case. However, we are postulating that the authority has erred in not classifying Y as a member of X's family. Surely it may be said, the authority was created to administer the benefit correctly, not incorrectly. Here the authority is incorrect, so it has gone outside its remit: it has overstepped the mark. Which is the right approach?

Before considering that question, take a quite different case. Statute empowers local authorities to grant to applicants licences to use premises for certain public entertainments and authorises

[65] See Chap. 5, p. 168 *et seq*.

[66] Example suggested by *Dyson Ltd.* v. *Fox* [1976] Q.B. 503. (But the dispute in that case was between a private landlord and his tenant concerning Rent Act protection vouchsafed to members of a deceased tenant's family—see Chap. 3, p. 106).

the imposition of conditions for certain specified purposes only, including preventing persons in the neighbourhood being unreasonably disturbed by noise.[67] Suppose that P applies to his local authority which grants him a licence to run a discotheque on every day of the week except Sunday. The authority justifies the Sunday ban by reference to its noise control power and to what it describes as the need to retain Sunday as a day of rest and quiet. P maintains that the authority ought not to impose a total ban on any particular day but must confine itself to considering what level of noise is acceptable, and for what period, on every day of the week. He shows that licensing authorities elsewhere in the country commonly grant discotheque licences for certain periods on Sundays. Now, one can easily postulate a case where an authority would have overstepped its noise control power: an authority which, relying on that power, refused to license any discotheques at all would clearly have done so. No licensing authority can be heard to say that all noise of this sort constitutes unreasonable disturbance when Parliament, by conferring the power, has indicated otherwise. Can our authority say that all such noise on Sundays is unreasonable?

This example is a far cry from our parcels service case: it seems clearly to be about "the way in which" the authority may act, rather than about "the kind of thing" it may do. In this respect it resembles our "member of the family" example; but it differs in that the issue for decision in that case seemed to be capable of either a correct or an incorrect answer. Here, on the contrary, one would not say that a certain licence condition is "correct" and another "incorrect." The case seems, indeed, to fall squarely within what would commonly be regarded as the authority's own province of policy-making and execution. On the other hand, it may be open to argument here as much as in the "member of the family" case, that the authority has gone wrong in its selection of factors upon which to base its decision. So, the question is, as in the previous example: does that kind of mistake (if established) carry an authority beyond the boundaries of its power?

This question, which each of the last two examples has posed, can be generalised as follows: may it ever be said that a public authority has crossed the boundaries of its competence—has gone outside its remit—by making a mistake in the course of doing the kind of thing it exists to do? If the answer is yes, the whole notion of "boundaries" to public authority power seems to be cast into

[67] Local Government (Miscellaneous Provisions) Act 1982, s.1 and Sched. 1, para. 4(4).

doubt. That notion, as we have seen, conjures up the image of a playing-field with the courts acting as linesmen with power to decide only when a boundary has been crossed: linesmen who have no jurisdiction over what happens on the field of play. But in our last two examples, the questions "is Y a member of the family?" and "may the licensing authority prohibit discotheques on Sunday?" seem to be questions about what is happening on the field of play. If we say they are "boundary" questions, therefore, the analogy collapses.

Now, that may demonstrate simply that analogies are good servants but bad masters: that they cannot be pressed too far. But we should recall what led us to adopt the analogy in the first place. Our description of judicial review as the jurisdiction of courts to keep public authorities within their remit seems to imply that judicial review is concerned precisely with establishing and policing boundaries of official power; but that it does not enable the courts to intervene where those boundaries have not been crossed. Do we, then, adhere to our "boundary" analogy and say that our "member of the family" and "Sunday licensing" issues are not "boundary" issues? If we do that, we accept that the law of judicial review is not in any way concerned with the way in which a public authority does what it was created to do. No matter how grievous the error in failing to classify Y as a member of X's family; no matter how eccentric the licensing authority's attitude to Sunday discotheques, the law of judicial review would have nothing to say. This would amount to accepting that whenever in the course of doing what it was created to do a public authority encounters an issue which must be resolved before it can proceed, the authority's resolution of that issue should be incapable of being challenged in the courts. On the other hand, it is plain that if every alleged error of a public authority were challengeable in the courts, that authority would have no effective decision-making power.

As we shall see, the courts are empowered, in the exercise of their judicial review jurisdiction, to entertain some but not all such challenges. In terms of our analogy, the courts are not only linesmen but also, to an extent, referees.[68] The question is, to what extent? What sort of error counts as taking a public authority outside its remit, and what not? What sorts of error are reviewable, and what immune from review? And who decides? It is essentially with these questions and with others arising from them that this book is concerned.

[68] *cf. per* Lawton L.J. in *Laker Airways Ltd.* v. *Dept. of Trade* [1977] Q.B. 643 at 724.

E. Scheme of the Book

Of the questions just put we tackle first, in Chapter 2, the question who decides what is the scope of judicial review. We observe first that judicial review jurisdiction flows from both common law and statutory sources; we then describe (section A) the circumstances in which a remit issue may come before the courts. Broadly, where the resolution of a remit issue is crucial to the resolution of a liability issue, the remit issue is said to arise "collaterally;" otherwise it is said to arise "directly." We consider the courts' jurisdiction to entertain both direct (section B) and collateral (section C) challenges. Next we discuss judicial review and the royal prerogative (section D). Finally (section E) we consider some features of the relationship between the remit of a public authority and its legal capacity to sustain criminal and civil liability.

In Part II of the book we tackle the central question raised above—essentially, what action or inaction of a public authority will take it outside its remit. In Chapter 3 we examine the notion of error of law which (as appears in Chapter 2) is crucial in answering this question. In Chapters 4, 5 and 6 we look at the different kinds of transgression or error which may carry an authority outside its remit. Chapter 4 deals with alleged errors of law, fact or degree; Chapter 5 with the boundary between matters of law and matters of policy; and Chapter 6 with alleged transgressions of procedural requirements.

Part III of the book is concerned with the machinery of judicial review—the remedies and procedures by which public authorities may be kept within their remit. In Parts I and II of the book we use the distinction between "liability" and "remit" issues to explain the nature of judicial review and the circumstances in which it may operate. Although at a general descriptive level the distinction appears readily intelligible, difficult questions may arise as to its true juridical nature and effects, particularly as regards the procedures by which judicial review may be sought and the remedies which those procedures may yield. These questions are tackled in Chapter 7. In Chapter 8 we will look at the remedies themselves, and at the form of procedure known as application for judicial review introduced in 1977. Finally, in Chapter 9, we will consider the extent to which the availability of other forms of legal redress may influence the exercise of the court's discretion to allow an application for judicial review to be made.

Chapter 2

REVIEW JURISDICTION

As already indicated, the question in this chapter is who decides what is the scope of judicial review jurisdiction; or, more conventionally, what are the sources of the jurisdiction whose extent and operation we shall examine in Parts II and III of the book.

Briefly, the sources are two: common law and statute. From the common law source flows the so-called "supervisory" review jurisdiction of the High Court over a wide range of public authorities. This jurisdiction began to develop towards its modern forms in the seventeenth century. From the statutory source flows the modern jurisdiction of courts to hear appeals—"appellate" review jurisdiction. We must also consider the particular circumstances in which Parliament has by statute ousted or modified review jurisdiction which would otherwise have existed in those circumstances.

In section B of this chapter we give some account of the common law and statutory review jurisdictions just mentioned. But we have so far made no reference to the circumstances in which it may fall to a court to rule on the question of whether a public authority has gone outside its remit. As we are about to see, a litigant may raise a remit issue either "directly" or "collaterally." In order to understand the true extent of review jurisdiction it is necessary first to explain the notions of direct and collateral challenge (section A). We can then see how the common law and statutory review jurisdictions operate in the context of, first, direct and, then, collateral challenge (sections B and C respectively). In section D we consider judicial review of Crown action under what is claimed to be its prerogative power. Finally, in section E, we notice some aspects of the relationship between the legal notions of remit, capacity and liability of public authorities.

A. Direct and Collateral Challenge

The issue of whether a particular public authority has gone outside its remit—*i.e.* what we have labelled a "remit issue"—may arise in litigation either (i) directly or (ii) indirectly (or, as it is said, "collaterally").[1] An assertion that an authority has exceeded its remit

[1] On the distinction between "collateral" and "direct" challenge see Wade A.L. p. 296, Craig, p. 384. See also A. Rubinstein, *Jurisdiction and Illegality*, Chap. III where, however, the distinction is drawn differently.

may be said to be a "direct challenge" where the proceedings in which a remit issue arises are designed specifically to settle that issue. The challenge may be said to be "collateral" where, on the contrary, the proceedings in which the issue arises are designed to settle another issue in the context of which the remit issue arises.

(1) Remit issue arising collaterally

Here, as we have just said, the proceedings are designed to settle an issue other than the remit issue which arises. Most commonly[2] the issue which the proceedings are designed to settle is the liability in civil or criminal law[3] of one of the parties. If it transpires that the resolution of the liability issue depends on whether or not a public authority has, at some stage prior to the proceedings, gone outside its remit, this remit issue arises "collaterally." The public authority in question may or may not be a party to the litigation. If it is a party it may be either defendant or plaintiff/prosecutor. The following examples indicate how a liability issue may depend on a remit issue.

Public authority defendant

1. A public authority (D) with statutory powers to enter and "inspect" private land[4] enters P's land and (relying on its powers) undertakes some minor excavations by way of "inspection." P sues in trespass. D's defence is that the excavations were permitted by the statutory power to inspect. P maintains that D has gone outside its remit. D's liability thus turns, or depends, on the success or failure of P's collateral challenge.[5]

Public authority plaintiff

2. Local authority landlord (P) takes possession proceedings against council house tenant D for failure to pay rent increase. D

[2] *cf.* Rubinstein *op.cit.*, pp. 39 *et seq*: the proceedings are not always on a "liability" issue. See, *e.g. Westminster City Council* v. *British Waterways Board* [1985] A.C. 676. Issue was whether Board as landlords of premises tenanted by council had grounds under landlord and tenant legislation for opposing new tenancy. This turned on whether council, as planning authority had exceeded its remit in refusing planning permission for change of use so as to protect its tenancy. The House of Lords held that it had.

[3] For discussion of civil and criminal liability and their relationship to the notion of remit, see Chap. 7.

[4] *e.g.* for the purpose of discovering sites of archaeological interest: National Heritage Act 1983, s.36.

[5] For a case law example of this type of challenge, see *Cooper* v. *Wandsworth Board of Works* (1863) 14 C.B. (N.S.) 180, below p. 66, note 45.

admits his failure to pay but argues that P has gone outside its remit in making the increase. D's liability to the possession order turns on the success or failure of his collateral challenge.[6]

Public authority not a party to proceedings:

Criminal prosecution

3. D is prosecuted for breach of a bye-law made by a local authority and forbidding a person to sing in any public place after having been required by a police constable to desist. D admits singing but defends himself by asserting that the authority exceeded its remit in making the bye-law. Again, D's liability turns on the success or failure of his collateral challenge.[7]

Civil action

4. The Commons Commissioners purporting to act under their statutory powers amend the Commons Register by removing Blackacre from it. D nevertheless continues to assert that he has rights of common over Blackacre and continues to graze his sheep. P, the owner of Blackacre, sues D in trespass. D's defence is that the Commissioners exceeded their remit in removing the land. D's liability in trespass will thus depend on the success or failure of his collateral challenge.[8]

Such is the notion of collateral challenge. In section C of this chapter we shall consider the approach of the courts to such challenges. It is to be observed that very many criminal and civil proceedings against public authorities do not turn upon or raise any

[6] See *Wandsworth London Borough Council* v. *Winder* [1985] A.C. 461 (facts as in example). Note that in *Winder* Lord Fraser said (at p. 508) that the remit issue was not "truly collateral" because it was "the central issue which has to be decided." But its centrality does not prevent its being collateral, or incidental, to the issue for whose resolution the proceedings were commenced.

[7] See *Kruse* v. *Johnson* [1898] 2 Q.B. 91 (facts as in example). Note that criminal prosecutions are commonly (as in *Kruse*) initiated by the police. For a case where the public authority whose remit was in issue was also prosecutor, see, *e.g. Rogers* v. *Essex County Council* [1985] 2 All E.R. 39 (education authority prosecuted parents for failure of their school age child to attend school. By way of defence, parents successfully challenged authority's ruling that school was within walking distance of child's home).

[8] For a case law example of this type of challenge, see *Bunbury* v. *Fuller* (1853) 9 Ex.111. See below, p. 66 (note 45).

remit issue. We consider later[9] aspects of the relationship between the notions of remit, capacity and liability. Now, however, we turn from the notion of collateral challenge to that of "direct" challenge—*i.e.* from cases where a remit issue arises collaterally to cases where it arises "directly."

(2) Remit issue arising directly

Here, as we said, the proceedings are designed specifically to settle a remit issue. We may distinguish two common types of circumstance in which the issue of whether a particular public authority has gone outside its remit arises directly.

(a) A public authority (A) is in dispute with another party (P). The dispute raises the issue of whether A has gone outside its remit. In proceedings in which no question of liability arises, P asks a review court to rule that A has gone outside its remit.

(b) Two parties (P and D) are in dispute. A court or tribunal (A) has decided the dispute in favour of (say) D. P asks a review court to rule that A has gone outside its remit.

We consider each type of situation in turn.

(a) *Dispute between public authority and another party*

In this situation a dispute has arisen in which one party alleges that the other party, a public authority, has gone outside its remit. The challenge is directed solely to this issue, and no question of liability arises in the proceedings. The absence of any liability issue in the proceedings distinguishes this type of direct challenge from collateral challenge.

We may take the three examples already given in Chapter 1 (section D) when discussing the "boundary" analogy.

1. Recall the case of the authority empowered to provide a bus service, for *inter alia* the carriage of parcels. Here the Post Office or dissentient rate-payer might wish to ask a review court to rule simply that the transport authority has exceeded its remit and should not continue to operate the doorstep delivery service. No issue of liability arises. The challenge would therefore be direct.
2. Recall the case of the woman (Y) who was claiming state benefit as a "member of the family" of X. Y may wish to

[9] See below, pp. 82–90.

ask a review court to rule that the benefit authority has gone outside its remit in refusing to classify her as a member of X's family. The ruling would then entitle Y to claim benefit on the basis that she is a member. Y is not alleging that the authority has committed a civil wrong against her. The only issue is the remit issue and it would arise directly in the proceedings.

3. Finally, recall the case of the discotheque licence subject to the Sunday ban. The applicant, P, may wish to ask a review court to rule that the licensing authority has exceeded its remit in imposing the ban. Again, no issue of liability in either party need arise. In those circumstances, again, P's challenge would be a "direct" challenge of the kind under discussion.

In each of the above examples the public authority said to have gone outside its remit is the defendant in the proceedings. But, as will appear later, the authority itself may be able to bring proceedings seeking from the review court a declaration that it has not (as is alleged) gone outside its remit.

(b) *Public authority (court or tribunal) has decided dispute between two other parties*

In this situation two parties, P and D, are in dispute. The dispute has been brought before a court or tribunal,[10] for resolution. The authority has decided in favour of D but P wishes to have the matter reconsidered—reviewed—by a higher court or tribunal. Suppose, for example, that P sues D in a county court to recover a contract debt. The court gives judgment for D. P takes the view that the decision is wrong and appeals to the Court of Appeal. If P is able to reopen the dispute in this way he is challenging directly the decision of the county court, a public authority. He is asserting that, in deciding as it has, the court has gone outside its remit. So, a remit issue will arise directly in the proceedings before the review court—in our example, the Court of Appeal.

Two objections might be levelled at this analysis. First, it might be said that in the Court of Appeal P is asserting not that the county court has "gone outside its remit" but simply that it was wrong. But if an authority is wrong in circumstances where a higher authority can correct the error, the error carries the first

[10] Commonly a statutory tribunal of the type referred to in Chap. 1, pp. 9–11.

authority outside its remit. We may say that a county court's remit is to decide a particular dispute or type of dispute. But if a higher court is empowered to correct certain types of error made by it in the course of deciding such disputes, we may truly say that the county court's remit to decide does not extend to making those types of error. Of course, if an authority's remit is to decide a particular dispute, the intention is that the authority should decide correctly. In that sense, a remit to decide never includes a remit to err. However, there are many cases where a deciding authority's error cannot be corrected: where there is no authority with corrective power. An umpire's decision that a batsman is "out" cannot be corrected by any higher authority even though a video re-play shows quite plainly that the batsman ought not to have been adjudged "out." In such cases the deciding authority's remit, or power to decide (be the authority cricket umpire or court or tribunal) may be said to include a power to err. Where, on the other hand, there is a superior authority with power to correct certain of the inferior[11] authority's errors, the inferior authority goes outside its remit if it makes errors of that description.

The second objection which might be levelled at our analysis of the nature of the proceedings before the Court of Appeal in our contract debt example is this. The real issue before the Court of Appeal, it might be said, is not (as we have characterised it) whether the county court has exceeded its remit—or made an error which the Court of Appeal may correct. The real issue is, quite simply, whether D is or is not liable in debt to P: it is that, and not the remit issue, which the proceedings are "designed specifically to settle." Now, that is certainly the case; but it should not be allowed to obscure what is also the case which is that in the Court of Appeal P must show that the decision of the county court was wrong in a way in which the Court of Appeal may correct. P cannot, as it were, start afresh and proceed in the Court of Appeal as he did in the county court. P cannot, for example, expect the Court of Appeal to rehear his witnesses and make its own findings of fact on that basis. In short, the issue before the Court of Appeal is whether the county court has committed an error of a sort which the Court of Appeal may correct. If it has committed such an error, the Court of Appeal will correct it and, commonly, will then decide the issue between D and P on the correct basis; but,

[11] In legal usage "inferior" is not pejorative: it merely indicates that one authority is below, or subject to, another in a jurisdictional hierarchy. For "inferior" and "superior" courts, see Chap. 4, pp. 152–154.

alternatively, it may send the issue back to the county court for retrial.[12]

Let us now return to our general description of the sort of direct challenge with which we are here concerned. It is alleged before a review court that a lower court or tribunal has gone outside its remit. The court or tribunal has decided a dispute which has arisen between parties P and D. The review court is asked by one of the parties to rule that the inferior tribunal has exceeded its remit in deciding in favour of the other. The circumstances in which a remit issue can arise in this way are very numerous. They include all cases where a dispute between parties has been taken for resolution to a court or tribunal and where the decision of the court or tribunal is subject to review (whether supervisory or appellate) by a higher court. Consider the following examples.

1. The disputants (P and D) may be private individuals, *e.g.* plaintiff and defendant in a civil action (as in the contract debt example given above); or prosecutor and defendant in criminal proceedings. If either party can challenge before a review court a ruling given in the proceedings by the inferior court, the challenge is a direct challenge of our type (b).
2. Either or both of the disputants (P and D) may be public authorities. As in the previous example, the issue before the inferior court may be solely as to one party's liability in either civil or criminal law—*e.g.* the liability in tort of a local authority for injury caused to a pedestrian by inadequately fenced roadworks; or the criminal liability of a local authority prosecuted for breach of anti-pollution regulations. Here again, if either party can challenge before a review court a ruling given in the proceedings by the inferior court, the challenge is a direct challenge of our type (b).
3. Suppose that the disputants (P and D) are public authorities, or that one of them is. Suppose also that, as in our first two examples of collateral challenge, the issue between them is a liability issue in which a remit issue arises collaterally: *e.g.* a public authority's liability in trespass depends on the extent of its statutory power to enter and "inspect" private land. A court of first instance decides the collateral remit issue, and therefore the liability issue, against the plaintiff landowner, P. If P can challenge that decision, the issue for the review court will be whether the lower court,

[12] County Courts Act 1984, s.81. For "appeal" generally, see below pp. 41 *et seq.*; for correction of error on appeal, see pp. 57–60.

in deciding as it has, has exceeded *its* remit: has made a reviewable error. P's challenge will thus be a direct challenge of our type (b).

4. Suppose that a review court hears and determines a direct challenge of our type (a): *e.g.* it rejects our discotheque owner, P's, assertion that the licensing authority has exceeded its remit in imposing the Sunday ban. If P can challenge that decision in a higher court, the issue for that court is, as in the previous example, whether the lower court has made a reviewable error. And the challenge, likewise, will be a direct challenge of our type (b).
5. Suppose finally a case where our disputants, P and D, have taken their dispute not to a court but to a statutory tribunal or other authority. The dispute may be, for example, whether the Department of Health and Social Security (D) should pay supplementary benefit to a claimant (P); or whether a taxpayer (P) should pay tax demanded by the revenue (D). Suppose that the benefit dispute has been decided against P by a supplementary benefits appeal tribunal,[13] and the tax dispute against P by tax commissioners.[14] If in either case P can challenge the tribunal's decision before a review court, the challenge will be a direct challenge of our type (b). For the question will be whether the tribunal has made a reviewable error in deciding as it has.

In each of the five examples just considered, the dispute between P and D remains the same dispute which the parties took to the lowest court or tribunal even if, via the hierarchical structure of the courts, the matter is eventually considered by the House of Lords. As the parties to the dispute proceed up the review structure, the aim of each is to "win his case." In that light it may appear artificial to characterise the issue before a review court as whether or not an inferior tribunal has exceeded its remit. However, to do otherwise would be misleading. It is true that a review court will usually appear to be addressing itself to the issue between the parties. But its jurisdiction is a jurisdiction to review the decision of the inferior tribunal: to correct such errors of the inferior tribunal as the review court is empowered to correct. We shall see[15] that

[13] See Chap. 1, p. 10.
[14] *Ibid.*
[15] See below, pp. 57–60.

the correction of error by a review court may or may not settle the issue between the parties.

So much for the circumstances in which a party may wish to raise a remit issue by way of direct challenge. We must now move away from our general, non-technical, vocabulary of "review" and "remit" so as to examine the various different review jurisdictions vested in the English courts. So far, we have described judicial review as the jurisdiction of courts to keep public authorities within their remit. But in any particular case, the question whether a particular public authority has gone outside its remit can be answered only in terms of the particular review jurisdiction or jurisdictions to which it is subject. In terms of the law of judicial review, then, a public authority goes outside its remit if its act or decision is subject to legal challenge by a party invoking one or other of the review jurisdictions which we now turn to consider.

B. Direct Challenge—Supervisory and Appellate Review

(1) Common law: supervisory review

Since the seventeenth century the High Court[16] and the courts above it in the judicial hierarchy (today the Court of Appeal and the House of Lords) have developed a network of remedies available by way of direct challenge to a party who establishes that a public authority has gone outside its remit. The historical basis of this jurisdiction is the common law role of the Court of King's Bench as supervisor of the legality of the acts and proceedings of all manner of public authorities exercising statutory powers.[17] Hence this jurisdiction is commonly referred to as "supervisory review." The jurisdiction did not, and does not, extend to reviewing the decisions of the very courts in whom it is vested: judicial review of decisions of the High Court and the Court of Appeal is by way of statutory appeal only.[18] Decisions of the House of Lords are not subject to judicial review; but, as we have already

[16] Until 1874 the jurisdiction was vested in the Court of King's (or Queen's) Bench. The Judicature Act 1873 created the High Court (see ss.3–5) and transferred to it, *inter alia*, the jurisdiction of the Court of King's Bench. Today applications for judicial review (see text below) are made to a single judge (except that in a criminal cause or matter and in non-criminal matters of special importance or difficulty applications are made to a Divisional Court of the Queen's Bench division: Ord. 53, r. 5 (as amended)); and see *The Supreme Court Practice 1985*, p. 767. A "divisional" court is a court of not less than two judges: Supreme Court Act 1981, s.66.

[17] For review of the exercise of prerogative powers, see section D below.

[18] See *Re Racal Communications Ltd* [1981] A.C. 374: see below Chap. 4, p. 152.

observed[19] their effect may be reversed by statute. "Supervisory review" must be distinguished from "appellate review" which is of statutory origin and with which we deal in the next section. As a common law jurisdiction, supervisory review is subject to such general or particular restrictions or modifications as Parliament may by statute choose to make.[20]

The chief[21] remedies of supervisory review are five: certiorari, prohibition, mandamus, injunction and declaration. Since 1977 they have been available by way of a procedure known as Application for Judicial Review.[22] That procedure was introduced by the judges themselves—the rule committee of the Supreme Court making a new Order 53.[23] The procedure was put on a statutory basis by section 31 of the Supreme Court Act 1981. We shall deal in some detail with remedies and procedure at a later stage.[24] Here we shall simply indicate the nature and scope of the five remedies referred to. The first three, certiorari, prohibition and mandamus, were fashioned by the Court of King's Bench specifically for the purpose of keeping public authorities within their remit. They are referred to as "prerogative" remedies because they were originally available only to the Crown to enable it to keep inferior authorities within bounds. The Crown is today still nominally plaintiff in proceedings for the remedies[25] but, as we shall see, the actual plaintiff is the party making the direct challenge. The effect of certiorari[26] is to "quash," *i.e.* to render or declare legally ineffective a public authority decision which carries the authority outside its remit.

[19] See Chap. 1, p. 9.
[20] See below, pp. 46–56.
[21] "Chief" in the sense of application to a wide range of official action. The prerogative remedy of habeas corpus is, of course, of high constitutional importance but applies only in the narrow field of unlawful detention of persons. For habeas corpus as an instrument of judicial review, see Wade A.L., pp. 542–546.
[22] Certiorari, prohibition and mandamus are available only by this procedure (Supreme Court Act 1981, s.31(1)(*a*)). For where injunction and declaration may be sought by way of other procedures, see Chap. 7.
[23] R.S.C., Ord. 53: see now *The Supreme Court Practice 1985*.
[24] Part III of the book.
[25] As appears from the title of cases, *e.g. R.* v. *Blankshire County Council* [public authority] *ex p. Smith* [applicant for judicial review].
[26] Latin, to be informed or apprised. Historically the writ of certiorari embodied a demand by the Crown to be apprised of details of the inferior tribunal's proceedings so that they could be scrutinised. In procedural reforms accomplished by the Administration of Justice (Miscellaneous Provisions) Act 1938 the writs of certiorari, prohibition and mandamus (but not habeas corpus) became "orders" (R. M. Jackson, *The Machinery of Justice in England* (7th ed.), pp. 42–44): see now Supreme Court Act 1981, s.29.

Prohibition is an order of the court to a public authority to desist from a particular course of action which is beyond its remit. Mandamus[27] is an order to a public authority to discharge a duty remitted to it.

Unlike the prerogative remedies, the other two chief remedies of supervisory review—injunction and declaration—play a dual role in our legal system. The injunction, originating in the Court of Chancery, is a familiar remedy in the resolution of what we have referred to as liability issues[28] (whether or not involving public authorities). But, in addition it was adapted by the superior courts to supplement the prerogative remedies as a remedy of supervisory review: to prohibit or, as the case may be, to order where, for historical and technical reasons, prohibition or mandamus were less readily available. The declaration is of nineteenth century statutory origin.[29] It is today a means of obtaining an authoritative court ruling on a particular issue where, for some reason,[30] a mandatory remedy is not appropriate. Like the injunction, the declaration is used in the resolution of both liability and remit issues.

We said that our five remedies are available by way of direct challenge to a party who establishes that a public authority has "gone outside its remit." As we have already observed, this is a convenient general term reflecting the notion that a public authority exists for a particular purpose or purposes and the fact that there exists legal machinery by which the courts may ensure that an authority pursues proper purposes and does not pursue improper ones. But in order to articulate the extent of each of the different types of review jurisdiction we must now adopt more precise terminology: the terminology in which the courts (in the case of supervisory review) or Parliament (in the case of appellate review and statutory modification of supervisory review) have defined the jurisdiction in question.

(a) *Ultra vires*

In the context of common law supervisory review a public authority goes outside its remit if it acts "*ultra vires*" (beyond its powers) or "without jurisdiction." "Acting *ultra vires* and acting without jurisdiction have essentially the same meaning, but it is usual to speak of *vires* when considering administrative and subordinate legislative orders, and of jurisdiction when considering

[27] Latin, we order.
[28] See Chap. 1, p. 15.
[29] Via the 1883 Rules of the Supreme Court. See now R.S.C., Ord. 15, r. 16.
[30] See Chap. 8.

judicial decisions, or orders having a judicial flavour."[31] Why the distinction? Recall our discussion of the "boundary" analogy in Chapter 1, section D. It appeared there that a key question in defining the notion of remit is: may it ever be said that a public authority has crossed the boundaries of its power[32] by making a mistake in the course of doing the kind of thing it exists to do?

Until recently the answer given by the courts in exercising their supervisory review jurisdiction depended in part on whether the public authority in question was or was not discharging a "judicial" function. If it was not, then broadly any material error of law or fact would take it *ultra vires* or outside its jurisdiction.[33] If, however, it was discharging a "judicial" function, only errors "going to the jurisdiction" would do so. Now, the distinction between judicial and non-judicial functions, as well as the distinction (in the case of judicial functions) between errors going to the jurisdiction and those not so going, were at least fiendishly difficult if not impossible to draw with any precision. Fortunately, in recent years the courts have tended to abandon these distinctions. Today:

> "[t]he scope of judicial review is more likely to turn on the wording of the grant of power, the subject-matter and the context, than on the question whether the function is analytically administrative or judicial. *The current tendency is for the courts to review all questions of law but to show self-restraint in reviewing findings of fact.*"[34]

So, as we shall see,[35] the notion of error of law is today the key to the problem of what takes a public authority *ultra vires* or outside its jurisdiction: the tendency is for all errors of law to be regarded as "going to the jurisdiction"—in modern parlance, as *jurisdictional error*. We shall analyse the notion of error of law in the next chapter, but in this chapter we shall see that the notion is of central importance not only in supervisory review but also in the other major branch of judicial review: appeal. However, before we turn from supervisory to appellate review we must glance at an area of supervisory review jurisdiction once of great, but now of declining, importance: error on the face of the record.

[31] De Smith J.R.A.A., p. 106.
[32] *i.e.* in the present context, acted *ultra vires* or without jurisdiction.
[33] De Smith J.R.A.A., p. 107.
[34] *Op.cit.*, p. 108 (italics added).
[35] Chap. 4 (Law, Fact and Degree), 5 (Law and Policy) and 6 (Irregular or Unfair Procedure).

(b) *Patent error*

We have just seen that, until recently, only certain ill-defined types of error by a public authority discharging a "judicial" function (itself ill-defined) would take the authority outside its jurisdiction. However, the Court of King's Bench had developed an alternative basis upon which to review erroneous decisions. If the record of the proceedings of a statutory authority revealed that the authority had erred in law or in fact, the Court would quash the erroneous decision by certiorari. If, then, an error was *patent* it could, in principle, be quashed. "In principle" because, as always, Parliament could (and, in the nineteenth century in particular, often did) remove this jurisdiction in particular circumstances. Now, as we shall see,[36] because of the nature of an authority's "record," the errors which most commonly appear thereon are errors of law. Substantially, then, the patent error jurisdiction is a jurisdiction to correct patent errors of law. The jurisdiction is of declining importance precisely because, as we have seen, today any error of law (whether patent or not) may well carry a public authority outside its jurisdiction. Furthermore, as we are about to see, statute very commonly makes provision for a party to appeal against any alleged error of law, thus again tending to render resort to the patent error jurisdiction unnecessary.

(2) Statute: appellate review

We have just seen that supervisory review jurisdiction is the creature of common law and is vested in the High Court. Appellate review jurisdiction, on the contrary, is the creature of statute and is vested in such courts as Parliament may deem appropriate in the circumstances of particular types of case. Of course, courts are not the only public authorities invested by statute with jurisdiction to hear appeals from the decisions of other public authorities. As we saw in Chapter 1, statutory tribunals and public inquiries, for example, provide machinery by which persons may seek to challenge public authority decisions other than in the courts. Our subject, however, is *judicial* review and our present concern is with the appellate review jurisdiction which Parliament has conferred upon courts.

Substantial accounts of appellate jurisdiction (judicial and otherwise) must be sought elsewhere.[37] For present purposes we may note that there is statutory provision for appeals to courts

[36] The patent error jurisdiction is examined in Chap. 4, pp. 164–167.

[37] For a concise account, see P. F. Smith and S. H. Bailey, *The Modern English Legal System* (1984), Chap. 19. See too, de Smith C. & A., pp. 542–545; de Smith J.R.A.A., pp. 17–18, 126–127 and 281–283.

from: (a) other courts; (b) statutory tribunals; (c) other public authorities.

(a) *Appeals to courts from other courts*

There has been since the nineteenth century a comprehensive system of statutory appeals from the decisions of courts of first instance to higher courts in ordinary civil and criminal proceedings.[38]

In civil matters an unsuccessful party is commonly entitled to an appeal "by way of rehearing" from the court of first instance (county court or High Court) to the Court of Appeal (Civil Division). The rehearing is commonly "on documents": *i.e.* the Court of Appeal does not rehear witnesses but proceeds on the basis of transcripts or notes of their evidence. Consequently, on such appeals, the court will rarely differ from the first instance judge's assessment of the credibility and reliability of witnesses. On the other hand, the Court of Appeal is in as good a position as the trial judge to draw inferences of fact from witnesses' testimony and will also substitute its own rulings on questions of law when it finds that the lower court has erred.[39] A party may appeal from the Court of Appeal[40] to the House of Lords with the leave of either court. Leave is commonly given only where a case raises a point of law of some doubt or difficulty.

Turning to criminal matters, a person convicted in a magistrates' court is entitled to a complete witness rehearing in the Crown Court from which he or the prosecution may appeal by case stated[41] on point of law to the High Court and thence to the House of Lords (with leave of either court) on a point of law of general

[38] Smith and Bailey, *op.cit.* pp. 701–736; Walker and Walker, *The English Legal System* (6th ed., 1985), Chaps. 22, 25 and 27.

[39] For appellate review of exercises of discretion, see Chap. 5, pp. 204–205.

[40] On occasions a party may appeal from the High Court direct to the House of Lords, thus "leap-frogging" the Court of Appeal: Smith and Bailey, *op.cit.* p. 734.

[41] Supreme Court Act 1981, s.28(1). "Case stated" is a form of appeal on point of law commonly prescribed by statute—see further, *e.g.* Magistrates' Courts Act 1980, s.111(1) (next note); Tribunals and Inquiries Act 1971, s.13 (referred to below). Under this procedure the authority whose decision is impugned is required to state facts found and decision reached, and to formulate the point of law for decision by the appeal court. The procedure was originally used on application for certiorari (Wade A.L., p. 599). As we shall see in Chap. 3, a tribunal errs in law if, *inter alia*, it reaches a conclusion which cannot properly be drawn from the facts of the case in hand. To detect such an error a review court must have access to the facts found by the tribunal. It follows that the case stated procedure is particularly suitable where an error of law of this sort is alleged: *R.* v. *Ipswich Crown Court ex p. Baldwin* [1981] 1 All E.R. 596.

public importance. Either prosecutor or defendant may appeal directly from a magistrates' court to the High Court on point of law.[42] As for trials on indictment in the Crown Court, there is no appeal against an acquittal by a jury.[43] But a convicted person may appeal to the Court of Appeal (Criminal Division) as of right on point of law and otherwise with leave of that court. Either prosecutor or defendant may appeal from the Court of Appeal to the House of Lords if the Court of Appeal certifies that a point of law of general public importance is involved and, in addition, either court gives leave.

We have already observed that the Court of Appeal has appellate review jurisdiction over the High Court's exercise of its supervisory review jurisdiction. This derives from the general statutory provision[44] that "the Court of Appeal shall have jurisdiction to hear and determine appeals from any judgment or order of the High Court." The appellate jurisdiction of the House of Lords over the Court of Appeal derives from the general statutory provision[45] that "an appeal shall lie to the House of Lords from any order or judgment of . . . [the] Court of Appeal . . ."

This system of appeals within the ordinary court structure is, of course, a constituent part of the law of judicial review. The courts appealed from are public authorities, and when they perpetrate an error which can be corrected on appeal we may say that they have gone outside their remit.[46] Notice, of course, that they have not necessarily acted *ultra vires* or without jurisdiction. In the first place, as we noted, the superior courts themselves are not subject to the common law supervisory jursidiction: so the notions of *ultra vires* and lack of jurisdiction have no application to them.[47] In the second place, in the case of an authority which is subject to supervisory review, we saw that the current tendency is for errors of law, but not other errors, to be regarded as carrying it outside its jurisdiction. We consider later[48] how far this approach applies to

[42] Magistrates' Courts Act 1980, s.111(1) (previous note). The sub-section extends to "Any person who . . . is aggrieved by the conviction, order, determination or other proceeding of the court . . ."

[43] But under the Criminal Justice Act 1972, s.36 the Attorney-General may refer a point of law to the Court of Appeal after an acquittal on indictment. The acquittal is not affected by any ruling which the Court of Appeal or House of Lords may make.

[44] Supreme Court Act 1981, s.16(1). The restrictions in s.18 are not here material.

[45] Appellate Jurisdiction Act 1876, s.3(1). The requirement of leave is in the Administration of Justice (Appeals) Act 1934, s.1(1).

[46] See above, pp. 33–37.

[47] See further Chap. 4, p. 152.

[48] *Ibid.*

inferior courts. Now we may simply note that where an inferior court does make an error which carries it outside its jurisdiction, such error is in principle subject to attack under either supervisory or appellate review jurisdiction.[49]

(b) *Appeals to courts from statutory tribunals*

We saw in Chapter 1 that Parliament has created a large number of statutory tribunals with jurisdiction to decide a wide range of disputes—disputes arising both between private individuals and between a private individual and a public authority. On occasions, as we saw, Parliament has made provision for appeal from such tribunals to a higher tribunal such as the Social Security Commissioners and the Employment Appeal Tribunal.

During the last 30 years Parliament has displayed an increasing tendency to provide for a right of appeal on point of law from statutory tribunals to the High Court or (in the case of tribunals of particular eminence such as those just mentioned) directly to the Court of Appeal. The Tribunals and Inquiries Act 1958 (now replaced by the Tribunals and Inquiries Act 1971) was a landmark. It provided,[50] as section 13 of the 1971 Act now provides, for appeal on point of law from specified[51] tribunals to the High Court (from which, under the ordinary appellate structure, appeal lies to the Court of Appeal and, ultimately, the House of Lords). There had been similar isolated provisions in earlier statutes, but since 1958 such statutory provisions have become commonplace.[52]

(c) *Appeals to courts from other public authorities*

There is no clear pattern of rights of appeal (to courts or otherwise) in the administrative law field.[53] Nevertheless, one may say that "in general, no appeal will be provided against discretionary decisions involving questions of national policy or the allocation of scarce resources"[54]—at either central or local government level. On the other hand, statute commonly makes provision for appeal against public authority decisions on licensing matters, including land use and development as well as the many commercial and other activities (*e.g.* possession of fire arms) requiring a licence. What appellate jurisdiction do the courts have in these contexts?

[49] On choice of jurisdiction, see Chap. 9.
[50] Tribunals and Inquiries Act 1958, s.9.
[51] 1958 Act, s.9 and Sched. 1; 1971 Act, s.13 and Sched. 1.
[52] For many examples under the Tribunals and Inquiries Acts and earlier and later statutes, see Table of tribunals in Wade A.L., pp. 824–828.
[53] De Smith C. & A., p. 543.
[54] *Ibid.*

We saw that appeals to courts from statutory tribunals are commonly on point of law only. Likewise, such appeals as there are to courts from public authorities other than courts or statutory tribunals are commonly restricted to point of law. So, for example, there is provision for appeals in many planning matters from the Secretary of State (himself often acting as an appellate tribunal from a local authority) to the High Court on point of law[55]; and in certain social security matters one may appeal on point of law to the High Court from the Secretary of State.[56]

There is a major exception to our proposition that appeals to courts from statutory tribunals and other authorities are commonly restricted to point of law. Many[57] administrative functions of a sort discharged in the past by justices of the peace are today remitted by statute to local authorities. Examples are the licensing of public entertainments,[58] of street trading[59] and of a variety of trades or occupations.[60] No doubt because of local courts' experience in discharging such functions, and albeit that their discharge involves considerable elements of discretion, Parliament commonly provides for an appeal on the merits from the local authority to a magistrates' court and, thence to the Crown Court.[61] Further appeal (commonly to a Queen's Bench Divisional Court) is, however, invariably restricted to point of law.

Such in outline are the supervisory and appellate judicial review jurisdictions under which courts may adjudicate upon direct challenges—*i.e.* direct assertions that a public authority has gone outside its remit. To invoke the supervisory jurisdiction by way of application for judicial review is plainly to mount a direct challenge: the issue before the court is whether or not a particular public authority has gone outside its remit in the sense that it has acted *ultra vires* or without jurisdiction or is guilty of patent error. To appeal is also to mount a direct challenge. The appellant is inviting the appeal court to exercise its jurisdiction to correct an error alleged to have been made by the inferior court or tribunal. As already explained, a tribunal's remit cannot be said to include

[55] Town and Country Planning Act 1971, ss.246, 247.
[56] Social Security Act 1975, ss.93, 94.
[57] But not all, *e.g.* liquor licensing: Licensing Act 1964.
[58] Local Government (Miscellaneous Provisions) Act 1982, s.1 and Sched. 1.
[59] *Ibid.* s.3 and Sched. 4.
[60] *e.g.* offensive trades: Public Health Act 1936, s.107; sale of certain foods: Food Act 1984, ss.16–19.
[61] Appeals on some matters, *e.g.* rating (General Rate Act 1967, s.7) are to the Crown Court direct. See *Investors in Industry Ltd.* v. *Norwich City Council* [1986] 2 All E.R. 193.

power to make such errors as may be corrected by a superior tribunal. We saw that judicial appellate jurisdiction may extend to correcting any error made by an inferior court or tribunal; or it may be, and in the administrative law context commonly is, restricted to the correction of errors of law.

Both application for judicial review and appeal are thus means by which judicial review jurisdiction may be invoked directly. We consider in section D of this chapter the extent to which the supervisory and appellate review jurisdictions may be invoked collaterally. Now, however, we may focus on an important feature of the two jurisdictions.

We saw that under the supervisory jurisdiction the courts may grant certain remedies to restrain public authorities from acting *ultra vires* or without jurisdiction.[62] We saw too that the courts are now tending to treat all errors of law as carrying an authority *ultra vires* or outside jurisdiction. Error of law is also, as we have just said, the usual basis for appellate judicial review of the acts and decisions of public authorities other than courts of first instance.[63] Judicial review jurisdiction is thus in very many cases a jurisdiction to correct errors of law. In Part II of this book we shall first examine the notion of error of law.[64] We shall then identify various types of substantive and procedural errors of law and consider how far each type may be subject to supervisory or appellate review.[65]

Any account of judicial review jurisdiction is, however, incomplete without reference to the manner in which Parliament has intervened in particular cases to oust or modify the review jurisdictions described above. To this we now turn.

(3) Statute: ouster clauses[66]

A statutory provision expressly removing (ousting) or curtailing review jurisdiction is referred to as an ouster clause. Parliament's power to oust or to modify review jurisdiction is, of course, in law unlimited. The courts have tended to interpret ouster clauses restrictively—*i.e.* as cutting down the courts' jurisdiction as little as the interpretation of the words of the statute will allow. It is always open to Parliament to respond to a restrictive judicial interpretation by enacting a patently wider clause. Broadly speaking Parliament has tended not to

[62] As well as to correct patent error.

[63] From courts of first instance, as we have seen, there is commonly an appeal by way of rehearing.

[64] See Chap. 3.

[65] See Chaps. 4 and 5 (substantive); Chap. 6 (procedural).

[66] De Smith J.R.A.A., pp. 364–376; Wade A.L., pp. 598–622; Craig, Chap. 14.

respond in this fashion, no doubt on an estimate of the constitutional value of largely preserving the review jurisdiction of the courts.

Since the end of the seventeenth century Parliament has often provided by statute for the curtailment of review jurisdiction in particular areas. We say "review" rather than solely "supervisory review" because sometimes Parliament has chosen to exclude in a particular class of case a statutory right of appeal which would otherwise have been available under a general statutory provision.

(a) *"Finality" clauses*

Often a statute will provide that a determination by a particular authority is "final" or "final and conclusive" (or similar words). Such a clause may or may not be intended to oust or curtail review jurisdiction. A ruling may be made "final" by statute with the intention merely of distinguishing it from a ruling which is only interlocutory[67]; or to indicate that it is to be binding on another authority with jurisdiction on a different aspect of the same case.[68] In other contexts, on the contrary, a "finality" clause is plainly intended to curtail review jurisdiction. The courts have always interpreted finality clauses of this sort as merely prohibiting appeal. Such a clause does not oust the common law supervisory jurisdiction. Why is this?

From the end of the seventeenth century, while some statutes contained finality clauses, others provided specifically that a decision should not be "removed by certiorari." The courts took the view that since a finality clause did not specifically mention certiorari (whereas other clauses did) a finality clause was not intended to affect the availability of that remedy. So, in a case where (the finality clause apart) there would have been a statutory appeal, the sole effect of the clause is to remove the appeal.[69]

[67] See, *e.g.* Supreme Court Act 1981, ss.29(2); 60.

[68] See, *e.g. R.* v. *Nat. Ins. Commissioner ex p. Hudson* [1972] A.C. 944 (in considering claim to disablement benefit, medical authorities bound by "final" decision of national insurance tribunal on question of injury benefit).

[69] See, *e.g. Pearlman* v. *Keepers of Harrow School* [1979] Q.B. 56 (county court's determination of whether alterations were "structural" was, by statute, "final and conclusive." Court of Appeal held that sole effect of this finality clause was to oust appeal. See further on this case Chap. 4, p. 156. Against the flow of authority was the Court of Appeal's ruling in *Tehrani* v. *Rostron* [1972] 1 Q.B. 182 that since the availability of certiorari was unaffected by a finality clause, a right of appeal by way of case stated also survived because the difference between the two was merely "a matter of procedure."

Further, as Lord Parker said in *R.* v. *Medical Appeal Tribunal, ex p. Gilmore*[70]

> "Sometimes, as here, the statute provides that subject to a specific right of appeal the decision shall be final. In such a case it may be said that the expression 'shall be final' is merely a pointer to the fact that there is no further appeal . . .. Since, however, appeal is the creature of statute the expression is strictly unnecessary."

Lord Parker continued[71]:

> "In other cases the expression is used in the statutes when no rights of appeal are provided. In such a case it could be said that the expression was of no effect unless it was intended to oust the remedy by way of certiorari. Be that as it may, I am satisfied that such an expression is not sufficient to oust this important and well-established jurisdiction of the courts."

As Lord Parker acknowledged, it is difficult to see that in the latter case the courts are doing other than to render a statutory provision nugatory. The approach may be justified only on the basis that in other contexts, as we have just seen, finality clauses have been construed as merely precluding appeal and have thus taken on a fixed meaning.

We consider below the effect of a statutory provision that a certificate or other instrument (as distinct from a decision) shall be "conclusive" or "conclusive evidence" of certain matters.

(b) *"No certiorari" and "conclusive" clauses*

From the end of the seventeenth century Parliament quite frequently enacted clauses providing that a decision of a court or tribunal should not be removed by certiorari. This was in response to a tendency in the Court of King's Bench to exercise the patent error review jurisdiction on excessively technical and trivial grounds. What was the effect of a "no certiorari" clause? Here Parliament quite plainly intended to curtail the supervisory juris-

[70] [1957] 1 Q.B. 574 at 589. For this case, see Chap. 4, p. 165.
[71] *Ibid.*

diction. But the courts again construed the clause narrowly, holding that it ousted the patent error jurisdiction but did not prevent review of decisions held to be *ultra vires* or without jurisdiction. The reasoning was that, while it was plain that Parliament intended to immunise from challenge even patently erroneous decisions, it could not have intended to immunise a decision which was in reality no decision at all, being outside jurisdiction. In *ex p. Bradlaugh* a magistrate had ordered the destruction of certain books on the basis that they were obscene. But under statute he had jurisdiction to make the order only where, in addition, he considered that publication of the books would be a criminal offence. Since he had not considered that question his order was quashed notwithstanding a "no certiorari" clause. As Mellor J. said,[72] "The consequence of holding otherwise would be that a . . . magistrate could make any order he pleased without question." He could, for example, order the destruction of books which he considered "distasteful" rather than obscene.

In modern times Parliament has abandoned the use of clauses specifically excluding certiorari and other remedies.[73] It continues to use finality clauses in some statutes and has adopted[74] in others a new formula providing that a determination of a particular authority "shall not be called in question in any court of law" (or similar words). The House of Lords held in *Anisminic Ltd.* v. *Foreign Compensation Commission*[75] that (except in one important class of case[76]) the new formula goes no further in ousting judicial review than did the old "no certiorari" clause. It immunises from challenge (by way of either appellate or supervisory review) any determination which is not *ultra vires* or outside jurisdiction. But any determination which is *ultra vires* or outside jurisdiction remains vulnerable to supervisory review on that basis.

The *Anisminic* case arose as follows. Under International Law one government must pay compensation to another in respect of injuries which have been sustained by nationals of the latter and for which the paying government accepts liability. The Foreign Compensation Act 1950 charges the Foreign Compensation Commission (FCC) with the distribution to U.K. nationals of compen-

[72] (1878) 3 Q.B.D. 509 at 513.
[73] De Smith J.R.A.A., p. 368.
[74] Infrequently since the enactment of the Tribunals and Inquiries Act 1958, s.11: see text below.
[75] [1969] 2 A.C. 147.
[76] *i.e.* "time-limited" ouster clauses: see (c), below.

sation so received by the U.K. government. The *Anisminic* case concerned a claim by A. Ltd. to compensation for damage to its property in Egypt during the Suez crisis. On the interpretation adopted by FCC of the relevant Order in Council, A. Ltd.'s claim failed. By a bare majority the House of Lords held that the interpretation was wrong and that the error of law carried FCC outside its jurisdiction.[77]

The Act provided[78] that: "The determination by the Commission of any application made to them under this Act shall not be called in question in any court of law." This provision notwithstanding, the house granted A. Ltd. a declaration that the determination was a nullity (*i.e.* outside FCC's jurisdiction) and that FCC should treat A. Ltd.'s claim as established. The House was unanimous on the effect of the ouster clause. In Lord Reid's words[79]:

> "Undoubtedly such a provision protects every determination which is not a nullity. But I do not think that it is necessary or even reasonable to construe the word 'determination' as including everything which purports to be a determination but which is in fact no determination at all."

So, a finality clause is held merely to preclude appeal. A "shall not be questioned" clause is held both to preclude appeal and to oust the patent error jurisdiction; but not to preclude supervisory review of determinations which are *ultra vires* or without jurisdiction. As we saw, most appeals to courts in the administrative law context are appeals on points of law and most patent errors are errors of law: it follows that the ouster clauses under consideration appear designed to restrict review for error of law. Add these observations to our proposition[80] that the courts are tending today to treat all errors of law as carrying an authority outside its jurisdiction—as jurisdictional errors—and the result is as follows. Since neither of these common forms of ouster clause is held to exclude supervisory review based on jurisdictional error, and since errors of law are commonly held to be jurisdictional, neither form of ouster clause commonly excludes review based on error of law. It follows that the clauses are in effect nugatory in the case of a public

[77] The ruling on jurisdictional error is discussed in Chap. 4(D).
[78] Section 4(4).
[79] [1969] 2 A.C. 147 at 170.
[80] See above, p. 40.

authority whose errors of law are held to carry it outside its jurisdiction.[81]

We must postpone consideration of the constitutional propriety of the courts' emasculation of ouster clauses until we have examined the proposition that errors of law are commonly held to be jurisdictional.[82] But what has been Parliament's response? Far from taking any general steps[83] to provide that a "shall not be questioned" clause means what it appears to say, Parliament has since 1958 made little use of such clauses. Furthermore, in the Tribunals and Inquiries Acts[84] it has provided in effect (and subject to some exceptions) that clauses of this nature in pre-1958 legislation shall operate only as finality clauses.[85] As for the *Anisminic* decision itself, Parliament responded by providing an appeal from the Foreign Compensation Commission to the Court of Appeal[86] (but no further[87]) on points of statutory interpretation. Subject to that, the ouster clause was strengthened by immunising from chal-

[81] But note that if Parliament provides that the validity of a notice or decision shall not be questioned except by way of a specific (*e.g.* appeal) procedure, the court may hold that that procedure is the sole method of challenge: see, *e.g. R* v. *Greenwich London Borough Council ex p. Patel* [1985] *The Times*, July 5 (Town and Country Planning Act 1971, s.243(1)). But *cf. McDaid* v *Clydebank D.C.* [1984] J.P.L. 579 (Scottish equivalent of TCPA, s.243(1) held not to oust review jurisdiction where, through the fault of the planning authority, applicant had had no opportunity to use appeal procedure). See further (c) below.

[82] See Chap. 4.

[83] But consider the particular form of ouster clause in the Interception of Communications Act 1985. Section 7(8) provides: "The decisions of the Tribunal [established by s.7(1)] (*including any decisions as to their jurisdiction*) shall not be subject to appeal or liable to be questioned in any court." (Emphasis added).

[84] 1958 Act, s.11; 1971 Act, s.14.

[85] The Acts provide that "shall not be questioned" clauses (or provisions "which by similar words" exclude supervisory jurisdiction) in acts prior to the 1958 Act shall not have the effect of ousting the High Court's jurisdiction to grant certiorari and mandamus. We have seen that "shall not be questioned" clauses differ from finality clauses solely in their removal of the remedies of supervisory review in the case of patent error. The Tribunals and Inquiries Acts remove that difference with the effect stated in the text. The two chief exceptions to the Act's provision on "shall not be questioned" clauses (see 1958 Act, s.11(3); 1971 Act, s.14(3)) are (i) time-limited ouster clauses: see next heading in text below; (ii) "any order or determination of a court of law" to which, accordingly, a "shall not be questioned" clause will still apply with full force. The 1958 Act excepted also "any order or determination of the Foreign Compensation Commission" with the effect in the *Anisminic* case related in the text above. For the aftermath to *Anisminic*, see text immediately below.

[86] Foreign Compensation Act 1969, s.3(2).

[87] *Ibid.* s.3(8).

lenge[88] not only any determination by the Commission[89] but also "anything which purports to be a determination."[90] But since, as we shall see,[91] most errors of law by a statutory authority can be characterised as errors of interpretation, it follows that most errors of law by the Commission are appealable and, so, that the ouster of supervisory review may be of no great significance.

Finally, we must consider in this context the effect of a statutory provision that a certificate or other instrument shall be "conclusive," or "conclusive evidence," of certain matters. To what extent, if at all, does such a provision oust the court's supervisory jurisdiction?

In the first place, for an instrument to have the prescribed effect, it must be what it purports to be. So, for example, a local authority may, in certain circumstances, serve on the person having control of a house a notice requiring him to make repairs. Unless appealed within a given time the notice "shall be final and conclusive as to any matters which could have been raised on such an appeal . . . "[92] But if the notice is served on the wrong person it is a nullity: "simply not a notice on which the [statutory] provision . . . can bite."[93] If, then, it appears from the instrument itself that it is not what it purports to be, the statute will not immunise it from challenge.[93a]

But may it be argued that a certificate which contains an error of law is, on that account alone, a nullity? If so, a statutory provision relating to the conclusiveness of "a certificate" would seem not to protect what (to adapt Lord Reid's words in *Anisminic*) purports to be a certificate but is in fact no certificate at all. In *R.* v. *Registrar of Companies ex p. Central Bank of India*[93b] an application to quash the company registrar's registration of a charge failed. The Court of Appeal found that the registrar had acted without jurisdiction in that the original instrument of charge had not been delivered in time. But the statute[93c] provided that the registrar's

[88] Except on the basis of denial of natural justice: *ibid* s.3(10). For natural justice, see Chap. 6, (B).
[89] 1969 Act, s.3(9).
[90] *Ibid* s.3(3). Would our hypothetical magistrates' order to destroy distasteful books "purport to be" a determination of the sort he was empowered to make?
[91] Chap.3, p. 115 *passim*.
[92] Housing Act 1957, s.37(1).
[93] *Per* Oliver L.J. in *Pollway Nominees Ltd.* v. *Croydon L.B.C.* [1985] 3 All E.R. 24, 28; aff'd. (H.L.) [1986] *The Times*, July 19 (facts as in text).
[93a] *Ibid*. See also *R.* v. *Registrar of Companies ex p. Central Bank of India* [1986] 1 All E.R. 105 at 123 *per* Slade L.J.
[93b] Previous note.
[93c] Companies Act 1948, s.98(2); see now Companies Act 1985, s.401(2).

certificate of registration should be "conclusive evidence that the requirements of . . . [the] Act as to registration [had] been complied with." The court held unanimously that no contrary evidence could be adduced. It is submitted that this conclusion can be supported on the basis that "The whole point of creating the register . . . is to give security to persons relying on the certificate. If it were possible to go behind the certificate . . . no lender . . . could be secure . . . "[93d] On that basis one may conclude that the statutory provisions:

> confer on the registrar the power to decide finally and conclusively *all* ancillary questions, whether they be questions of fact or law, or mixed fact and law, which fall to be decided in determining whether the requirements of . . . the . . . Act as to registration have been complied with . . . [93e]

Consider by way of contrast section 1(3) of the European Communities Act 1972 which provides that an Order in Council declaring that a treaty is a Community Treaty "shall be conclusive that it is to be so regarded." In *R.* v. *H.M. Treasury ex p. Smedley*[93f] Slade L.J. said that the subsection would not "empower [the Crown] to purport to bring into the ambit of the 'Community Treaties' an international agreement which demonstrably had no connection whatever with 'the Treaties' as defined . . . "[93g] The purpose of the "conclusive" provision was to avoid judicial intervention "in borderline cases." Its purpose was not to empower the Crown to confer the legal status of a Community Treaty upon, say, a U.K. trade agreement with Saudi Arabia. Similar observations, surely, could be made about the purpose of section 40(3) of the Crown Proceedings Act 1947 which provides:

> "A certificate of a Secretary of State: (*a*) to the effect that any alleged liability of the Crown arises otherwise than in respect of His Majesty's Government in the United Kingdom . . .

[93d] *Per* Harman L.J. in *Re C.L. Nye Ltd.* [1971] Ch. 442 at 469.

[93e] *Per* Slade L.J. in the *Bank of India* case at [1986] 1 All E.R. 122. Note that it appears from the judgments in the case that the statute (1) does not operate to confer validity on a transaction which is invalid for reasons other than failure to comply with the statutory requirements; (2) will not preclude challenge by the Attorney General where the statute in question does not bind the Crown; (3) may well not preclude challenge on the ground either of fraud or of patent error.

[93f] [1985] Q.B. 657.

[93g] *Ibid.* p. 673.

shall, for the purposes of this Act, be conclusive as to the matter so certified."[93h]

Suppose that an anti-nuclear protester who had been shot near a British military establishment in the United Kingdom by a member of the British armed services were to sue in tort, alleging that the Crown was vicariously liable for the act of its servant. Surely Parliament did not intend the above provision to empower the Home Secretary to issue (albeit in good faith) an unchallengeable certificate immunising the Crown from liability.

Unfortunately, in *R.* v. *Secretary of State for Foreign Affairs ex p. Trawnik*[93i] the Court of Appeal seems to have ruled to the contrary. The court dismissed an application for judicial review of a section 40(3)(*a*) certificate relating to prospective liability of the Crown in nuisance for the establishment of a machine gun range in West Berlin. May L.J. (with whom Gibson L.J. agreed) said:

> "[A]n application for judicial review . . . if based upon the proposition that that which has been certified is so clearly wrong that the certificate must be a nullity, would be bound to fail because the evidence which counsel would wish to call to prove this very thing could not be adduced."

It is submitted that the reasoning in *Trawnik* cannot be reconciled with that in *Anisminic*. In *Trawnik* the court distinguished *Anisminic*, apparently on the basis that the ouster clause there referred to a "determination" whereas in *Trawnik* what was protected was a certificate.[93j] Surely, though, where a certificate is the legal vehicle of a decision, it is inconsistent with *Anisminic* to hold that a certificate which can be shown to be a nullity is immunised from challenge by a conclusiveness provision.

(c) *Time-limited ouster clauses*

It is one thing for the courts to have jurisdiction to entertain challenges to official acts or decisions whose effect upon the challenger is purely financial, as, *e.g.* in the *Anisminic* case. It is quite another thing when the effect of the act or decision is to set in train what may be a vastly expensive and practically irreversible alter-

[93h] Thus precluding any proceedings being taken: s.40(2)(*b*).
[93i] [1986] *The Times*, February 21.
[93j] It was on this basis that the court held also that the "similar words" provision in the Tribunals and Inquiries Act, s.14 (above, note 85) did not apply. But *cf.* de Smith J.R.A.A., pp. 369–70.

ation of the environment, as, *e.g.* in the case of compulsory purchase orders or planning decisions. If the courts are to have review jurisdiction in such cases, there is a clear public interest in imposing a time limit beyond which no challenge may be entertained. What was once Smith's house may now have been for some years a pile of rubble beneath a motorway. One need not dwell on the consequences of permitting him now to challenge the validity of a compulsory purchase order under which his land was acquired.

In such cases as compulsory purchase and planning, Parliament usually provides (by a more or less standard formula[94]) that the validity of an order or decision may be challenged within six weeks[95] of its being made. Subject to that, it is provided that the order or decision "shall not be questioned in any legal proceedings whatsoever." We have seen how the courts interpret those words in statutes which make no provision whatever for review. How do they interpret them in statutes, such as we are now considering, which make express provision for review but impose a time limit?

Smith v. *East Elloe Rural District Council*[96] concerned a compulsory purchase order. The question was whether the ouster clause precluded challenge, even on the ground of fraud, after six weeks. By a majority of 3:2 the House of Lords held that it did: the words of the ouster clause were "wide enough to cover any kind of challenge which any aggrieved person may think fit to make."[97] The words ("shall not be questioned . . ." etc) are, of course, substantially identical to those in the *Anisminic* statute. In the *Anisminic* case the House of Lords cast doubt on *Smith* v. *East Elloe*, observing that the authorities on the effect of "no certiorari" clauses had not been cited there. This disapproval suggested that the *Anisminic* approach might in the future be held to apply as much to the time-limited ouster clause as to the absolute one.

[94] See, *e.g.* Acquisition of Land Act 1981, s.25; Town and Country Planning Act 1971, ss.242, 244, 245. Perhaps strangely there is no statutory restriction on challenges to the validity of local authority decisions on planning applications. These are therefore subject to review under the common law supervisory jurisdiction—see, *e.g. Steeples* v. *Derbyshire C.C.* [1984] 3 All E.R. 468. Decisions on appeal to the Secretary of State from local authority decisions are subject to the time-limited procedure; but *cf. Greater London Council* v. *Environment Secretary* [1985] *The Times* July 18; s.242 held not to oust supervisory jurisdiction where challenge is to reasoning underpinning decision. (The challenge failed: *R.* v. *Environment Secretary ex p. G.L.C.* [1985] *The Times* December 30).

[95] A period described by Lord Radcliffe in the *East Elloe* case (below) at p. 769 as "pitifully inadequate." On proposals for reform, see Wade A.L., p. 614.

[96] [1956] A.C. 736.

[97] *Per* Viscount Simonds, *ibid.* p. 751.

But this took no account of the different contexts, referred to above, of the two types of clause. Seven years later in *R.* v. *Secretary of State for the Environment ex p. Ostler*[98] the Court of Appeal applied the *East Elloe* decision in a case on similar facts. Lord Denning M.R. (whose reasons Shaw L.J. adopted[99]) observed:[1]

> "In the *Anisminic* case the . . . Act ousted the jurisdiction of the court altogether. It precluded the court from entertaining any complaint at any time about the determination. Whereas in *Smith* v. *East Elloe* the statutory provision has given the court jurisdiction to inquire into complaints so long as the applicant comes within six weeks. The provision is more in the nature of a limitation period than of a complete ouster."[2]

It seems, then, that the courts will treat themselves as having no jurisdiction to entertain any challenge whatever outside the time limit specified, just as they have no jurisdiction to hear actions time-barred by the Limitation Act 1980.

We should notice finally that the "standard formula" used by Parliament in time-limited ouster clauses defines what challenges may be made within the six week period. The grounds of challenge are either that the order is not within the powers of the Act or that any requirement of the Act has not been complied with to the substantial prejudice of the applicant for review. The case law shows[3] that there are some differences between the common law *ultra vires* jurisdiction and this statutory version. Reference will be made to these differences as points arise.

(4) Supervisory and appellate review compared and contrasted

We now consider some differences and some similarities between the common law and statutory review jurisdictions outlined above.

(a) *Source of jurisdiction*

Appellate review jurisdiction is solely the creature of statute. Supervisory review jurisdiction is the creature of common law but, as we have just seen, its extent in any given case may be deter-

98 [1977] Q.B. 122.
99 *Ibid.* p. 140.
1 *Ibid.* p. 135.
2 See Wade A.L., p. 613; de Smith J.R.A.A., p. 374.
3 See Wade A.L., pp. 615–622.

mined not only by judicial development but also by statutory intervention. The rule is, then, that

> "[Supervisory review] always lies, unless it is expressly taken away, and an appeal never lies, unless it is expressly given by . . . statute . . ."[4]

(b) *Extent of power to correct error*

Broadly, a statute confers appellate review jurisdiction on a court to enable the court to correct error—error made by an inferior authority in the course of deciding an issue remitted to it. As we have observed, an authority's remit cannot be said to extend to making such errors as may be corrected on appeal. Supervisory review jurisdiction too is concerned with the correction of error by public authorities. As we have seen, some errors carry an authority outside its jurisdiction and are subject to supervisory review on that basis. Other errors are subject to supervisory review because they are patent.

Although one may characterise both jurisdictions as being concerned with the correction of public authority error, nevertheless appellate review and supervisory review often appear to be radically different processes. Take, on the one hand, an appeal "on the merits." This exists where a statute grants simply an "appeal" (not confining the appeal to point of law only) so that the appeal court has jurisdiction to rehear the whole case and make such order as ought to have been made in the first instance.[5] As we have observed, appeals of this nature are common within the ordinary court structure—*i.e.* where the first instance decision is that of a court. An example might be an appeal to the Court of Appeal from a county court or High Court decision in a running-down or other negligence case.

On the other hand, consider the case of a local authority with statutory power to charge such local public transport fares as it

[4] *Per* Abbott C.J. in *R.* v. *Cashiobury Hundred Justices* (1823) 3 Dow. & Ry. 35. Abbott C.J. actually said "certiorari," not "supervisory review;" but the principle applies to supervisory review generally. It must, of course, be recalled that supervisory review jurisdiction does not extend to Parliament itself or to the superior courts. As to Crown prerogative power, see below, pp. 74–81.

[5] See, *e.g.* R.S.C., Ord. 55 (High Court); Order 59 (Court of Appeal). As an alternative to deciding the issue itself, an appeal court will commonly be empowered either to remit the issue to the trial court for decision on the proper basis or to order a retrial. Where an appeal is on point of law only an appeal court will very commonly remit the issue: see text below.

thinks fit. Suppose that it decides to permit unemployed persons to travel free of charge.[6] A ratepayer may feel that an extra burden is being cast upon him and that the power does not entitle the authority to charge no fares at all to one section of the community. He has no statutory avenue of appeal but may seek to challenge the decision under the supervisory review jurisdiction. Now, in this case, all the court may do is in effect to rule whether or not the authority's grant of free rides is *intra* or *ultra vires*. It has no jurisdiction itself to determine what fares should be charged.

These contrasting examples illustrate the difference between the jurisdiction of an appeal court with full power to rehear a case and the jurisdiction of the High Court in the exercise of its supervisory role. The difference in the examples relates to the manner of the court's correction of error. In the first example it corrects the error and decides the case. In the second it merely corrects the error and leaves the authority to fix reasonable fares. It is on the basis of such contrasting examples that it is sometimes said that appellate review is concerned with the "merits" of a case whereas supervisory review is concerned only with "legality."[7] However, as we are about to see, the contrast between the two examples is attributable not to a fundamental difference between supervisory and appellate review as such but rather to a difference between, on the one hand, supervisory review and appeal on point of law and, on the other, appeal not confined to point of law.

Very often the extent of a court's jurisdiction to review a decision is the same irrespective of whether it acts under appellate or supervisory jurisdiction. We have observed that many appeals are on point of law only. In order to succeed, the appellant must show that the court or tribunal below erred in law. We have observed too that errors of law will in many cases take an authority *ultra vires* or outside its jurisdiction. In such a case the task of an applicant invoking the supervisory jurisdiction is the same as the task of an appellant—simply to establish an error of law. How in these circumstances does the manner in which the appeal court

[6] *cf. Prescott* v. *Birmingham Corporation* [1955] Ch. 210 (see Chap. 5, p. 184).

[7] See, *e.g.* Wade A.L., p. 34. For recent judicial pronouncements, see *R* v. *Chief Constable of North Wales Police ex p. Evans* [1982] 1 W.L.R. 1155: "Judicial review is concerned, not with the decision, but with the decision-making process" *per* Lord Brightman at p. 1173. See too *R.* v. *Entry Clearance Officer ex p. Amin* [1983] 2 A.C. 818 at 829 *per* Lord Fraser; *Council of Civil Service Unions* v. *Minister for the Civil Service* [1985] A.C. 374 at 401 (Lord Fraser), 414 (Lord Roskill). While emphasising the nature of review jurisdiction as a jurisdiction to correct only certain errors of an inferior authority (see above, pp. 33–35), these dicta tend to obscure the kinship between supervisory review and appeal on point of law—see text following.

may correct the error compare with the manner in which a supervisory court should proceed?

Take two examples:

1. Consider the basis on which in the *Anisminic* case[8] the Foreign Compensation Commission rejected A. Ltd.'s claim. A. Ltd.'s property in Egypt had been sequestrated by the Egyptian government and sold on to an Egyptian government agency ("T.E.D.O."). The legislation governing A. Ltd.'s claim to F.C.C. provided that both the claimant and any "successor in title" of the claimant must be British nationals. F.C.C. interpreted "successor in title" broadly to mean "next owner." On that basis T.E.D.O. was A. Ltd.'s successor in title: it was not a British national, so A. Ltd.'s claim failed. The House of Lords held, on the contrary, that "successor in title" meant, more narrowly, "person succeeding to property on death or (in the case of a company) liquidation." On that basis A. Ltd. had no successor in title, T.E.D.O.'s nationality was immaterial and F.C.C.'s rejection of A.'s claim was shown to be wrong in law.

In a case of this sort, the correction of the error of law (the misconstruction of the legislation[9]) so to speak "decides" the case. No issue remains. Thus, if the direct challenge in such a case is made under the supervisory jurisdiction (as it was in *Anisminic*) the review court may either (as it did in *Anisminic*) declare that the decision is void and that the claim is established or (if it thinks necessary) issue a mandamus to the public authority to satisfy the claim.[10]

If a direct challenge of this sort were by way of appeal on point of law (as it would be under the Foreign Compensation Act 1969[11]) the ruling of the appeal court would have precisely the same effect as the remedy granted under the supervisory jurisdiction.

2. Suppose that in determining that a landowner, P, requires planning permission for certain proposed operations, the Secretary of State[12] specifies the factors on which he has based his decision. P appeals to the High Court on point of law[13] and argues

[8] [1969] 2 A.C. 147.

[9] See Chap. 3, p. 100 *et seq*.

[10] *e.g.* as the Court of Appeal did in *R.* v. *Eastleigh Borough Council ex p. Betts* [1983] 1 W.L.R. 774 (reversed by House of Lords on grounds not affecting this point—[1983] 2 A.C. 613).

[11] See above, p. 51.

[12] Acting under Town and Country Planning Act 1971, ss.53 and 35 or 36.

[13] *Ibid.* s.247.

successfully that the minister has erred in law in his selection of factors.[14] What order should the High Court make on the appeal?

This case is unlike that in the previous example. Here, the mere correction of the error of law cannot be said to "decide" the case. It merely establishes that the factor in question should have been considered. In such a case the court must "remit the matter to the Secretary of State with the opinion of the Court for rehearing and determination by him."[15] Likewise, a court exercising supervisory jurisdiction in a case where the correction of an error of law does not "decide" the case would proceed similarly. It would quash the erroneous determination, leaving the first instance tribunal to determine the issue on the correct basis.[16]

These examples show that the correction of an error of law may or may not settle the issue between the parties. Whether it does settle the issue (as in the first example) or not (as in the second) the manner of correction is substantially the same whether on appeal on point of law or by way of supervisory review. In a case such as our transport fares example the correction of any error of law cannot possibly settle the question of what fare must be charged. It can settle only the issue whether or not no fare may be charged. But, were there some form of statutory appeal on point of law against the fare-fixing of a transport authority, the appeal court would be placed in substantially the same position as the supervisory court in our example.

So, as regards the extent to which a review court may correct error, there is a clear distinction between, on the one hand, review (whether supervisory or appellate) confined to correction of error of law and, on the other, review (*i.e.* appellate) not so confined. In this context that distinction is of more significance than the distinction between supervisory review and appellate review.

[14] For this type of error of law, see Chap. 5, p. 179 *passim*.

[15] R.S.C., Ord. 94, r. 12(5): see *Green* v. *Minister of Housing and Local Government* [1967] 2 Q.B. 606. See similarly R.S.C., Ord. 94, rr. 10(4), 10A(4). For general power of High Court on appeal to remit matter to first instance tribunal, see Ord. 55, r. 7(5). For cases where statute provides for appeal on point of law direct to the Court of Appeal (*e.g.* from the Employment Appeal Tribunal—Employment Protection (Consolidation) Act 1978, s.136(4)) see *Dobie* v. *Burns International Security Services (U.K.) Ltd.* [1985] 1 W.L.R. 43. Where the first instance tribunal has erred in law but the correction of that error does not settle the issue, "then it is for an appellate tribunal to remit the case to the only tribunal [*Sc.* the first instance tribunal] which is charged with making findings of fact," *per* Donaldson M.R., *ibid.* p. 49.

[16] As, *e.g.* if the High Court were to quash by certiorari a local authority's refusal of planning permission on the basis that the authority had erred in law (*cf.* note 94 above).

(c) *Choice of jurisdiction*

Official action may be subject to either supervisory or appellate review or both. We consider later[17] the criteria according to which, in cases where both jurisdictions are in principle available, one is preferred.

(d) *Standing*

We deal later[18] also with the question of standing: who may appeal? Who may invoke supervisory jurisdiction? Since appeals are always statutory, statute prescribes in each case who may appeal—*e.g.* any party to a proceeding or any person aggrieved. Although statute[19] now provides that for application for judicial review a person must have a sufficient interest, the body of the law relating to standing to invoke supervisory jurisdiction is substantially judge-made.

(e) *Void or voidable?*

Finally we must consider the vexed distinction between "void" and "voidable" official action. The courts have commonly characterised as "void" an act or decision which is *ultra vires* or outside jurisdiction. Contrastingly, action which (while not being *ultra vires* or outside jurisdiction) is vitiated by patent error or by error which may be corrected on appeal may be labelled "voidable."[20] In the context of our present comparison between supervisory and appellate review, the labels seem to suggest a distinction between, on the one hand, action which is subject to supervisory review because *ultra vires* or without jurisdiction and, on the other, action which is subject either to supervisory review for patent error or to appellate review. The former is "void"; the latter "voidable." What is the difference?

The labels void and voidable are applied by the courts to describe the legal consequences of official action so labelled. Broadly, void means of no legal effect; voidable means legally valid and effective until "avoided"—*i.e.* in the context of judicial review, until held invalid by a court exercising review jurisdiction. If the distinction as just stated were rigorously and consistently applied

[17] See Chap. 9.
[18] See Chap. 8.
[19] Supreme Court Act 1981, s.31(3).
[20] See generally de Smith J.R.A.A., p. 151 *et seq.*; Wade A.L., p. 310 *et seq.*; Craig, p. 388 *et seq.*

by the courts it would follow that a void order or decision could be ignored with impunity at all times and by all persons for all purposes. Whereas voidable action (although by definition so tainted as to be liable to avoidance via appropriate legal proceedings) would have to be treated as perfectly valid by all persons for all purposes unless and until avoided.

Fortunately, the distinction between void and voidable is not applied with this degree of logical rigour. We say "fortunately" because it would seem absurd to make different categories of review jurisdiction the basis of so stark a distinction as to the legal consequences of different official acts all of which, from a commonsense point of view, are (by definition) in some sense invalid or beyond remit. Less fortunately, however, the courts have retained the void/voidable distinction but have blurred its application to such an extent that any simple exposition of this area of law is impossible.[21] All that we can do here is to indicate broadly how the distinction operates for certain practical purposes.

1. We have already noted how a statutory ouster clause may be held to immunise from challenge official action which would otherwise be subject to appeal or review for patent error ("voidable"); but to confer no such immunity upon official action which is *ultra vires* or outside jurisdiction ("void").[22]
2. If action which is *ultra vires* or outside jurisdiction remains unchallenged "it will remain as effective for its ostensible purpose as the most impeccable of orders."[23] Furthermore, if such action is challenged the challenge may fail for a variety of reasons. "[An] order may be hypothetically a nullity, but the court may refuse to quash it because of the plaintiff's lack of standing, because he does not deserve a discretionary remedy, because he has waived his rights, or for some other legal reason."[24] In this sense, then, *ultra vires* action is voidable rather than void[25] (and if not

[21] See, *e.g.* de Smith J.R.A.A., p. 152 referring to "terminological and conceptual problems of excruciating complexity."

[22] See above, p. 50.

[23] *Per* Lord Radcliffe in *Smith* v. *East Elloe R.D.C.* [1956] A.C. 736 at 769 (above, p. 55).

[24] Wade A.L., p. 314. For standing and remedial discretion, see Part III; for waiver, see Chapter 6(B)(iv). "Other legal reason" might include the expiry of a time limit as, *e.g.* in the *East Elloe* case (above) or where an applicant is tardy in applying for judicial review.

[25] See, *e.g. per* Lord Morris in *Ridge* v. *Baldwin* [1964] A.C. 40 at 125 (see Chap. 6, p. 215 *passim*).

avoided will be valid[26]). And in this sense also there is no distinction between the consequences of *ultra vires* action and action which is reviewable for patent error or on appeal.

3. There does appear to be a distinction, however, with regard to collateral challenge.[27] It is said that "in principle, void but not voidable decisions are open to collateral attack."[28] This appears to reflect the notion that void acts and decisions are of no legal effect, whereas voidable ones are valid until avoided by direct challenge. We shall consider the scope of collateral challenge shortly,[29] but may observe at once that the void/voidable distinction is no more rigorously applied and is no more satisfactory in the context of collateral challenge than elsewhere.
4. There is an apparent distinction between the respective consequences of void and voidable official action during the period between the action itself and a successful challenge to its validity. If the action is said by the review court to have been *ultra vires* and void, it follows that it must be treated as "incapable of ever having had any legal effect on the rights or duties of the parties to the proceedings."[30] So, for example, any interim loss inflicted by a public authority on the basis that an order of the authority was valid would be recoverable from the authority as if the order had never existed[31]; but if the order is said to have been voidable only, then, pending proceedings to avoid it "the order would remain good, and a support for all that had been done under it."[32]

The difficulty with this aspect of the void/voidable distinction, however, is that the courts have tended to fit the label (void or voidable) to the desired consequence.[33] As Lord Wilberforce has said: "In truth when the court says that an act of administration is voidable, or void but not *ab initio*, this is simply a reflection of a conclusion, already

[26] Wade, *loc.cit.* above note 24.
[27] See above, p. 30.
[28] De Smith J.R.A.A., p. 155.
[29] See below, p. 65 *et seq.*
[30] *Per* Lord Diplock in *Hoffman-La Roche & Co.* v. *Secretary of State for Trade and Industry* [1975] A.C. 295 at 366 (see below).
[31] See, *e.g. per* Lord Denning in *D.P.P.* v. *Head* [1959] A.C. 83 at 111 (see section (C) below).
[32] *Ibid.*
[33] For examples, see Craig, pp. 393, 402 *passim.*

reached on unexpressed grounds, that the court is not willing in the case to give compensation or other redress to the person who establishes the nullity."[34]

Reverting now to general consideration of the void/voidable distinction it may well be desirable for a legal system to prescribe different consequences for different varieties of invalid official action. So, for example, a statutory instrument may be arguably *ultra vires*; but one would not necessarily expect that the law would permit it to be flouted with impunity before the question had been settled in court.[35] On the other hand, an inspector of taxes may make an invalid demand which one might expect could be ignored without the necessity and expense of resorting to a court to have its invalidity formally established.[36] Surely, though, common sense suggests that such different consequences as may be attached to different varieties of invalid official action should be attached by reference to considerations other than a technical legal distinction between "void" and "voidable" flowing inexorably from an equally technical distinction between one variety of review jurisdiction and another.

In this connection one may welcome recent authoritative judicial acceptance of the shortcomings of the void/voidable distinction as a basis for describing the legal consequences of invalid official action.[37] But to discard outmoded conceptualism only to replace it with wide judicial discretion may be thought a remedy worse than the disease.[38] It is to be hoped that the courts will recognise the need to formulate coherent principles for assessing the consequences of invalidity. Meanwhile, clarity of thought might be assisted by referring to official action which has been subject to

[34] [1975] A.C. 295 at 358–359.

[35] In the *Hoffman-La Roche* case (above) the company was suing for a declaration that a price-restraint order was *ultra vires*. But the House of Lords granted the minister an interlocutory injunction (without requiring an undertaking as to damages) preventing the company from selling drugs at prices higher than those prescribed until the *ultra vires* issue had been resolved.

[36] One might, of course, choose to resort to court for the sake of certainty—*cf. Dyson* v. *Att.-Gen.* [1911] 1 K.B. 410.

[37] See, *e.g. per* Lord Wilberforce in *Calvin* v. *Carr* [1980] A.C. 574 at 589–590 (see Chap. 6, pp. 222, 241); *per* Lords Hailsham and Keith in *London & Clydeside Estates Ltd.* v. *Aberdeen District Council* [1980] 1 W.L.R. 182 at 189, 203. Council's issue of certificate which failed to inform company of right to appeal was breach of mandatory procedural requirement (see Chap. 6, p. 207). But House of Lords held certificate not a complete nullity; so council's failure did not subject company to statutory consequence (loss of right to appeal) which would in the circumstances have followed the council's total failure to issue a certificate.

[38] See Craig, pp. 403–407.

review (of whatever sort) as simply "invalid"[39] and attempting to state the consequences of that invalidity in particular contexts.

We shall revert to the void/voidable issue in the context of both collateral challenge[40] and procedural unfairness[41] where, as we shall see, particular difficulties arise.

C. Collateral Challenge

As already explained,[42] we are now envisaging legal proceedings which are designed to settle an issue other than whether or not a particular public authority has gone outside its remit. Commonly, as in the examples given earlier,[43] that issue will be as to the criminal or civil liability of one of the parties to the proceedings. As those examples illustrate, the resolution of the central issue in the proceedings may turn on the separate (or "collateral") issue of whether or not a public authority has exceeded its remit. The question to which we now turn is in what circumstances will a party to proceedings be permitted to raise a remit issue collaterally?

We begin with the principle (noticed during our discussion of the void/voidable distinction[44]) that void but not voidable decisions are open to collateral attack. The proposition that void decisions are open to collateral attack may be illustrated by reference to the four examples given earlier:

(1) the landowner suing in trespass an authority relying on its statutory power to enter and inspect private land;
(2) the local authority tenant being sued for possession of his house by the authority which is relying on its statutory power to demand increased rent;
(3) the accused challenging the validity of a bye-law under which he is charged with an offence of singing in a public place;
(4) the alleged trespasser challenging the validity of the Commons Commissioners' removal of land from the Commons Register.

In each of the four cases the party wishing to make the collateral

[39] See, *per* Lord Wilberforce, *loc.cit.* above note 37.
[40] See below.
[41] See Chap. 6, p. 241.
[42] See above, p. 30.
[43] *Ibid.*
[44] Immediately above.

challenge would be permitted to do so if he could show that the public authority in question had acted *ultra vires*.[45]

As examples 2, 3 and 4 illustrate, collateral challenge is often by way of defence to proceedings brought in the wake of the defendant's disregard of an allegedly void order or decision. But there are circumstances in which this form of collateral attack will not be permitted even though the defendant maintains that he can establish that certain official action is *ultra vires* and void. In the *Hoffman-La Roche* case,[46] for example, the company was prevented by injunction from disregarding a statutory instrument pending the resolution of the company's claim that the instrument was *ultra vires*. Another circumstance in which the proposition that void decisions are open to collateral attack may be subject to qualification, is where the fundamental issue in the proceedings is not one of liability but one of status. So, for example, in *Skinner* v. *Carter*[47] a man had entered into a bigamous marriage on the basis of which he and his "wife" obtained an adoption order. In proceedings in a magistrates' court he was ordered to pay maintenance for the adopted child. The Court of Appeal (while not deciding whether or not the adoption order was void) upheld the magistrates' refusal to allow the man to raise that issue by way of collateral challenge in the maintenance proceedings.

These exceptions to the proposition that void decisions are open to collateral challenge illustrate our observation[48] that the void/voidable distinction is no more rigorously applied, and is no more satisfactory a basis for predicating the consequences of a public

[45] For authority on example 1 see, *e.g. Cooper* v. *Wandsworth Board of Works* (1863) 14 C.B. (N.S.) 180. Local authority demolished house under order which was void because made without giving owner a hearing. Owner raised remit issue collaterally in his successful action for trespass. For collateral challenge to compulsory purchase orders today see *Smith* v. *East Elloe R.D.C.*, below, note 59). Example 2—see *Wandsworth L.B.C.* v. *Winder* [1985] A.C. 461: facts as given in text. D permitted to assert by way of defence to possession proceedings (*i.e.* collaterally) that rent increase was *ultra vires*. Example 3—see *Kruse* v. *Johnson* [1898] 2 Q.B. 91: facts as given in text. Accused permitted to raise *vires* issue in defence; but by-law held valid. Example 4—*cf. Bunbury* v. *Fuller* (1853) 156 E.R. 47 where P sued D to enforce commutation order by Tithes Commissioners. D permitted to defend on basis that Commissioners' decision was void; but defence failed. There is nothing in any of these cases to suggest that for the purposes of allowing collateral challenge the critical distinction is "void or voidable" rather than "valid or invalid." But in 1 and 3 the only basis for direct challenge would have been *ultra vires*; and in 2 and 4 the defence was argued in terms of *vires* or jurisdiction.

[46] [1975] A.C. 295 (see above, note 35).

[47] [1948] Ch. 387.

[48] See above, p. 63.

authority's going outside its remit, in the context of collateral challenge than elsewhere. That observation is further illustrated when we turn to examine the correlative proposition that voidable decisions are not open to collateral challenge.

The prime example of that proposition is the so-called *Marshalsea* rule[49] from which stems the immunity of courts and their officers from liability in tort for damage inflicted in the enforcement of erroneous decisions except where the decision is outside or in excess of the court's jurisdiction. We shall examine the extent of judicial immunity shortly but we may notice here that "the *Marshalsea* rule has been applied to courts which were never considered to be courts of record[50] as well as to judicial institutions far removed from the ordinary law courts."[51] Now, as is shown by our example of a land owner's action in trespass against an authority relying on its statutory power to enter and inspect private land, to sue in tort alleging that the defendant authority has acted *ultra vires* is an important form of collateral challenge to "void" decisions. But where the decision of a court or tribunal, though erroneous and challengeable (say, on appeal) is within jurisdiction (and so merely "voidable") that form of collateral challenge is excluded by the *Marshalsea* rule.

The effect of the law of judicial immunity is thus severely to limit the availability of one important form of collateral challenge. Indeed, the limit is even more severe than we have indicated; for as we shall see, a court or tribunal may have exceeded its jurisdiction for purposes of direct challenge but be held not to have done so for purposes of collateral challenge of this type.

However, we should not forget that collateral challenge may take many forms other than an action in tort whose success depends on demonstrating the invalidity of a particular official act or decision. Case law is scanty, but one should not conclude that because a particular public authority is protected from suit in tort (except where it acts outside jurisdiction in the special sense just

[49] *Case of the Marshalsea* (1612) 77 E.R. 1027 (see below, note 69): see Rubinstein, *op.cit.* above, p. 56 *passim.*

[50] To which the rule was originally restricted: Rubinstein, *ibid.* "A court of record is one of which the acts and judicial proceedings are enrolled in its archives and are conclusive evidence of what is recorded," Jervis on *Coroners* (9th ed., 1957), p. 23.

[51] Rubinstein, *op.cit.* p. 60, *e.g.* tribunals empowered to authorise detention of the mentally ill: *Everett* v. *Griffiths* [1921] 1 A.C. 631; *D.P.P.* v. *Head* [1959] A.C. 83 at 111–112 *per* Lord Denning. For a statutory grant of immunity from suit (not precluding *direct* challenge) see Mental Health Act 1983, s.139, considered in *R.* v. *Hallstrom ex p. W* [1985] 3 All E.R. 775.

referred to) it follows that its invalid acts within jurisdiction are immune from other forms of collateral challenge. In *Director of Public Prosecutions* v. *Head*,[52] for example, the House of Lords ruled that one constituent of the statutory offence of unlawful sexual intercourse with which the defendant was charged[53] was that the woman concerned should have been lawfully detained as a mental defective. A majority of the House held that accordingly the defendant had a good defence if he could show that the woman was not lawfully detained, and that it was immaterial whether the detention order was void rather than voidable.[54] Only Lord Denning[55] regarded that distinction as crucial to the admissibility of the defendant's collateral challenge. But as Lord Somervell asked[56]:

> "Is a man to be sent to prison on the basis that an order is a good order when the court knows it would be set aside if proper proceedings were taken? I doubt it . . . . The distinction between void and voidable is by no means a clear one . . . I am not satisfied that the question whether a man should go or not go to prison should depend on the distinction."

One might ask, likewise, whether in other circumstances the right to mount a collateral challenge by way of defence should depend on the distinction: *i.e.* on whether an order or decision is, on the one hand, *ultra vires* or outside jurisdiction or, on the other, simply liable to be set aside on appeal or on the basis of patent error. Suppose that in our Commons Register example[57] the alleged trespasser could show that the Commissioners had erred in law in that they had misconstrued the legislation. Surely his freedom to raise this issue by way of defence should turn not on whether the error was jurisdictional but, rather, on whether it could have been subject to any form of direct challenge.

The question when will collateral challenge be permitted cannot satisfactorily be answered by recourse to the void/voidable distinction. In so far as there is a short answer to the question it may be

[52] [1959] A.C. 83.
[53] Under Mental Deficiency Act 1913, s.56(1)(*a*). Under the current law the offence is sexual intercourse with a woman who is a defective: Sexual Offences Act 1956, s.7.
[54] Lords Reid and Tucker concurred on this point with Lord Somervell: [1959] A.C. at 98, 103 and 104.
[55] *Ibid.* p. 112.
[56] *Ibid.* p. 104.
[57] Above, example 4.

that there is a presumption in favour of allowing collateral challenge in the absence of cogent reasons to the contrary. There are a number of circumstances, at any rate, where it is clear that collateral challenge will not be permitted.

(1) Express statutory exclusion

Some statutes expressly preclude any challenge whatever other than that for which the statute itself provides. See, *e.g.* the time-limited ouster clause cases considered above.[58] Here no collateral challenge will be permitted. In *Smith* v. *East Elloe R.D.C.*[59] the claim against the council was itself a case of collateral challenge which failed on this basis.

Of course, there are many circumstances in which the need to mount a collateral challenge may arise outside time limits prescribed for direct challenge by way of either supervisory or appellate review. Subject to express statutory provision of the sort just referred to, this alone should not affect the availability of collateral challenge.[60] If it were otherwise, private rights would be extinguished not (as Parliament has enacted) by the running of limitation periods but, in effect, by time limits imposed on particular kinds of direct challenge to the validity of public authority action.

(2) Implied statutory exclusion

There are some reported cases where a court has refused to permit a collateral challenge because the court finds that a statute has impliedly excluded any challenge other than what it has provided for expressly.[61] While all will depend on the words of the statute in question, we may observe that such cases are likely to be rare. As we have seen, the courts interpret express ouster clauses restrictively. They are likely to be even less sympathetic to arguments based on implication.

[58] See above, pp. 54–56. See also, *e.g.* Local Government Finance Act 1982 s.4(1) (below, Chap. 9): validity of rates and precepts "shall not be questioned except by an application for judicial review." Would this oust collateral challenge?

[59] [1959] A.C. 736 (see *ibid.*) The challenge in *Smith* was out of time. Their lordships held that the ouster clause deprived the courts of all jurisdiction in the matter, except as provided.

[60] See *e.g. R.* v. *Jenner* [1983] 1 W.L.R. 873 (invalidity of planning authority's "stop" notice good defence to criminal prosecution. Time limit for application for judicial review had expired), *cf. R.* v. *Smith* [1985] J.P.L. 183 (statutory ouster clause prevented invalidity of enforcement notice being used as defence to criminal prosecution).

[61] Wade A.L., pp. 298, 595.

(3) Orders of courts

It is contempt of court to fail to comply with an order of a superior court of record.[62] So, in contempt proceedings, it is not a defence to assert (*i.e.* collaterally) that the order would have been reversed on appeal. In such a case, then, the only possible method of challenge is direct.[63] Similarly, in proceedings taken to enforce an order of an inferior court it may be supposed that a collateral challenge to the validity of the order in question would not be permitted.[64]

Notice that this principle applies only to preclude collateral challenge to a court order in contempt or enforcement proceedings. In other circumstances, of course, a party may initiate or defend proceedings on the basis that a court order made in different proceedings should be set aside,[65] as, for example, where a judge who acts without jurisdiction is held liable for false imprisonment.[66]

(4) De facto officers and judges

Acts and decisions of officers and judges whose appointment is defective in law may not be challenged collaterally, at any rate until the defect becomes plain for all to perceive. However, the rule is not confined to collateral challenge as normally understood but extends to any challenge, direct or collateral, other than pro-

[62] Courts of record (see above, note 50), both superior and inferior, had common law jurisdiction to punish for contempt in the face of the court; but only superior courts of record had jurisdiction to punish for contempt out of court—see *R* v. *West Yorkshire Coroner ex p. Smith (no. 2)* [1985] 2 W.L.R. 332 (coroner's court inferior court of record). County courts and magistrates' courts, not being courts of record, had to be given statutory power to punish contempts (*ibid.*). For superior and inferior courts, see Chapter 4, p. 152.

[63] *Isaacs* v. *Robertson* [1984] 3 W.L.R.705; *Hadkinson* v. *Hadkinson* [1952] P. 285. Sometimes even direct challenge may be excluded—as in the case of a court whose order is not subject to supervisory review (see, *e.g.* Supreme Court Act 1981, s.29(3), Crown Court's jurisdiction in matters relating to trials on indictment) and is not appealable. In *R.* v. *Central Criminal Court ex p. Crook* [1984] *The Times* November 8, judge ordered no disclosure of rape victim's name outside court. Divisional Court indicated that order was probably outside jurisdiction (this point confirmed *re* magistrates' court in *R.* v. *Arundel Justices ex p. Westminster Press Ltd.* [1985] 2 All E.R. 390) but held that it had no jurisdiction to interfere. In such a case the order of the lower court is without legal basis but nevertheless cannot be challenged. This is plainly unsatisfactory. For proposals to reverse *Crook* by statute see [1985] N.L.J. 404.

[64] In *Munks* v. *Munks* (1985) 129 S.J. 65 the Court of Appeal assumed that the principle in *Isaacs* v. *Robertson* (above) would apply to a county court order.

[65] See, *e.g. Munks* v. *Munks* (previous note).

[66] See generally *Re McC (a minor)* (below, note 70); but *cf. Re F.* [1977] Fam. 165; and see *Skinner* v. *Carter* (above, note 47).

ceedings to remove the official.[67] Details of this doctrine of *de facto* officers and judges must be sought elsewhere.[68]

(5) Judicial immunity

We have already referred to the rule that a person who wrongly suffers loss of liberty or property under the order of a court may not sue in tort unless he can show that the court acted without or in excess of jurisdiction. On that basis no judge (except possibly a magistrate) is liable in tort for anything done within his jurisdiction. And, despite equivocal statutory provision,[69] a majority of the House of Lords has indicated, albeit obiter, that the same rule now applies to magistrates.[70]

As to want of jurisdiction, judges of superior courts will rarely be liable in tort since superior courts are deemed to have power conclusively to determine the limits of their own jurisdiction.[71] But "the Lord Chief Justice himself" could be liable in damages if he were to "act in bad faith, doing what he knows he has no power to do."[72]

Inferior courts[73] are not, of course, judges of their own jurisdiction. A magistrate who, without or in excess of jurisdiction, imprisons a person or causes him to make a money payment is liable in damages to that person.[74] "Without jurisdiction" means "no juris-

[67] Rubinstein, *op.cit. above*, p. 208.

[68] Wade, p. 300; Craig, p. 387; Rubinstein *ibid.*

[69] Justices of the Peace Act 1979, s.44—the equivocality is explained by Lord Bridge in *Re McC (a minor)* [1985] A.C. 528 at 539–540.

[70] *Re McC* (*ibid.*) pp. 540–541 (Lord Bridge with whom Lord Elwyn-Jones concurred at p. 533), 559 (Lord Templeman).

[71] See Buckley L.J. in *Sirros* v. *Moore* [1975] Q.B. 118 at 138; de Smith J.R.A.A., p. 121, n. 66. In *Sirros* v. *Moore* at 134 Lord Denning said that the "root decision" for superior courts is *Hamond* v. *Howell* (1674) 86 E.R. 816 at 1035 (judge fined members of "perverse" jury and imprisoned them for failing to pay fines. Jurors failed to recover damages for false imprisonment because judge believed, albeit erroneously, that he had jurisdiction to act as he did).

[72] *Per* Lord Bridge in *Re McC op.cit.* p. 540 (see note 69); see too *Sirros* v. *Moore* at pp. 135 and 140. Note that acting in bad faith (maliciously) does not of itself carry a judge outside jurisdiction for these purposes; so, provided that he remains within his jurisdiction, it seems that a judge is immune from suit even if he acts maliciously: see de Smith J.R.A.A., p. 121, *cf.* p. 338. This seems to belie the rationale of judicial immunity which is said to be "to strengthen [judges'] independence, so that their decisions may not be warped by fear of personal liability" (Wade A.L., p. 674).

[73] In *Sirros* v. *Moore* (above) at 133 Lord Denning M.R. said that for inferior courts "the root decision is the *Marshalsea Case*" (above, note 49: bail recognisancer imprisoned by Marshalsea Court. He recovered damages for false imprisonment on the basis that the court had no jurisdiction over the party for whom he had stood bail).

[74] Justices of the Peace Act 1979, s.45.

diction to entertain the proceedings at all,"[75] *e.g.* because of territorial considerations or lapse of time.[76] "Excess of jurisdiction" here does not include every "jurisdictional" error which would attract the exercise of the High Court's supervisory review jurisdiction. It is a narrower concept extending only to a case where a court (having jurisdiction to entertain proceedings) does "something quite exceptional"[77] in the course of them. In *Re McC (a minor)*[78] for example, magistrates were alleged to have imposed a custodial sentence without informing the defendant, as they were by statute bound to do, of his right to apply for legal aid. The House of Lords held unanimously that if the allegation were proved the magistrates would be liable for false imprisonment as having acted in excess of jurisdiction.[79] It may, of course, be difficult on occasion to say precisely what is and is not "quite exceptional" for these purposes. But the speeches in *Re McC* and the cases there cited perhaps indicate that if the judge ought to have known that he had no authority to act as he did, he may be held to have exceeded his jurisdiction.[80]

It is plain, at any rate, that no matter how gross an irregularity of procedure, there will be no liability if, in the actual circumstances, the court could lawfully have done precisely what it did, had it followed the correct procedure. It was on this basis that their lordships in *Re McC* explained *Sirros* v. *Moore*[81] where a Crown Court judge caused the detention of an appellant from a magistrates' court. The detention was irregular in that the judge had acted under a misapprehension as to the effect of the order he had made: but had he properly understood his jurisdiction he could lawfully have ordered the detention.

[75] *per* Lord Bridge, [1985] A.C. 528 at 546.

[76] See cases cited, *ibid.* pp. 544–545.

[77] *Per* Lord Bridge, *ibid.* p. 546.

[78] [1985] A.C. 528. The case concerned the law of Northern Ireland; but the House confirmed that in respect of magistrates' liability for acts outside jurisdiction, the law is in substance the same as that of England and Wales.

[79] Justices of the Peace Act 1979, s.53 provides for a magistrate to be indemnified out of local funds where he acted reasonably and in good faith. Note also section 52 which limits damages to one penny where it is proved that the plaintiff was actually guilty of the offence or liable to pay the sum in question and accordingly underwent no greater punishment than that assigned by law. The section may refer only to the possible liability of magistrates for acts done within jurisdiction (see text above); but *cf. R.* v. *Waltham Forest JJ. ex p. Solanke* [1985] 3 W.L.R. 788 where Woolf J. held that the section applied even where justices had no jurisdiction.

[80] See also *per* Buckley L.J. in *Sirros* v. *Moore* [1975] Q.B. 118 at 140–141.

[81] Previous note.

In *Sirros* v. *Moore* a majority of the Court of Appeal held that judges of inferior courts, including magistrates, had the same degree of immunity as judges of superior courts. In *Re McC* Lord Bridge observed that, because of the relevant statutory provisions[82] this approach "cannot possibly be supported in relation to justices."[83] He continued[84]:

> "The narrower question whether other courts of limited jurisdiction can and should be given the same immunity from suit as the superior courts . . . is one on which I express no concluded opinion, though my inclination is to think that this distinction is so deeply rooted in our law that it certainly cannot be eradicated by the Court of Appeal and probably not by your Lordships' House, even in exercise of the power declared in the [1966] Practice Statement made by the House. So fundamental a change would, in my present view, require appropriate legislation."

It appears, then, that, at present, inferior courts generally enjoy no more immunity than magistrates' courts in respect of acts and decisions made without or in excess of jurisdiction. In *Re McC* Lord Templeman observed[85] that it might be desirable to legislate to give magistrates the same immunity as superior courts but to create a state-funded compensation scheme for appropriate cases. The same may no doubt be said for inferior courts generally.

Finally we must consider the effect of a successful collateral challenge. The principal issue (in the four examples with which we began, the liability issue) may have been decided on the basis that the public authority act impugned is indeed beyond the remit of the authority. On the basis, that is to say, that a direct challenge would have succeeded or (if in time) still would succeed. But there has been no direct challenge. The proceedings in which the successful collateral challenge was made resolve only the liability issue between the parties concerned. The public authority whose act is impugned may not even be a party to the proceedings.[86] How, in any event, should the success of the collateral challenge be regarded by the public authority concerned and by other parties?

[82] See above, notes 69, 74.
[83] [1985] A.C. 528 at 550.
[84] *Ibid.*
[85] *Ibid.* p. 559.
[86] As in our examples 3 and 4; and in *D.P.P.* v. *Head* (above, note 52).

Where the public authority was a party to the proceedings in which the collateral challenge succeeded,[87] no doubt the authority (having pursued such avenues of appeal as are available and as it chooses) would be prudent to deal with other potential plaintiffs and defendants on the basis that the collateral challenge would succeed for them too.

Where the public authority was not a party, its attitude to the success of the challenge will depend in part upon the status of the court concerned and upon the probability of other, perhaps higher, courts taking the same view. The issue may be of particular importance to a public authority in a case such as *D.P.P.* v. *Head*[88] where the implication of the success of the collateral challenge is that the authority may be liable to other parties on other bases.[89]

D. The Royal Prerogative and Review

We saw earlier[90] that the Crown's unlimited legal capacity together with its residual prerogative powers, provide the legal basis for a wide field of executive activity. To what extent may official action which purports to be an exercise of the legal capacity or prerogative power of the Crown be subject to judicial review? We must distinguish two questions: (1) How far may the courts rule upon the lawfulness of such action? (2) Under what heads of review jurisdiction—direct or collateral, supervisory or appellate—may challenge be mounted?

(1) Extent of review jurisdiction

The seventeenth century constitutional settlement established the principle "that the King hath no prerogative but that which the law of the land allows him . . . "[91] In modern times that principle has been understood to mean that "whilst the courts are empowered to determine the existence, scope and form of a prerogative power, that power is absolute, in the sense that the courts have disclaimed jurisdiction to review the propriety or adequacy of the grounds on which it has been exercised."[92] Although there are

[87] As in *Cooper* v. *Wandsworth Board of Works* (above, note 45); see too *Wandsworth L.B.C.* v. *Winder* (*ibid.*).
[88] [1959] A.C. 83.
[89] *Ibid.* p. 111, *per* Lord Denning.
[90] See Chap. 1, pp. 12–14.
[91] *Case of Proclamations* (1611) 12 Co. Rep. 74 (extracted in Keir and Lawson, *Cases in Constitutional Law*, 6th ed., p. 108).
[92] *Laker Airways Ltd.* v. *Dept. of Trade* [1977] Q.B. 643 at 678–679 *per* Mocatta J. Similarly Lord Fraser in *Council of Civil Service Unions* v. *Minister for the Civil Service* [1985] A.C. 374 at 398 (see below).

many historical uncertainties about the precise extent of the prerogative,[93] it is clear that Parliament has legislated in many areas which were previously covered by prerogative. So the courts' jurisdiction to determine the scope of prerogative power often falls to be exercised where the question is how far a statute has superseded the prerogative. For example, where Parliament by statute, and subject to limitations, has authorised official action in an area previously covered by the prerogative, the courts hold that the prerogative is superseded and that the government can act only subject to the statutory limitations.[94] Again, even where it is accepted that the Crown has acted under prerogative power, the courts may hold that the power is less wide than the Crown had believed, so, for example, entitling a subject to compensation for loss of property.[95]

Until 1984, however, it appeared that the courts disclaimed jurisdiction to review the manner in which an established prerogative power was exercised. Whereas, as we shall see,[96] the courts have exercised their review jurisdictions so as to prevent abuse of discretionary powers conferred by statute on public authorities, it seemed that the exercise of discretionary powers deriving from the prerogative could not be reviewed. But in 1984 in a case[97] concerning union membership at government communications headquarters (G.C.H.Q.) a majority in the House of Lords took a radically different approach. The Minister for the Civil Service (the Prime Minister) was empowered by prerogative Order in Council[98] to regulate the conditions of service of civil servants. Without consulting the unions concerned, she announced a ban on union membership by staff at G.C.H.Q. When the unions applied

[93] See, *e.g.* Viscount Radcliffe's speech in *Burmah Oil Co.* v. *Lord Advocate* [1965] A.C. 75 at 114–115 *passim.*

[94] *Attorney-General* v. *De Keyser's Royal Hotel Ltd* [1920] A.C. 508 (wartime requisition: statutory power held to have superseded prerogative; and subject entitled to compensation provided for by statute). *Laker Airways* case (above) (detailed statutory provision for government licensing of international air traffic fettered absolute prerogative power to grant or withdraw such licences): see also Court of Appeal at [1977] Q.B. 684 at 721–722 (Roskill L.J.); 728 (Lawson L.J.). *cf.* Lord Denning M.R. at 705–706 in effect anticipating the *G.C.H.Q.* case, below.

[95] *Burmah Oil Co.* v. *Lord Advocate* (above): during Second World War U.K. Government destroyed company's installations in Burmah to deprive enemy of their use. Company admitted destruction was lawful but sued for compensation. The ruling of a bare majority in the House of Lords in favour of compensation was reversed by the War Damage Act 1965 (see Chap. 1, p. 18).

[96] See Chap. 5.

[97] *Council of Civil Service Unions* v. *Minister for the Civil Service* [1985] A.C. 374.

[98] See Chap. 1, p. 13.

for judicial review of the ban, the government argued that the courts could no more review the exercise of prerogative power delegated to a minister by Order in Council than they could a direct exercise of prerogative power. The House of Lords unanimously rejected the argument. In Lord Fraser's words[99]:

> "[W]hatever their source, powers which are defined, either by reference to their object or by reference to procedure for their exercise, or in some other way, and whether the definition is expressed or implied, are . . . normally subject to judicial control to ensure that they are not exceeded."

However, the House held, again unanimously, that this was not a "normal" case; and although the ban had been imposed unfairly, the minister had justified her action by reference to considerations of national security.

In the present context, perhaps the most important feature of the *G.C.H.Q.* case is that three[1] of the five law lords did not confine their rulings on review of prerogative action to the case of delegated power. They indicated that it is no longer good law that the exercise of discretionary powers deriving from the prerogative cannot be reviewed. There was "no reason why simply because a decision-making power is derived from a common law and not a statutory source it should *for that reason only* be immune from judicial review."[2]

Now, it is clear that the:

> "nature and subject matter [of many prerogative powers] is such as not to be amenable to the judicial process. The courts are not the place wherein to determine whether a treaty should be concluded[3] or the armed forces disposed in a particular manner[4] or Parliament dissolved on one date rather than another."[5]

[99] [1985] A.C.374 at 399.
[1] *Ibid. per* Lord Scarman at 407; Lord Diplock at 410–411; Lord Roskill at 417–418.
[2] Lord Diplock, *ibid.* (his lordship's emphasis).
[3] See *e.g. Blackburn* v. *Att.-Gen.* [1971] 1 W.L.R. 1037. (Even if U.K. accession to Treaty of Rome involved surrender of U.K. Parliamentary sovereignty, accession not challengeable in courts).
[4] See, *e.g. Chandler* v. *D.P.P.* [1964] A.C. 763. (Anti-nuclear protesters charged under statute with acting prejudicially to national interest were not permitted to call evidence to establish that maintenance of nuclear weapons in U.K. was against national interest).
[5] *Per* Lord Roskill [1985] A.C. 374 at 418; footnotes added.

By the nature of the judicial process the courts are not equipped to adjudicate on the legality of the exercise of what we have referred to as the prerogatives of state.[6] The rules or conventions governing the exercise of these prerogatives are insufficiently precise to enable a litigant wishing to challenge their exercise to formulate issues of law and fact of the sort with which the courts are equipped to deal. Further,

> "[t]he reasons for the decision maker taking one course rather than another do not normally involve questions to which, if disputed, the judicial process is adapted to provide the right answer, by which I mean that the kind of evidence that is admissible under judicial procedures and the way in which it has to be adduced tend to exclude from the attention of the court competing policy considerations which, if the executive discretion is to be wisely exercised, need to be weighed against one another, a balancing exercise which judges by their upbringing and experience are ill-qualified to perform."[7]

In short, the issues are not justiciable.

The same may be true of many aspects of the exercise of the prerogatives of government. In the *G.C.H.Q.* case the House of Lords indicated[8] that the exercise of the discretions inherent in, *e.g.* the grant of honours or the exercise of the prerogative of mercy[9] would be unlikely to be considered justiciable. But these limitations on judicial review derive from the nature of the powers concerned and not from their source in prerogative rather than statute.[10] The *G.C.H.Q.* case indicates that "[t]oday . . . the controlling factor in determining whether the exercise of prerogative power is subject to judicial review is not its source but its subject matter."[11] As the *G.C.H.Q.* case itself indicates, where the Crown has delegated prerogative power in specific terms, the question of whether or not the power has been exercised within those terms may be eminently justiciable. Furthermore, there are

[6] See Chap. 1, p. 12.
[7] *Per* Lord Diplock [1985] A.C. 374 at 411.
[8] See, *e.g.* Lord Diplock *ibid.* at 411; Lord Roskill at 418.
[9] *cf.* A.T.H. Smith in (1983) *Public Law* 398 at 432–434.
[10] Indeed many *statutory* duties of public authorities are expressed so widely as probably to make them non-justiciable. Wade A.L., p. 625, cites, *e.g.* the Secretary of State's duty under the National Health Service Act 1977 to continue the promotion in England and Wales of a comprehensive health service.
[11] *Per* Lord Scarman at [1985] A.C. 374 at 407.

indications in the judgments[12] that the courts may be especially willing to intervene on the basis of unfair exercise of prerogative power—*i.e.* for breach of the so-called rules of natural justice.[13]

There are indications too in the *G.C.H.Q.* case that the availability of judicial review of Crown action will not turn on what Lord Diplock described[14] as "esoteric" distinctions between prerogative power strictly so-called and the Crown's legal capacity.[15] In this connection we may observe that their lordships approved *R.* v. *Criminal Injuries Compensation Board ex p. Lain*[16] in which a Divisional Court held that decisions of the Board were subject to supervisory review even though the Board was set up "under the prerogative." But, as Professor Wade has observed,[17] the Criminal Injuries Compensation Board was set up not by the exercise of prerogative power strictly so-called but by the Crown in the exercise of "its ordinary powers as a natural person." It seems then to follow from the *G.C.H.Q.* case that the government can no longer regard itself as immune from judicial review simply because it is acting through the Crown's common law capacity rather than exercising either prerogative or statutory powers. Subject, then, to the overriding issue of justiciability, the government's actions in such fields as the award of contracts, the issuing of passports and the grant of extra-statutory tax concessions may be suitable candidates for challenge by way of judicial review.[18]

Further discussion of the notion of justiciability may be postponed until we have observed its development and operation in the context of judicial review of the exercise of statutory powers.[19] But it must not be forgotten that the most frequently advanced and most effective governmental rebuff to attempts to secure judicial review in this field is likely to be, as in the *G.C.H.Q.* case, "considerations of national security." Their lordships did hold that in order to rely on this ground the government must produce evi-

[12] *Ibid.* p. 411 (Lord Diplock); 419 (Lord Roskill).
[13] See Chap. 6 (B).
[14] [1985] A.C. 374 at 409.
[15] For this distinction, see Chap. 1, p. 12.
[16] [1967] 2 Q.B. 864.
[17] Constitutional Fundmentals, pp. 47–48.
[18] To bring such government action within the reach of judicial review may be regarded as a desirable consequence of what Professor Wade argues is an over-wide conception of "prerogative." But a paradoxical consequence may be to entitle government employees to apply for judicial review where non-government employees cannot: see Professor Wade's article in (1985) 101 L.Q.R. 180 at 190–197.
[19] See especially Chapter 5 (*Law and Policy*) p. 189 *passim*.

dence that the decision was in fact based on security considerations. But it seems unlikely that the courts will go further than to require a minister to establish that he did, as a matter of fact, characterise as "security considerations" the grounds on which he acted. It seems that the question of the propriety of this characterisation is "par excellence a non-justiciable question."[20]

This last observation does prompt the aside that there are some circumstances in which government claims of security considerations are treated as, in varying degrees, justiciable. So, security considerations may be the basis of a government claim to "public interest immunity"—*i.e.* to resist in the context of litigation the other side's demand for discovery[21] of certain documents by arguing that non-disclosure is in the public interest.[22] On the one hand, the House of Lords has indicated[23] that the courts are never absolutely bound to accept a government claim to immunity, no matter what its basis. On the other, it is plain from the judgments that the courts would be most unlikely to question a claim based in good faith on security considerations. Nevertheless, one could no doubt envisage circumstances where the courts might scrutinise the credentials of a bland assertion that documents should not be disclosed on grounds of national security.

Indeed, in a different context, Parliament has made courts the arbiters of whether disclosure of information is necessary in the interests of, *inter alia*, national security. Section 10 of the Contempt of Court Act 1981 provides that no court may require a person to disclose the source of information which he has published "unless it be established to the satisfaction of the court that disclosure is necessary in the interests of . . . national security . . . " In *Secretary of State for Defence* v. *Guardian Newspapers Ltd*[24] the Ministry of Defence claimed that a newspaper should surrender a document "leaked" to it by a civil servant and concerning the sit-

[20] *Per* Lord Diplock [1985] A.C. at 412. Only Lord Scarman (at 406) supported views expressed by Lord Devlin in *Chandler* (above, note 4) that, within broad limits, the question of the interests of national security may be justiciable.

[21] *i.e.* disclosure of the contents.

[22] It was at one time thought that such a claim could be made only by the government by virtue of "crown privilege." But in *Rogers* v. *Home Secretary* [1973] A.C. 388 the House of Lords held that a claim to non-disclosure could be made by any person interested in the proceedings and, therefore, was properly described as a claim to "public interest immunity." For accounts of this branch of the law, see Wade A.L., pp. 721–730; Craig, pp. 609–620.

[23] See especially *Conway* v. *Rimmer* [1968] A.C. 910; *Burmah Oil Co. Ltd.* v. *Bank of England* [1980] A.C. 1090 (Craig, pp. 611, 615).

[24] [1985] A.C. 339.

ing of nuclear missiles in the U.K. The document indicated the source of the leak and the House of Lords held by a bare majority that the ministry had provided "just enough"[25] evidence to justify its claim that it was in the interests of national security that the source of the leak should be disclosed. But Lord Bridge said[26]:

> "I understand all your Lordships to be of one mind, first, that in such a case it is eminently desirable that all relevant material should be spelled out in the evidence put before the court with the utmost particularity, secondly, that the evidence relied on by the Crown in the instant case fell significantly short of that counsel of perfection."

In the context of judicial review of the exercise of prerogative power the conclusion from the foregoing is, perhaps, that unqualified statements about the non-justiciability of security issues should be taken with some reserve.

(2) Modes of challenge

Under what heads of review jurisdiction may a party challenge the legality of action taken by the Crown in reliance upon its prerogative power?

(a) *Appellate review*

Generally speaking, of course, the exercise of prerogative power will not be subject to appeal. Prerogative power is by definition non-statutory, whereas rights of appeal are created by statute as a means of challenging decisions made by authorities whose power derives from statute. Although the jurisdictions of the superior and certain other courts derive ultimately from the royal prerogative to dispense justice,[27] those jurisdictions have long since been put on a statutory basis; and the network of appeals is entirely statutory. However, the superior courts do continue to exercise the prerogative jurisdiction of wardship. Although jurisdiction relating to care and control of children is today largely statutory "[t]he courts have asserted the continued existence of the

[25] *Per* Lord Diplock *ibid.* p. 346.
[26] *Ibid.* p. 372.
[27] De Smith C. & A., pp. 141, 150.

prerogative but are reluctant to invoke it."[28] In a case where the court did invoke that jurisdiction its exercise could be challenged by way of the ordinary statutory appellate machinery.[29]

(b) *Supervisory review*

Challenge under the supervisory jurisdiction may be direct or it may be collateral.

If direct, the appropriate remedy will usually be a declaration. For the prerogative remedies are not available against the Crown[30]: nor is the injunction.[31] However where the Crown has by prerogative Order in Council delegated prerogative power to a minister it may perhaps be possible to obtain a prerogative remedy against the minister in respect of unlawful exercise of the power.[32]

Turning to collateral challenge, many reported cases raising questions of the reviewability of prerogative power have been cases where an issue as to the extent of a litigant's private law rights or criminal liability have turned on the lawfulness of Crown action relying on prerogative power.[33]

[28] *Ibid.* p. 144, n. 90. See, *e.g. A.* v. *Liverpool City Council* [1982] A.C. 363. Of the relationship between the prerogative jurisdiction of the courts and the statutory powers of local authorities with regard to care and control of deprived children, Lord Roskill said (at p. 377) "I am of the clear opinion that, while prerogative jurisdiction of the court in wardship cases remains, the exercise of that jurisdiction has been and must continue to be treated, as circumscribed by the existence of the far-ranging statutory code . . . " See too *Re W (A Minor)* [1985] 2 W.L.R. 892. Where there is a *lacuna* in the statutory code, the court may exercise the prerogative jurisdiction: *Re J. (A Minor)* [1984] 1 W.L.R. 81; but *cf. Re M. (A Minor)* [1985] 2 W.L.R. 811 (*lacuna* filled by later statutory provision).

[29] R.S.C., Ord. 58; see Halsbury, *Laws of England* (4th ed.), Vol. 24, para. 592.

[30] These remedies were originally available only to the Crown; and even today the Crown remains nominal plaintiff—see p. 38 above.

[31] Crown Proceedings Act 1947, s.21. But *cf.* Chap. 8 below.

[32] In the *G.C.H.Q.* case Lord Fraser (at [1985] A.C. 397) noted simply that "the remedy of certiorari [originally sought before Glidewell J.] is no longer sought."

[33] See, *e.g.* the *De Keyser* case (above, note 94): the action was by petition of right, now abolished. Today it would be simply an action in quasi-contract turning on the prerogative point; the *Burmah Oil Co.* case (above, note 95) was a Scottish case under the Crown Suits Act 1857. Under English law the action would have been in tort, turning likewise on the prerogative point. The *Chandler* case (above, note 4) may be characterised as a case of unsuccessful collateral challenge: D's criminal liability turned on the success or failure of his challenge to the Crown's assessment of what was prejudicial to the national interest. As observed above, the court refused to consider evidence on this issue, so the challenge failed *in limine*.

E. Note on the Remit, Capacity and Liability of Public Authorities

A public authority is treated in English Law as having a limited remit or competence. From this notion flows the law of judicial review. But how does the notion of limited remit relate to the principles upon which a public authority may be held liable for a civil or criminal wrong? In particular:

(1) How does the notion of limited remit relate to the capacity of a public authority to commit civil and criminal wrongs?
(2) How far may a public authority's remit protect it from liability?
(3) To what extent may a public authority's transgression of the limits of its remit constitute the basis of civil liability?

A comprehensive account of the law of public authority liability must be sought elsewhere.[34] This note is confined to indicating the relationship between limited remit and liability at the points just mentioned.

(1) The capacity of public authorities to commit civil and criminal wrongs

(a) *Torts*

If on ordinary tort law principles a public authority would be liable in tort it cannot escape liability simply by establishing that the action in question carried it outside its remit and arguing that, on that basis, it had no capacity to commit the tort. There is no doubt that if in the course of discharging a duty or exercising a power of a public authority an employee of the authority commits, say, the tort of negligence, the authority is vicariously liable on the usual master/servant principles—as, for example, if a local authority workman, while demolishing a building which the authority has power or a duty to demolish, negligently injures a passer-by.[35] It would indeed be strange if in another case the authority could escape liability simply by demonstrating that it had no power to undertake the demolition.[36]

Again, if the authority acts directly through an officer rather than an employee, it may be liable for his torts. Suppose, for

[34] *e.g.* Wade A.L., Chaps. 20 and 21; Craig, Part 4.
[35] For a selection of reported cases, see Wade A.L., p. 656.
[36] If the employee's contract of employment is *ultra vires* (*cf.* (c) below) there could be no vicarious liability. But there might be primary liability if the action is authorised by its officials—see text below and next note.

example, that the officers of a water authority authorise the supply of water through lead piping, thus injuring consumers. If negligence can be shown, the authority will be liable: not vicariously but primarily.[37] It should make no difference whether or not, in using lead piping, the authority acts *ultra vires*. Indeed, in the context of our treatment of collateral challenge we have already met a number of cases in which public authorities acting through their officers or their employees may be liable in tort where the action complained of is *ultra vires*.[38]

The truth is, surely, that capacity to commit legal wrongs is an incident of legal personality shared alike by legal entities with a limited remit and those with no such limit. Giving judgment for a plaintiff house-owner in a nuisance action[39] against a public authority in respect of the unauthorised construction of a stand for the viewing of a procession, Avory J. observed[40]:

> "To say that, because the [corporation] had no legal right to erect it, therefore the corporation cannot be sued, is to say that no corporation can ever be sued for any tort or wrong."[41]

Of course, just as an employer (whether a public authority or not) will not be vicariously liable for the torts of his employees committed "outside the scope of their employment," so a public authority would not be liable for the torts of an officer or an employee when he is, in the old phrase, "on a frolic of his own." The authority would not be liable, for example, for negligent injuries inflicted either by an employee or by an officer who, without colour or claim of authority, drove the authority's vehicle while engaged entirely on his own concerns.

(b) *Crimes*

The *ultra vires* doctrine appears to have had as little impact in relieving public authorities of criminal liability as it has in the law

[37] See *Barnes* v. *Irwell Valley Water Board* [1938] 1 K.B. 21 " . . . [I]f a corporation acts in the only way in which a corporation, being an artificial person, can act—that is, if the central governing body of the corporation orders or ratifies an act—then the act must be attributed to the corporation itself" Winfield and Jolowicz on *Tort* (12th ed.), p. 693.

[38] Recall, *e.g. Cooper* v. *Wandsworth Board of Works* (above, note 45). The authority acted *ultra vires* in demolishing the plaintiff's house. It was nonetheless liable in damages for trespass.

[39] The nuisance was a public nuisance. The plaintiff had a private law tort action because it caused special damage to her.

[40] *Campbell* v. *Paddington Corporation* [1911] 1 K.B. 869 at 875.

[41] *i.e.* any tort or wrong committed while acting *ultra vires*.

of tort. It would appear[42] that the principles of public authority criminal capacity are similar to those for tort except that vicarious liability for crime is far less extensive. At common law the *mens rea* of an employee cannot generally be attributed to his employer: in such case there is no vicarious liability. It is often otherwise under statute; and, in addition, statute has created many regulatory offences of strict liability for which an employer (whether public authority or not) may be vicariously liable.[43]

A corporation, including, presumably, a public authority, may be a principal even to a crime requiring *mens rea* if the offence is perpetrated by an officer who is the "directing mind and will" of the corporation.[44]

(c) *Breaches of contract*

The duty not to commit a tort or a crime may be said to lie automatically on all legal persons with capacity to commit such wrongs. But the duty not to commit a breach of contract lies only upon a person who has, and has chosen to employ, the capacity to make a binding contract. The notion of limited remit yields the principle that a public authority is empowered to make only such contracts as "relate to functions which the authority is authorised expressly or impliedly to perform."[45] Any other contract is *ultra vires*. Can a public authority be liable for breach of an *ultra vires* contract?

Clearly the courts will not force a public authority to perform a contract where the performance would entail the authority acting *ultra vires*—*e.g.* a contract fettering discretion[46]; a contract interfering with the attainment of a particular statutory purpose[47]; a contract purportedly made in the exercise of a particular statutory power but which does not accord with limitations imposed on the power.[48]

[42] On criminal capacity of corporations, see Smith and Hogan, *Criminal Law* (5th ed.), pp. 155 *passim*, on which this summary relies. The reported cases are mostly on limited companies; but there is no reason in principle why the position of a public authority should differ. Smith and Hogan (p. 160) observe that the arguments in favour of imposing corporate criminal liability are hardly compelling.

[43] Smith and Hogan, *op.cit.* pp. 148–149.

[44] *Op.cit.* p. 156.

[45] Chitty on *Contracts* (25th ed.), p. 702.

[46] See Chap. 5, p. 196, *Fettering by Contract.*

[47] *Ayr Harbour Trustees* v. *Oswald* (1883) 8 App.Cas.623 (discussed, *ibid.*).

[48] *Rhyl U.D.C.* v. *Rhyl Amusements Ltd* [1959] 1 W.L.R. 465 (no power to lease corporation land without ministerial consent—"lease" held void).

Equally clearly, surely, the right to damages for breach of a public authority contract should not turn on complex *vires* issues which, to a party contemplating entering into contractual relations, may be quite inscrutable. No doubt there are cases where it should have been plain that a particular contract would be *ultra vires*. But there are many *ultra vires* contracts of which that could not be said. Suppose that a local authority resolves to expand a public transport service for which it is responsible, and at the same time to reduce fares. Assume that the scheme is *ultra vires*[49] but that before any legal action is taken to challenge the validity of the scheme the authority enters into a number of contracts in pursuance of it. It employs new staff; it enters into building contracts for the extension of existing premises; it contracts to purchase new vehicles and new office machinery and stationery. Now, if the scheme itself is *ultra vires*, all these contracts must be *ultra vires*. Surely, though, if, for example, the authority is forced to break its undertakings because the scheme is held to be *ultra vires*, the authority should be liable for their breach.[50] It is surely in the public interest that public authorities should retain commercial credibility. Should they not be liable at any rate for breach of contracts which, although *ultra vires* could not have been expected to be perceived by the other party to be so? The obvious juridical difficulties in the notion of liability for breach of an *ultra vires* contract[51] may suggest that it is for Parliament rather than the courts to find a solution here. Perhaps what is required is a modified version of the type of statutory provision made with respect to limited companies in the European Communities Act 1972.[52] The statute might protect a public authority from specific enforcement of *ultra vires* contracts while entitling deserving plaintiffs to recover damages for their breach.

(d) *Immunity from suit*

At common law the Crown enjoyed complete immunity from suit. This immunity has now largely been removed although some vestiges remain.[53] We have already referred to the law of judicial

[49] *cf. Bromley London Borough Council* v. *Greater London Council* [1983] 1 A.C. 768 (below, Chap. 5, p. 184).
[50] *cf.* Hogg, *Liability of the Crown*, Chap. 5.
[51] See Craig, p. 601.
[52] s. 9, *cf. Re Jon Beauforte Ltd.* [1953] Ch. 131.
[53] *e.g.* the exemption of premises occupied by government departments from the enforcement provisions of food hygiene legislation (to be removed: see National Health Service (Amendment) Bill 1986). For the law of Crown Proceedings, see Wade A.L., Chap. 21 and works there cited.

immunity.[54] Those cases apart, statute may confer upon a public authority a substantial (and sometimes doubtfully justifiable) immunity from liability.[55]

(2) Remit to do "wrong"

(a) *Tort and crime*

Clearly there are innumerable situations where a public authority is remitted to do what, if it were done by a private individual, would be a tort or a crime: demolition in pursuance of compulsory acquisition of land is a prime example. In cases of this sort Parliament judges that the community is better served by the extension of public power than by the preservation of private rights. It would be fatuous to characterise this aspect of democratic government as a remit to do wrong.

There are, however, many cases where it is highly debatable whether or not a statute is to be taken to have authorised the infliction of particular harm on a plaintiff. For example, the statute may have authorised the construction of a sewage works. But need the works have been at the bottom of P's garden? And has P no remedy for the nuisance of the smell? Essentially the question in each case is a matter of interpretation of the statute concerned. If in all the circumstances what the statute has authorised will inevitably cause the injury complained of, then there is no redress at common law. Details of the principle of "inevitable injury" must be sought elsewhere.[56] Here we may note that the common law's inadequacy in this context has been somewhat mitigated by the Land Compensation Act 1973 which provides for the payment of compensation to those whose land value is "depreciated by physical factors [*e.g.* noise, smell, fumes] caused by the use of public works."[57]

(b) *Contract*

We shall see later[58] how a public authority may fall under a statutory duty to break a binding contract.

[54] See above, p. 71.
[55] Commonly cited is the position of the Post Office under (now) the Post Office Act 1969.
[56] Wade A.L., pp. 650–655; Craig, pp. 527–533.
[57] Section 1(1).
[58] See Chap. 5, p. 197.

(3) Power, duty and liability in tort

If in the course of discharging a duty or exercising a power a public authority commits a recognised tort such as nuisance or negligence it will be liable, subject to what has been said above about immunity and inevitable injury. Furthermore, as we have seen, it should be no defence for the authority to show that when the tort was committed the authority was acting *ultra vires*. But suppose that an authority has a power which, on a particular occasion, it does not exercise; and that, as a consequence, a person suffers damage to himself or his property. Suppose, for example, that a local authority has statutory power to inspect the foundations of any building in course of construction in its area but that the authority did not inspect the foundations of a house which P has just bought from the builder. Later, it appears that the foundations were negligently constructed so that the building is seriously defective. The builder is bankrupt. Assuming that the defective construction would have been apparent on inspection, can P recover the cost of reconstruction from the local authority? It is settled that a plaintiff may recover for such damage where the authority has made a negligent inspection, albeit that the authority had merely a power to inspect.[59] *A fortiori*, surely, if the authority had a duty to inspect and either inspected negligently or failed to inspect at all. But what is the position where, as in our example, the authority has merely a power to inspect and has not inspected at all?

First, it is perhaps misleading to speak of a public authority having "merely a power." For powers are conferred on a public authority for a public purpose; and the authority always has a duty to consider according to all relevant criteria whether or not to exercise a power conferred.[60] This duty, as we shall see, may be enforced by way of judicial review.[61] Now, the authority in our example may have decided for impeccable administrative reasons to exercise its power of inspection on a selective basis with the consequence that P's foundations are not inspected. In this event, P has no cause of action.[62] But suppose that the authority has failed to give either any or proper consideration to the exercise of its power of inspection; or that its failure to inspect P's foundations is

[59] *Dutton* v. *Bognor Regis U.D.C.* [1972] 1 Q.B. 373 as explained by the House of Lords in *Anns* v. *Merton London Borough Council* [1978] A.C. 728.
[60] See Chap. 5, pp. 171–172 *passim*.
[61] See Chap. 5, p. 201 *et seq*.
[62] See, *e.g. per* Lord Wilberforce in *Anns* v. *Merton L.B.C.* (above) at 753–754 distinguishing between the "policy area" and the "operational area."

the consequence of a policy which has been adopted without regard to all relevant criteria. In either event, the authority has acted *ultra vires* and is in breach of such duty of care as it owes to P. But can P recover? The House of Lords has indicated[63] that if in such circumstances P can establish all the other ingredients of the tort of negligence, he may recover.

One ingredient, of course, is that the authority's negligent (and *ultra vires*) failure to inspect must have caused P damage. *i.e.* P must show that had the authority acted *intra vires*, P would not have suffered the damage. This is a burden which P may find very difficult to discharge. We are supposing that the authority has a power, not a duty, to inspect. We are supposing too that it has abused that power. Had it not done so P's foundations might well have been inspected. But to succeed in his action what P must show, surely, is that had it not abused the power, the defect in P's foundations would certainly have been discovered. Possibly there may be features of the situation which will enable P to show this (*e.g.* the size and importance of P's building; or the fact that it is one of many similarly defective buildings and it is clear that, under a proper policy, some would have been inspected, leading to the discovery of the defect in all). It is a heavy burden; nevertheless a plaintiff may be able to discharge it.[64]

If P recovers damages here, then, the root of his case will be that the authority went *ultra vires* by abusing its power. Notice, though, that to show abuse of power, though essential, is only the first step. In these circumstances "liability cannot exist *unless* the act complained of lies outside the ambit of the power."[65]

> "A plaintiff complaining of negligence must prove, the burden being on him, that action taken was not within the limits of a discretion bona fide exercised, *before he can begin to rely* on a common law duty of care. But if he can do this, he should, in principle, be able to sue."[66]

So, a plaintiff who can establish *ultra vires* may sue; but he will suc-

[63] In *Anns* v. *Merton L.B.C.* (above). *cf. Peabody Fund* v. *Parkinson Ltd.* [1985] A.C. 210 (no duty of care owed to developers); *Investors in Industry Commercial Properties Ltd.* v. *S. Beds D.C.* [1986] 1 All E.R. 787 (no duty of care to original building owner even though not personally careless).

[64] *Anns* was concerned only with preliminary points of law: *i.e.* with the question of what a plaintiff must establish in order for the authority to be liable. It does not appear, therefore, whether the plaintiff was able to discharge the burden in that case.

[65] *Per* Lord Wilberforce in *Anns* (see note 62) at p. 758. Emphasis added.

[66] *Per* Lord Wilberforce, *ibid.* p. 755. Emphasis added.

ceed only if in addition he can discharge the heavy burden described above.[67]

Are there any other circumstances in which a public authority's liability in tort in the event of the non-exercise of a power may turn on a *vires* issue? There are many situations today where an authority has some sort of statutory licensing power, *e.g.* power to license sales of liquor and other items; to license entertainments of various sorts; to license (*i.e.* give planning permission for) development of land; to license imports and exports; to license or certificate an individual to carry on a particular trade or profession. Suppose that in the purported exercise of such a power a public authority either refuses to grant or revokes a licence of some description. Suppose that P, the applicant or erstwhile licensee, can show that the refusal or withdrawal was *ultra vires*; and that he has suffered loss as a consequence. May he recover that loss from the authority?

Of course, the principle in *Anns* v. *Merton L.B.C.*[68] could apply here. If P can show that the authority was negligent and that, had it acted lawfully, it would certainly have granted or refrained from revoking P's licence, P should succeed. But there is a different basis upon which, alternatively, P may succeed. The cases[69] indicate that if P can show either that the authority was maliciously disposed towards him or, simply that it knew that its action was *ultra vires* and would injure P, P can recover on that basis. He can recover here without discharging the heavy burden of showing that the authority would certainly have exercised its discretion in his favour. For here he has shown "misfeasance in public office" which is recognised as a tort in its own right.[70] On this basis, for example, it has been held[71] that a government department would be liable in tort for loss inflicted on the plaintiff by the revocation of a poultry import licence if the plaintiff could show that the department knew both that the revocation was *ultra vires* and that it would damage the plaintiff. Here too, then, *ultra vires* may be the basis of a public authority's liability in tort for failure properly or at all to exercise a statutory power.

[67] For an example of a plaintiff's failure to discharge the burden, see *West* v. *Bucks C.C.* [1984] *The Times*, November 13 (road accident where council had not painted double white lines not caused by absence of lines).

[68] Discussed above.

[69] See Wade A.L., pp. 669–674; Craig, pp. 548–554.

[70] In *Dunlop* v. *Woollhara Municipal Council* [1981] 2 W.L.R. 693 at 703, Lord Diplock said that the tort was "well established." But there are remarkably few English cases and the nature of "misfeasance" is not clear in all respects.

[71] *Bourgoin S.A.* v. *Minister of Agriculture etc.* [1985] 3 All E.R. 585. But *cf.* the law of judicial immunity (see above, p. 71, note 72).

The tort of misfeasance in public office relates to the abuse of statutory power. If, of course, a plaintiff can show that a statute has imposed upon a public authority a duty to confer upon him a benefit which it has withheld he may sue to recover that benefit. But, as we shall observe later,[72] it is often difficult to show that the statute imposes a duty actually to confer the benefit as distinct from a duty to consider according to proper criteria whether to confer it. This distinction has acute consequences in the field of remedies and procedure, in which context we shall consider it.

[72] See Chap. 7.

Part II

Grounds for Review

In the *G.C.H.Q.* case[1] Lord Diplock remarked[2] that today

> "one can conveniently classify under three heads the grounds on which administrative action is subject to control by judicial review. The first ground I would call 'illegality,' the second 'irrationality' and the third 'procedural impropriety.' That is not to say that further development on a case by case basis may not in course of time add further grounds."

This classification has already proved popular with the courts.[3] It encapsulates neatly the well-established varieties of error of law[4] which are grounds for judicial review and with which we deal in this part of the book under the headings "Law, Fact and Degree,"[5] "Law and Policy"[6] and "Irregular or Unfair Procedure."[7] As to possible further grounds, one possible candidate has already emerged. In *Gillick* v. *West Norfolk Area Health Authority*[8] Lord Bridge suggested[9] that the promulgation by a public authority in a public document (*e.g.* a ministerial circular) of advice which is erroneous in law may be a ground for judicial review even though the authority has not relied upon (and therefore has not exceeded or abused) a particular statutory power. We consider this suggestion later.[10]

1 *Council of Civil Service Unions* v. *Minister for the Civil Service* [1985] A.C. 374.
2 *Ibid.* p. 410.
3 See, *e.g.* *Wheeler* v. *Leicester City Council* [1985] 3 W.L.R. 335 (H.L.); *R* v. *Transport Secretary ex p, G.L.C.* [1985] 3 All E.R. 300; *R.* v. *Social Services Secretary ex p. Westhead* [1985] *The Times*, October 17 (Q.B.D.)
4 See Chap. 3.
5 See Chap. 4.
6 See Chap. 5.
7 See Chap. 6.
8 [1985] 3 All E.R. 402.
9 *Ibid.* p. 427.
10 See Chap. 8, p. 301.

Chapter 3

ERROR OF LAW

We observed in Chapter 2 that judicial review jurisdiction (both supervisory and appellate) is in very many cases a jurisdiction to correct errors of law.[1] We shall examine in Chapters 4, 5 and 6 the different circumstances in which public authorities may be said to have erred in law and the bases upon which those errors may be corrected by way of judicial review. In this chapter we examine the notion of error of law itself.[2]

Section A sketches an analytical framework within which the question "what counts as error of law?" may be considered by reference to the notions of "fact-finding," "rule-stating" and "rule application." Section B shows how the process of applying law to facts differs in its nature from both "fact-finding" and "rule-stating;" and how applying law to facts may be said to involve questions of "degree" as distinct from questions of "law" or of "fact."

Using the conceptual framework established in sections A and B, the remaining sections consider, by reference to decided cases, the question "what counts as error of law?" Section C considers how a tribunal may err in law while purporting to find facts. Section D contains a discussion of errors in stating relevant legal rules. And Section E answers the question: when may a tribunal's alleged errors in applying law to facts be characterised properly as errors of law?

A. Deciding an Issue: a Three-Stage Process

Where the essence of an issue is whether or not a particular set of facts falls within a general category or concept, one may identify three stages in the resolution of the issue. The three stages are: (i) fact-finding; (ii) rule-stating; (iii) rule application. So, *e.g.* the question may be whether X has a contract of service with Y: whether X is in law the servant, or employee, of Y. In order to decide the issue one must first describe what are conceived to be the relevant features of the relationship. These are commonly

[1] See Chap. 2, p. 46.

[2] This chapter reproduces with amendments and additions our article on "Error of Law in Administrative Law" (1984) 100 L.Q.R. 612. On error of law, see de Smith J.R.A.A., pp. 126–139; Wade A.L., pp. 814–823; Craig, pp. 167–170, 313–315; W. A. Wilson (1963) 26 M.L.R. 609; (1969) 32 M.L.R. 361.

called the "primary facts . . . facts which are observed by the witnesses and proved by testimony."[3] In this case those primary facts would include, for example, findings as to the length and continuity of X's service, the degree of control exercised by Y over X in the course of his work, and the manner of payment.[4] That is the "fact-finding"[5] stage of the decision. One may then say that the "second stage" of the issue-deciding process is the elucidation of the concept of "contract of service," *i.e.*, the statement of the law's criteria of a contract of service. And then, again, that the "third stage" is the application of the legal concept to the facts found.

It will be immediately apparent that the three "stages" of the process do not in practice occur consecutively or even separately. For instance, one's perception of what are the "relevant" features of X and Y's relationship is, of course, conditioned by one's awareness and understanding of the question to whose answer the features are relevant; that is to say, by one's more or less precise notion of the legal meaning of "contract of service."[6] But the purpose of this analysis is not to suggest that the three stages do in practice occur consecutively or separately. It is, rather, to show that all three may be identified as constituents of the process of resolving an issue. If that is accepted, one then has an analytical framework—our three "stages"—within which to identify and characterise the types of error which may occur.[7]

We shall first consider generally the notions of error of law, of fact and of degree. We shall then look in some detail at each of our three "stages" and see how at each stage an error of law may occur.

[3] *Per* Denning J. in *Bracegirdle* v. *Oxley* [1947] K.B. 349 at 358.

[4] See, *e.g. O'Kelly* v. *Trusthouse Forte plc* [1984] Q.B. 90 at 104–105.

[5] Facts are "what happened:" actual occurrences. But actual occurrences are invariably described or recounted in conceptual terms: "The *man threw* his *gun* into the *river*." In a particular case, the characterisation of the individual as "man," his action as "throwing," the object as "gun" and its destination as "river" might be both relevant and contested. In such a case, one issue might then be, *e.g.* whether a particular observed sequence of anatomical movements was to be characterised as "[deliberately] throwing" as opposed, say, to "[accidentally] dropping." But where the characterisation—or "conceptualisation"—of specific observed phenomena as "man," "threw," "gun," "river," or whatever, is not in issue, the description of an actual occurrence in those terms will be treated as a statement of "facts."

[6] On this, see *Cross on Precedent* (3rd ed.), p. 179, n. 3.

[7] It is perhaps thus that one may justify indulging in an exercise apparently considered by Lord Diplock (in *Re Racal Communications Ltd* [1981] A.C. 374 at 383) as appropriate only to a "scholiast."

B. Law, Fact and Degree

As we have observed, the existence of a court's review jurisdiction will often turn on the answer to the question "error of law or no?" A tribunal would naturally be said to have erred in law if in some fashion it had misstated or misinterpreted a relevant legal rule: if it had erred at the "rule-stating" stage. Again, it would naturally be said to have erred in fact if, in its finding of "the facts," it treated as having occurred what in truth did not occur. Often, however, a decision will be attacked on the ground that the tribunal has erred at our "third stage"; in its application of the law to the facts. Take again the contract of service example. Suppose that the tribunal concludes that X is Y's employee. Its statement of both the facts and of the relevant rules may be unexceptionable. Yet X may still argue that the decision should have gone the other way: that the tribunal erred in classifying the facts found under the legal category "contract of service." Is X alleging that the tribunal has erred in law? This question is considered at length later.[8] Here it is important to observe simply that the process of applying the law to the facts is of a different nature from either "fact-finding" or "rule-stating."

In terms of syllogism we may treat the statement of the relevant rule as the major premiss: "a contract of service exists where . . . " (state criteria to be fulfilled). The statement of the facts is the minor premiss: "X works for twenty hours each week in Y's hotel . . . [etc.]." The conclusion is that X is (or is not) Y's servant. Now, a conclusion may follow indisputably from given premisses, *e.g.* All men are mortal. Socrates is a man. Socrates is mortal. In formal logic of this kind there is no problem of classification—of applying "law" (the major premiss) to facts (the minor). The form of the premisses dictates the conclusion. But our contract of service case is different. The difference arises from the manner in which the law defines "contract of service." Strictly, the law provides not a definition but, rather, a number of criteria which, if all were present, would represent the paradigm notion of contract of service. But the law does not decline to characterise as a contract of service every relationship which does not display all the criteria and so is not the paradigm. In the non-paradigm case the application of law to facts involves a weighing and balancing of considerations pointing in different directions. The conclusion cannot be said to be "correct" or "incorrect" as a finding of fact or statement of a rule may be. That being so, if it is alleged that in

[8] See below, section E.

such a case a tribunal has erred in its application of law to facts it may be unhelpful to insist that the error be labelled with one or other of the labels commonly used to describe errors in the other processes. If our contract of service case were of this sort[9] one might more usefully describe the question whether or not X was Y's servant as one neither of law nor of fact but of degree.[10]

Before turning to the question how at each of the three "stages" of the decision-making process an error of law may occur, we may at the outset recall the practical purpose of the distinction between on the one hand questions of law and on the other questions of fact and of degree. The editor of de Smith's *Judicial Review of Administrative Action* writes[11]:

> "In administrative law the most common reason for drawing the distinction is to identify the matters upon which a reviewing court is empowered to substitute its view for that of the body that made the initial decision. It would seem a reasonable working hypothesis to assume that when a court has jurisdiction to review the decisions of an administrative tribunal on questions of law, its intervention should extend to those matters upon which its decisions are likely to be better than those of the tribunal under review."

As we have seen, the characterisation of an error as "of law" or otherwise provides the criterion upon which in a wide variety of circumstances the superior courts have or do not have review jurisdiction. It is, so to say, the "shorthand" adopted by Parliament (in the case of many statutory rights of appeal) or by the courts themselves (in the case of supervisory review) to indicate what is conceived to be the "proper" area for control by the superior courts. Since the law uses the notion of error of law as a criterion of review jurisdiction, it is clearly desirable that the criterion should be capable of clear exposition and certain and consistent application.

It should at once be said that any attempt to show that the English courts have adopted a consistent approach to this matter appears to be doomed to certain failure. The writings of distinguished commentators abound with warnings to the unwary.

[9] As was *O'Kelly* v. *Trusthouse Forte plc* (see note 4 above). The case is discussed below, pp. 118, 125.

[10] In "The Application of Rules: Law or Fact?" (1982) 98 L.Q.R. 587 Etienne Mureinik defends the thesis that questions of application are questions of law. For critique of this thesis, see further below, p. 122.

[11] De Smith J.R.A.A., pp. 127–128 (Professor J. M. Evans).

Professor Wade writes[12] that "There can hardly be a subject on which the courts act with such total lack of consistency as the difference between fact and law." More cautiously, Professor de Smith wrote[13] "The criteria adopted by the courts for distinguishing between questions of law and questions of fact have not been uniform." It has even been suggested[14] that "which view is taken seems to depend on how much control an appellate court wishes to exercise over an inferior court or tribunal, rather than by reference to principle"; and Lord Denning has on occasion given at least extra-judicial support to this point of view.[15]

If there is no principle, no consistency, in the manner in which the courts approach this important issue, that is a serious blot on our jurisprudence. However, it may be argued that there is something less than that "total lack of consistency" discerned by Professor Wade. In any event, this chapter attempts to show that the materials are available from which an approach of considerable coherence and consistency may be manufactured.

C. Error of Law at the Fact-Finding Stage

We are concerned here with alleged error by a tribunal in finding the primary facts. These facts are "observed by the witnesses and proved by testimony."[16] Clearly, testimony may lead the tribunal to find that certain events occurred which, in truth, did not. Here, the tribunal makes an error of fact. Does it follow from that that a superior court with jurisdiction to correct only errors of law cannot intervene? Briefly, the answer is that the fact-finding process will be said to display an error of law if the facts are found on the basis of "no evidence." However, before considering the meaning of "no evidence" we may notice that on this "no evidence" principle, a tribunal may err in law in finding facts which in truth did occur. So, the question may be whether A is B's father. Suppose that in truth he is. A tribunal which found on the basis of no evidence that he was would err in law (but not, of course, in fact) in its finding of that fact.

We turn now to the meaning of "no evidence." The books are full of references to dicta of high authority to the effect that, as du

[12] Wade A.L., p. 817.
[13] De Smith J.R.A.A., p. 129.
[14] By Bailey, Cross and Garner in *Cases and Materials in Administrative Law* (1977), pp. 472–473.
[15] *The Discipline of Law*, p. 66. And see Beatson and Matthews, *Administrative Law : Cases and Materials*, p. 372.
[16] *Per* Denning J. in *Bracegirdle* v. *Oxley* [1947] K.B. 349 at 358.

Parcq L.J. said in *Bean* v. *Doncaster Amalgamated Collieries Ltd*,[17] "to come to a conclusion which there is no evidence to support is to make an error in law." However, many of these dicta, including that just cited, relate to circumstances where what was at issue was not a finding of primary fact but, rather, the application of legal rules to facts found: what we have characterised as a "third stage" question. In *Bean's* case,[18] for example, the question was whether certain expenditure fell into the category of capital or, on the contrary, income expenditure. Now, as we shall see, the third stage question, in so far as it is one of law, is often best expressed as "Are the facts found *capable of falling* within the relevant legal concepts?" rather than as "*Do they* so fall?" The question thus formulated in terms of capability may be answered, as it was in effect in *Bean's* case,[19] in the form that there is (or is not) "evidence" to support the conclusion that the facts found do (or do not) fall within the legal concepts. But "evidence" here means "material tending rationally to lead to or support" the conclusion. It does not mean testimony to the occurrence of events: evidence of primary facts.[20] Nevertheless, there are dicta of the highest authority to the effect that to find a (primary) fact with no evidence to support the finding is to err in law.[21] But are there only dicta? Is there no clear authority on the question?

(1) Complete absence of witness statement

Reviewing relevant authorities in *R.* v. *Nat Bell Liquors Ltd*[22] Lord Sumner said that the point was "by no means settled on authority."[23] The difficulty is, of course, that tribunals of fact will only rarely purport to find facts on the basis of "no evidence" where that phrase imports a complete absence of any witness statement relating to the alleged events. As Lord Sumner said,[24]

> "It is evident that this exact point must be one of rare occurrence . . . Only when it appears that no witness whatever has said a thing that must be said by someone will it fall to be discussed."

[17] [1944] 2 All E.R. 279 at 284.
[18] *Ibid.*
[19] *Ibid.*, see especially *per* Scott L.J. at 283.
[20] For further examples of the *Bean* usage of "evidence" see cases cited in de Smith J.R.A.A., p. 133, n. 24.
[21] See, *e.g. Cababé* v. *Walton-on-Thames U.D.C.* [1914] A.C. 102 *per* Lord Dunedin at 114.
[22] [1922] 2 A.C. 128 at 150–151.
[23] *Ibid.* p. 150.
[24] *Ibid.* pp. 149–150.

Although on the facts of the *Nat Bell* case the point did not there arise,[25] Lord Sumner considered what the position would be where a record of justices' proceedings actually showed (although it need not have done so) a finding of fact based on no witness statement. He referred[26] to *R.* v. *Cheshire Justices*[27] where

> "it actually appeared on the affidavits filed . . . that, in making their order, [the justices] had acted on a view of the facts not testified to at all, but merely stated to them by one of their own body as being within his knowledge. The Court of Queen's Bench nevertheless . . . declined to interfere."

Later, however, he observed[28] that

> "If justices state more than they are bound to state, it may, so to speak, be used against them, and out of their own mouths they may be condemned . . ."

It appears, then, that today a court with jurisdiction to correct error of law would be unlikely to decline to interfere with a finding of fact based on "no evidence" where that phrase means a complete absence of witness statement relating to the alleged fact.[29]

(2) Insubstantial evidence

The phrase "no evidence" has an extended meaning. As Professor Wade has written[30]

> " 'No evidence' does not mean only a total dearth of evidence. It extends to any case where the evidence, taken as a whole, is not reasonably capable of supporting the finding."

[25] A Canadian company had been convicted of unlawful liquor sales. The company applied for certiorari to quash the conviction on the basis that the prosecution had relied solely on the evidence of a highly unreliable witness. The Privy Council (overturning the Supreme Court of Alberta) held that certiorari should not be granted where, as in the case, there was some (albeit weak) evidence to support the facts found.

[26] [1922] 2 A.C. at 151.

[27] (1838) 8 Ad. & E. 398.

[28] *Ibid.* p. 155.

[29] As, *e.g.* in *Mahon* v. *Air New Zealand* [1984] A.C. 808 : Royal commission into air disaster found airline guilty of deception. New Zealand Court of Appeal (upheld by Privy Council) quashed costs order based on the finding. The Court found that there was no evidence of certain facts upon which the Commission had relied in finding deception.

[30] Wade A.L., p. 287.

Now, while, as we shall see,[31] this extended meaning of "no evidence" appears to be taking firm root as a criterion of error of law at the "third stage," it cannot be said to be established in the context of errors at the fact-finding stage. In the *Nat Bell* case Lord Sumner considered whether "no evidence" in this sense could constitute an error of law which, if it appeared on the record, could be quashed by certiorari. He said[32]

> "On certiorari, so far as the presence or absence of evidence becomes material, the question can at most be whether any evidence at all was given on the essential point referred to. Its weight is entirely for the inferior court."

It has been observed that even where the jurisdiction of an appellate court is not limited to point of law only, "the findings of the judge of first instance as to the credibility and reliability of witnesses cannot normally be disturbed."[33] It is *a fortiori* where the jurisdiction is so limited.[34] Furthermore, Lord Sumner's notion of "weight" would no doubt extend not only to credibility and reliability but also to inferences from what witnesses observed to what else occurred, although not observed. It appears that only if there is an error as to the law of evidence[35] (*e.g.* rules as to admissibility or corroboration) will a tribunal's bona fide finding of fact on even the lightest-weight evidence be disturbed on the basis that it is erroneous in law.[36]

D. Misstating the Law

A misstatement of a rule of law is, by definition, an error of law. The notion of "misstatement," however, requires some elucidation.

[31] See below, p. 116, note 7 *passim*; and see *Bean's* case, above (note 17).
[32] [1922] 2 A.C. 128 at 144.
[33] W. A. Wilson in (1963) 26 M.L.R. 609 at 613.
[34] See, *e.g. Hollier* v. *Plysu Ltd* [1983] I.R.L.R. 260 (C.A.); *Martin* v. *Glynwed Distribution Ltd* [1983] I.C.R. 511 (C.A.).
[35] See *per* Lord Sumner in *Nat Bell* [1922] 2 A.C. at 144; de Smith, J.R.A.A., pp. 136–137. In *Rowing* v. *Minister of Pensions* [1946] 1 All E.R. 664 Denning J. held that a Pensions Appeal Tribunal erred in law where it found against the evidence that R's war service had not aggravated an ear condition from which he was suffering. But here the tribunal erred as to the location of burden of proof: it took it to be on R: whereas on the proper construction of the legislation there was a presumption in R's favour to which the tribunal had given no weight. Accordingly, it had erred in law in this respect.
[36] See, *e.g. per* Lord Diplock in *Mahon* (above note 29) at pp. 832–833.

In the course of deciding an issue, a tribunal may say in effect: "The facts are these, the law is that. The facts fall within the legal rules as stated." Here, clearly, there has been a statement of the legal rules which, it is conceived, govern the issue. This statement of legal rules may be erroneous in any of a number of different ways, depending on the form which the statement takes.

The statement may be simply a recitation of what are taken to be applicable statutory provisions. Clearly there will be error of law here if for some reason—*e.g.*, repeal, amendment, further provision—the recitation is defective. Equally plainly, a statement of a common law rule *per incuriam*, or inconsistent with, binding authority would be an error of law.

But where the relevant rule is statutory, a misstatement is most likely to be in the nature of a misinterpretation of statutory words correctly stated. Here, in an attempt to nip confusion in the bud, a caveat must be made. The word "misinterpretation" opens a Pandora's box. For, as we shall see, if a tribunal has erred in applying the law to the facts, a superior court may draw the inference that the tribunal must have misinterpreted a relevant legal rule. Suffice it to say here that our present concern is with the case where a tribunal chooses to elucidate formally its understanding of statutory words. We are not here concerned with the case where a review court purports to discern, from its own juxtaposition of the applicable rule and the first instance decision, that the tribunal must be taken to have misinterpreted the rule, although no formal elucidation of the rule appears in the adjudication.[37]

Turning then to misinterpretation—in the sense of erroneous elucidation—of statutory words. It is well known that the courts distinguish between words in statutes used in their popular or "ordinary" sense and words used in a "technical" sense.[38] Since "the proper construction of a statute is a question of law,"[39] it is a question of law in which kind of sense words in a statute are used. The distinction is often not easy to draw.[40] However, our principal

[37] See *per* Lord Radcliffe in *Edwards* v. *Bairstow* [1956] A.C. 14 at 36: cited and discussed below, p. 114 *et seq*.

[38] Craies, *Statute Law* (7th ed.), pp. 162–174; Maxwell, *Interpretation of Statutes* (12th ed.), pp. 81–85; Cross, *Statutory Interpretation*, pp. 52–57.

[39] *Per* Lord Reid in *Brutus* v. *Cozens* [1973] A.C. 854 at 861.

[40] See, *e.g. Cinzano (UK) Ltd* v. *Customs and Excise Commissioners* [1985] 1 W.L.R. 484. The House of Lords held that the blending of wines of different strengths did not involve the "production" of wine for purposes of the Alcoholic Liquor Duties Act 1979, s.54. The question was, essentially, whether or not the statutory draftsman had endued the notion of "production" with a restricted meaning for purposes of the statute. In holding that he had, the House in effect treated "production" in the statute as a legal term of art (see text below).

concern here is not with the drawing of the distinction but with its consequences in the context of the law-fact issue. In that context one may begin by considering, on the one hand, words used in a technical legal sense and on the other, words not so used. In what follows, words of the latter type are referred to as "ordinary" words (distinguishing them from legal "terms of art"[41]). But, we shall see that words which are in this sense "ordinary" may be used either in a popular (or "everyday") sense or in a sense peculiar to a particular trade, business, science or other specialised activity with its own technical vocabulary.

What is the correct approach to the elucidation of words of each of our two types?

(1) Legal terms of art

Here the question is: with what meaning is the statutory draftsman to be understood to have endued the word? Now, clearly, this question can be answered only by one or more of the familiar techniques of statutory construction. It is a question for legal argument and judicial decision. If a tribunal errs in this exercise, it errs in law. So, for example, in the *Anisminic* case[42] the Foreign Compensation Commission was under a statutory duty to treat a claim as established if (*inter alia*) "the applicant [was] . . . the owner of the [sequestrated] property or [was] the successor in title of such person." Moreover, both applicant and successor in title (if any) had to be British nationals. In dismissing Anisminic Ltd.'s claim, the Commission "construed this provision as requiring them to inquire, when the applicant is himself the original owner, whether he had a successor in title."[43] A majority of the House of Lords held that, on the contrary:

> " 'successor in title' must . . . mean some person who could come forward and make a claim in his own right. There can only be a successor in title where the title of its original possessor has passed to another person . . . [T]herefore . . . the words . . . have no application to a case where the applicant is the original owner"[44]

[41] See *per* Lord Scarman in *Shah* v. *Barnet L.B.C.* [1983] 2 A.C. 309 at 340.

[42] *Anisminic Ltd* v. *Foreign Compensation Commission* [1969] 2 A.C. 147. See above, Chap. 2, p. 49, below, Chap. 4, p. 140.

[43] *Ibid. per* Lord Reid at p. 173.

[44] *Ibid. per* Lord Reid at pp. 174–175; see too, *per* Lord Pearce at pp. 204–205; *per* Lord Wilberforce at pp. 213–214.

On the basis that the Commission had erred in law by asking itself the wrong question, the House of Lords granted a declaration that the Commission's determination was a nullity.[45] The Commission's error of law in the *Anisminic* case was an error of construction; for the question of the meaning of a legal term of art is purely a question of construction: *i.e.* how is Parliament to be taken to have used this word in this context?

(2) Ordinary words

Turning now to "ordinary" words as above defined: the question of the meaning of such words resolves itself ultimately into a question of common usage. Where the word is used in its popular (or "everyday") sense, the question is: how in fact do people generally use the word? So too where a word is used in a sense peculiar to a particular trade, business etc. The question there is: how in fact is the word commonly used in that trade or business? Now, of course, a question as to common usage is a question of fact. And the courts are apt to express the distinction between legal terms of art and "ordinary" words by insisting that "The meaning of an ordinary word of the English language is not a question of law."[46] "[It] is . . . a question of fact."[47] However, the treatment of the question of the meaning of an ordinary word as a question of fact cannot be pressed too far.

On the one hand, where an ordinary word is used in a "trade" sense "evidence with regard to that meaning is unquestionably admissible."[48] On the other, where an ordinary word is used in its "everyday" sense, the question as to common usage is answered in the courts not by evidence but by judicial notice.[49] The judges may refer to dictionaries[50]; or rely upon common usage as discerned by courts over an extended period of time[51]; or the meaning may be treated simply as common knowledge.[52]

One common objection to this approach to elucidation of

[45] See below, p. 140 *et seq*.
[46] *Per* Lord Reid in *Brutus* v. *Cozens* [1973] A.C. 854 at 861.
[47] *Per* Lord Scarman in *Shah* v. *Barnet L.B.C.* [1983] 2 A.C. 309 at 341.
[48] Cross, *Statutory Interpretation* (1976) p. 54.
[49] *Ibid.*
[50] *Per* Lord Scarman in *Shah's* case (above note 47) at p. 342.
[51] In *Shah's* case (above note 47) the House of Lords proceeded in this fashion.
[52] Such was the approach of the Court of Appeal in *Dyson Holdings Ltd* v. *Fox* [1976] Q.B. 503 (discussed below) and of the House of Lords in *Presho* v. *Insurance Officer* [1984] A.C. 610 (meaning of "directly interested" in a trade dispute). In *Shah's* case (above) the House of Lords was prepared in principle to admit evidence of a change in English usage: [1983] 2 A.C. 309 at 342.

"everyday" words is that it obscures the fact that commonly such words have no one single meaning. So, for example, it is in certain circumstances a statutory offence to "indicate," except in a prescribed form, that one is willing to provide credit facilities.[53] In ordinary parlance "to indicate" may or may not include implied as well as express intimations: a motorist would be said to have made a right turn "without indicating" if he had made no hand or automatic signal, even though prior to the manoeuvre he slowed down and moved towards the centre of the road; on the other hand no such formal intimation would be required before it could be said of a person that he had "indicated" his annoyance. In a criminal case no doubt the court must decide which meaning is correct.[54] But are there not many situations in administrative law where the choice of meaning would be better made by a specialist tribunal rather than a court? This raises issues of constitutional principle referred to later.[55] We may here observe that it is possible for a court to establish the boundaries of meaning of a particular statutory concept while preserving for an administrative authority great flexibility in the application of the concept to particular facts[56]; and that the superior courts show no general inclination to interpret statutory words in a way which would rob them of their inherent breadth and flexibility of meaning.[57] Nevertheless, it is plain that the "judicial notice" approach to ascertaining common usage may founder if not used with great perspicacity.[58] But what is its importance in the context of the law-fact issue?

Clearly the approach brings what is said to be a fact-finding exercise much nearer to the exercise of construing a legal term of art than to the exercise of evidence-based fact-finding. May we nevertheless say that since the question of usage is a question of

[53] Consumer Credit Act 1974, ss.43, 44, 167(2).

[54] As in *Jenkins* v. *Lombard North Central plc* [1984] 1 W.L.R. 307 (indication of willingness to provide credit facilities must be express).

[55] Chap. 4 pp. 162–164, below.

[56] See next section.

[57] See *Shah* and *Dyson* cases discussed below.

[58] Some might question the accuracy of the Court of Appeal's discernment of the popular meaning of "family" in *Dyson Holdings Ltd* v. *Fox* considered below. And, in a different context, the Court of Appeal's ruling (in *Simpson* [1983] 1 W.L.R. 1494) that a flick knife is an offensive weapon *per se* for the purpose of s.1 of the Prevention of Crime Act 1953 may give rise to concern. The basis of the ruling was that the court could take judicial notice that flick knives are made for the purpose only of causing injury. But, as a matter of fact, that appears not to be the case: see [1983] Crim.L.R. 114 (J.C.S).

fact, a tribunal which errs in its finding as to current usage will err in fact and not in law? It seems not. The characterisation of a question of usage as one of fact appears to relate only to the question "*where* is the meaning to be sought?" (answer: in common usage). We have just seen that (at any rate in the case of ordinary words used in their everyday sense) it appears not to relate to the question "*how* is it to be sought?" (answer: via judicial notice and not via evidence). Nor, it seems, does it (in any case) relate to the question "what is the status (law or fact) of a finding as to how a word is used?" So, in *Shah* v. *Barnet L.B.C.*[59] the House of Lords quashed the decisions of a number of education authorities that certain overseas students were not (as for grant purposes the statute required them to be) "ordinarily resident" in the authorities' areas. The words "ordinarily resident" were used in their ordinary (everyday) sense and indicated habitual and normal abode. The authorities had erred in law by ruling that the words connoted a degree of permanency[60] which the applicants' residences lacked. As Lord Scarman said[61]:

> "Though the meaning of ordinary words is, as Lord Reid observed in *Brutus* v. *Cozens*,[62] a question of fact, the meaning to be attributed to enacted words is a question of law, being a matter of statutory interpretation."

There is no contradiction here. In that the inquiry is as to the existence of facts (common usage) the question is one of fact. However, in that the inquiry will determine the meaning of a particular word in a particular statute, the question (being as to the elucidation of a legal rule) is one of law.[63] This entitles a superior court to substitute its view for that of the inferior tribunal. Furthermore, as Professor Cross pointed out "decisions with regard to [the ordinary meanings of statutory words], unlike other decisions on questions of fact, become binding precedents so far as the construction

[59] [1983] 2 A.C. 309.
[60] In *Hipperson* v. *Electoral Officer* [1985] 3 W.L.R. 61 the presence of anti-nuclear protesters who camped outside Greenham Common airbase was held to be sufficiently permanent to count as residence for electoral purposes.
[61] [1983] 2 A.C. 309 at 341.
[62] [1973] A.C. 854.
[63] See *per* Lord Scarman in *Lees* v. *Secretary of State* [1985] 2 W.L.R. 805 at 806 (meaning of "walk" in Social Security Act 1975, s.37A).

of the statute in question is concerned."[64] In this respect too, the matter is of law and not of fact.[65]

Why, then, it may be asked, call the question one of fact at all? The reasons are, first, as already observed, so as to prescribe the correct approach to elucidating the statutory words; and, secondly, so as to cater for changes in common usage. Consider *Dyson Holdings Ltd.* v. *Fox*.[66] A county court judge had held that for the purposes of the Rent Act 1968 the defendant was not a member of the family of the man with whom she had lived as if she were his wife for 40 years. It followed that the defendant was not entitled to Rent Act protection as statutory tenant by succession when the man died. On appeal by the defendant on point of law the Court of Appeal reversed the county court. The judge had erred in law in treating the word "family" in the statute as a legal term of art whose meaning was fixed by a Court of Appeal decision in 1950.[67] The majority of the Court of Appeal (James and Bridge L.JJ.) reasoned as follows. The word "family" bore its ordinary meaning. That meaning might change from time to time, and at any given time was to be established by judicial notice of how (at that time) the word was commonly used. The common usage of the word family had changed since 1950 so as to include a person such as the defendant.[68]

This reasoning, it may be suggested, indicates the value of treating the meaning of an ordinary word as a matter of fact for the purpose of answering the question "where is the meaning to be sought?" However, once a superior court has ruled on ordinary meaning, that ruling will bind inferior tribunals but will not convert the word into a term of art. Thus the statutory meaning may change if there is evidence of change in common usage. As observed above, there is no contradiction here.

Lord Denning M.R.'s judgment in *Dyson Holdings Ltd* v. *Fox* is problematical, according as it does with the result reached by the

[64] Cross, *Statutory Interpretation*, p. 55. See too Cross, *Precedent* (3rd ed.), pp. 223–224.

[65] So, *e.g.* (subject to possible proof of change in common usage—see text below), an education authority would err in law if, after *Shah's* case, it purported to find as a fact that the words "ordinarily resident" are commonly used in a sense other than that indicated by the House of Lords in *Shah*.

[66] [1976] Q.B. 503.

[67] *Gammans* v. *Ekins* [1950] 2 K.B. 328 (holding that "family" did not include common law spouse).

[68] *cf.* Cross, *Statutory Interpretation*, p. 47. But even in 1985 a homosexual couple were not members of the same family: *Harrogate B.C.* v. *Simpson* (1985) 25 R.V.R. 10.

majority but not with their reasoning.[69] Lord Denning took the proposition that the meaning of an ordinary word is a question of fact and inferred from it that a review court with jurisdiction to correct only errors of law cannot normally interfere with an elucidation of an ordinary word with which it disagrees. This approach, as we have seen, has now been firmly rejected by the House of Lords in *Shah* v. *Barnet L.B.C.*[70] The analysis in the paragraphs above shows that one may usefully, coherently and consistently treat the question as one of fact for one purpose but as one of law for others.

To summarise on the elucidation of "ordinary" words in statutes: a tribunal must approach the question of the meaning of an ordinary word as a question of fact. That is, it must establish how in fact the word is used in its "everyday" sense or in a particular "trade" sense as the case may be. The tribunal will err in law if it approaches the question otherwise. A tribunal will err in law also if its finding as to ordinary usage does not accord with a ruling of a superior court unless there is evidence of change of usage subsequent to that ruling. The justification for treating the meaning of an ordinary word as a question of law is as follows. The question is: what do the statutory words mean? One may say that they mean what they are in fact commonly used to mean. Usage is fact; but Parliament has made it law in the statute in question. Parliament has, so to say, placed the stamp of legislative authority upon, *i.e.* incorporated into law, whatever is (from time to time) contemporary usage. The usage (and so the content of the law) may change. Its quality as law remains until Parliament changes the statutory

[69] In "Law and Fact" [1976] Crim.L.R. 472 at 478 *et seq.*, Professor Glanville Williams criticised both Lord Denning's judgment and aspects of the House of Lords' approach to the law/fact issue in *Brutus* v. *Cozens* [1973] A.C. 854 upon which Lord Denning relied. In *Brutus* v. *Cozens* magistrates had found B not guilty of insulting behaviour when he demonstrated against apartheid during a Wimbledon tennis match. The Divisional Court (on case stated) held that the magistrates had erred in law in their understanding of the statutory phrase "insulting behaviour." The House of Lords (reversing the Divisional Court) held that no such error appeared. The actual decision in *Brutus* v. *Cozens* is regarded as unexceptionable; but their Lordships' analysis of the law-fact distinction has given rise to concern. Professor Williams' chief criticism of the case was that by precluding judicial definition of ordinary words (on the basis that their meaning was purely a question of fact) the House of Lords had endangered future consistency of decision (*loc.cit. above* at p. 479). As appears from the text, the House's ruling in *Shah* appears to have averted that danger.

[70] [1983] 2 A.C. 309 (above).

provision. And it is precisely its quality as law which enables, indeed requires, the courts to treat an error in elucidating the meaning of an ordinary (as well as of a legal technical) word in a statute as an error of law.

We turn now from the elucidation of statutory words to their application.

E. Error of Law in Applying Law to Facts

A decision may display no palpable error in either statement or elucidation of legal rule or finding of primary fact. The decision may nonetheless be wrong: the tribunal may have erred at the stage of "ultimate inference"[71]: it may have erred in its application of the law to the facts. For example, compulsory purchase legislation may exempt from its provisions land which is "part of any park."[72] The authority may describe accurately the salient features of, say, Windsor Great Park; and it may display no palpable error in its elucidation of the word "park" (taking it to be used in the statute in the sense of parkland as commonly understood). But it is clear in the case postulated that if the authority were to decide that a portion of land comprised within Windsor Great Park were not "part of a park" it would decide erroneously. Now, the word "park" is clearly sufficiently precise for one to be able to say without fear of contradiction of most pieces of land either that they are or that they are not a park or part thereof. But the word is not sufficiently precise for one to be able to say without fear of contradiction of every piece of land that it is or is not parkland. Blackacre may display some and lack others of the characteristics of a park. If the question arose whether Blackacre was a park one might legitimately dissent from the answer that it was, or, as the case may be, was not. But whereas to maintain (if one knew the topography of the place) that Windsor Great Park was not a park would unarguably be to display some misunderstanding of the meaning of the word park, to maintain that Blackacre was (or was not) could be said to display only a difference of emphasis or degree as to what count as the distinguishing features of a park. Now, as a moment's reflection will show, Parliament very fre-

[71] De Smith J.R.A.A., p. 130.
[72] See *White and Collins* v. *Min. of Health* [1939] 2 K.B. 838.

quently employs in statutes concepts with at least as great a degree of "open texture" as "park." Suppose one were asked starkly: "Is the question whether a piece of land (correctly described in its physical features) is for the purposes of the statute a park (correctly defined) a question of fact or of law?" Surely in this, as in many similar cases, one could reply in terms of Professor de Smith's observation that "This ultimate finding or inference could as well be styled one of law as one of fact."[73] As we shall see, the courts tend today to characterise an alleged error in making the final inference as one of law in a case such as our Windsor Great Park example; as one of fact or degree in a case such as our Blackacre example.[74]

There are at least two distinct characteristics of the concept "park" which might illustrate Professor de Smith's observation. One we have noticed and characterised as its "open texture." The other is the fact that it is a term in everyday use, so that we may say that a layman would be likely to be no less capable than a lawyer of deciding whether a particular piece of land is or is not a park. By no means all statutory concepts are of this sort. To say whether X is tenant for life of Whiteacre for purposes of the Settled Land Act 1925 is, even if the relevant facts and legal rules are stated with limpid clarity and unexceptionable accuracy, a task for a trained lawyer only. An error here could hardly be characterised as other than an error of law.

We are here concerned with the question: "Is an error in applying law to facts properly to be characterised as an error of law or as one of fact or degree?" The above observations suggest that an appropriate method of proceeding towards an answer would be first to consider the distinction between those applications or "final inferences" which require a trained lawyer to make them, and those which do not. Then, secondly, to consider when it may be said that a tribunal has erred in law in making a final inference of the sort which could be made as well by a layman as by a lawyer. This approach reflects the well-known analysis of Denning L.J. in the *British Launderers' Research Association* case[75]:

[73] De Smith, *loc.cit.* above note 71.

[74] See the analysis of Woolf J. in *England* v. *Secretary of State* (1981) 3 F.L.R. 222 at 224, approved and applied by the Court of Appeal in *R* v. *Birmingham Juvenile Court ex p. N.* [1985] 2 All E.R. 688.

[75] *British Launderers' Research Association* v. *Hendon Rating Authority* [1949] 1 K.B. 462 at 471–472.

"The conclusions from primary facts are . . . inferences[76] deduced by a process of reasoning from them. If, and in so far as, those conclusions can as well be drawn by a layman (properly instructed on the law) as by a lawyer, they are conclusions of fact for the tribunal of fact: and the only questions of law which can arise on them are whether there was a proper direction in point of law; and whether the conclusion is one which could reasonably be drawn from the primary facts . . . . If, and in so far, however, as the correct conclusion to be drawn from primary facts requires, for its correctness, determination by a trained lawyer—as, for instance, because it involves the interpretation of documents, or because the law and the facts cannot be separated, or because the law on the point cannot properly be understood or applied except by a trained lawyer—the conclusion is a conclusion of law on which an appellate tribunal is as competent to form an opinion as the tribunal of first instance."

(1) Where a trained lawyer is required

We turn first to those inferences, or applications of law to facts, which require a trained lawyer to make them. The clearest case of this type is, in Denning L.J.'s words where "the law on the point cannot properly be understood or applied except by a trained lawyer."[77] Our Settled Land Act example is one in point, and many similar examples will come to mind in such fields as trusts,

[76] One must guard here against possible confusion between two of the three "stages" of the process of deciding an issue: the "fact-finding stage" (considered above) and the "rule application stage" (now being considered). As already observed (note 3 above) Denning L.J. used the term "primary facts" to mean "facts which are observed by witnesses and proved by testimony." The term extends, therefore, not only to what the witnesses observed but also to inferences from what the witnesses observed to what else occurred, although not observed. Since the term "primary facts" includes inferences of this sort it follows that the "inferences" to which Denning L.J. referred in the text above this note are of the type described by Professor de Smith as the "ultimate finding or inference" and treated in this article as characterising the "third stage" of the process of deciding an issue: the application of law to facts.

[77] For this, and Denning L.J.'s other criteria, see extract from *British Launderers'* case immediately above.

revenue,[78] conveyancing and commercial law. The *British Launderers' Research Association* case itself furnishes an example. Quarter Sessions had decided that the Association was (for purposes of a rating statute) "instituted for the purposes of science . . . exclusively." On case stated, the Divisional Court found in effect that Quarter Sessions had erred in law. The Court of Appeal upheld the Divisional Court. The question required a construction of rating legislation in the light of case law in that and kindred areas and the interpretation of formal legal documents,[79] the memorandum and articles of association of the plaintiff. In such a case, the question of whether a particular association falls within a statutory category encrusted with authority of a high degree of legal technical complexity cannot be expected to be answered correctly other than by a trained lawyer. In this sense one might say that in such a case "the law and the facts cannot be separated."[80] Since in effect both Divisional Court and Court of Appeal had jurisdiction to correct errors of law, they had jurisdiction to consider whether the conclusion of Quarter Sessions was correct and, as it was not, to reverse it.

Although there are no doubt many questions which are unarguably of the type which require determination by a trained lawyer, judges have differed as to whether certain questions fall into the category. Lord Denning has treated the question of causation as purely a question of law:

> "Once [the primary facts] are found, then the question whether one or more of the preceding events is a 'cause' or not of the occurrence is a question of law. It was so treated by the House of Lords in *Baker* v. *Willoughby*[81] . . . . The

[78] For an example of a case where the application of a rule of trusts law in a revenue context quite clearly required a lawyer's expertise, see *Watson* v. *Holland* [1985] 1 All E.R. 290: taxpayer's liability to tax depended on whether, in the circumstances, he could claim the benefit of the rule in *Lassence* v. *Tierney* (1849) 1 Mac & G 551 that where an absolute gift is "engrafted" with trusts which fail, the absolute gift takes effect to the exclusion of a resulting trust. Gibson J. held that the Special Commissioners had erred in law in deciding that the rule did not apply.

[79] Another of Denning L.J.'s criteria of where a trained lawyer is required—see notes 75, 77 above.

[80] The third of Denning L.J.'s criteria.

[81] [1970] A.C. 467.

> reason is because the problem . . . requires for its correct solution to be determined by a trained lawyer.[82] It is too difficult for a layman.[83]"

However, the question for the House of Lords in *Baker* v. *Willoughby*, in so far as it was one of causation, was whether act A was in law *capable* of being regarded as a cause of situation B in a case where act C (which followed act A) would by itself have produced situation B. The House of Lords has indicated[84] that when, as a matter of law, act A is held to be capable of being regarded as a cause of situation B, the question whether it *is* is a question of fact (or degree) for the jury: "In a court of law this question must be decided as a properly instructed and reasonable jury would decide it."[85]

Again, there are differences of approach, this time within the House of Lords, in *Tsakiroglou* v. *Noblee Thorl*[86] on whether the question "is a contract frustrated?" is a question purely of law or, on the contrary, a mixed question of law and fact.[87]

It is difficult to see how either the question of causation or that of frustration can be purely one of law: for the former is often and the latter used frequently to be put to a jury. The approach of the House of Lords on causation in *Stapley* v. *Gypsum Mines*[88] and of their Lordships taking a similar approach in the frustration context in the *Tsakiroglou* case is surely to be preferred: the question what is capable of being a cause or a frustrating event is a question of law; the question of whether certain events (held to be so capable) are the cause of others or do constitute frustration is a question of fact or degree.[89] If a jury can answer a question, that question plainly does not require a trained lawyer to answer it. Similarly, where Parliament has conferred a particular jurisdiction on a tribunal consisting of non-lawyers, it will be relatively rarely that questions falling to be answered in the exercise of that jurisdiction will be of the sort that can be answered only by a trained lawyer.

[82] Lord Denning cited his judgment in the *British Launderers'* case (above).
[83] *Per* Lord Denning M.R. in *Hoveringham Gravels* v. *Environment Secretary* [1975] 1 Q.B. 754 at 763. See, to the same effect, *R* v. *Criminal Injuries Compensation Board ex p. Ince* [1973] 1 W.L.R. 1334 at 1341.
[84] See, *e.g. Stapley* v. *Gypsum Mines* [1953] A.C. 663.
[85] *Per* Lord Reid in *Stapley's* case, *ibid.* 681. And see *per* Megaw L.J. in *ex p. Ince* (note 83) at 1344.
[86] [1962] A.C. 93.
[87] Pure law: *ibid., per* Lord Reid at p. 119; *per* Viscount Simonds at p. 116. *cf.* Lords Radcliffe, at pp. 123–125, Hodson, at pp. 129–130 and Guest at p. 134.
[88] See above, notes 84 and 85.
[89] *i.e.*, within *Edwards* v. *Bairstow* limits: see text below.

The same may be said of tribunals whose membership includes both a legally qualified and lay element. Such tribunals will commonly have to deal with issues of great complexity[90]; but it is the tribunal (and not just its legally qualified members) which must decide the issue.

(2) Where a layman is as good as a lawyer

In administrative law Parliament often confers jurisdiction upon tribunals which, although they may be advised by, are not composed, or not wholly composed, of lawyers.[91] Such tribunals will encounter problems in the application of law to facts. Where Parliament has provided for a lay element in the tribunal's membership one may suppose that most such problems will be of Denning L.J.'s second type: problems which can as well be solved "by a layman (properly instructed on the law) as by a lawyer."[92] For example, a tribunal may have to determine whether facts found do or do not fall within statutory words such as "park," "trade" or "plant" or expressions such as "intentionally homeless" or "ordinarily resident." Within the limit indicated by Denning L.J. in the *British Launderers' Research Association* case[93] and considered below, the application of such words is treated by the courts as matter of fact for the tribunal of fact. The question of fact here is, in effect: do the primary facts found fall within the ordinary notion of "park," "trade" or whatever it may be? Strictly, of course, the question is not one of fact but, as Denning L.J. pointed out,[94] of inference from (or classification of) fact. But to the extent that a

[90] See Wade A.L., p. 785.

[91] See de Smith J.R.A.A., p. 16 *passim*.

[92] This is not to suggest that the problems "do not involve much law" (see Gwyneth Pitt's criticism of our approach in (1985) 101 L.Q.R. 217 at 235). The relevant law may be highly complex and non-lawyers will require the advice of lawyers in order to frame the question which the tribunal is required to answer. As we have seen, any error at this stage is an error of law. Our argument relates to the process of answering the question once properly framed. The argument is that where Parliament has conferred jurisdiction on a tribunal composed wholly or in part of non-lawyers it would seem strange to maintain that the questions of application with which the tribunal is commonly faced are questions which can be answered only by a trained lawyer. For discussion of what might be the appropriate ambit of a specialist appeal tribunal's jurisdiction, see below pp. 124–127.

[93] [1949] 1 K.B. 462 at 471–472.

[94] *Ibid.*

lawyer is no better equipped than a layman to perform the exercise, it is characterised as a question of fact—or degree[95]—rather than of law. On this basis "the only questions of law which can arise . . . are whether there was a proper direction in point of law and whether the conclusion is one which could reasonably be drawn from the primary facts."[96]

The leading authority on this kind of error of law in this kind of case is *Edwards* v. *Bairstow*.[97] There, taxpayers had been assessed to income tax on profit made in the course of the purchase and sale of a spinning plant. The assessment was based on the view of the Revenue that the transaction was an "adventure in the nature of trade." The General Commissioners discharged the assessment, holding that the transaction was not to be so classified. The Revenue appealed to the High Court, contending that the Commissioners had erred in law. The High Court and the Court of Appeal held that the question "trade or no?" was one of fact, so that the Commissioners' decision could not be disturbed. The House of Lords reversed the courts below and allowed the Revenue's appeal. The decision of the Commissioners was one to which "no person acting judicially and properly instructed as to the relevant law could have come."[98] It is to be observed that there was no alleged error in the Commissioners' statement of the facts and no erroneous statement of the relevant legal rule, or erroneous elucidation of the notion of trade. How, then, did the error of law appear? As Lord Radcliffe said[99]:

> ". . . the law does not supply a precise definition of the word 'trade' . . . . In effect it lays down the limits within which it would be permissible to say that a 'trade' . . . does or does not exist. But the field so marked out is a wide one and there are many combinations of circumstances in which it could not be said to be wrong to arrive at a conclusion one way or the other. If the facts of any particular case are fairly capable of

[95] See above, p. 96 and *per* Lord Radcliffe in *Edwards* v. *Bairstow* [1956] A.C. 14 at 33, discussed below.
[96] *Loc.cit.* above, note 93.
[97] [1956] A.C. 14.
[98] *Ibid.* p. 36, *per* Lord Radcliffe. See too *per* Viscount Simonds at p. 29.
[99] [1956] A.C. 14 at 33. Lords Tucker and Somervell agreed with Lord Radcliffe, and Viscount Simonds' judgment is to the same effect.

> being so described, it seems to me that it necessarily follows that the determination . . . that a trade does or does not exist is not 'erroneous in point of law' . . .
> All these cases in which the facts warrant a determination either way can be described as questions of degree and therefore as questions of fact."[1]

This case, though, was not one where in Lord Radcliffe's words "it could not be said to be wrong to arrive at a conclusion one way or the other." As Viscount Simonds said of the Commissioners' decision: "Everything pointed the other way"[2]; and as Lord Radcliffe asked[3]:

> "What detail does [the transaction] lack that prevents it from being an adventure in the nature of trade, or what element is present in it that makes it capable of being aptly described as anything else?"

Consequently, given that there is no challenge to the finding of primary fact, and although there is no express error in the statement or elucidation of the legal rule

> " . . . the court must intervene. It has no option but to assume that there has been some misconception of the law and that this has been responsible for the determination."[4]

This, then, is a case where the existence of a "second-stage" error of law (a misconstruction of a legal rule) must be inferred. The process of inference is as follows. Reverting to our syllogistic framework,[5] we have a statement of the minor premiss (the facts of the case) to which no exception is taken. We have a conclusion ("not a trade") which is plainly wrong. The only possible explana-

[1] See further below, p. 122.
[2] [1956] A.C. 14 at 29.
[3] *Ibid.* p. 37.
[4] *Ibid.* p. 36 *per* Lord Radcliffe. For another case where the House of Lords found no option but to assume misconception of the law, see *Presho* v. *Insurance Officer* [1984] A.C. 310, *per* Lord Brandon at p. 319.
[5] See above, p. 95.

tion of the error in the conclusion is the existence of an error in the unarticulated major premiss (the meaning of "trade").[6]

Reverting to our earlier example of whether land was or was not part of a park: surely the *Edwards* v. *Bairstow* analysis would today apply *mutatis mutandis* to that question,[7] as it has been held to apply to many other such questions[8] arising in administrative law as to the proper characterisation of an alleged error in applying law to facts.

Professor Wade observes[9] that:

> "The House of Lords' doctrine [*scil.* in *Edwards* v. *Bairstow*] that the error must be one which a reasonable tribunal could not make is frequently disregarded, and judges willingly revert to the simpler and more logical doctrine . . . [that] 'where all the material facts are fully found, and the only question is whether the facts are such as to bring the case within the provisions properly construed of some statutory enactment, the question is one of law only.' "[10]

Leaving aside for the present the question of the greater logicality of the simpler doctrine,[11] it may be suggested with respect that the House of Lords' doctrine in *Edwards* v. *Bairstow* now commands a very wide degree of judicial acceptance in many areas of administrative law. The following examples may be considered.

[6] In *Council of Civil Service Unions* v. *Minister for the Civil Service* [1985] A.C. 374 at 410 Lord Radcliffe's analysis in *Edwards* v. *Bairstow* was described by Lord Diplock as "ingenious" and "today no longer needed." But it remains a cogent explanation of how a court may infer a misconstruction of a legal rule in circumstances where an inferior tribunal has not ventured to provide a formal elucidation. It also mitigates the apparent oddity of, say, the House of Lords reversing the Court of Appeal and the High Court on the basis that "no reasonable tribunal properly instructed in the law" could have reached the decision in question. (See, *e.g. Reed* v. *Nova Securities Ltd* [1985] *The Times*, February 5.) Lord Radcliffe's explanation shows that the basis of the reversal is that the House of Lords differs from the lower courts on the proper interpretation of a relevant legal rule. Had the lower courts taken the same view as the House of Lords, then, no doubt, they too would accept that "no reasonable tribunal . . ."

[7] As Harman L.J. said in *Ashbridge Ltd* v. *M.H.L.G.* [1965] 1 W.L.R. 1320, of the *White and Collins* case (above, note 72) in which the question arose: "the decision eventually was that there was no evidence on which the Minister could have come to his conclusion." In *Edwards* v. *Bairstow* at p. 36 Lord Radcliffe said that the type of error in that case could be similarly so described.

[8] For examples, see text following.

[9] Wade A.L., p. 819.

[10] Citing Lord Parker in *Farmer* v. *Cotton's Trustees* [1915] A.C. 922 at 932, and other cases.

[11] As to this, see below, p. 123.

First, in the context of statutory provision in the field of employment, the question has often arisen of the ambit of two phrases hallowed by statutory usage: "course of employment" and "contract of service." An employee who is injured in the course of his employment may claim statutory compensation.[12] He may appeal to the Court of Appeal on a point of law from a decision of the Social Security Commissioner.[13] In what circumstances may a commissioner's decision that an injury did or did not occur in the course of employment be said to be wrong in law? In *R.* v. *Industrial Injuries Commissioner ex p. A.E.U. (No. 2)*[14] a workman had been injured in his place of employment some five minutes after the end of his ten-minute tea break. He had deliberately and without permission extended the break and, at the time of the injury, was showing no signs of returning to his work. The commissioner decided that although "course of employment" would cover acts "reasonably incidental" to work (*e.g.* a legitimate tea break) consciously to overstay one's break time by fifty percent or more was not reasonably incidental, so the claim failed. The Court of Appeal held that the commissioner had asked himself the correct question and that his answer was not one to which he could not reasonably come.[15] This was a case, to adopt Lord Radcliffe's formulation in *Edwards* v. *Bairstow*,[16] inside "the limits within which it would be permissible to say" that the workman was, or was not, in the course of his employment. The question was one of degree "dependent on the particular circumstances of each case."[17] Accordingly, the commissioner not having erred in law, his decision could not be challenged.[18]

In the *A.E.U.* case the Court of Appeal emphasised[19] the need

[12] See now Social Security Act 1975, s.50.
[13] Social Security Act 1980, s.14.
[14] [1966] 2 Q.B. 31.
[15] See especially *per* Salmon L.J. at p. 52.
[16] [1956] A.C. 14 at 33; discussed above.
[17] [1966] 2 Q.B. 31 at 52, *per* Salmon L.J. See too *per* Davies L.J. at 51.
[18] Compare *R.* v. *Insurance Cmr. ex p. Michael* [1977] 1 W.L.R. 109 where the Court of Appeal indicated certain reported decisions of commissioners on the "course of employment" point which, in the Court's view, were wrong in law on the *Edwards* v. *Bairstow* test. See too *Nancollas* v. *Insurance Officer; Ball* v. *Insurance Officer* [1985] 1 All E.R. 833: itinerant employees whose work time included time taken to travel to assignments were injured while travelling from home to an assignment. Allowing the employees' appeal against the Social Security Commissioner's refusal of injury benefit the Court of Appeal held that the only decision consistent with the facts was that the claimants were injured in the course of their employment. The Commissioners had therefore erred in law in the *Edwards* v. *Bairstow* sense.
[19] [1966] 2 Q.B. at 45 (Lord Denning M.R.), 50 (Davies L.J.).

to avoid the tendency into which superior courts had fallen in dealing with the "course of employment" problem as it had arisen under the Workmen's Compensation Acts. That tendency was in effect to treat as a question of law the question "was the plaintiff acting in the course of his employment?" The Court of Appeal took the view that the question of law was, rather, "may it fairly be said that the plaintiff was acting in the course of his employment?"[20] Once answered in the affirmative, the question "was he?" is entirely for "the arbitrators [*scil.* the commissioners] to whom the legislature ha[s] entrusted the administration of compensation."[21]

The Court of Appeal has now adopted an exactly similar approach to the vexed question of the meaning and application of the phrase "contract of service." In *O'Kelly* v. *Trusthouse Forte Plc.*[22] an industrial tribunal had held that certain waiters hired by the company on a week by week basis at the Grosvenor House Hotel did not have contracts of service with, *i.e.* were not employed by, the company: their contract was "for services" rather than "of service."[23] They were thus not entitled to an employee's protection under the Employment Protection Act 1978. An individual may appeal from an industrial tribunal to the Employment Appeal Tribunal "on a question of law."[24] The waiters appealed to the Employment Appeal Tribunal which, on the basis of certain Court of Appeal dicta, treated the question "contract of service or contract for services?" as one of pure law and reversed the industrial tribunal. The company appealed to the Court of Appeal. Donaldson M.R. and Fox L.J. held that the Appeal should be allowed. The only points of law for the Employment Appeal Tribunal were whether the industrial tribunal had asked itself the right question and, if so, whether its answer was one which a tribunal, properly instructed, could reasonably reach.[25] Here, the approach of the industrial tribunal was impeccable on both points. It followed that the industrial tribunal had not erred in law and that its decision should stand. Ackner L.J., on

[20] See Lord Denning M.R. *ibid.* pp. 48–49.
[21] *Ibid.* p. 45.
[22] [1984] Q.B. 90.
[23] See *per* Ackner L.J. *ibid.* p. 100.
[24] For discussion of the appellate jurisdiction of specialist appeal tribunals, see below, pp. 124–127.
[25] [1984] Q.B. 90 *per* Fox L.J. at p. 121; Donaldson M.R. at p. 123.

the other hand, although concurring in the result, regarded it as "axiomatic"[26] that the question was purely one of law. Here again, the majority view accords with and expressly applies the House of Lords' doctrine in *Edwards* v. *Bairstow*.[27]

In recent years the House of Lords has itself applied the *Edwards* v. *Bairstow* doctrine in the revenue law field on such

[26] *Ibid.* p. 114.

[27] See also *Gunning* v. *Mirror Group Newspapers* [1986] 1 All E.R. 385 (no evidence on which contract for newspaper distribution could be said to require distributor "personally to execute any work"). For a case whose facts fell as clearly outside "contract of service" as those of *Edwards* v. *Bairstow* fell within "trade," see *Davies* v. *Presbyterian Church of Wales* [1986] 1 All E.R. 705. The House of Lords (approving earlier decisions including that of the Court of Appeal in *Methodist Conference* v. *Parfitt* [1984] Q.B. 368) held that "by no stretch of imagination" (p. 710) could the agreement between a Presbyterian minister and his Church constitute a contract of service. It had been argued for the minister that the ruling of the industrial tribunal that he was an employee disclosed no error of law "because the tribunal instructed itself correctly as to the law, took into account all relevant circumstances and reached a conclusion which was reasonable." But (at p. 709) Lord Templeman (delivering the unanimous judgment of the House) made it clear that the conclusion was not "reasonable" in that it failed to take account of a fundamental feature of the relationship between the minister and the Church, *i.e.* that "the duties owed by the Church to the [minister] are not contractual"; or, as the Court of Appeal held in *Parfitt*, that there was no intention to create a contractual relationship.

It cannot be too strongly emphasised that under the *Edwards* v. *Bairstow* doctrine no conclusion is "reasonable" if it can be reached only by failing to take account of a crucial consideration. For such failure, had it been explicit in the judgment below, would have constituted a "second-stage" error: as, for example, if an industrial tribunal were to state explicitly that intention to create legal relations was not an essential ingredient of a contract of employment. But even though in *Davies* the error did not appear in this way, the conclusion that Davies was an employee itself disclosed that the error must, in truth, have occurred.

In *Davies* Lord Templeman said (at p. 709) that "[t]he decision in *Edwards* v. *Bairstow* has nothing to do with this case . . . . The question to be determined is a question of law, namely, whether upon the true construction of the book of rules a pastor of the church is . . . under a contract of service." It is submitted that his lordship is not to be taken as holding that the question "contract of service or no?" is always a pure question of law: that would be to overrule *O'Kelly* v. *Trusthouse Forte* (text above) to which his lordship did not refer. Rather, it is submitted, Lord Templeman was indicating that the case in question was not of the "open-textured" type where (according to *Edwards* v. *Bairstow*) "the facts warrant a determination either way." The question in *Davies* was "whether a pastor of the Presbyterian Church of Wales is an employee under a contract of service." That question was purely one of law because, in law, there was only one possible answer. Intention to create legal relations is, in law, a prerequisite of any contract. To hold that there is a contract of service in the absence of such intention is to err in law.

questions as the application of the statutory term "plant" for income tax purposes and the term "alteration" in the context of value-added tax legislation. In *I.R.C.* v. *Scottish and Newcastle Breweries Ltd*[28] the House of Lords refused to treat as erroneous in law a decision by the Special Commissioners that hotel decor was "plant" (as being the means by which—attracting customers—as opposed to the place where the hotel business was carried on). As Lord Lowry[29] said,[30] referring to "the classic statement of Lord Radcliffe in *Edwards* v. *Bairstow*":

> ". . . the law does not supply a definition of plant or prescribe a detailed or exhaustive set of rules for application to any particular set of circumstances, and there are cases which, on the facts found, are capable of decision either way; a decision in such a case is a decision on a question of fact and degree and cannot be upset as being erroneous in point of law unless the commissioners show by some reason they give or statement they make in the case stated that they have misunderstood or misapplied the law in some relevant particular . . ."[31]

Again, in *A.C.T. Construction Ltd* v. *Customs & Excise Commissioners*[32] the House of Lords followed Brandon L.J. in the Court of Appeal in the same case[33] in applying the *Edwards* v. *Bairstow* approach to the characterisation of certain building work as "maintenance" (which was not "zero rated" for value-added tax purposes) rather than "alteration" (which was[34]). The work was the insertion of new concrete foundations beneath buildings whose original foundations had never been adequate. The V.A.T. tribunal held that the work was maintenance. Drake J., the Court of Appeal and the House of Lords held, on the contrary, that it was alteration. In the Court of Appeal Lord Denning M.R. took the view that "Once you have the primary facts established, as you have here, about the underpinning, then the question whether the

28 [1982] 1 W.L.R. 322.
29 With whom (and with Lord Wilberforce) Lords Salmon, Fraser and Bridge agreed.
30 [1982] 1 W.L.R. 322 at 327.
31 See too *Cole Bros. Ltd* v. *Phillips (Inspector of Taxes)* [1982] 1 W.L.R. 1450 (H.L.).
32 [1981] 1 W.L.R. 1542.
33 [1981] 1 W.L.R. 49.
34 Until June 1984: Finance Act 1984, s.10 and Sched. 6.

work comes within the word 'maintenance' or not is a question of law for the judges to decide."[35] Brandon L.J., on the other hand, said that the question of law was whether the work was "capable of coming within the expression 'maintenance'."[36] The work, he said,

> "involved a radical and fundamental alteration to the construction of the building as it had been before. It involved an extension of the existing building in a downward direction. Such work in my view is not capable of coming within the expression 'maintenance' in the ordinary and natural meaning of that word."[37]

In effect, surely, the new foundations were as much "alteration" (and as little "maintenance") as the provision of a second course of brickwork to a building originally constructed with one course only. Brandon L.J., unlike Lord Denning M.R., took the *Edwards* v. *Bairstow* approach. And it was Brandon L.J.'s reasoning which the House of Lords cited and found "compelling."[38]

Examples of the current growth of judicial acceptance of the *Edwards* v. *Bairstow* approach could be multiplied. The House of Lords adopted it in 1981 in the context of a local authority finding of intentional homelessness for purposes of the Housing (Homeless Persons) Act 1977[39]; and the Court of Appeal in 1983 with reference to the court's jurisdiction over awards of arbitration tribunals.[40]

(3) The Edwards v. Bairstow doctrine: rationale and objections

As already noted, Professor de Smith observed[41] that in many cases the "ultimate finding or interference could as well be styled one of law as one of fact." One may venture to suggest that clarity of analysis would be advanced if it were recognised that the pro-

[35] [1981] 1 W.L.R. 49 at 54.
[36] *Ibid.* p. 56.
[37] *Ibid.* p. 57.
[38] [1981] 1 W.L.R. 1542 at 1546 *per* Lord Roskill with whom Lords Diplock, Elwyn-Jones, Keith and Scarman agreed. See too *Customs & Excise Cmrs* v. *Viva Gas Appliances* [1983] 1 W.L.R. 1445 (H.L.). And, in the context of Capital Gains Tax: *Furniss* v. *Dawson* [1984] A.C. 474.
[39] *Islam* v. *London Borough of Hillingdon* [1983] 1 A.C. 688, see esp. Lord Lowry at p. 717.
[40] *Uni-Ocean Lines* v. *C-Trade of Geneva S.A.* [1984] 1 Lloyd's Rep. 244.
[41] De Smith J.R.A.A., p. 130.

cess of "ultimate inference"—the application of law to facts—is of a different nature from either "fact-finding" or "rule-stating."[42] There are, as the examples above show, many cases where the application of law to facts involves a weighing and balancing of considerations pointing in different directions; cases where, because of the "open-texture" of the concepts in which Parliament has chosen to cast its legislation, there is no logically or mathematically "correct" answer to a question of application of law to facts. Suppose that in such a case the statutory authority has decided the issue and that the court has jurisdiction to correct only an error of law. If the court applies the *Edwards* v. *Bairstow* doctrine here it is in effect distinguishing between a decision which shows that the statutory authority has erred in its drawing of the boundaries of meaning of the statutory words; and a decision which (while the court itself might have decided otherwise) shows no such error. The court treats a decision of the latter kind as not displaying error of law. Mureinik says[43] that in such a case the court is treating the question of rule application as posing "only issues of fact." Rather, surely, the court is recognising that the final inference involves a process of reasoning distinct from both fact-finding and rule-stating.[44] In *Edwards* v. *Bairstow* Lord Radcliffe said[45] that it raises what "can be described as questions of degree and therefore as questions of fact." It is submitted that the words "and therefore as questions of fact" mean "and therefore as questions to be determined by the statutory authority rather than by the court."[46]

The *Edwards* v. *Bairstow* doctrine does not reflect a failure by the courts to understand the epistemological kinship between one type of reasoning and another (rule-stating and rule-applying are indeed kindred but nonetheless distinct processes). Rather, the

42 See above, p. 95.

43 (1982) 98 L.Q.R. 615.

44 See above, pp. 95, 108. It does not seem helpful to refuse (as Mureinik does, *ibid.* 618) to treat this process as *sui generis* on the basis that "if the decision is the judgment of the law, it says what the law is. That is all that we mean by an answer to a question of law. So questions of law and questions of fact, together exhaust the sorts of questions that can be judicially disposed of."

45 [1956] A.C. 14 at 33.

46 For other examples of courts characterising questions of application as questions of "fact," see *South West Water Authority* v. *Rumbles* [1985] 2 W.L.R. 405 (H.L.) (whether occupier of premises "had the use" of drainage facilities for rating purposes); *Cresswell* v. *Board of Inland Revenue* [1984] I.C.R. 508 (whether change in employees' work practices amounted to a different job). In neither case did the court's jurisdiction turn on the law/fact distinction. But one could evisage circumstances where it would do so and where a decision on either question could be characterised as erroneous in law in the *Edwards* v. *Bairstow* sense.

doctrine is one application of a "reasonable working hypothesis"[47] about the basis of a review court's jurisdiction: "its intervention should extend to those matters upon which its decisions are likely to be better than those of the tribunal under review." Professor Wade argues[48] that the *Edwards* v. *Bairstow* doctrine:

> "may be vulnerable to logical analysis in that, once the facts of the case are established, the application to them of some legal definition or test is in its nature a matter of law."

It is submitted with respect that Professor de Smith's view is to be preferred—the application of law to facts is "in its nature" neither a matter of law nor a matter of degree. It may in a particular case be characterised as the one or the other according to the criteria set out above.

What objections are there to the *Edwards* v. *Bairstow* doctrine? One general objection is that its operation is too uncertain.[49] First, it is said, there is no acid test to distinguish cases where a non-lawyer can apply law to facts from cases where a trained lawyer is required. Secondly, even if it is plain that the doctrine applies in a particular case, it is impossible to predict where precisely a court will draw the boundaries of meaning of statutory words.

There are, of course, uncertainties in both these respects. But it is submitted that the uncertainties are by no means so great as to justify the assertion that the *Edwards* v. *Bairstow* notion of error of law is incapable of operating as "an organising principle."[50] As to the first point above, the cases discussed earlier suggest that the doctrine is now very widely applied in the administrative law field where decisions are commonly made by non-lawyers. As to the second, it is merely a particular statement of the general proposition that there is always a penumbra of uncertainty in the meaning of statutory words. But the very notion of penumbra implies the existence of areas which clearly are, and others which clearly are not, in shade. The precise extent of the penumbra, of the open-texture of statutory provision, can be established only by authoritative rulings in particular cases.

[47] See passage from de Smith J.R.A.A., pp. 127–128 set out above p. 96.
[48] Wade A.L., p. 819.
[49] See J. Beatson, *The Scope of Judicial Review for Error of Law* (1984) 4 Ox.J.-Leg. Stud. 22 at 43 *passim*.
[50] *Ibid.*

Another, quite distinct, general objection to the *Edwards* v. *Bairstow* doctrine is that a review court is seen to be accepting that the first instance tribunal could have reached an opposite conclusion and yet would still not have erred in law. It is argued that for a court to proclaim that there is in law no single right answer to questions such as those arising in the cases considered above "smacks of abdication of responsibility" and is a failure to take rights seriously.[51] As a general objection to *Edwards* v. *Bairstow* this surely fails. If one accepts that because of the open-texture of language there will be many cases of application of law to facts where there is not a uniquely correct answer, it seems then to be an open question whether or not a particular review court should be invested with jurisdiction to determine in particular types of case which of the possibly correct answers is to be treated as actually correct. One sensible answer to that question is, as Professor Evans intimates,[52] that a review court should be invested with such jurisdiction where "its decisions are likely to be better than those of the tribunal under review." In cases such as those considered above, where the application of law to facts does not require the specific skills of a lawyer it is not to be assumed that the decision of a court of law on the application issue will probably be better than that of the first instance tribunal. The *Edwards* v. *Bairstow* doctrine acknowledges this.

Now, as we are about to see, this does not suggest that the first instance tribunal's application of law to facts (if within *Edwards* v. *Bairstow* parameters) should necessarily be immune from review by an authority other than a court of law. It suggests merely that, in confining the review jurisdiction of a court to the correction of errors of law, Parliament may be taken as indicating that the court is not the appropriate tribunal to undertake that particular exercise. That being the case, resort by a court in appropriate circumstances to the *Edwards* v. *Bairstow* doctrine may be seen not as an abdication of responsibility but as a correct perception that the responsibility does not lie with it. This general objection to *Edwards* v. *Bairstow* thus appears to fail.

But there is a cogent particular objection to the application of the doctrine to determine the extent of the jurisdiction vested in a specialist appeal tribunal (such as the Employment Appeal Tri-

[51] Gwyneth Pitt in (1985) 101 L.Q.R. 217 at 233.
[52] De Smith J.R.A.A., p. 128.

bunal[53] or the Social Security Commissioners[54]) to which an appeal lies on point of law only. This objection has been well demonstrated[55] by reference to the jurisdiction of the Employment Appeal Tribunal to correct only errors of law by industrial tribunals. We observed earlier that in *O'Kelly* v. *Trusthouse Forte plc*[56] the Court of Appeal reversed the Employment Appeal Tribunal where it had differed from an industrial tribunal on the question "contract of service or contract for services?" The Court held that the jurisdiction of the Employment Appeal Tribunal was limited to correction of errors of law of the *Edwards* v. *Bairstow* type. This means, for example, that if a company had an arrangement of the *O'Kelly* type with workers in different parts of the country, different industrial tribunals might (within *Edwards* v. *Bairstow* parameters) reach opposite conclusions on the contract of service issue; but the Employment Appeal Tribunal would have no jurisdiction to correct the tribunal whose application of the relevant criteria to the facts of the case it considered wrong. So, absurdly and unjustly, the same contract might be a contract of service in Cleveland but a contract for services in Devon.[57]

Surely the jurisdiction of the Employment Appeal Tribunal should extend to the resolution of such differences. We have seen that the *Edwards* v. *Bairstow* doctrine may be taken to reflect the hypothesis that the intervention of a review court should extend to those matters on which its decisions are likely to be better than those of the tribunal under review. The doctrine acknowledges that when application of law to facts requires a balancing of many, often opposed, considerations in a particular field of law and practice, the decision of a specialist tribunal is likely to be better than that of a court of general jurisdiction. But it can hardly be suggested that the decision of an industrial tribunal is likely to be better than that of the Employment Appeal Tribunal. For the Employment Appeal Tribunal, consisting as it does of a High

53 Employment Protection (Consolidation) Act 1978, s.136(1).

54 *e.g.* Supplementary Benefits Act 1976, s.15A; S.I. 1980 No. 1605 (appeals from Supplementary Benefit Appeal Tribunals; appeals to the Commissioner from Local Social Security Tribunals are not restricted to point of law—see note 58 below).

55 By Pitt, *loc.cit.* above note 51.

56 [1984] Q.B. 90. Apparently not affected by the decision of the House of Lords in *Davies* v. *Presbyterian Church of Wales* [1986] 1 All E.R. 705 (note 27 above).

57 (1985) 101 L.Q.R at 231–232, citing *Nethermere Ltd* v. *Taverna* [1984] I.R.L.R. 240, discussed at *ibid.* pp. 221–223.

Court judge on full-time secondment and two (or more) appointed members with special knowledge or experience of industrial relations on employers' and workers' sides respectively, is a tribunal of unique expertise in its field.

We have seen that a question of application of law to facts may be treated as a question of law or, on the contrary, as one of degree according to whether or not the expertise of a trained lawyer is required in order to answer the question. Could one not say similarly that as between a local tribunal and a specialist appeal tribunal whose jurisdiction is confined to questions of law, a question of application should be regarded as a question of law where it requires special expertise in the particular field of law and practice concerned? So, for example, the expertise of the Employment Appeal Tribunal may be regarded as superior to that of individual industrial tribunals. On this basis, the Employment Appeal Tribunal should have jurisdiction to rule authoritatively in a case such as that just envisaged of conflict between different industrial tribunals. On the other hand, the expertise of the Court of Appeal cannot be said to rival that of the Employment Appeal Tribunal in matters of application of this sort. On that basis, an appeal on point of law from the Tribunal to the Court of Appeal should continue to be governed by the *Edwards* v. *Bairstow* doctrine.

Commonly, of course, appeals to specialist appeal tribunals are not confined to point of law,[58] so that the problem discussed above does not arise.[59] But the problem might arise where jurisdiction in a particular field is conferred on each of a large number of local tribunals from which the sole avenue of appeal is to a court on point of law only. The General Commissioners of Income Tax are an example.[60] If it became apparent that taxpayers in different parts of the country were faring differently at the hands of different tribunals of Commissioners, it might be thought desirable for Parlia-

[58] *e.g.* appeals to the Social Security Commissioners from Local Social Security Tribunals : Social Security Act 1975, s.101, but *cf.* now Social Security Bill 1986, Sched. 3 para. 7: appeal to be limited to point of law; to the Immigration Appeal Tribunal from an adjudicator: Immigration Act 1971, s.20; to the Betting Levy Appeal Tribunal under Betting, Gaming and Lotteries Act 1963, s.28(6); to the Transport Tribunal under Transport Act 1968, s.70.

[59] Although such tribunals as the Immigration Appeal Tribunal and the Social Security Commissioners sit in a number of divisions, there should be sufficient "comity" between them to ensure that different divisions do not commonly reach opposite conclusions on materially the same facts.

[60] There are over 400 tribunals. Appeal from them is to the High Court on point of law only : Taxes Managment Act 1970, s.56. *Edwards* v. *Bairstow* itself was an appeal from General Commissioners.

ment to interpose a specialist appeal tribunal between the Commissioners and the court.

F. Summary

A superior court commonly has jurisdiction to correct an alleged error by an inferior tribunal only where the error is error of law. We have suggested that a tribunal errs in law in each of the following cases.

(i) If the tribunal purports to find that particular events occurred although it is seised of no admissible evidence that the events did in fact occur. Where, however, admissible evidence has been led, its assessment is entirely for the tribunal. To conclude, on even the slenderest evidence, that particular events occurred is not to err in law.

(ii) If the tribunal approaches the construction of a legal term of art in a statute on the erroneous basis that the statutory wording bears its "ordinary" meaning (*i.e.* its "everyday" or "trade" meaning, as the case may be).

(iii) If the tribunal approaches the construction of a statutory word or phrase bearing an "ordinary" meaning (see (ii), above) on the erroneous basis that it is a legal term of art.

(iv) If the tribunal, though correctly treating a statutory word or phrase as a legal term of art (or, as the case may be, bearing an "ordinary" meaning), errs in its elucidation of the word or phrase.

(v) If the tribunal errs in its conclusion (*i.e.* in applying the law to the facts) in a case where this process requires the skill of a trained lawyer. Here, the error is error of law because the issue is purely one of law.

(vi) If, in a case where a conclusion can as well be drawn by a layman (properly instructed on the law) as by a lawyer, the tribunal reaches a conclusion which cannot reasonably be drawn from the facts as found. In that event, the superior court has no option but to assume that there has been some misconception of the law and that this has been responsible for the conclusion. But the issue may admit of more than one possible resolution. The inferior tribunal's conclusion may be one of the possible resolutions; yet it may be a conclusion which the superior court (had it been seised of the issue) would not have reached. Nevertheless, the inferior tribunal does not err in law. The matter is one of degree; and a superior court with jurisdiction to correct only errors of law will not intervene.

It is to be noted that the above analysis of the notion of error of law may be applied in the context of the exercise of discretionary power as well as to the resolution of the types of issue already considered. Take any common type of discretionary power, *e.g.* to impose on the grant of a licence such conditions as the authority may think fit; or to charge such fares or rents, or to pay such wages as the authority may determine. In the course of exercising such a power the need will arise for the authority to "find facts." Accordingly, it may err in law in sense (i) above. Again, the authority may, in articulating its decision, choose to elucidate the meaning of the statutory words conferring the power. If it errs in its elucidation it will err in law in sense (iv) above. However, as in the cases already discussed, it will often be argued that an error of law consisting of a misinterpretation of the scope of the statutory power must be inferred from the circumstances of its exercise. Here, as we shall see,[61] there is an obvious parallel between the *Edwards* v. *Bairstow* doctrine in (vi) above and the *Wednesbury*[62] analysis of unreasonableness. On that analysis, as we shall see, a purported exercise of a discretionary power can be upset if it is proved to be unreasonable in the sense, not that it is what the court considers unreasonable, but that it is what the court considers is a decision that no reasonable body properly instructed on the law could have come to.

In this chapter we have sought to show that the notion of error of law can be elaborated with some precision. In the ensuing chapters we shall see how errors of law in different circumstances may be corrected by way of judicial review (whether supervisory or appellate). We postpone until later[63] consideration of the question whether or not it may be thought satisfactory that in administrative law the review jurisdiction of courts should be, broadly speaking, a jurisdiction to correct errors of law.

[61] See Chap. 5, pp. 181–182.

[62] *Associated Picture Houses Ltd* v. *Wednesbury Corporation* [1948] 1 K.B. 223—see Chap. 5.

[63] See Chaps. 4 and 5, pp. 161–164 and 183–190.

Chapter 4

LAW, FACT AND DEGREE

The question in this chapter[1] is: in what circumstances and on what bases may a public authority be said to have gone outside its remit in the course of resolving an issue of law, fact or degree?[2]

A. Supervisory and Appellate Review

(1) Supervisory review

We saw in Chapter 2[3] that in the context of common law supervisory review a public authority exceeds its remit if either (i) it acts *ultra vires* or, in a phrase bearing essentially the same meaning, "without jurisdiction," or (ii) the record of its proceedings contains patent error. We consider below[4] the extent and current importance of the patent error jurisdiction. Now we ask what will take a public authority *ultra vires* or outside jurisdiction.

(a) We may start by recalling our discussion of the "boundary" analogy in Chapter 1.[5] We began there by observing that a public authority may cross a line clearly drawn by Parliament and indicating the boundary of the authority's competence. Our example was of a public authority charged solely with the provision of a public transport service which purported to branch out into the provision of houses for the homeless. This is a clear case of *ultra vires*. We then saw that there are circumstances where an issue is plainly a "boundary" issue but where Parliament appears not to have drawn the boundary with precision. Our example there was of a local authority empowered by statute to provide a bus service and to supplement the passenger service by the carriage of parcels. We supposed a dispute as to whether the power extended to the provision by the authority of a doorstep delivery service for those par-

[1] For the issues discussed in this chapter, see de Smith J.R.A.A., Chap. 3; Wade A.L., Chap. 9; Craig, Chap. 9.

[2] For issues of policy, see Chap. 5. For circumstances in which procedural irregularity will carry an authority outside its remit see Chap. 6.

[3] See Chap. 2, pp. 39–41.

[4] See pp. 164–167.

[5] See Chap. 1, pp. 23–27.

cels carried between bus termini. The courts treat "boundary" questions of this sort as self-evidently questions of *vires*. As we shall see in section B of this chapter, the courts resolve such questions by applying a test somewhat reminiscent of the *Edwards* v. *Bairstow* test[6] of error of law.

(b) A question may arise as to whether a public authority, usually a court or statutory tribunal, charged with deciding issues of law, fact or degree has jurisdiction to embark on the consideration of a particular case. Here if an authority asserts jurisdiction where it has none, or declines a jurisdiction which it has a duty to assume, it by definition acts (or decides not to act), "without jurisdiction." Under the heading "Threshold Jurisdictional Issues" in section C below we consider some reported cases where questions of this type have fallen to be resolved by the courts in the exercise of supervisory review jurisdiction.

(c) We distinguish "Threshold" from "Substantive" Jurisdictional Issues, with which we deal in section D. Under this head we take cases where, while it may be accepted that an authority may or must embark on the consideration of a particular case, it is argued that its jurisdiction to decide the case does not extend to making errors of a particular kind. If this argument succeeds, it follows that any such error may be corrected by the exercise of supervisory review jurisdiction. Recall our example in our discussion of the boundary analogy of the state benefit payable to a "member of the family" of a particular individual. We there asked whether it may ever be said that a public authority has crossed the boundaries of its power (in the present context, has acted without jurisdiction) by making a mistake in the course of doing the kind of thing it exists to do. In Chapter 2 we observed that in answering the question "what errors take an authority outside jurisdiction?" "the current tendency is for the courts to review all questions of law but to show self-restraint in reviewing findings of fact."[7] In section D of this chapter we examine the proposition that error of law counts as jurisdictional error—a proposition which, we shall see, raises acute questions as to the proper scope of supervisory review.

(2) Appellate review

We have observed that error of law is the usual basis for appellate judicial review of the acts and decisions of public authorities

[6] See Chap. 3, p. 114.
[7] De Smith J.R.A.A., p. 108—cited in Chap. 2, p. 40.

other than courts of first instance.[8] And we have explained[9] how it may be said that such error carries the authority concerned outside its remit. Where, then, a court has statutory appellate jurisdiction to correct error of law by an inferior authority, the basis of its intervention is plain; and nothing more need be said about the manner of that intervention than has been said already.[10]

B. Acts Incidental or Consequential

The problem here is that in conferring powers and imposing duties on public authorities Parliament commonly legislates in terms whose generality tends to raise the question whether a particular activity which is not expressly authorised may nevertheless fairly be said to be impliedly authorised. If so, the activity is *intra vires*; if not, *ultra vires*. The problem is illustrated by the "carriage of parcels" example, referred to above, where the dispute was whether or not the power extended to the provision by the authority of a doorstep delivery service. On what principles will a court resolve such a dispute? It is a dispute which, clearly, cannot be resolved purely by reference to the express words of the statute; for it is the very imprecision of those words which engenders the dispute.

As with the *Edwards* v. *Bairstow* doctrine[11] and, as we shall see later,[12] with the *Wednesbury* doctrine in the context of discretionary power, the courts give full recognition to the inherent flexibility of the terms in which Parliament has chosen to legislate. The governing principle, laid down by the House of Lords and applied in case after case is

> "that whatever may fairly be regarded as incidental to, or consequential upon, those things which the legislature has authorised, ought not (unless expressly prohibited) to be held, by judicial construction, to be *ultra vires*."[13]

[8] See Chap. 2, p. 46. From courts of first instance, as we saw, there is commonly an appeal by way of rehearing. We saw also that from magistrates' courts, as an alternative to appeal to the Crown Court by way of rehearing, statute provides for appeal on law by way of case stated so that a point of law may be taken straight to the High Court.
[9] See Chap. 2, pp. 33–37.
[10] See Chap. 2, pp. 57–60.
[11] See Chap. 3, p. 114.
[12] See Chap. 5, p. 179.
[13] *Att.-Gen.* v. *Gt. Eastern Rly. Co.* (1880) 5 App.Cas. 473, *per* Lord Selborne L.C. at p. 478.

A key phrase is "whatever may fairly be regarded." There are (as we have seen with the *Edwards* v. *Bairstow* doctrine) limits to the flexibility deriving from the open-texture of legislation. And Parliament may legislate in terms which are less rather than more open-textured. But to give full recognition to such open texture as there may be, is to recognise that Parliament has granted to the conferee of the power, and not to the courts, the right to determine (within the open texture) what activities should be pursued.

Thus in our parcels service example it might be expected that the authority's view would prevail and that the doorstep delivery service would be held *intra vires.*[14] On the other hand, our authority could not rely on the statutory power in question to run a general parcels delivery business apart from the bus service.[15] Two much-cited cases, one either side of the line, are *Att.-Gen.* v. *Smethwick Corporation*[16] and *Att.-Gen.* v. *Fulham Corporation.*[17] In the *Smethwick* case a local authority set up a printing department so as to service the work of its other departments more cheaply than by contracting work out to local printers. The Court of Appeal held that the expenses of the department were, in the terms of the statute, "necessarily incurred in carrying this Act into effect" in that the enterprise was incidental to or consequential upon those functions expressly remitted to the authority. But in the *Fulham* case a statutory power to provide municipal "wash-houses" (fore-runners, it seems, of the modern "launderette") did not extent, incidentally or consequentially, to the establishment of a municipal laundry.

Att.-Gen. v. *Crayford U.D.C.*[18] shows clearly how the courts will refrain from too restrictive a construction of a statutory word of broad meaning. The Court of Appeal held that local authority

[14] In *Att.-Gen.* v. *Manchester Corporation* [1906] 1 Ch. 643 a statutory power to run tramways for the purpose, *inter alia*, of carrying parcels was held to extend to the provision of ancillary services including doorstep collection and delivery.

[15] *Ibid.* See also *London County Council* v. *Att.-Gen.* [1902] A.C. 165 (power to work tramways did not extend to provision of bus service linking tram termini across the River Thames but not confined to tramway passengers).

[16] [1932] 1 Ch. 562.

[17] [1921] 1 Ch. 440.

[18] [1962] Ch. 575. It will be observed that cases in this area have commonly been brought by way of an Attorney-General's relator action (see Chap. 7). This is explained by difficulties (now largely superseded) of the law relating to the prerogative remedies and to *locus standi.* In the *Crayford* case the court found the willingness of the Attorney to lend his name to a competitor of the insurance company used by the council "curious" (p. 585), even "odd" (p. 590), but accepted (what has since been confirmed by the House of Lords in *Gouriet* v. *U.P.O.W.* [1978] A.C. 435) that his decision to grant or withold his name in this context is non-justiciable.

"management" powers over council houses extended to arranging for insurance of tenants' household effects. Evidence showed that council tenants sustaining uninsured losses tended to become bad tenants. Thus "the risk insured against closely affect[ed] the productiveness of the houses"[19] and the insurance arrangements were part of management.

The test applied by the courts is whether the activity concerned is incidental to or consequential upon what is expressly authorised; it is not whether the activities can conveniently be run in harness.[20] However, the Local Government Act 1972[21] now empowers a local authority "to do anything . . . which is calculated to facilitate, or is conducive or incidental to, the discharge of any of their functions." This power, where it applies, would clearly legitimise many of the kinds of activity held not to be incidental or consequential in the reported cases. Wide though this power is, even it has its limits: it has been held not to empower a local authority to conduct a campaign against central government policy even where the policy was to abolish the authority.[22]

Finally, we may observe that action which might ordinarily be regarded as incidental or consequential, and so as impliedly authorised, may nevertheless be held unlawful if it impinges on a basic constitutional right of the individual such as the right to unimpeded access to the courts. In *Raymond* v. *Honey*[23] a prison governor prevented a prisoner from applying by letter to the High Court to commit the governor for contempt of court. The governor relied on rules made under statute "for the regulation and management of prisons." But the House of Lords held that nothing in the statute or the rules authorised restriction of the prisoner's right of access to the courts. So basic a right may be taken away only by express enactment.[24]

[19] *Per* Donovan L.J., *ibid*. p. 592.
[20] *L.C.C.* v. *Att.-Gen.* (above): see *per* Lord Macnaghten at p. 169.
[21] s.111(1).
[22] *R* v. *G.L.C. ex p. Westminster City Council* [1984] *The Times*, December 27. See now Local Government Bill 1986, cl. 2.
[23] [1983] A.C. 1. *Raymond* v. *Honey* was applied in *R.* v. *Home Secretary ex p. Anderson* [1984] 2 W.L.R. 725: Divisional Court held *ultra vires* prison rule preventing prisoner from complaining about prison treatment to his lawyer (a prisoner's mode of access to the courts) unless complaint was simultaneously made through prison procedure.
[24] Note that prisoner's right of access to courts does not extend to a right to be personally present in court as opposed to being legally represented there: *R* v. *Governor of Brixton Prison ex p. Walsh* [1985] A.C. 154; but if authorities do exercise statutory discretion to produce prisoner in person they may claim from prisoner expenses of production incidentally to or consequentially upon the exercise of the power: *Becker* v. *Home Office* [1972] 2 Q.B. 407 (C.A.).

C. Threshold Jurisdictional Issues

A "threshold jurisdictional issue" may arise as follows. It may be either plain under a particular statute[25] or not disputed in a particular case that Parliament has made the existence of a certain state of affairs a condition precedent to the existence of jurisdiction in an authority. Here, then, the statute in effect provides that if the prescribed state of affairs exists, but not otherwise, the authority (*e.g.* a court or tribunal) shall have jurisdiction to decide an issue of law, fact or degree and take appropriate action. It may nevertheless be disputed in such a case whether or not the state of affairs exists. Such a dispute we label a threshold jurisdictional issue. The threshold is crossed if the condition precedent is fulfilled. Beyond the threshold the authority had jurisdiction to consider the case[26]; but the threshold issue is, precisely, whether the threshold has been crossed—whether the authority may enter upon jurisdiction and embark on the consideration of the case. We are supposing a case where it is not disputed that the authority's jurisdiction exists only *if* a prescribed state of affairs exists. It follows that the jurisdiction does not extend to deciding *whether* that state of affairs exists. As already observed, if an authority asserts jurisdiction where it has none, or declines a jurisdiction which it has a duty to assume, it by definition acts (or decides not to act) "without jurisdiction." Accordingly, the authority is subject to correction by the High Court in the exercise of its supervisory review jurisdiction or by any court before which the issue may be raised by way of collateral challenge.

We should at once make the obvious point that on every occasion on which an authority assumes jurisdiction (*i.e.* embarks on the consideration of a case) it expressly or impliedly asserts that any conditions precedent to its doing so are fulfilled. This obviously necessary assertion will in most cases be patently correct and so unassailable. When we say that the authority's jurisdiction does not extend to deciding whether a condition precedent is fulfilled we mean that in cases where the assertion that it is fulfilled is questionable, the authority's ruling may be reversed by a court

[25] See, *e.g.* Magistrates' Courts Act 1980, s.127(1): " . . . *a magistrates' court shall not try an information* . . . *unless* the information was laid . . . within 6 months from the time when the offence was committed" (emphasis added): what counts as laying information treated as threshold jurisdictional issue in *Hill* v. *Anderton* (see text to note 30 below).

[26] How far that jurisdiction extends is, of course, another matter—considered below, p. 136 *et seq*.

exercising supervisory review jurisdiction.[27] For, as explained above, the ruling relates to a question—the extent of the authority's jurisdiction—which (we are supposing) the authority accepts it has no jurisdiction authoritatively to resolve.

We now take some case law examples of "threshold" issues. The prescribed condition precedent to the authority's jurisdiction may relate, for example, to the territorial limits of the jurisdiction, to the persons falling under the jurisdiction or to other circumstances governing the existence of jurisdiction. Territorial limits were in issue where the father of Helen Smith, an English nurse who died in obscure circumstances in Saudi Arabia, applied for judicial review of the West Yorkshire coroner's refusal to hold an inquest even though the body had been brought within the coroner's district.[28] Statute required the coroner to hold an inquest "whether the cause of death arose within his jurisdiction or not." Quashing the coroner's refusal, the Divisional Court held by a majority that those words contemplated cases of death both within and outside the jurisdiction of the English courts. In *Re Daley*[29] the issue was whether or not magistrates had jurisdiction to proceed to summary trial of a young person without allowing him to elect between summary and jury trial. The accused attained the age of 17 (and so became entitled to elect) after he had first appeared before the court but before the occasion when the election issue fell to be considered. Quashing the magistrates' refusal to allow the election, the House of Lords held that the statutory provision as to the accused's age when he "appeared" referred to the appearance at which the election issue was considered.

Reported cases raising what we have labelled threshold jurisdictional issues are legion: statute provides that a magistrates' court shall not try an information unless it has been laid within six months of the alleged offence. The House of Lords held that an information had been "laid" if delivered in time to the office of the magistrates' clerk even though not considered by the clerk or magistrates within the six-month period.[30] Under statute a county

[27] See the observations of Devlin J. in *R.* v. *Fulham Rent Tribunal ex p. Zerek* [1951] 2 K.B. 1 at 10–11. As to the exercise of supervisory jurisdiction in cases of this sort, Devlin J. observed (*ibid.*): "Where the question of jurisdiction turns solely on a disputed point of law, it is obviously convenient that the court should determine it then and there. Where, however, the dispute turns on a question of fact, about which there is a conflict of evidence, the court will generally decline to interfere."

[28] *R.* v. *W. Yorks. Coroner ex p. Smith* [1982] 3 W.L.R. 920.

[29] [1983] A.C. 347.

[30] *Hill* v. *Anderton* [1983] A.C. 328.

court judge must hear an appeal from any "order or decision" of a registrar. The Divisional Court quashed a judge's refusal to entertain an appeal from a registrar's refusal of a certificate under the special divorce procedure: the registrar's refusal was in substance an interlocutory order from which, accordingly, an appeal lay.[31] Prison visitors inquiring into a charge of serious misconduct by a prisoner have no jurisdiction to entertain a lesser charge if that has not been specifically laid.[32]

It must be emphasised that in none of these cases was it argued that the court or tribunal subject to the challenge had jurisdiction to decide the issue at stake. It is on that basis that the issue may be characterised as a "threshold" issue; for it is accepted, as we said, that statute, by prescribing circumstances in which jurisdiction exists, has imposed a condition precedent to its existence—a threshold which must be crossed before jurisdiction exists. As will appear in the next section, however, there are many circumstances where (a) statute provides in effect that an authority may or must act in a particular way *if* certain criteria are fulfilled; but (b) it is disputed whether or not the authority has jurisdiction to determine *whether* the criteria are fulfilled.

D. Substantive Jurisdictional Issues

(1) Jurisdictional error

In our example[33] of the state benefit payable to a "member of the family" of a particular individual we supposed that Y who had lived with X for ten years as his wife (although not married to him) claimed benefit as a member of the family of X. If the benefit authority reject Y's claim, holding that she is not a member of X's family, is there any basis upon which Y can assert that the authority has gone outside its jurisdiction?

There is no doubt that the authority is properly seised of the issue of Y's entitlement to benefit. No threshold jurisdictional issue arises. The threshold having been crossed, the issue is as to the substance or extent of a jurisdiction which falls to be exercised: hence our label "substantive jurisdictional issue." The authority must pay benefit to Y *if* she is a member of X's family; but it claims jurisdiction to decide *whether* or not she is. The question is

[31] *R.* v. *Nottingham County Court ex p. Byers* [1985] 1 W.L.R. 403.
[32] *R.* v. *Board of Visitors of Dartmoor Prison ex p. Smith* [1986] 2 All E.R. 651.
[33] See Chap. 1, p. 25.

whether, from the proposition that the authority is properly seised of the issue, it follows that the authority has jurisdiction to decide every question which may need to be resolved before the issue can be disposed of.

We may repeat here the obvious point made with regard to threshold issues. The benefit issue in our example cannot be disposed of unless it is settled whether or not Y is a member of X's family. It follows that the authority must make a pronouncement on that question. But it does not follow that no matter how wrong that pronouncement may be, the authority remains within the confines of its jurisdiction.[34] The English courts have consistently taken the view that, even where a statutory authority is properly seised of an issue, certain errors will carry the authority outside its jurisdiction—*i.e.* that the authority's power to err is limited. An obvious difficulty thus arises.

If it were held that every error carried an authority outside its jurisdiction it would follow that the authority had no jurisdiction to *decide* anything. For to *decide* is to choose between alternatives. If a person is entitled to make only that selection which another will endorse, he has no true power of choice: no power to *decide* the issue. Parliament plainly does not intend that the many authorities to which it has remitted issues of law, fact or degree should have no true power to decide, *i.e.* no power to err. So the question is: what errors do, and what do not carry an authority outside jurisdiction? In short, what counts as "jurisdictional error?"

In tackling the question "what counts as jurisdictional error?", the *Anisminic* case[35] is a "legal landmark."[36] To understand its impact we must first refer to the law as it was prior to *Anisminic*.

(2) Before Anisminic

Before *Anisminic* the courts solved the jurisdictional error problem very much on a case by case basis. It was difficult or impossible to extract from the reported cases criteria which one could apply with any certainty to solve later cases as they arose. By way of

[34] According to what has been labelled the "pure" theory of jurisdiction (expounded principally by D. M. Gordon in (1929) 45 L.Q.R. 459 and elsewhere) an authority can never be said to have gone outside its jurisdiction by erring in its determination of an issue of law or fact of which it is properly seised. The theory is much discussed in the textbooks (*e.g.* de Smith J.R.A.A., pp. 108–113 finds it "coherent"; Wade A.L., pp. 267–270; "not so much pure as simple") all of which agree that it does not represent English Law.

[35] *Anisminic Ltd.* v. *Foreign Compensation Commission* [1969] 2 A.C. 147: see above, Chap. 2, pp. 49, 59.

[36] *Per* Lord Diplock in *Re Racal Communications Ltd.* [1981] A.C. 374 at 382.

illustration we may take a number of reported cases of the pre-*Anisminic* era.

An Act of 1836[37] empowered commissioners to order payment of a lump sum in lieu of tithe, but excluded from its provisions "lands [whose] tithes have been already commuted." In *Bunbury* v. *Fuller*[38] P sued to recover from D a sum awarded by the Commissioners. D maintained that the tithes in question had been already commuted and that the Commissioners' contrary decision was wrong and carried them outside jurisdiction. The court found for P on the basis that the tithes had not been already commuted; but held that, as D had argued, the question whether or not they had been commuted was not a question for the Commissioners. That question was "collateral to the merits of the case."[39] Now, of course, to label an issue "collateral"[40] is merely to assert that the authority has no jurisdiction to decide it; it does not explain why. What, then, was the test or criterion of what was and was not a "collateral" issue?

In *R.* v. *Lincolnshire Justices ex p. Brett*[41] B failed in his application for certiorari to quash a paternity order made against him by magistrates. The statute authorised an order to be made only "if the evidence of the mother be corroborated . . . " In the Court of Appeal Warrington L.J. said:

> "It seems to me plain that one of the things [the justices] had to decide, in hearing the complaint was whether the evidence of the mother was corroborated . . . . Therefore it cannot be said that the existence of corroborative evidence was a collateral matter."[42]

The test offered here, then, is whether the issue had necessarily to be decided: if so, it could not be collateral. But under this test, neither would the commutation issue in *Bunbury* v. *Fuller* have been collateral. Nor would the issues which were held in effect to be collateral in *R.* v. *Bradford*[43] and in *White and Collins* v. *Minis-*

37 Commutation of Tithes Act.
38 (1853) 156 E.R. 47.
39 *Ibid.* p. 60.
40 The term "collateral" is used here in a quite different sense from its use in the phrase "collateral challenge" (see Chap. 2, p. 29). Here it means in effect "outside jurisdiction"; there, "incidental"—*i.e.* incidental to the remit issue.
41 [1926] 2 K.B. 192.
42 *Ibid.* p. 201.
43 [1908] 1 K.B. 365.

ter of Health.[44] In both cases statute authorised certain public use of private land other than "park" land. In *White and Collins* Luxmoore L.J. regarded it as:

> "almost self-evident that the Court which has to consider whether there is jurisdiction to make . . . the [compulsory purchase order] must be entitled to review the vital finding on which the existence of the jurisdiction relied upon depends."[45]

In *Bradford*, Channell J. characterised the park issue as "a preliminary question which arises before [the justices] begin to exercise, their jurisdiction."[46] Under the *Brett* test, however, the question "park or no?" (being one which it was necessary to resolve) would not be collateral.

Then, contrast the approach in the "park" cases with that of the Privy Council in *Colonial Bank of Australia* v. *Willan*[47] where the statutory Court of Mines had ordered the winding-up of a company on the petition of a creditor. The company challenged the validity of the order on the basis that the winding-up jurisdiction could be exercised only in favour of a "creditor to whom [the Company] is indebted in a sum exceeding £50" and that the existence of the debt (which the company contested) was a collateral issue. Rejecting the challenge, the Privy Council observed that the existence of the debt was "essential to the order"[48] and fell to be decided by the judge. "Essential," however, seems hardly different from "vital," the *White and Collins* criterion of what counts as a collateral issue. And is it at all clear that the park issue in *Bradford* was "preliminary" in a sense in which the debt issue in *Willan* or the corroboration issue in *Brett* were not?

The truth is that on the question of what matters fall within, and what outside an authority's jurisdiction, many[49] statutes are inscrutable. Judicial rulings based on criteria as elusive as those referred to above are both impressionistic and calculated to pro-

[44] [1939] 2 K.B. 838.
[45] *Ibid*. p. 855.
[46] [1908] 1 K.B. at 371.
[47] (1874) L.R. 5 P.C. 417.
[48] *Ibid*. p. 446.
[49] Many—but not all: in a particular statutory context a matter may be regarded as unarguably a "threshold" issue (see above, p. 134).

duce inconsistent authorities. Such rulings serve only to obscure the fact that in reality Parliament has not anticipated the jurisdictional issue which has arisen and has provided no criteria for its resolution. A signal contribution of the judicial approach initiated in *Anisminic* is that it recognises and caters for this fact of legislative life.

(3) Anisminic and after

It appears that since *Anisminic*, any error of law by an administrative tribunal or authority (as distinct, perhaps, from a court of law[50]) is prima facie jurisdictional. Issues of fact, degree or policy, on the contrary, are for the authority to decide.

This statement is based substantially on *obiter dicta* of Lord Diplock in *Re Racal Communications Ltd.*[51] decided 12 years after *Anisminic*. Lord Diplock said:

> "The breakthrough made by *Anisminic* was that, as respects administrative tribunals and authorities, the old distinction between errors of law that went to jurisdiction and errors of law that did not was for practical purposes abolished. Any error of law that could be shown to have been made by them in the course of reaching their decision on matters of fact or of administrative policy would result in their having asked themselves the wrong question with the result that the decision they reached would be a nullity."

As we shall see, these dicta take account of case law development since *Anisminic*; and their thrust was substantially endorsed by a unanimous House of Lords in *O'Reilly* v. *Mackman*.[52] In this section we shall see how *Anisminic* began this new judicial approach to what counts as jurisdictional error and how later cases have built on the *Anisminic* foundation; also we shall consider whether the development is a satisfactory one. We turn first to the case itself.

(a) *The Anisminic case*

It will be recalled[53] that Anisminic Ltd. claimed compensation for loss of property sequestrated during the Suez crisis by the Egyptian government and sold on to a government agency

[50] For separate considerations relating to courts of law, see sub-section (c) below.
[51] [1981] A.C. 374 at 383.
[52] [1983] 2 A.C. 237 at 278, 286 (for this case, see Chap. 7).
[53] See Chap. 2, p. 49.

(T.E.D.O.). Under the relevant statutory instrument the Foreign Compensation Commission (F.C.C.)[54] were directed to treat a claim as established if the claimant satisfied them that, *inter alia*, both he and any "successor in title" of his were British nationals. F.C.C. interpreted "successor in title" to mean "subsequent owner" or "assignee." On that basis T.E.D.O. was A Ltd.'s successor in title: it was not a British national, so A Ltd's claim failed. A majority (3:2) of the House of Lords held, on the contrary, that "successor in title" meant "person succeeding to property on death or (in the case of a company) liquidation." On that basis A Ltd had no successor in title, and T.E.D.O.'s nationality was immaterial. F.C.C. had, accordingly, erred in its construction of the statutory instrument. The majority of the House held that that error was jurisdictional: why?

The statutory instrument directed F.C.C. to award compensation if they were satisfied that prescribed conditions, including one relating to the nationality of the applicant and any successor in title, were fulfilled. Clearly the question whether the conditions were fulfilled was remitted to F.C.C. So under the pre-*Anisminic* approach[55] to jurisdictional error, the court could hardly have characterised the issue as "collateral," *i.e.* outside F.C.C.'s jurisdiction. But the crux of the new approach adopted in *Anisminic* is a shift of focus from the substance of an issue as being "collateral" or otherwise to the juridical nature of an issue as being onc of law or otherwise. Accept that it is for F.C.C. to say whether the prescribed conditions are fulfilled. That issue is within their remit. But it does not follow that F.C.C. has jurisdiction to interpret authoritatively the statutory words prescribing the conditions—*i.e.* to construe the relevant statutory instrument. The majority in *Anisminic* held that F.C.C.'s remit did not extend to authoritative determination of the meaning of the statutory conditions of entitlement. F.C.C.'s erroneous construction of the "successor in title" condition thus carried them outside their jurisdiction. The Commission "failed to deal with the question remitted to it and decided some question which was not remitted to it."[56]

It may be plain from what has just been said that the *Anisminic* case establishes that certain errors of law of our "second-stage" type[57] are jurisdictional. For the error in the case was plainly of

[54] Established by Foreign Compensation Act 1950, s.1.
[55] See above, p. 137.
[56] [1969] 2 A.C. at 171, *per* Lord Reid.
[57] See Chap. 3, p. 93.

that type: an erroneous elucidation of the phrase "successor in title." But one will look in vain in the judgments in *Anisminic* for any general proposition that error of law as such prima facie carries an administrative tribunal outside its jurisdiction.[58] As already intimated however, the case law has advanced considerably since *Anisminic*. The signal contribution of that case appears in retrospect to have been, as Lord Diplock said in *O'Reilly* v. *Mackman*,[59] that it

> "liberated English public law from the fetters that the courts had theretofore imposed on themselves . . . by drawing esoteric distinctions between errors of law committed by such tribunals that went to their jurisdiction, and errors of law committed by them within their jurisdiction."

But it is only by examination of reported cases since *Anisminic* that we can see how it may now be suggested that all errors of law prima facie carry a public authority outside its jurisdiction. We shall consider the cases under our three-stage classification of errors of law at the fact-finding stage, errors of elucidation and errors in applying law to facts. Before turning to the cases, however, we should highlight two points of importance.

First, an alternative way of stating the proposition that generally speaking any error of law will carry a public authority outside its jurisdiction is to say that generally speaking a public authority has no jurisdiction to decide issues of law. But this may seem strange in that, in the course of discharging their statutory functions, a vast number of public authorities are every day faced with issues of law. How can one say that they have no jurisdiction to decide

[58] Both Lords Reid (p. 174) and Pearce (p. 195) pointedly refrained from identifying jurisdictional error with error of law generally. And Lord Wilberforce (p. 209) eschewed "any necessary predisposition . . . that questions of law, or questions of construction, are necessarily for the courts" (although, with Lord Pearson (p. 215) he agreed with Lords Reid and Pearce that any error in construing the relevant provisions of the statutory instrument in the case would go to jurisdiction—only Lord Morris dissented on this point). But by 1981 Lord Wilberforce was able to refer to the "well-known principle [that] there [may be] no appeal to a court against . . . a decision [of an administrative authority] but it may be subject to 'judicial review' for error in law including no doubt absence of any material on which the decision could reasonably be reached" *Din* v. *London Borough of Wandsworth* [1983] 1 A.C. 657, (see below p. 145).

[59] [1983] 2 A.C. 237 at 278.

these issues? We must recall our earlier discussion of the notion of *deciding*.[60] We pointed out that an authority will have to pronounce upon many issues which arise in the course of disposing of a matter of which it is properly seised, but that it does not follow that its pronouncements on all such matters are to be regarded as authoritative when challenged. Plainly, if an authority errs in law but its decision is not challenged it is idle to maintain that the authority's decision is outside jurisdiction, and so "void" or a "nullity", on the basis that, had it been challenged, a court would have treated it as such.[61] On the other hand, our proposition that an error of law carries an authority outside jurisdiction does mean that if the authority errs in law it exposes itself to supervisory review on the basis that it has gone outside jurisdiction.

Our second point is to recall that the proposition is that all errors of law prima facie carry an authority outside jurisdiction, and to focus on the phrase "prima facie." This phrase indicates that we are dealing with a rebuttable presumption rather than a rule of law. The constitutional basis of supervisory review is the jurisdiction of the courts to interpret the legislative enactments of a sovereign Parliament.[62] There is no legal limit to the extent of power to decide and to act which Parliament may choose to confer on a particular statutory authority.[63] For the courts to state as a rule of law that certain types of statutory authority have no power to decide issues of law, would be to ignore this constitutional axiom. The most the courts may properly do is, so to speak, to indicate to Parliament that they will make certain presumptions about the scope of the powers of statutory authorities: presumptions which, by their very nature, can be rebutted if Parliament shows clearly that it intends to do so. To quote Lord Diplock again:

> "Parliament can, of course, if it so desires, confer on administrative tribunals or authorities power to decide questions of law as well as questions of fact or of administrative policy; but this requires clear words, for the presumption is that where a

[60] See above, p. 137.
[61] *cf.* Chap. 2, p. 62 (void/voidable).
[62] See Chaps. 1 and 2, pp. 5, 37.
[63] "Although in theory perhaps, it may be possible for Parliament to set up a tribunal which has full and autonomous powers to fix its own area of operation, that has, so far, not been done in this country" *per* Lord Wilberforce in *Anisminic* at p. 207. But *cf.* now Interception of Communications Act 1985, s.7(8) providing that the decisions of the tribunal established by the Act, "including any decisions as to their jurisdiction" shall not be liable to be questioned in any court.

decision-making power is conferred on a tribunal or authority that is not a court of law, Parliament did not intend to do so."[64]

We shall consider later how faithfully the courts have responded to statutory indications that the presumption is not to apply; and also whether it is constitutionally proper for the courts to have adopted the presumption at all. Now we turn to examine the post-*Anisminic* case law on administrative tribunals and authorities ((b) below) and on courts of law ((c) below).

(b) *Administrative tribunals and authorities*

The post-*Anisminic* case law relates largely to errors of law at our second and third stages, *i.e.* misstatements and misapplications of legal rules. Accordingly, we deal first with errors of these types and postpone until last consideration of whether errors of law at the fact-finding stage may be held to be jurisdictional errors.

(i) *Misstating the law.* An authority errs in law if it errs in its statement of a rule or its elucidation of a statutory word or phrase.[65] Will the error be jurisdictional? An authority will commonly elucidate (*i.e.*, indicate its understanding of the meaning of) statutory words by addressing itself to certain questions which appear to it to require answers if the rule is to be applied to the facts before it. So, *e.g.*, in the *Anisminic* case F.C.C. decided that "as T.E.D.O. was not a British national and as T.E.D.O. was the 'successor in title' or assignee of the appellants [the claim failed]."[66] F.C.C. had asked themselves whether T.E.D.O. was the assignee of the company on the basis that "successor in title" meant "assignee." This, then, was the error of elucidation which, as the majority of the House of Lords held, caused F.C.C. to ask

[64] *Re Racal* [1981] A.C. 374. It will be recalled (see Chap. 2., p. 51) that in its response to *Anisminic* Parliament did use clear words to rebut the presumption, enacting that, for the future, F.C.C. should "have power to determine any question as to the construction or interpretation of any provision of an Order in Council [under the 1950 Act]" (Foreign Compensation Act 1969, s.3(1)). But Parliament also provided an appeal on questions of law to the Court of Appeal (*ibid.* s.3(2)).

[65] See Chap. 3, p. 100 *et seq.*

[66] [1969] 2 A.C. at 179 *per* Lord Morris.

themselves the wrong question and carried them outside jurisdiction. Since *Anisminic*, and despite Lord Wilberforce's reservations in that case,[67] the courts appear to have proceeded, often *sub silentio*,[68] on the basis that if an authority errs in law by asking the wrong question, the authority goes outside jurisdiction.

Among the reported cases germane to this point since *Anisminic* are a number concerning the interpretation of the "intentionally homeless" provisions of the Housing (Homeless Persons) Act 1977, two of which reached the House of Lords. In one, *Din* v. *Wandsworth London Borough Council*,[69] the House held, by a majority, that the local authority had correctly construed the statute. However, the case proceeds on the basis that error of construction would have carried it outside its jurisdiction and contains an apparent acknowledgment by Lord Wilberforce that "error of law" is indeed now the basis of supervisory review for jurisdictional error.[70] In *Islam* v. *Hillingdon L.B.C.*[71] the applicant had been evicted from one-room rented accommodation when he was joined by his wife and children from Bangladesh. The local authority decided that he had become homeless intentionally "having deliberately arranged for his wife and children to leave accommodation [in Bangladesh] which it would have been reasonable for them to continue to occupy."[72] The statute, however, referred to "accommodation . . . which it would have been reasonable for [the applicant] to continue to occupy"[73]: so the authority had asked itself the wrong question; and on this basis alone the House would have quashed the decision.[74]

[67] See note 58 above.

[68] See, *e.g.* *Woodling* v. *Secretary of State* [1984] 1 W.L.R. 348 (H.L.); *Cinzano U.K. Ltd.* v. *Customs and Excise Cmrs.* [1985] 1 W.L.R. 484. Second-stage errors will commonly appear on the face of the record. It may thus be unnecessary for a court to specify whether the error is subject to correction because it goes to jurisdiction or, rather, because it is patent: see further section (E) below.

[69] [1983] 1 A.C. 657.

[70] See note 58 above.

[71] [1983] 1 A.C. 688.

[72] *Ibid.* p. 710.

[73] 1977 Act, s.16.

[74] See *per* Lord Lowry, *loc. cit.* at p. 715. Admittedly, the error of construction appeared on the face of the record; but, as we shall see, the House asserted jurisdiction to review a further (third-stage) error which did not (see p. 717). *Islam* thus seems to be authority for treating error of law as jurisdictional. See too *R.* v. *Reigate etc. B.C. ex p. Paris* [1984] *The Times* July 19; *R.* v. *Ealing L.B.C., ex p. McBain* [1986] 1 All E.R. 13 (error of construction appeared from affidavit—*i.e.*, not on face of record).

In similar vein, the Court of Appeal quashed an immigration officer's refusal of entry clearance to a would-be student on the basis that if an authority errs in law by asking itself the wrong question it goes outside jurisdiction. In *R.* v. *Chief Immigration Officer ex p. Kharrazi*[75] K had been refused leave to enter the U.K. because an immigration officer was not satisfied (as the rules[76] required him to be) that K intended to leave the country on completion of "a full-time course of study." To a majority of the Court of Appeal it appeared from the officer's affidavit that he had interpreted that phrase to mean a specific course for which definite arrangements had been made. K had arranged for a three year "O" level course but hoped to remain in the U.K. for "A" level and, perhaps, undergraduate study. The court held that "a full-time course of study" should be more broadly interpreted to comprehend a coherent plan of the kind entertained by K. The officer's decision was quashed because, having asked himself the wrong question, he had gone outside his jurisdiction.[77]

Finally we may recall *Shah* v. *Barnet L.B.C.*[78] We saw earlier that local authorities were held to have erred in law in their construction of the phrase "ordinarily resident" in a statute relating to student grants. Lord Scarman, delivering the substantial judgment of the House, took only a few sentences to indicate that if such an authority fails to direct itself properly in law—fails to ask the right questions—it goes outside its jurisdiction.[79]

As already observed, *Anisminic* itself was a case where an error of law of the type we are considering was characterised by the House of Lords as jurisdictional. After *Anisminic* it seemed probable that such errors, at any rate when perpetrated by an administrative tribunal or authority, and subject to specific contrary indications in particular statutes, would be held to be jurisdic-

[75] [1980] 1 W.L.R. 1396.

[76] The rules are not statutory (see de Smith J.R.A.A., pp. 75–76). But they are "parastatutory" and it appears that immigration authorities' decisions under them can be reviewed by the courts on the normal principles—see *per* Lord Wilberforce in *Zamir* v. *Home Secretary* [1980] A.C. 930 at 947.

[77] *Ibid*. p. 1403 (Lord Denning M.R.) and p. 1408 (Dunn L.J.).

[78] [1983] 2 A.C. 309: see above Chap. 3, p. 105.

[79] *Ibid*. p. 350. Lord Scarman referred to *Associated Provincial Picture Houses Ltd.* v. *Wednesbury Corporation* [1948] 1 K.B. 223 rather than to *Anisminic* for this proposition. As we shall see in Chap. 5, the *Wednesbury* principle relates to error of law in the exercise of a discretion: such error carries an authority *ultra vires* or outside jurisdiction. Lord Scarman observed that the error in *Shah* related to a mandatory duty, thus making it "a stronger case for judicial review."

tional. The case law since *Anisminic* suggests strongly that this is the position.[80]

(ii) *Errors of law in applying law to facts.* To the extent that a particular authority's misstatements of law carry that authority outside jurisdiction,[81] to the same extent should its errors of law in applying law to facts do so. The reasoning is as follows. If the error of application is on a point where applying the law to the facts requires the skill of a trained lawyer[82] the error is error of law because the issue is purely one of law.[83] The error is as much by definition an error of law as is a misstatement of a rule of law. Accordingly, it would appear artificial to distinguish here between the effects of second-stage and third-stage error. In administrative law, though, as already explained,[84] the application of law to facts will commonly be a matter as much for a layman properly instructed on the law as for a lawyer. Here, as we have seen, the *Edwards* v. *Bairstow*[85] doctrine is gaining increasing judicial acceptance as the criterion for what counts as error of law.

We saw that in *Edwards* v. *Bairstow* Lord Radcliffe explained why reaching a conclusion which could not reasonably be drawn from the facts should be characterised as error of law. As appears from examples given earlier,[86] a tribunal may state the facts of a case with unexceptionable accuracy. It may state correctly (without venturing to elucidate) the relevant legal rule. Its conclusion,

[80] In *R.* v. *Deputy Governor of Camphill Prison ex p. King* [1985] Q.B. 735 a prison deputy governor was held by the Court of Appeal to have misconstrued a prison rule in convicting a prisoner of an offence, but the prisoner was held not entitled to judicial review. The court observed that the prisoner's proper recourse was to the Home Secretary (whose own decision might be subject to judicial review). This may be regarded as a case where review was sought against the wrong authority (see further, Chap. 9) rather than as a case where a statutory authority's misconstruction is immune from review. In *R.* v. *Sheffield Supplementary Benefits Appeal Tribunal ex p. Shine* [1975] 1 W.L.R. 624 the Court of Appeal refused certiorari even though the tribunal had misconstrued a statutory provision. The refusal was based on the discretionary nature of certiorari (see below Chap. 8) but the court did indicate (see p. 632) that it did not regard the error as jurisdictional: it is submitted that this is weak authority against the existence of what we may label the *Anisminic* presumption because (a) the issue "jurisdictional or no?" was not argued, the application for certiorari being based on the appearance of the error on the face of the record; and (b) the case was decided before the presumption had passed into judicial currency after *Re Racal*.

[81] See immediately above.

[82] See Chap. 3, p. 110.

[83] *Ibid.*

[84] See Chap. 3, p. 113.

[85] [1956] A.C. 14.

[86] See Chap. 3, p. 117 *et seq.*

its application of rule to facts, may nevertheless be a conclusion which implies an interpretation of the rule which, had that interpretation been express, would have amounted to an error of elucidation. In these circumstances a court, as Lord Radcliffe said[87] "has no option but to assume that there has been some misconception of the law and that this has been responsible for the determination." There is, in short, an implied misinterpretation of the relevant legal rule. Here, then, second and third-stage error of law are identical in their juridical nature; they are distinct only in the manner of their detection. It would surely be artificial to distinguish between them as regards their liability to review. If a particular authority's second-stage error carries the authority outside jurisdiction, so should that authority's third-stage error.

In *Edwards* v. *Bairstow* itself the question for the House of Lords was "error of law or no?" There was statutory appellate jurisdiction to correct error of law, so that the case is of no authority on whether third-stage error of law is jurisdictional and thus subject to common law supervisory review jurisdiction. Nevertheless, since *Anisminic*, the courts have tended to characterise errors of law of the *Edwards* v. *Bairstow* type as jurisdictional errors when perpetrated by administrative tribunals and authorities. So, for example, Lord Bridge, summarising in *Cocks* v. *Thanet District Council*[88] the grounds for supervisory review, gave as one[89] "[reaching] a conclusion of fact which can be impugned on the principles set out in the speech of Lord Radcliffe in *Edwards* v. *Bairstow*."[90]

Before referring to some reported cases in which this approach appears actually to have been taken we may, to avoid confusion, dwell briefly on Lord Bridge's reference to reaching a conclusion of *fact*. Courts do sometimes characterise as matters of "fact" the whole range of findings which, under the *Edwards* v. *Bairstow* doctrine, it may fall to a statutory authority to make. This includes not only findings of "primary fact"[91] but also rulings that facts found do or do not fall within a relevant legal category.[92] We reiterate

[87] [1956] A.C. at 36.
[88] [1983] 2 A.C. 286 at 292.
[89] The other two being procedural impropriety—see Chap. 6; and "*Wednesbury*" unreasonableness—see Chap. 5.
[90] For similar references, see *O'Reilly* v. *Mackman* [1983] 2 A.C. 237 at 282 (*per* Lord Diplock); *R.* v. *Police Complaints Board ex p. Madden* [1983] 1 W.L.R. 447 at 467. (*Per* McNeill J.).
[91] See Chap. 3, p. 94.
[92] See, *e.g.* Lord Denning M.R. and Sachs L.J. in *Coleen Properties Ltd.* v. *M.H.L.G.* [1971] 1 W.L.R. 433 at 438, 439. (The case is considered below).

here the suggestion made earlier[93] that where (because of statutory open texture) particular facts are capable of falling either within or outside a particular legal category, the question "in or out?" should be characterised as one of "degree" rather than of "fact."

Turning to reported cases, *Islam* v. *Hillingdon London Borough Council*[94] is clear House of Lords authority for the application of the *Edwards* v. *Bairstow* doctrine to identify jurisdictional error of law in the application of law to facts. We saw[95] that the local authority had asked itself the wrong question. But the House of Lords went on to consider whether (even had the authority asked itself the right question) its conclusion that Islam was intentionally homeless could be sustained. Now, if a man lives in a single room from which he is evicted when joined by his wife and four children, there is plainly no basis for concluding that he has ceased to occupy "accommodation which is *available* for occupation both by him and by any other person who might reasonably be expected to reside with him" (a constituent of the statutory test[96] of intentional homelessness). Accordingly, as Lord Lowry said in *Islam*[97] a decision to the contrary is:

> "one in which, as Lord Radcliffe put it [in *Edwards* v. *Bairstow*] 'the true and only reasonable conclusion contradicts the determination,' which is another way of saying that there was *no* evidence to support the panel's decision and that it ought therefore to be reversed by judicial review and suitable declarations granted."[98]

The application of the *Edwards* v. *Bairstow* doctrine to identify jurisdictional error is further illustrated by a contrasting pair of Court of Appeal decisions on similar statutory provisions. In *Coleen Properties Ltd.* v. *Minister of Housing and Local Government*[99] a local authority had clearance powers over land adjoining a slum-clearance area if the acquisition of the adjoining land was "reasonably necessary for the satisfactory development or use of the cleared area." At a public inquiry the authority had simply asserted the necessity of the acquisition of particular adjoining

93 See Chap. 3, pp. 121–122.
94 [1983] 1 A.C. 688.
95 See above, p. 145.
96 Housing (Homeless Persons) Act 1977, s.16 (emphasis added).
97 [1983] 1 A.C. 688 at 717.
98 See also *R.* v. *Gloucs. City Council ex p. Miles* [1985] *The Times*, March 6.
99 [1971] 1 W.L.R. 433.

land whereas the owner of that land had led contrary expert opinion. The Minister confirmed the order against the inquiry inspector's recommendation. But the Court of Appeal quashed[1] the order because there was no material upon which the Minister could have come to his conclusion.

In *R.* v. *Environment Secretary ex p. Powis*[2] on the other hand, the Court of Appeal refused to quash the Secretary's ruling under a similar statutory provision that the acquisition of certain land was reasonably necessary[3] for the authority's purposes. The minister had considered material on the basis of which that conclusion could properly be reached.

(iii) *Error of law at the fact-finding stage.* If an authority finds that particular events occurred, although it is seised of no admissible evidence that they did in fact occur, the authority errs in law.[4] But is the error jurisdictional? In 1922 in *R.* v. *Nat Bell Liquors Ltd.*[5] Lord Sumner was emphatic that it was not: "To say that there is no jurisdiction to convict without evidence is the same thing as saying that there is jurisdiction if the decision is right, and none if it is wrong . . . "[6] But this view, oft-cited as it is and authoritative as it appears, must now be treated with reserve. First, Lord Sumner's statement is clearly not necessarily true. Convicting "without evidence" is not the only way in which the decision may be "wrong": it may be wrong because, *e.g.*, it proceeds on findings of fact which are erroneous, albeit based on some evidence. It is true that such a decision, although wrong, would not commonly[7] carry an authority outside jurisdiction. But it does not follow that the same is true where findings are based on no evidence whatever. Secondly, not only was Lord Sumner's dictum strictly obiter (there was admissible evidence in the case[8]) but *Nat Bell* was a Privy Council case, and in a later Court of Appeal decision the jurisdictional issue was treated as not having been

[1] The court's jurisdiction arose under a "statutory *ultra vires*" provision (see Chap. 2, p. 56): "not within the powers of this Act." But the applicable principles seem the same as for common law *ultra vires* or jurisdictional error—see *ex p. Powis* (next note). See too *Ashbridge Investments Ltd.* v. *M.H.L.G.* [1965] 1 W.L.R. 1320, in which at p. 1326 Lord Denning M.R. anticipated the post-*Anisminic* equation of jurisdictional error and error of law.

[2] [1981] 1 W.L.R. 584.

[3] The statutory word was "requisite"; but the court interpreted that as meaning "reasonably necessary" (p. 592).

[4] See Chap. 3, pp. 98–99.

[5] [1922] 2 A.C. 128 (P.C.).

[6] *Ibid.* p. 152.

[7] *cf. Khawaja's* case, see below note 12.

[8] [1922] 2 A.C. at 144–145.

settled.[9] Moreover, in 1922 there was no doctrine that errors of law as such were prima facie jurisdictional. As we have just seen, there is now substantial authority for this proposition as it relates to errors of law of our second and third-stage types. The courts have referred generally to "errors of law," and there is no obvious reason why errors of law at the fact-finding stage should not be included. Indeed, there is one class of case where it is well-established that an authority which in effect finds facts on no admissible evidence thereby goes outside its jurisdiction. That is where a criminal conviction is secured by fraud or perjury and the review court is satisfied that the trial court would have acquitted but for the fraud or perjury—which thus "eliminate[s] the only admissible evidence pointing to guilt."[10]

Whatever may be the effect of a finding of fact based on no admissible evidence, it seems clear that other findings of fact, though erroneous, will in general be held to fall within an authority's jurisdiction.[11] But in *Khawaja* v. *Home Secretary*[12] the House of Lords, overruling an earlier decision of its own,[13] created an exception to this proposition. Where the freedom of the individual is concerned, the courts will not readily construe a statute to have empowered an administrative authority to find facts on which the power to restrict that freedom depends. Subject to clear contrary wording in the statute, the courts will tend to regard the existence of the requisite facts as a condition precedent to the exercise of the power and to ask whether, on a balance of probabilities, the evidence shows that the condition precedent exists. In *Khawaja* the House quashed a Home Office determination that an individual was an illegal entrant to the U.K. when it appeared that the evidence failed to prove that (as the Home Office asserted) he was guilty of deception.[14] The *Khawaja* exception to the general reluctance of review courts to re-open issues of fact may or may

[9] In *ex p. Brett* [1926] 2 K.B. 192 (see text to note 41, above) Bankes L.J. expressly left the point open: pp. 199–200. Atkin L.J.'s approach (p. 201) seems nearer to Lord Sumner's.

[10] *Per* Watkins L.J. in *R* v. *Knightsbridge Crown Court ex p. Goonatilleke* [1985] 3 W.L.R. 553 at 561 referring to a line of authority stemming from *R.* v. *Gillyard* (1848) 12 Q.B. 527. See also *R.* v. *Kingston upon Thames JJ. ex p. Khanna* [1985] *The Times* November 21: conviction quashed because based solely on inadmissible evidence; (inadmissibility appeared only after the trial).

[11] See above, p. 140 *et seq.*

[12] [1984] A.C. 74.

[13] *Zamir* v. *Home Secretary* [1980] A.C. 930.

[14] See also *Ali* v. *Home Secretary* [1984] 1 W.L.R. 663; but *cf. R.* v. *Home Secretary ex p. Bugdaycay* [1986] 1 All E.R. 458 (court has no jurisdiction to investigate refugee status and entitlement to asylum).

not be justifiable on the basis that the freedom of the individual is at stake. However, judicial review is generally not an appropriate procedure for the trial of issues of fact[15] and "[i]t is for consideration whether it would not be more sensible and more efficient to arrange that [cases of the *Khawaja* type] be heard by specialist adjudicators."[16]

(c) *Courts of law*

We turn now to consider how far the *Anisminic* approach to jurisdictional error may be said to apply to courts of law as distinct from administrative tribunals and authorities. We must first distinguish between superior and inferior courts; for only the latter are subject to supervisory review.

(i) *Superior courts.* To classify an error as jurisdictional is to assert that it is a ground for supervisory review. Decisions of the High Court and of certain other courts, likewise denominated "superior" courts, were never and are not today subject to supervisory review. It follows that such courts cannot be said to be guilty of jurisdictional error.[17]

Supervisory review jurisdiction in essentially its modern form has been vested in the High Court (or its predecessor, the Court of King's Bench) since the seventeenth century. Being a jurisdiction *of* the High Court, it cannot be exercised *over* that court: High Court judges have, for obvious reasons, never sought to exercise the jurisdiction over their brethren; nor over the courts above them in the judicial hierarchy. Moreover, the jurisdiction of those Courts (the Court of Appeal and the House of Lords) is almost entirely appellate, deriving (as all appellate jurisdiction does) wholly from statute. Accordingly, those courts are not only immune from the common law supervisory jurisdiction, but also possess no such jurisdiction[18]; although they do have appellate jurisdiction over judgments and orders of the High Court in its exercise of the supervisory jurisdiction. These basic jurisdictional principles were underscored by the House of Lords in *Re Racal Communications Ltd.*[19] There, the Director of Public Prosecutions

[15] See *per* Hodgson J. in *R.* v. *Home Secretary ex p. Addo* [1985] *The Times*, April 18.

[16] *Per* Donaldson M.R. in *Ali* (above note 14) at p. 666.

[17] *Re Racal Communications Ltd.* [1981] A.C. 374 (considered below).

[18] For the original jurisdiction of the Court of Appeal to hear renewed applications for leave to apply for judicial review, see Gordon, *Judicial Review: Law and Procedure* (1985) para. 7–16.

[19] [1981] A.C. 374.

had applied unsuccessfully to a High Court judge for authority to inspect the books of a company in connection with criminal proceedings. The statute[20] provided that the High Court judge's decision "shall not be appealable." Nevertheless, the Court of Appeal purported to reverse the decision, holding that the judge had erred in law and that the error was, on the *Anisminic* approach, jurisdictional. Since the "no appeal" clause did not oust supervisory review jurisdiction,[21] the Court of Appeal had jurisdiction to hear the challenge. The House of Lords unanimously and emphatically reversed the Court of Appeal holding, for the reasons given above, that the High Court was not subject to supervisory review and that the Court of Appeal's appellate jurisdiction was ousted by the "no appeal" clause.[22]

There are certain other courts which are not subject to supervisory review either because they are by statute denominated "superior" courts, *e.g.* the Courts-Martial Appeal Court[23] and the Restrictive Practices Court[24]; or because their "constitution, jurisdiction and powers and . . . relationship with the High Court"[25] are such as to have led the High Court to disclaim supervisory jurisdiction over them, *e.g.* the Central Criminal Court.[26] The Crown Court also is a superior court[27] but is in certain circumstances subject by statute to supervisory review.[28] County courts, on the other

[20] Companies Act 1948, s.441. (See now Companies Act 1985, s.721).
[21] See Chap. 2, p. 47.
[22] Also by Judicature Act 1925, s.31(1)(*d*) (now Supreme Court Act 1981, s.18(1)(*c*)) providing that no appeal shall lie to the Court of Appeal from any High Court decision which by virtue of any statutory provision (however expressed) is final.
[23] Courts-Martial (Appeals) Act 1968, s.1(2).
[24] Restrictive Practices Court Act 1976, s.1(1).
[25] *Per* Goff L.J. in *R.* v. *Cripps ex p. Muldoon* [1984] Q.B. 68 at 87.
[26] *R.* v. *Central Criminal Court Justices ex p. L.C.C.* [1925] 2 K.B. 43. The Central Criminal Court was abolished by the Courts Act 1971; but the Act retained the name for the Crown Court sitting in London: s.4(7), (see now Supreme Court Act 1981, s.8(3)).
[27] Supreme Court Act 1981, s.45(1).
[28] *Ibid.* s.29(3) provides that "In relation to the jurisdiction of the Crown Court, other than its jurisdiction in matters relating to trial on indictment, the High Court shall have all such jurisdiction to make [the prerogative orders] as the High Court possesses in relation to . . . an inferior court." (See also s.28(2): no appeal by way of case stated to High Court from Crown Court judgment or decision relating, to trial on indictment). On what matters "relate to trial on indictment," see *Re Smalley* [1985] A.C. 622. A "helpful pointer" is whether they "affect the conduct of the trial" (*per* Lord Bridge at pp. 643–644). So (as held in the case) a Crown Court order to estreat (*i.e.* forfeit) a bail recognisance, and, probably, a legal aid contribution order, do not relate to trial on indictment. An order as to costs or as to the composition of a jury or a witness summons (*ex p. Rees* [1986] *The Times*, May 7) does so relate.

hand, are for most purposes inferior courts and therefore, like magistrates' courts, subject to the supervisory jurisdiction.[29] But in the exercise of certain specific powers conferred upon them by statute they have been treated as superior courts and therefore immune from supervisory review.[30] There are some courts (such as local election courts) whose status is not entirely clear. In these circumstances, as the Divisional Court has observed:[31]

> "it is difficult to extract [from the cases] any precise principle. The most that can be said is that it is necessary to look at all the relevant features of the tribunal in question . . . to decide whether [it] should properly be regarded as inferior to the High Court, so that its activities may appropriately be the subject of judicial review[32] by the High Court."

The distinction between superior and inferior courts is in most situations, at any rate, easily made. We turn now to consider how far the *Anisminic* approach to jurisdictional error applies to inferior courts.

(ii) *Inferior courts.* In *Re Racal*[33] Lord Diplock, having observed that since *Anisminic* any error of law by an administrative tribunal or authority is prima facie jurisdictional, asserted that the presumption did not extend to inferior courts: "what limits are imposed on the kinds of questions of law they are empowered to decide depends on the construction of the statute unencumbered by any such presumption."[34] This suggestion that the extent of supervisory review may be determined in part by a hard-and-fast distinction between inferior courts on the one hand and administrative tribunals and other administrative authorities on the other has attracted little support. Both its rationale and its workability have been questioned by learned authors[35]; and it was not endorsed in *Re Racal* by the three other law lords who delivered

[29] See County Courts Act 1984, ss.83, 84.

[30] *Skinner* v. *Northallerton County Court Judge* [1899] A.C. 439 (bankruptcy jurisdiction).

[31] *R.* v. *Cripps ex p. Muldoon* [1984] Q.B. 68 at 87: local election court held "inferior" for purposes of supervisory review. The Court of Appeal ([1984] Q.B. 686) upheld the Divisional Court on a different ground and found it unnecessary to consider the superior/inferior issue.

[32] *i.e.* supervisory review [footnote added].

[33] [1981] A.C. 374.

[34] *Ibid.* p. 383.

[35] Wade (1980) 96 L.Q.R. 492 at 494–497; Beatson [1984] Ox.Jo.Leg.Stud. 22 at 37–39; *cf.* Christie (1981) 131 N.L.J. 707 at 708.

reasoned speeches[36]; and it appears to have been abandoned by Lord Diplock himself in *O'Reilly* v. *Mackman*.[37] Indeed, the considerations which, as we shall see,[38] may be said to argue in favour of the adoption by the courts of the *Anisminic* approach to jurisdictional error do seem to apply no less, in general, to inferior courts than to administrative tribunals and authorities. However, there is a feature of Parliament's manner of providing for appeals from courts to higher courts which calls for separate consideration here.

The jurisdiction of courts of first instance tends to extend over wide and disparate fields: consider the multifarious issues within the jurisdictions of magistrates' courts and county courts, to say nothing of the High Court itself. Statutes commonly provide in quite general terms for appeals from the decisions of such courts but make the general provision subject to specific restrictions in the same or later statutes.[39] Accordingly, where in particular types of case Parliament wishes the decisions of such courts to be immune from appeal it must make specific provision to that effect. For administrative tribunals and authorities the position tends to be different. Their jurisdiction is usually highly specialised, and Parliament decides with specific reference to that jurisdiction whether or not to confer a right of appeal to the courts. If, then, there is in a particular case no appeal to the courts from an administrative tribunal or authority, the reason will commonly be that no appellate provision whatever has been made for appeals from that authority. If, by contrast, there is no appeal from a court to a higher court, the reason will commonly be that there is an express statutory restriction of a general appellate provision. This observation enables us now to identify a type of situation in which the *Anisminic* presumption that all errors of law are jurisdictional appears not to apply to inferior courts. But, as we shall see, this is

[36] Indeed, Lord Salmon at [1981] A.C., p. 386 bracketed together tribunals and inferior courts.

[37] [1983] 2 A.C. 237 at 278, bracketing together inferior courts and statutory tribunals. And see also *R.* v. *Greater Manchester Coroner ex p. Tal* [1984] 3 W.L.R. 643 (considered below).

[38] See below, p. 161 *et seq*.

[39] See, *e.g.* Magistrates' Courts Act 1980, s.111(1) conferring right of appeal by case stated on, *inter alia*, "any person who was a party to any proceedings before a magistrates' court"; County Courts Act 1984, s.77: "any party to any proceedings in a county court . . . may appeal . . . to the Court of Appeal"; Supreme Court Act 1981, s.16(1): appeal to Court of Appeal "from any judgment or order of the High Court." These provisions are all subject to exceptions in the statutes themselves or later statutes.

not because there is any fundamental difference for present purposes between inferior courts on the one hand and administrative tribunals and authorities on the other. Rather, it is because in the type of situation in question the *Anisminic* presumption is plainly rebutted by contrary statutory intention.

Suppose that, as in *Pearlman* v. *Keepers of Harrow School*,[40] a statute has conferred upon a county court jurisdiction in a particular matter but has provided expressly that the court's decision on that matter shall be "final." Without this "finality clause"[41] there would in *Pearlman* have been an appeal to the Court of Appeal on point of law (now[42] on both fact and law). But Parliament has quite explicitly withdrawn that right of appeal. In such a case it is hardly plausible for the High Court to exercise its supervisory jurisdiction on the basis of a presumption of statutory interpretation that all errors of law are jurisdictional. For, by explicitly withdrawing a statutory means of challenging all errors of law Parliament has surely indicated that it wishes to immunise at any rate some such errors from challenge. In the face of such clear indication it can hardly be proper for a court to apply the *Anisminic* presumption and to hold that all errors of law *ipso facto* carry the inferior court outside jurisdiction.

In *Pearlman* a majority of the Court of Appeal nevertheless did apply the presumption in these circumstances. A tenant of a house had installed gas-fired central heating. By statute the county court's decision was "final and conclusive" on whether this counted as a "structural alteration" for purposes of the Leasehold Reform Act 1967.[43] The county court ruled against the tenant who then applied to the High Court for leave to apply for judicial review of the ruling. The Court of Appeal, by a majority, allowed the tenant's appeal against the High Court's refusal to grant leave. The majority held that the county court judge's ruling was wrong in law and *ipso facto* carried him outside jurisdiction. But subsequently both the Privy Council in *South East Asia Fire Bricks* v.

[40] [1979] Q.B. 56.

[41] See Chap. 2, p. 47.

[42] County Courts Act 1984, s.77(1): *cf.* 1959 Act, ss.108, 109 which it replaced.

[43] The Act entitles long-leaseholders of houses below a specified rateable value to purchase the freehold. In order that such leaseholders would not refrain from making structural alterations or extensions (whose effect would be to raise the rateable value of the house and possibly to take it outside the 1967 Act limits) the Housing Act 1974 in effect provided that such increases in rateable value could be ignored for purposes of the 1967 Act.

Non-Metallic etc. Union[44] and the House of Lords in *Re Racal*[45] strongly disapproved the majority view in *Pearlman* and endorsed the dissent of Geoffrey Lane L.J. It appears, then, that where statute has expressly excluded a right of appeal on point of law which would otherwise have existed[46] it is not open to a court exercising supervisory review jurisdiction to apply the *Anisminic* presumption. In such a case, as Lord Diplock said in *Racal*, there may survive "those subtle distinctions formerly drawn between errors of law which go to jurisdiction and errors of law which do not."[47]

It may well be, however, that Lord Diplock's dicta on inferior courts in *Racal* are confined to the type of case just considered. For, take by contrast a case where there is no statutory ouster of a right of appeal from an inferior to a higher court or, equally, a case where there is simply no statutory provision for appeal. Here, surely, the *Anisminic* presumption may be applied with no less propriety[48] than in a similar situation involving an administrative tribunal or other authority. In both *R* v. *Surrey Coroner ex p. Campbell*[49] and *R* v. *Greater Manchester Coroner ex p. Tal*[50] the question arose whether the *Anisminic* approach should apply in considering an application for judicial review of a coroner's verdict from which there is no right of appeal as such.[51] In *Campbell* the Divisional Court, following Lord Diplock in *Racal*, held not.[52] But in *Tal* the same court (differently constituted), preferred Lord Diplock's later approach in *O'Reilly* v. *Mackman*, and, declining

44 [1981] A.C. 363.
45 [1981] A.C. 374.
46 As in *Pearlman*. In the *S.E. Asia Firebricks* case (previous note) the statute contained special provisions on the resolution of questions of law, making it plain that the inferior court had jurisdiction on certain matters of law. In both cases there was a "no certiorari" clause (see Ch. 2(B)(iii)), so the question of whether the alleged error of law went to the jurisdiction was crucial. In the *S.E. Asia* case the Privy Council held that an alleged error of law by the Industrial Court of Malaysia did not go to the jurisdiction.
47 [1981] A.C. at 383.
48 On this, see below, p. 158 *et seq*.
49 [1982] Q.B. 661.
50 [1985] Q.B. 67.
51 Coroner's Act 1887, s.6 confers on the High Court wide powers to quash a coroner's rulings on an application by or under authority of the Attorney-General but s.35 of the Act preserves the general common law supervisory jurisdiction of the court. The question in the two cases cited was, in effect, how far that jurisdiction extends.
52 Relatives of prisoner who died in custody held not entitled to challenge coroner's directions to jury as being erroneous in law.

to follow the earlier decision, held that the *Anisminic* presumption applied in principle as much to inferior courts as to tribunals.[53]

(d) *Constitutional considerations*

We have seen that recent case law suggests that where a question arises as to the extent of the statutory powers of an inferior court or administrative tribunal or authority, there is a rebuttable presumption (which we label "the *Anisminic* presumption") that such authorities are not intended by Parliament to have power to decide questions of law.[54] This means that where the presumption is not rebutted, error of law will carry such an authority outside jurisdiction and, on that basis, render its decision liable to supervisory review. If this correctly states the current law, that law is new law; and it is judge-made. Is this judicial law-making acceptable?

The United Kingdom constitution assigns to the superior courts the task of authoritatively interpreting statute. To the extent that the judges adopt clear and consistent canons of statutory interpretation, to a corresponding extent can Parliament be sure at the time it legislates of the effect which the courts will give to its legislation. In particular, the parliamentary draftsman will know what he must do to avoid (or ensure) the judicial application of a particular presumption of legislative intent in the interpretation of a particular statute. Of course, every time the superior courts adopt a new canon of statutory interpretation, such as the *Anisminic* presumption, they do so in the context of interpreting an existing statute. With regard to that and other statutes then in force the courts are, from the parliamentary draftsman's point of view, positioning the goal posts after the ball has been kicked. On the other hand, as changes occur in the political and social context in which Parliament legislates, the canons of statutory interpretation must also change; and, under current arrangements, the judges can change

[53] Relatives of two prisoners who died with a third prisoner in a prison cell fire held entitled to challenge coroner's directions to jury as being erroneous in law. But challenge failed because applicants held not to have shown that coroner had erred in law. The *Anisminic* presumption may, of course, be held not to apply in specific circumstances where a statutory provision has been construed to confer jurisdiction notwithstanding certain irregularities which may be characterised as errors of law. See, *e.g. R.* v. *Ipswich JJ. ex p. Edwards* (1979) 143 J.P. 699: for lawful committal of accused for trial on indictment, statute (Indictable Offences Act 1848, s.17, now replaced by Magistrates' Courts Act 1980, s.4 and rules made under *ibid.* s.144) requires only that justices take sworn depositions in prescribed manner. Accordingly, if these provisions are fulfilled, committal is lawful; and justices do not go outside jurisdiction by admitting inadmissible evidence—an error of law.

[54] For doubts as to how far this presumption applies to inferior courts, see subsection (c) above.

them only when considering existing statute law in a particular case.

We must now consider how faithfully the courts appear to accept clear statutory indications that in a particular context the *Anisminic* presumption is not to apply. This, of course, will bear on whether the courts may truly be regarded as confining themselves to their constitutional role as interpreters of statute. We shall then turn to the broader issue of whether the changes precipitated by the *Anisminic* case are constitutionally acceptable.

(i) *The Anisminic presumption as a presumption of legislative intent.* We have seen that the *Anisminic* presumption appears to apply in principle as much to inferior courts as to administrative tribunals and other administrative authorities. But that in the case of an inferior court the presumption may be regarded as having been rebutted where both (a) there is a general statutory provision of a right of appeal from the decisions of the court in question and (b) Parliament has expressly withdrawn that right of appeal in a particular type of case. If the court errs in law in deciding a case of that type, the error will not necessarily be jurisdictional. This is because Parliament can hardly be said to have intended that all errors of law will carry a court outside jurisdiction where one statute has expressly withdrawn a mode of challenging error of law (*i.e.* appeal) which would otherwise have existed under another statute. Here, then, the superior courts seem to be accepting clear indications that the *Anisminic* presumption is not to apply.

What then of the *Anisminic* case itself? We have already noticed[55] that the relevant statute contained an ouster clause which, as the House of Lords unanimously accepted, was intended to exclude the common law supervisory jurisdiction based on patent error. But since most patent errors are errors of law,[56] it would appear that the ouster clause should be taken to have indicated Parliament's intention to curtail challenges based on error of law. Yet in the *Anisminic* case an error of law was held to be jurisdictional; and it is from that case that the presumption is said to have emerged that all errors of law are jurisdictional. Nevertheless, while it is plain that the presumption itself is new law, *Anisminic* need not be seen as presaging a refusal by the courts to yield to parliamentary intimations that the presumption is not to apply.

Ouster clauses of the *Anisminic* variety indisputably are not to be taken as indicating that Parliament intends to exclude supervi-

[55] See Chap. 2, p. 50.

[56] For the patent error jurisdiction, see section (E), following.

sory review jurisdiction based on jurisdictional error.[57] So, even though jurisdictional error seems to have been re-defined by the adoption of the *Anisminic* presumption, it would still appear that an ouster clause of the "shall not be called into question" type should not be taken as indicating that Parliament intends to rebut the presumption. This argument may be thought disingenuous; but it is intended solely to suggest that the courts' adoption of the *Anisminic* presumption should not be treated as constitutionally improper on the basis that the courts have created a new rule of law under the guise of a presumption of statutory interpretation. We turn shortly to consider whether constitutional impropriety may be alleged on any other basis; but we conclude this section on the *Anisminic* presumption as a presumption of legislative intent by considering a further question.

We turn now to cases where no ouster clause is involved. It appears that the effect of the *Anisminic* presumption (unless rebutted) will be to characterise as jurisdictional any error of law by an authority which is subject to supervisory review but from whose decisions Parliament has simply not provided an appeal.[58] Consider, however, cases where a statutory right of appeal on point of law is available. Will this by itself be sufficient to rebut the presumption that all errors of law by the authority concerned are jurisdictional?

The argument would be as follows: Parliament is said (according to the *Anisminic* presumption) to know and to accept that, unless it provides otherwise, the authority concerned will be treated by the courts as having gone outside jurisdiction if it errs in law. But if error of law is thus already open to challenge in the courts why should Parliament provide, by way of appeal, what would on this basis appear to be a superfluous second mode of challenge? It may be argued therefore that one cannot in these circumstances presume that Parliament intended that all errors of law by the authority should be jurisdictional.

Now, it is true that the question will not commonly arise in practice. If there is an appeal on point of law a dissatisfied party will be inclined to use it, or else will probably be told by the High Court to use it in preference to application for judicial review[59] on the

[57] *cf.* time-limited ouster clauses which, after the time limit, are taken to exclude all challenge in the courts: see Chap. 2, p. 54; *cf.* also the recent case law on "conclusive" clauses, *ibid.* pp. 52–54.

[58] See, *e.g.* cases on Housing (Homeless Persons) Act 1977 cited on p. 145 *et seq.* above.

[59] On application for judicial review see Chap. 2, p. 38 above and Chaps 7 and 8 below.

"other convenient remedy" principle.[60] Through this principle the courts acknowledge that by providing appeal machinery Parliament has indicated that ordinarily this machinery will best dispose of challenges to the decisions of the authority concerned. But there is no reason why the courts should go further and infer that Parliament has intended to make the appeal procedure the exclusive mode of direct challenge—for there may be good reasons in a particular case why application for judicial review may be a more appropriate procedure.[61] Where this is so, it would be strange to suggest that the availability of appeal on point of law should be taken to diminish the extent of the supervisory review jurisdiction exercisable under what (we are supposing) is in the particular case the more appropriate procedure of application for judicial review. It follows, then, that if the *Anisminic* presumption is held to apply even where there is statutory provision for appeal on point of law, its status as a presumption of legislative intent is not compromised.

(ii) *Error of law as the touchstone of jurisdictional error.* In the period beginning with *Anisminic* the superior courts have in effect announced to Parliament that, generally speaking, if it wishes to endow a statutory authority with the capacity to perpetrate errors of law immune from supervisory review it must make that abundantly clear in the statute. We have thus passed from an era in which judicial identification of jurisdictional error was highly impressionistic[62] to one in which the courts have stated plainly the basis upon which they will characterise an error as jurisdictional. Whether it was constitutionally proper for the courts rather than Parliament to take this initiative is for commentators to debate and, ultimately, for Parliament itself to decide.[63] The initiative may be seen by some as a usurpation of legislative authority; by others, on the contrary, as a constructive attempt to clarify the boundaries of competence between courts and administration. One's choice of perspective will no doubt be affected by one's assessment of the substantial merits and demerits of this new approach to the characterisation of jurisdictional error.

The broad effect of the *Anisminic* presumption is to draw a line

[60] See Chap. 9 below.

[61] *e.g. R.* v. *Huntingdon D.C. ex p. Cowan* [1984] 1 W.L.R. 501 (case raised novel point of general importance: applicant permitted to proceed by A.J.R. instead of prescribed appeal procedure culminating in appeal on law to High Court).

[62] See pp. 137–140 above.

[63] For Parliament's response to the House of Lords' assertion of jurisdiction in the *Anisminic* case itself, see Chap. 2, p. 51.

of demarcation between, on the one hand, the jurisdiction of the superior courts and, on the other, that of most other statutory authorities. Generally speaking, questions of law are ultimately for the superior courts[64]; questions of fact and degree are for the authority to which an issue is in the first instance remitted.[65] Two crucial questions are:

(1) How clear is the line which the superior courts have drawn?
(2) Have the courts drawn the line in the right place?

The clarity of the line depends on the precision of the notion of error of law discussed in Chapter 3. The concepts of error of law in finding primary facts and in stating applicable rules are clear and can be applied with some precision.[66] What of the concept of error of law in applying law to facts? It has been shown that in administrative law the *Edwards* v. *Bairstow* doctrine usually provides the criterion of what counts as an error of law of this type. That doctrine is founded on the semantic truth that no matter how "open-textured" a particular statutory category may be, it is not infinitely so. There are limits to the openness of the texture: recall our example of "park" land.[67] As the reported cases show, it may require litigation to determine the boundaries of a concept such as "trade," "course of employment," "plant," "structural alteration" "family" and so on. But this does not of itself detract from the utility of the *Edwards* v. *Bairstow* doctrine.[68] As we have observed, the utility of that doctrine depends on the courts' readiness to give full effect to the possible range and shades of meaning of ordinary words. We suggested in Chapter 3 that the case law indicates such a readiness. We add here only the obvious point that the viability of the *Anisminic* identification of jurisdictional error with error of law depends substantially on the satisfactory operation of the *Edwards* v. *Bairstow* doctrine.

There is one consideration which, perhaps, links our first question about the clarity of the notion of error of law with our second about whether the line of demarcation between superior courts and other statutory authorities has been drawn in the right place.

64 An inferior court when considering a collateral challenge may rule that the authority whose action is challenged has erred in law. But the inferior court's ruling will itself commonly be subject to review by the superior courts.
65 Subject, of course, to any statutory right of appeal on such questions.
66 It is not to the point to object that often one cannot predict with any certainty how a superior court will elucidate particular statutory words. This is a feature of the relationship between legislation and adjudication not in any way peculiar to judicial review.
67 See Chap. 3, p. 108.
68 See Chap. 3, p. 114 *et seq*.

Parliament, as we have observed,[69] frequently confers jurisdiction on the superior courts to entertain appeals on point of law from inferior courts, tribunals and authorities. Our analysis of error of law in Chapter 3 is derived substantially from cases of the courts' exercise of this jurisdiction. Parliament continues to confer such jurisdiction on the superior courts: this surely indicates that Parliament regards "error of law" (thus understood) as not only a sufficiently clear but also a broadly satisfactory notion for demarcating the spheres of competence of superior courts and authorities subject to review jurisdiction.[70]

Focussing now on our second question, we may recall Professor Evans's "working hypothesis" that judicial review jurisdiction should extend to those matters on which a review court's decision is likely to be better than that of the tribunal under review.[71] Does the adoption of "error of law" as a general criterion of reviewability actually produce this result? Essentially, as our examination of "second" and "third stage" error of law shows,[72] the question is whether the superior courts are the most appropriate authorities to be charged with the definition of the limits of meaning of statutory language. We may take it for granted that a statute should be interpreted in the same way by all authorities who have to apply it.[73] So, there should be a means of establishing authoritatively which of two opposed interpretations of a particular provision is to prevail. But should that means be a ruling of a superior court or, rather, a ruling of a minister, a local authority or an expert tribunal?

Authorities functioning constantly in a particular field will undoubtedly be able to acquire a greater familiarity with the mass of law and practice in that field than will a High Court judge required to hear cases ranging over a far wider field of common and statute law. But, by the same token, the High Court judge's broad familiarity with the ever-growing bulk of legislation and with developments in legislative techniques and modes of statutory interpretation are qualifications to which particular administrative authorities can hardly aspire. The question is which kind of exper-

[69] See Chap. 2, p. 44 *et seq*.

[70] Other legislatures have indicated a similar attitude by making error of law a statutory ground for the exercise of supervisory review jurisdiction—see, *e.g.* Australian Administrative Decisions (Judicial Review) Act 1977, s.5(1); *cf.* too U.S. Federal Administrative Procedure Act 1974, s.706.

[71] De Smith J.R.A.A., p. 128; see Chap. 3, pp. 96, 123.

[72] See Chap. 3, pp. 104, 124.

[73] See also Chap. 3, p. 125.

tise is to be preferred. Detailed consideration of this political/constitutional issue is beyond the scope of this book. We may simply reiterate that to date Parliament has shown itself willing to confer expressly on the superior courts jurisdiction to correct errors of law perpetrated by a wide variety of public authorities in the course of exercising a great and disparate array of official powers. It must remain an open question whether the courts have been justified since *Anisminic* in taking to themselves an even broader jurisdiction to correct errors of law than Parliament has seen fit expressly to confer.[74]

Finally in this chapter, we turn from jurisdictional error to consider a quite different basis upon which supervisory review jurisdiction may be invoked—error on the face of the record.

E. Error on the Face of the Record[75]

The High Court has since the seventeenth century[76] exercised jurisdiction to quash by certiorari decisions of inferior courts and tribunals, the record of whose proceedings discloses error. In the nineteenth century Parliament's widespread use of "no certiorari" clauses[77] stultified the jurisdiction, but it was rediscovered by the Court of Appeal in 1951[78] at a time when Parliament's use of no certiorari clauses was in decline[79] and when the law on jurisdictional error was complex and obscure.[80]

The record of a tribunal's proceedings must contain the document initiating the proceedings, the pleadings if any and the adjudication[81]; also, it appears, documents referred to in, and thus incorporated by, those documents.[82] If the tribunal chooses or is

[74] For further discussion of constitutional considerations in this context, see Craig, pp. 334–349.
[75] De Smith J.R.A.A., pp. 400–408.
[76] De Smith J.R.A.A., p. 108 *passim*.
[77] See Chap. 2, p. 48.
[78] *R*. v. *Northumberland Compensation Appeal Tribunal ex p. Shaw* [1952] 1 K.B. 338.
[79] A decline ultimately reflected and endorsed by the Tribunals and Inquiries Act 1958, s.11 (1971 Act s.14).
[80] See above, pp. 137–140.
[81] The *Northumberland* case, above note 78, *per* Denning L.J. at p. 352.
[82] So decided by the Court of Appeal in *R* v. *Medical Appeal Tribunal ex p. Gilmore* [1957] 1 Q.B. 574; point left open by majority of House of Lords in *Baldwin & Francis Ltd.* v. *Patents Appeal Tribunal* [1959] A.C. 663.

under an express[83] or implied[84] statutory obligation to give reasons, the reasons will be part of the record.[85]

Suppose, for example, that as in *R.* v. *Medical Appeal Tribunal ex p. Gilmore*[86] the record shows (a) that X, who had been blind in one eye for some years, was claiming compensation when he lost the sight of the other eye in an industrial accident; and (b) that the tribunal awarded compensation to X on the basis that the accident caused X loss of the sight of only one eye rather than total blindness. If the relevant legislation required the tribunal to proceed on the latter basis rather than the former, the tribunal will, of course, have erred in law.[87] The error can be detected simply by scrutiny of the record in the light of the applicable law. It thus appears "on the face of the record."

Suppose by way of contrast that another claimant, Y, claimed compensation on the basis that he had previously been blind in one eye but that the tribunal found as a fact that he had not and awarded compensation on that basis. Any evidence on which the tribunal based its findings would not be part of the record[88]; so even if the tribunal based its finding on no evidence whatever (and so erred in law[89]) the error would not appear on the face of the record. Thus, while such errors as do appear on the record will almost invariably[90] be errors of law, not even all errors of law will appear.

[83] See, *e.g.* Tribunals and Inquiries Act 1971, s.12(1) (see Chap. 6, p. 207).

[84] "It is the function of professional judges to give reasons" *per* Griffiths L.J. in *R* v. *Knightsbridge Crown Court ex p. I.S.C. Ltd.* [1981] 3 W.L.R. 640 at 648. On the extent of the duty of public authorities generally to give reasons for their decisions, see Chap. 6, p. 234.

[85] *Per* Denning L.J. in *Northumberland* (above) at p. 352. Tribunals and Inquiries Act, s.12(4).

[86] [1957] 1 Q.B. 574.

[87] At our "second" or "third stage" (see Chap. 3), according to whether or not the tribunal formally stated or elucidated the rule. In *Gilmore* the error was of our "third" stage (*Edwards* v. *Bairstow*) type.

[88] *Per* Denning L.J. in *Northumberland* (above) at p. 352. This is subject, of course, to contrary statutory provision. In *R.* v. *Knightsbridge Crown Court ex p. The Aspinall Curzon Ltd.* [1982] *The Times*, December 16 Woolf J. suggested that since the procedural reforms of 1977 (see Chaps. 7 and 8) the court could look at evidence although not technically part of the record. *Sed quaere*: this seems to ignore the basis of the *patent* error jurisdiction.

[89] See Chap. 3, pp. 98–99.

[90] It is conceivable that if a particular record did contain an exhaustive statement of evidence of facts found, a review court might quash what it saw as an unjustified inference of fact, albeit based on some evidence.

The High Court's jurisdiction to correct patent error has in the past been of great importance. Today, however, it seems that its importance is dwindling to the point of obsolescence. Essentially this is because, as we have just seen, those errors which can be detected by a perusal of the "record" will almost invariably be errors of law. But the courts now have a very wide jurisdiction (whether by way of statutory appeal or via the *Anisminic* characterisation of error of law as jurisdictional) to correct errors of law as such, *i.e.* irrespective of whether or not they appear on the face of the record. If one may obtain review on the basis of error of law *simpliciter* there will be no need to invoke a jurisdiction which requires one to show not only error of law but also that the error appears on the face of the record.

But will there not be cases where there is no right of appeal and where the *Anisminic* presumption does not apply and where, consequently, one who seeks review will need to invoke the patent error jurisdiction? This seems unlikely. The *Anisminic* presumption will, apparently, be rebutted only where Parliament has indicated clearly that it is not to apply—as, for example, where Parliament has expressly withdrawn a right of appeal on point of law which would otherwise have been available.[91] The fact is, though, that the legislature is hardly likely to go to these lengths without taking steps to exclude the patent error jurisdiction also—as it did in both the *Pearlman*[92] and *South East Asia Firebricks*[93] cases referred to above. It is unlikely, then, that the patent error jurisdiction will remain unimpaired by Parliament in a case where the *Anisminic* presumption has been ousted. It follows that if the *Anisminic* presumption extends (unless rebutted) to all authorities subject to supervisory jurisdiction it is unlikely that there will be occasions where it will be strictly necessary for a litigant to resort to the patent error jurisdiction.

It would however be premature at this time to assert categorically that the *Anisminic* presumption is so wide-ranging as to render the patent error jurisdiction entirely obsolete. If an error of law does appear on the face of the record it may be sensible to put one's case in these terms rather than to invite dispute on whether the *Anisminic* presumption in principle applies and, if so, whether

[91] See p. 156.
[92] [1979] Q.B. 56.
[93] [1981] A.C. 363.

it is rebutted.[94] Nevertheless, "the artificial distinction between patent and latent errors of law . . . is very unsatisfactory"[95] and a Queen's Bench Divisional Court has pronounced it "obsolete."[96]

[94] In *R.* v. *Knightsbridge Crown Court ex p. I.S.C. Ltd.* [1981] 3 W.L.R. 640 the error (failure to take account of club re-structuring) was patent and was quashed on that basis; the Divisional Court was thus dispensed from deciding the "difficult question" whether the error was jurisdictional, a point on which the court was divided (see p. 652).

[95] De Smith J.R.A.A., p.139.

[96] *Per* Goff L.J. giving the judgment of the court in *R.* v. *Greater Manchester Coroner ex p. Tal* [1985] Q.B. 67 at 82.

Chapter 5

LAW AND POLICY

A. Policy Issues

In the last chapter we considered the courts' jurisdiction to review determinations by public authorities that particular facts fall within a certain legal category. The determination may have been made in a litigious or quasi-litigious context (*e.g.* whether X is "intentionally homeless" or "ordinarily resident"; or whether Y has a "successor in title"; or whether Z has made a "structural alteration" to his house); or in a purely administrative context (*e.g.* whether a power to carry parcels in conjunction with a bus passenger service extends to doorstep delivery of parcels). For ease of reference and distinction we may label these types of issue of law, fact and degree "issues of classification."

In this chapter we consider the courts' jurisdiction to review a decision of a public authority to follow a specific course of action which is admittedly of a kind which falls within general empowering words; but whose legality is attacked on the basis, essentially, that the decision was made without proper regard to the purpose for which the power was conferred by statute. Recall our example[1] of the authority, empowered to license premises for entertainments and to impose conditions, which licenses P's discotheque for every day of the week except Sunday. The Sunday ban is plainly a "condition" attached to a "licence." But P may be able to attack the validity of the condition on the basis that it is not a condition which may be imposed consistently with the purpose for which the power to impose conditions was conferred on the authority. As we observed, a challenge of this sort seems to relate to "the way in which" an authority may act rather than to "the kind of thing" it may do. More precisely it raises the issue of the legal limits of discretion,[2] *i.e.* of freedom to choose among often multifarious options which appear to be available within the broad limits of a general empowering provision. Questions as to the choice and nature of the criteria on which this freedom is to be exercised are commonly labelled "policy issues."

Plainly a public authority may be faced with both issues of classi-

[1] See Chap. 1, p. 25.
[2] See de Smith J.R.A.A., Chap. 6; Wade A.L., Part IV; Craig, Chap. 10.

fication and issues of policy in the course of a single enterprise. Take compulsory purchase legislation which exempts park land from its provisions. Whether Blackacre is or is not park land is an issue of classification.[3] Whether (if it is not park land) Blackacre should be the subject of a purchase order raises issues of policy. Furthermore, the distinction between issues of classification and issues of policy is not always easily made. Suppose that, as in the notorious case of *Roberts* v. *Hopwood*,[4] a public authority is empowered to pay its employees such wages as it thinks fit. It fixes the wages at levels substantially higher than the national average for work of the kind in question, apparently refusing to be guided by the "going rate" but awarding a sum representing what in its view a "model employer" should pay. Has the authority here resolved a policy issue or an issue of classification? It looks like a policy issue; but it may be said that rates of pay fixed without regard to factors commonly treated as crucial in this exercise are not "wages" at all[5]—on which basis the issue looks like one of classification. In challenging the lawfulness of an authority's decision in such a case either approach may be possible. It may be argued that the authority erred in law in its understanding of the term "wages"; or, alternatively that its error was in its failure to have regard to the purpose for which the power to pay wages was conferred upon it, *i.e.* to fix levels of remuneration by reference to criteria commonly used in that exercise.[6] In this chapter we consider the scope of challenge based on the notion that statutory power is confined not only by the terms in which but also by the purpose for which it is conferred. In other words, we consider the legal limits of the freedom of public authorities to resolve policy issues according to criteria of their own choosing.

We may begin by adverting to a certain fundamental objection to the very existence of judicial review jurisdiction in this area. Our brief survey in Chapter 1 of the current extent of official power gives some indication of the immense breadth and range of

[3] See Chap. 3, p. 108.

[4] [1925] A.C. 578. District auditor surcharged local councillors on the basis that wages payed to council employees were excessive, and so contrary to law. Councillors challenged surcharge. House of Lords held in effect that the excessive payments were *ultra vires* and the surcharge, therefore, proper.

[5] "They have not determined the payment as wages, for they have eliminated the consideration both of the work to be done and of the purchasing power of the sums paid . . . " *per* Lord Buckmaster, *ibid.* p. 590. See too Lord Atkinson at p. 600, Lord Wrenbury at p. 612 and Lord Carson at p. 618.

[6] In *Roberts* v. *Hopwood* the "purpose" approach is most strongly reflected in the speeches of Lords Sumner and Atkinson. On this issue generally, see G. D. S. Taylor [1976] C.L.J. 272.

policy issues which fall to be resolved by public authorities. Central government departments, local government and other authorities have wide and intertwined discretionary powers through whose exercise they may shape the fabric of society. In conferring these policy-making powers Parliament is substantially controlled by the central government. Its output of legislation largely reflects that government's current policies. So, any decision by the courts as to the extent of such powers (whether of central or local government or otherwise) is likely to be seen as a "victory" for one political point of view and a "defeat" for its opposite. In that sense the court's decision can hardly avoid being labelled "political." Even where a policy issue is not of a highly sensitive party-political nature (*e.g.* in the area of land development and planning control) or where the authority is not an elected authority (*e.g.* the police) any judicial pronouncement that this or that policy is unlawful tends to raise the hackles of those who believe that it is a general principle of representative government that policy decisions should be subject to political rather than to judicial controls and sanctions.

Now, as we shall see, the lynch-pin of judicial review of the exercise of statutory discretion is the notion that statutory power is conferred on public authorities for a purpose discernible from the statute itself. We shall consider shortly the difficulties associated with the discernment of statutory purpose. But assume for the moment that Parliament has indicated clearly the kind of purpose which particular legislation is designed to achieve. A public authority which used powers conferred upon it in this context without regard to the attainment of a purpose of that kind would, presumably, be acting contrary to the will of Parliament and in that sense "undemocratically." No doubt Parliament may wish to legislate in the knowledge that there is a constitutional means of restraining action of this sort without immediate recourse to amending legislation. The ordinary courts may or may not be thought to be an appropriate means to this end; but it is difficult to see that any basic principle of representative democracy is breached if the legislature chooses to rely upon some form of legal control as well as upon other (perhaps more remote and cumbersome) forms of political control to ensure that the purposes of its legislation are fulfilled. We have seen, indeed, that Parliament does confer on courts appellate review jurisdiction (commonly limited to point of law) over many public authorities, including those of central government, whose remit is to formulate and carry out policy.[7]

[7] See Chap. 2, p. 44 above; also p. 204 below.

This fact in itself tends to blunt the edge of a general assertion that judicial review is inappropriate in this field.

But it is supervisory review, founded on the notion of discernible statutory purpose, which arouses most criticism. The very range and diversity of statutory provision militates against the possibility of formulating accurate general statements of the principles governing this area of the law. As the leading work on judicial review reminds us, "the scope of judicial review will often be determined mainly by the wording of a power and the context in which it is exercised."[8] This in turn is seen as indicating uncertainty in the law and so becomes in itself a ground of criticism. It is plain at any rate that any assessment of the constitutional propriety of judicial review of policy decisions must begin with an examination of the notion of statutory purpose and the derivative notions of relevant and irrelevant consideration. To these matters we now turn.

B. Policy and Purpose—Relevant and Irrelevant Considerations

(1) The "Purpose Axiom"

In *Padfield* v. *Minister of Agriculture*[9] Lord Reid observed that

> "Parliament must have conferred the discretion with the intention that it should be used to promote the policy and objects of the Act; the policy and objects of the Act must be determined by construing the Act as a whole, and construction is always a matter of law for the court."[10]

The courts treat it as axiomatic that when Parliament confers statutory powers upon a public authority it does so to promote the achievement of a purpose or purposes ("policy and objects") which may be discovered from the statute. "If a power granted for one purpose is exercised for a different purpose, that power has not been validly exercised."[11] These statements, which together may be labelled the "purpose axiom," raise two distinct questions:

[8] De Smith J.R.A.A., p. 278. See also pp. 281, 348.

[9] [1968] A.C. 997.

[10] *Ibid*. p. 1030. For a similar approach in different areas of official power, see, *e.g.* *Roberts* v. *Hopwood* (above); *Newbury D.C.* v. *Secretary of State* [1981] A.C. 578 at 599; and *Westminster City Council* v. *Great Portland Estates plc* [1985] A.C. 661 at 670 ("planning purpose").

[11] De Smith J.R.A.A, p. 325, describing the proposition as "elementary."

(1) Should the courts adopt the purpose axiom at all? (2) How, in any event, do the courts apply the axiom?

Our principal concern will be with the second question. The first question encapsulates the issue to which we referred specifically in the opening section of this chapter and more generally in our earlier discussion of the question "do we need judicial review?"[12] Here we may simply note that the purpose axiom is commonly expressed by the courts in terms of a public authority's fiduciary duty to use its powers in a trustee-like fashion.[13] There is clearly some analogy between the legal position of a public authority and that of a trustee, particularly a public (or charitable) trustee. There are historical links between the social functions discharged by charities and those discharged by contemporary public authorities.[14] Furthermore, the vocabulary of trusteeship and fiduciary duty is apt to elucidate the notion of limited remit upon which, as we have seen, the whole law of judicial review is predicated.[15] Certainly the trusteeship analogy must not be pushed too far.[16] It will not be if its limited purpose is remembered. It is not designed to answer (as the law of trusts answers) detailed questions about rights and duties and those in whom they inhere.[17] It is designed only to reflect and, on the level of broad constitutional principle, to explain and to justify the purpose axiom.

Trustees (strictly so-called) hold on trust for their beneficiaries not only trust property but also their powers as trustees. As trustees of these powers they are duty-bound to consider according to proper criteria whether or not to exercise them.[18] So with public authorities.[19] But the purposes of a trust and, hence, the criteria which a trustee must apply in exercising his powers, are reasonably clear: he must manage the trust property for the benefit of his beneficiaries, whether private individuals or a section of the public. The purposes to be pursued by a particular public authority, on the other hand, will emerge only from the statute which creates it and its powers and duties.

[12] See Chap. 1, p. 15 *et seq*.
[13] See, *e.g. Roberts* v. *Hopwood* (above) at p. 596; *Prescott* v. *Birmingham Corpn.* [1955] Ch. 210, 235; *Bromley L.B.C.* v. *G.L.C.* [1983] 1 A.C. 768.
[14] See *Att.-Gen.* v. *Aspinall* (1837) 2 M. & C. 613, Chap. 7 below.
[15] See Chap. 1, pp. 14–15.
[16] Craig, p. 367 and references.
[17] In administrative law these questions are answered by construction of individual statutes (see below) and via the notions of public and private law right and *locus standi* (see Part III).
[18] See, *e.g. Halsbury's Laws of England* (4th ed.), Vol. 36, para. 885.
[19] See, *e.g. per* Lord Upjohn in *Padfield* [1968] A.C. at 1058–1061; Wade A.L., p. 355.

Just as judgment of the constitutional propriety of the *Anisminic* presumption may turn substantially on an assessment of the merits and demerits of its operation,[20] so perhaps with the purpose axiom. Accordingly, we turn to our second question: how do the courts apply the purpose axiom?

(2) Discovering the statutory purpose

Statutory power may be conferred either with or without express indication of the purpose for which it is conferred.

(a) *Purpose expressed in statute*

A statute may provide in terms that an authority "may exercise [specified] powers for the purpose of [achieving a specified result]."[21] But often the wording is more elliptical. The statute may say that the power must be exercised in a manner "best calculated to secure" or "expedient for the promotion of" a specified object. If the authority purports to exercise the power in disregard of that object it will have ignored the limit to its discretion expressly imposed by the statutory words. So, the Civil Aviation Authority was placed under a duty to exercise its functions, including licensing powers, in the manner it considered "best calculated to secure" (*inter alia*) a certain measure of competition in the provision of air services.[22] Ministerial "guidance" to the Authority not to permit competition on "long-haul" routes was declared *ultra vires* because it required the authority to disregard one of the purposes expressed in the statute.[23] Likewise, a local authority's statutory power to sue in exceptional circumstances for an injunction to prevent anticipated breaches of the criminal law is conferred expressly "for the promotion or protection of the interests of the inhabitants of their area."[24] Under that provision an authority obtained an injunction against a retailer who preferred to pay fines for breach of, rather than to observe, Sunday trading laws.

20 See Chap. 4, pp. 162–164.

21 As *e.g.* in Fair Trading Act 1973, s.73(2): considered in *R.* v. *Secretary of State for Trade ex p. Anderson Strathclyde plc* [1983] 2 All E.R. 233. See also Local Government (Miscellaneous Provisions) Act 1982, Sched. 1, para. 4(4) on which our example in Chap. 1, p. 25 of the discotheque subject to a Sunday ban was based. The Schedule provides that licences may be granted subject to conditions "imposed for all or any of [four specified] purposes, but no others." The purposes include preventing persons in the neighbourhood being unreasonably disturbed by noise. *Prima facie*, the authority in our example appears to have acted lawfully.

22 Civil Aviation Act 1971, s.3(1).

23 *Laker Airways Ltd* v. *Department of Trade* [1977] Q.B. 643.

24 Local Government Act 1972, s.222(1).

But the Court of Appeal discharged the injunction because the authority had not addressed itself to the question whether or not the proceedings were in the interests of the local inhabitants.[25]

In similar vein the statutory draftsman may express the purpose for which a power is conferred by providing that the power may be exercised on certain specified grounds, or if it appears to the authority that a certain result can be achieved. If the power is exercised on other grounds or to achieve another result the authority exceeds its remit. So, where a local education authority was empowered to direct school managers to dismiss teachers on "educational grounds" it acted *ultra vires* when it caused the managers to dismiss for financial reasons.[26] Again, a local authority was empowered to purchase compulsorily (instead of demolishing) a condemned house if it appeared that the house could be "rendered capable of providing accommodation which is adequate for the time being."[27] It acted *ultra vires* when it proposed to purchase a house with a view to permanent refurbishment.[28]

(b) *Purpose to be inferred*

A statute may confer discretion upon a public authority without any specific statement of purpose. In that event the purpose of the power can be discerned only by considering broadly the purpose of the legislation by which it is conferred. This doctrine of general statutory purpose is indeed a crude instrument with which to attempt to identify the particular purpose of specific statutory powers. There are, though, cases where, crude as it is, it works tolerably well to avoid the conclusion that a power may be used for any purpose which the authority cares to espouse.

Take, for example, an unqualified power conferred on a licensing authority to revoke licences already granted. A notorious and extreme example of abuse of such a power is the Canadian case where a liquor licensing authority, at the instigation of the Quebec Prime Minister, cancelled a restaurateur's licence because he had stood surety for bail in a large number of prosecutions of Jeho-

[25] *Stoke-on-Trent City Council* v. *B & Q (Retail) Ltd and other appeals* [1984] Ch. 1 (the *Barking and Dagenham L.B.C.* appeal).

[26] *Hanson* v. *Radcliffe U.D.C.* [1922] Ch. 490, *per* Lord Sterndale M.R. at p. 505.

[27] Housing Act, 1957, s.17(2); and see s.29(3): ". . . adequate for the time being pending its demolition. . . ."

[28] *Victoria Square Pty. Co. Ltd.* v. *Southwark L.B.C.* [1978] 1 W.L.R. 463, *per* Bridge L.J. at p. 472. The statute prescribed a different procedure for permanent refurbishment.

vah's Witnesses for various bye-law infringements.[29] It may be said that to concede that this cancellation was outside the purpose of the revocation power is merely to accept that there are indeed some purposes which could not conceivably be held to be authorised by a particular statute. Argument from such extremes, however, may be thought of little assistance in the majority of cases well away from the extreme. The case does nevertheless show the possible consequences of abandoning the notion that powers are granted for a purpose even where no purpose is expressed.

If our Canadian case is a plain example of a purpose beyond the pale, there is at the other end of the spectrum a series of English cases on council house rents which is generally regarded as a laudable example of judicial refusal to use the notion of statutory purpose to restrict the legitimate discretion of public authorities. Local authorities have statutory power to "make such reasonable charges for the tenancy . . . of [council] houses as they may determine."[30] Council tenants have failed to persuade the courts, on the one hand, that councils have no power to operate a means-tested rent rebate scheme for poor tenants[31]; and, on the other, that they have a duty to operate such a scheme.[32] The Divisional Court has observed that the general purpose of the legislation "is to provide houses for the classes of the community who cannot afford to pay economic rents . . . not to provide subsidised houses for people who can afford to pay economic rents."[33] Two salient points emerge. First, the courts would intervene in the unlikely event that any council purported to use its powers for the purpose of providing subsidised houses for people who could afford to pay economic rents. Secondly, the courts recognised that the notion of providing houses for those who cannot afford to pay economic rents is a wide one. If the purpose of the legislation cannot be expressed more precisely than this, that in itself is an indication

[29] *Roncarelli* v. *Duplessis* (1959) 16 D.L.R. (2d) 689. By 6:3 the Canadian Supreme Court held that the Prime Minister was liable in tort for the losses sustained by the restaurateur. Two of the majority based liability on the ground that the P.M. had caused the licensing authority to act *ultra vires* by using the power of revocation for an improper purpose.

[30] Housing Act 1957, s.111(1).

[31] *Leeds Corporation* v. *Jenkinson* [1935] 1 K.B. 168; *Smith* v. *Cardiff Corporation (No. 2)* [1955] 1 Ch. 159.

[32] *Luby* v. *Newcastle-under-Lyme Corporation* [1964] 2 Q.B. 64. (aff'd C.A. [1965] 1 Q.B. 214).

[33] *Per* Goddard J. in the *Leeds* case (above note 31) at p. 181. The purpose emerges both from the legislative history and from such provisions as s.113(2) of the 1957 Act (preference to be given to persons occupying insanitary or overcrowded houses [etc]).

that Parliament has intended to confer on housing authorities wide discretion on the policy issues arising—in particular, as the cases show, on the matter of whether a council tenant's inability to pay an economic rent is to be compensated for by ratepayers (via a means-tested rebate scheme) or by the general body of taxpayers (via the social security system).[34]

Whether in general (as in the council house cases) the courts have restricted their inferences of statutory purpose so as to give full rein to the discretion intended by Parliament to be exercised by public authorities is no doubt to an extent a question of impression. We may refer briefly to some well-known cases. Returning to our theme of licence revocation: in an English case reminiscent of the Canadian case already considered, a local authority had revoked a market stall-holder's licence substantially because, after the market had closed one day, the licensee had urinated in a side-street, the public lavatories being locked. Quashing the revocation, a majority of the Court of Appeal held in effect that whatever the purpose of the power to revoke, it was not to enable the council to mete out draconian punishment for an "isolated and trivial incident."[35] Again, the Court of Appeal declared *ultra vires* a decision by the Home Office to revoke television licences which the holders had purchased shortly before their existing licences were due to expire so as to avoid a fee increase which took effect on the expiry date. Whatever the purpose of the statutory revocation power, it could not be "to enable the Minister to raise more money."[36] The court relied chiefly on the well-established constitutional principle against taxation without clear Parliamentary authority.[37]

In the context of the grant of licences of a different sort, the courts have used the notion of "planning purpose"[38] to circum-

[34] See *per* Diplock L.J. in *Luby* (above note 32) at p. 73. But see now Social Security and Housing Benefits Act 1982, s.28.

[35] *R.* v. *Barnsley M.B.C ex p. Hook* [1976] 1 W.L.R. 1052 at 1063 *per* Sir John Pennycuick.

[36] *Congreve* v. *Home Office* [1976] Q.B. 629 at 652 *per* Lord Denning M.R. See also *Wheeler* v. *Leicester City Council* [1985] 3 W.L.R. 335. In order to punish rugby club for not pressing members to refrain from touring South Africa, council declined to renew club's licence to use municipal sports ground. House of Lords (reversing Forbes J. and a split Court of Appeal) held unanimously that council had abused the statutory powers on which it relied: for to punish club for acting lawfully, albeit in a manner which council deplored, was outside the purposes of the powers.

[37] [1976] Q.B. 652 at 655, 662.

[38] See *Newbury* and *Westminster* cases cited in note 10 above. Broadly, a planning purpose is one relating to the control of development in the interests of the preservation of environmental amenity.

scribe the power of a planning authority to make planning permission "subject to such conditions as they think fit."[39] In one case, observing that "those words are clearly too wide to be given their literal meaning"[40] the Divisional Court quashed (as *ultra vires*) conditions requiring a developer to make the flats available to persons who were on the local authority's housing waiting list and would obtain Rent Act security of tenure. The conditions were not imposed for a planning purpose but were "the equivalent of requiring the private developer to take on at his own expense a significant part of the duty of the local authority as housing authority."[41]

The cases considered above suggest that where the statutory purpose is to be inferred, the courts tend to refrain from inference more specific than the language and structure of the legislation permits. As we have seen, this tendency is often displayed by a review court saying, in effect, "whatever the purpose of a power of this sort (*e.g.* to revoke a licence) it cannot be (*e.g.*) to force individuals to purchase licences at a higher rate of tax than that in force when the now revoked licence was purchased." This approach is reminiscent of the *Edwards* v. *Bairstow* doctrine[42] where the court will often be saying in effect "whatever the meaning of (*e.g.*) 'park land,' it cannot extend to (*e.g.*) a small back garden." We consider shortly[43] cases where it is said that courts have gone much further than this in confining unjustifiably what appears to be the true breadth of statutory purpose. In any event, some of the sting could be taken out of the purpose axiom controversy if Parliament were more frequently to include specific statements of purpose in individual power-conferring provisions.[44]

(3) Identifying improper purpose—relevant and irrelevant considerations

The cases referred to in the previous section illustrate the operation of the purpose axiom and also indicate the difficulties of

[39] Town and Country Planning Act 1971, s.29(1).
[40] *R.* v. *Hillingdon L.B.C. ex p. Royco Ltd* [1974] Q.B. 720 at 729.
[41] *Ibid.* p. 732. See too *Westminster Renslade Ltd* v. *Environment Secretary* [1983] J.P.L. 454.
[42] See Chap. 3, p. 114 *et seq.*
[43] See below, p. 183.
[44] See Renton Committee on *The Preparation of Legislation* (1975) Cmnd. 6053, paras. 11.6–11.8. Also Lord Scarman in unpublished lecture (1983) quoted in Harlow & Rawlings, *Law and Administration* p. 344.

inferring statutory purpose when no purpose is expressed. Suppose, however, that it is established that Parliament has conferred a particular power for a certain purpose and that it is alleged that the conferee authority has used the power for a different purpose. We turn now to consider various ways in which that allegation may be substantiated.

(a) *Matters taken into account by authority*

Sometimes the purpose actually pursued by the authority will appear from what it or its officers have said or written. On the basis of this material it may emerge that the authority, in deciding to act as it did, took into account matters unconnected with or irrelevant to the attainment of the statutory purpose. Take for example the case from which we took our judicial exposition of the purpose axiom, *Padfield* v. *Minister of Agriculture*.[45] The minister was empowered to refer to a statutory committee of investigation complaints about the operation of the milk marketing scheme. Representatives of milk producers in the south-east region complained that the scheme treated them unfairly by comparison with producers in other areas. The minister declined to refer their complaint to the committee. Among his reasons were that the complaint raised "wide issues" and that if it were upheld by the committee he would be under pressure (which he would have found politically embarrassing) to give effect to its recommendations. The House of Lords held in effect that these reasons were irrelevant to the attainment of the statutory purpose for which the committee was created. That purpose was, essentially, to provide a forum for the ventilation of complaints unlikely to be dealt with satisfactorily by arrangements within the Milk Marketing Board—a purpose not advanced by a refusal based on grounds patently unconnected with it.

The presence of irrelevant considerations may thus indicate an improper purpose. The same may be said, obversely, of apparent failure to take into account relevant considerations—*i.e.* considerations which are germane to the achievement of the proper purpose. Another of the minister's reasons for declining to refer the complaint in *Padfield* was that the complaint could be dealt with internally. Given that the committee existed precisely to deal with complaints, like the one in *Padfield*, unlikely to be resolved inter-

[45] [1968] A.C. 997.

nally, this showed "that the minister was entirely misdirecting himself in law based on a misunderstanding of the basic reasons for the conferment on him of the power [to refer complaints]."[46]

In *Padfield*, the relevance, or irrelevance, of the minister's reasons had to be discerned by reference to what was held to be the statutory purpose of the power. But we should note that just as a statute may contain express indications of purposes for which powers are conferred, so it may list certain considerations to which an authority must have regard in the exercise of a power. So, *e.g.* a local authority may refuse or cancel registration of premises for the sale of certain foods if it appears that the premises are unsuitable "having regard to considerations of hygiene and in particular to the situation, construction or condition of premises, or to any activities carried on in them."[47] Here the statutory draftsman provides a list of considerations relevant to the attainment of whatever may be the statutory purpose of the power in question. So there is no need for a court to refer to that purpose in order to characterise a particular consideration as relevant to it. Furthermore, where in a statute a list of considerations appears to be exhaustive,[48] any other considerations are *ex hypothesi* "irrelevant."

(b) *Relevancy, error of law and "Wednesbury unreasonableness"*

The effect of the purpose axiom is to incorporate into the statutory words conferring a power the qualification that the power must be exercised only for a proper purpose. So, if the authority expressly states its purpose, and that purpose is improper, the statement is in effect a misstatement of the law—a "second-stage"[49] error of law. But, as we have just seen, there are many

[46] *Ibid*. p. 1060 *per* Lord Upjohn. For other examples of improper considerations indicating failure to pursue statutory purpose see *R*. v. *Cmr. of Met. Police ex p. Blackburn* [1968] 2 Q.B. 118: policy *re* prosecution of gaming law offences based on considerations of expense and manpower instead of on need to protect public from commercial exploitation of gambling impulse (but *cf. R*. v. *Cmr. of Met. Police ex p. Blackburn* (No. 3). [1973] 1 Q.B. 241); *R* v. *Immigration Appeal Tribunal ex p. Bastiampillai* [1983] 2 All E.R. 844: in refusing applicant's extension of leave to remain in U.K., Secretary of State failed to take account (as Immigration Rules required he should) of their financial dependence on their children settled in U.K.; *R*. v. *Home Secretary ex p. Benwell* [1985] Q.B. 554: in approving dismissal of prison officer on disciplinary charge minister took into account aspects of officer's record which on the proper construction of the regulations he should have ignored. But *cf. R*. v. *Home Secretary ex p. Broom* [1985] 3 W.L.R. 778 (not following *Benwell* on construction of regulations).

[47] Food Act 1984, s.19(1)(*b*). See also s.14(2), (6).

[48] See Taylor [1976] C.L.J. 276 *et seq*.

[49] See Chap. 3, p. 93.

cases where the impropriety of an authority's purpose may be inferred from an express statement of the considerations upon which the authority has relied in exercising, or declining to exercise, the power in question. If the specified considerations are substantially[50] irrelevant or do not include substantial relevant considerations, then again the authority is in effect guilty of second-stage error of law. For the authority has asserted mistakenly that the statutory power in question may be exercised on the basis of the improper considerations.

Today, failure to have regard to proper considerations is not uncommonly characterised by the courts as error of law.[51] It is a type of error of law more specifically and commonly characterised by reference to the principles articulated by Lord Greene M.R. in *Associated Provincial Picture Houses Ltd* v. *Wednesbury Corporation*.[52] There a local authority with statutory power to license Sunday cinema opening subject to such conditions as it thought fit had imposed the condition that children under 15 should not be admitted. The plaintiff licensee failed to obtain a declaration that the condition was *ultra vires* as being "unreasonable." But, accepting the plaintiff's contention that "discretion must be exercised reasonably" Lord Greene considered in what sense "unreasonableness" would carry an authority *ultra vires*:

> "[T]he word 'unreasonable' . . . is frequently used as a general description of the things that must not be done. For instance, a person entrusted with a discretion must . . . direct himself properly in law. He must call his own attention to the matters which he is bound to consider. He must exclude from his consideration matters which are irrelevant to what he has to consider. If he does not obey those rules, he may truly be said . . . to be acting 'unreasonably.' "[53]

Using for purpose B a power conferred for the pursuit of purpose A may be labelled "unreasonable" on much the same basis as using a chisel as a screwdriver may be so labelled: the means adopted are not designed to achieve the end desired. One manifestation of this sort of unreasonableness (epitomised in the maxim

[50] For effect of combination of relevant and irrelevant considerations, see p. 190 below.

[51] See, *e.g. per* Lord Lane C.J. in *R.* v. *Tottenham J.J. ex p. Joshi* [1982] 1 W.L.R. 631 at 635; *per* Lord Diplock in *Mohammed-Holgate* v. *Duke* [1984] A.C. 437 at 446; also see *per* Lord Upjohn in *Padfield*, at [1968] A.C., p. 1058.

[52] [1948] 1 K.B. 223.

[53] *Ibid.* p. 229.

about using a sledge-hammer to crack a nut) may be labelled "disproportionality." Lord Diplock has suggested that English law may one day expressly adopt this principle "which is recognised in the administrative law of several of our fellow members of the European Economic Community."[54]

Suppose now a case where nothing in what the authority or its officers have said or written can be characterised as an improper purpose or irrelevant consideration. In *Wednesbury* Lord Greene said[55]

> "Once that question is answered in favour of the . . . authority, it may be still possible to say that the . . . authority have nevertheless come to a conclusion so unreasonable that no reasonable authority could ever have come to it. In such a case, again, I think the court can interfere."

On what basis can the court interfere here? Clearly it may do so if "the decision [is] so perverse that no reasonable body *properly directing itself* could have reached such a decision."[56] The words emphasised are critical. There may be cases where it can be said by reference to the decision alone that it could not have been reached if the authority had confined itself to considerations germane to the purpose for which the power was granted. So, in *Williams* v. *Giddy*[57] commissioners had purported to exercise their discretion to award a gratuity not exceeding one month's pay for each year of a civil servant's service by awarding only one penny for each year of a certain period of his service. The reason for this award did not appear. But as Lord Macnaghten said[58]:

> "Whatever their motive may have been . . . , an illusory award such as this—an award intended to be unreal and unsubstantial—though made under guise of exercising discretion, is at best a colourable performance, and tantamount to a refusal by the Board to exercise the discretion entrusted to them by Parliament."

The error of law here is of our third-stage, *Edwards* v. *Bairstow*,

54 *Council of Civil Service Unions* v. *Minister for the Civil Service* (the *G.C.H.Q.* case) [1985] A.C. 374 at 410.
55 *Ibid*. p. 234.
56 *Per* Browne-Wilkinson L.J. in *Wheeler* v. *Leicester City Council* [1985] 2 All E.R. at 158 (emphasis added) referring to the *Wednesbury* case.
57 [1911] A.C. 381.
58 *Ibid*. pp. 385–386.

type.[59] There is no express pursuit of an improper purpose or reliance upon irrelevant considerations: no second-stage error. But the decision itself shows plainly that the purpose of the power (*i.e.* to introduce some flexibility into the making of a substantial award) must have been misconceived or ignored. Now, a decision-making process will seldom be so opaque as to conceal entirely the considerations on which an authority has proceeded.[60] And even where this is the case, it will seldom be proper to infer from the decision alone that it was taken without due regard to the statutory purpose.[61] There are, nevertheless, occasional reported cases in the *Williams* v. *Giddy* mould.[62]

But does *Wednesbury* unreasonableness go further than this? Judges sometimes speak as though it is possible to characterise a particular decision as "unreasonable" in an absolute sense: as though there were certain things that "no reasonable authority" could do even if its discretion were not limited by the purpose axiom.[63] But such an approach is supported by neither strict auth-

[59] See Chap. 3, p. 114.
[60] For duties to give reasons, see Chap. 6.
[61] The indications must be "overwhelming" *per* Lord Greene [1948] 1 K.B. at 230.
[62] *Ex p. Hook* (note 35 above) may be such a case—see *per* Hodgson J. in *R.* v. *Home Secretary ex p. Benwell* [1985] Q.B. 554 at 569. In *R* v. *Hillingdon L.B.C. ex p. Puhlhofer* (1985) 17 H.L.R. 278 Hodgson J. held that certain accommodation was so inappropriate to a family's needs that no reasonable authority properly exercising its Housing (Homeless Persons) Act 1977 powers could consider it appropriate. But the House of Lords held unanimously that on its proper construction the Act did not require the accommodation to be appropriate [1986] 1 All E.R. 467. The House indicated that there had been too many challenges "against local authorities who are endeavouring, in extremely difficult circumstances, to perform their duties under the 1977 Act . . . " (*ibid.* p. 474).
[63] See, *e.g. per* Lord Diplock in the *G.C.H.Q.* case at [1985] A.C. at 410: "By 'irrationality' I mean what can by now be succinctly referred to as '*Wednesbury* unreasonableness.' It applies to a decision which is so outrageous in its defiance of logic or of accepted moral standards that no sensible person who had applied his mind to the question to be decided could have arrived at it." Lord Greene's judgment in *Wednesbury* is susceptible of this construction: see *per* Willmer L.J. in *Hall & Co. Ltd.* v. *Shoreham U.D.C.* [1964] 1 W.L.R. 240 at 248–249. See too *Nottinghamshire C.C.* v. *Environment Secretary* [1986] 1 All E.R. 199 at 202 where Lord Scarman (expressing the unanimous view of the House of Lords) treated as separate grounds for review (i) error of statutory construction and (ii) "that the consequences of [the Secretary's] guidance were so absurd that he must have taken leave of his senses." But it seems both unnecessary and undesirable to treat the latter as a separate ground for judicial review. For if it appears that an official must have taken leave of his senses he has surely erred in his understanding of the limits of his powers. Further, it would be unfortunate if the dicta were taken to imply that the courts' jurisdiction to intervene on the basis of "absolute" unreasonableness is even wider where official action has not been approved (as it had in the case) by the House of Commons. *Cf. per* Lord Bridge in *Gillick* v. *D.H.S.S.* [1985] 3 All E.R. 402 at 426.

ority nor principle. The reported cases all exemplify the purpose axiom.[64] Indeed, without reference to some confining purpose, it cannot be said that even to dismiss a school teacher because she has red hair[65] is unreasonable. A notion of unreasonableness not confined by the operation of the purpose axiom would be a tool of unbridled judicial discretion.

(4) The boundary between law and policy[66]

The purpose axiom[67] is that statutory powers are conferred for a purpose; and that if a power granted for one purpose is exercised for a different purpose, that power has not been validly exercised. Are the notions of statutory purpose[68] and relevant consideration[69] sufficiently precise to enable public authorities, interested individuals and, where their jurisdiction is invoked, the courts to discern with certainty what actions fall within and what outside the legitimate field of official discretion? In short, how clear is the boundary between law and policy?

As we have seen, there will be cases where the statutory purpose is explicit and where an authority admits acting or is shown to have acted with a different purpose in view.[70] There are some cases too where, even though no statutory purpose is expressed, the action of a public authority is plainly directed to a purpose entirely unrelated to the whole thrust of the statute.[71] But many reported cases are less clear cut and arouse controversy, falling as they do into one of two broad categories. First, even where the statutory draftsman has given some express indication of purpose, the courts are not infrequently accused of discerning from very general words limitations far more specific than are warranted. Secondly, there

[64] *e.g. Hall* (see note 63). The court seemed to invoke a standard of "absolute" unreasonableness; but as *ex p. Royco* (note 40 above) shows, *Hall* plainly exemplifies the "purpose-related" notion defended in the text.

[65] A standard judicial example of "unreasonableness"—see *Wednesbury* at p. 229. To characterise such a dismissal as unreasonable is to assume (no doubt correctly) that any statutory power to dismiss must be exercised on grounds relating to the individual's employability or the authority's need to employ him. If a person could be dismissed at pleasure, then, no doubt, to dismiss him because he had red hair would be quite proper; and, if the employer had an intense dislike of red hair, perfectly reasonable.

[66] For a well-documented discussion of the "political" aspect of the judicial function, see *Policy Arguments in Judicial Decisions* (1983) by John Bell, esp. Chap. IV.

[67] See above, p. 171.

[68] See above, pp. 173–177.

[69] See above, pp. 177–183.

[70] See above, p. 173.

[71] See above, p. 174.

are many cases where either the purpose for which a power was conferred or the purpose for which an authority has exercised a power, or both, have to be inferred. Here the courts are sometimes said to have carried inference too far. We may now consider under these two heads some reported cases widely regarded as controversial.

(a) *Purpose expressed*

Bromley London Borough Council v. *Greater London Council*[72] raised questions about the degree of precision with which the statutory draftsman had indicated a statutory purpose by imposing on the GLC a duty to "promote the provision of integrated, efficient and economic transport facilities for Greater London . . ."[73] In carrying out an election pledge to cut public transport fares by 25 per cent. the GLC planned to meet the resulting deficit by a rate precept on the London boroughs. At the behest of Bromley Borough Council the Court of Appeal, upheld by the House of Lords, quashed the precept. The GLC was empowered to make grants "for any purpose" to the transport authority (London Transport Executive) but had to have regard to the Executive's duty to run its operation, so far as practicable, on a break even basis. The critical issue was whether the statute thus laid on the GLC an overriding duty to formulate its transport finance policy by reference to a need to break even or whether it could if it chose finance London transport substantially as a public service on the rates. Four of the five law lords opted for the former approach and referred not only to the provisions of the 1969 Act (including the "integrated, efficient and economic" provision) but also to earlier legislation and case law.[74]

The efforts of the majority to discern so clear a limitation on the GLC's policy-making powers may be thought less convincing than the approach of Lord Diplock who in effect applied the principle he had formulated in *Luby* v. *Newcastle-under-Lyme Corporation*,[75] one of the council house rent cases discussed above. Lord Diplock held that a "public transport as public service" policy was not of itself ruled out by the Act but that the specific policy of the GLC was unlawful because it failed to take account of the then

[72] [1983] 1 A.C. 768.

[73] Transport (London) Act 1969, s.1.

[74] *Prescott* v. *Birmingham Corpn*. [1955] Ch. 310 (power to charge such fares as authority think fit held to be subject to implied duty to run undertaking as business venture: free rides for pensioners *ultra vires*). Reversed on specific point by Travel Concessions Act 1964, s.1; and *cf*. now cases cited in note 76 below.

[75] [1964] 2 Q.B. 64.

current central government policy under which high council spending led to a reduction in the central government rate support grant, thus breaching the council's fiduciary duty to its ratepayers to use their money thriftily. Here, then, is a case where it may be felt that the majority judges endued a general statutory indication of purpose with greater precision (and so greater restriction on the discretion of the public authority) than was warranted by the statutory words themselves.[76]

(b) *Purpose to be inferred*

We turn now to our second head: cases where inference (whether of statutory purpose or of the purpose of an authority in exercising statutory power) figures prominently and controversially in the exercise of review jurisdiction. Of *Roberts* v. *Hopwood*[77] de Smith observed[78] that "most of the commentators agreed that [it] exceeded the proper limits of judicial review . . ." On one view the case decides merely that a power to pay "wages" does not authorise payment of gratuities.[79] On another view the House "came close to holding that expenditure by a local authority was contrary to law if in the opinion of the courts it was clearly unreasonable."[80] There is surely no justification for the courts inferring that Parliament intended the power to be thus confined. As already indicated, so unruly a notion of unreasonableness would turn judicial review into a jurisdiction to substitute a court's own judgment for that of an authority on whose judgment Parliament has chosen to rely.

Many of the more controversial cases of judicial review of the exercise of discretionary powers concern "default powers" of one sort or another. *Roberts* v. *Hopwood* centred on the then power of

[76] Contrast *R.* v. *L.T.E. ex p. G.L.C.* [1983] Q.B. 484; Div. Ct. declared later G.L.C. policy (achieving 25 per cent. fares reduction) within the powers of the Act in that it balanced L.T.E. duty to break even "so far as practicable" with its duty to "provide a service meeting the needs of Greater London." *cf.* also *R.* v. *Merseyside C.C. ex p. Gt. Universal Stores Ltd.* (1982) 80 L.G.R. 639 where (under a different statute) Woolf J. took an approach perhaps nearer to that of Lord Diplock than to that of the majority in the *Bromley* case.

[77] [1925] A.C. 578.

[78] De Smith J.R.A.A., p. 352.

[79] See *per* Forbes J. and Ormrod L.J. in *Pickwell* v. *Camden L.B.C.* [1983] Q.B. 962 at 986, 1000: local authority wage increases held lawful although considerably above (later agreed) national increase. Divisional Court declined to infer from size of increase a failure to consider relevant matters.

[80] De Smith J.R.A.A., p. 352 In *Pickwell* (previous note) Ormrod L.J. criticised the headnote to *Roberts* v. *Hopwood* which supports this interpretation but accepted that the speeches contain numerous expressions which could be used to support the headnote.

a district auditor to surcharge councillors for council expenditure contrary to law.[81] Today ministers are not infrequently empowered in certain circumstances to step in and override the policy and actions of a local or other authority. Default powers take many forms but they have in common that the conferee "is reviewing the action of another public body which itself has discretionary powers and duties."[82] Plainly, then, the conferment and exercise of default powers is in itself calculated to arouse controversy. When the courts are called upon to adjudicate between the conferee of the power and his victim they can hardly avoid being embroiled in controversy themselves. *Secretary of State for Education and Science* v. *Metropolitan Borough of Tameside*[83] illustrates both this point and our general point that in reviewing the exercise of discretionary power the courts may on occasion carry inference too far.

In the *Tameside* case the minister failed to obtain mandamus to compel a recently-elected Conservative education authority to go "comprehensive" in line with arrangements made by the outgoing Labour authority. The minister was empowered to issue directions to an authority if he was "satisfied . . . that [the] authority . . . [had] acted or [was] proposing to act unreasonably with respect to the exercise of any power." Three aspects of the House of Lords' decision call for comment.

First, the House took a now well-established view of the subjective "if satisfied" clause. Generally[84] where a statute uses subjective language such as "if the authority thinks fit" or "is satisfied" or "if it appears to the authority," the courts have required the authority to establish not merely that it thinks fit (etc.) but that there are grounds on which it could properly (*i.e.* having regard to the purpose for which the power is conferred) think fit (etc.).[85]

[81] For the current position of district auditors, see Local Government Finance Act 1982, sections 19 (replacing Local Government Act 1972, s.161, considered in *Pickwell* (above)) and 20 (replacing *ibid.* and applied in *Smith* v. *Skinner* [1986] *The Times*, March 6: Lambeth and Liverpool councillors surcharged and disqualified for "wilful misconduct" in failure to set lawful rate).

[82] *Per* Lord Wilberforce [1977] A.C. at 1047.

[83] [1977] A.C. 1014.

[84] Emergency or war-time legislation may be an exception: *Carltona* v. *Commissioners of Works* [1943] 2 All E.R. 560. In a war-time context the courts have gone so far as to treat as subjective statutory wording which was plainly objective ("if the minister has reasonable cause to believe"): *Liversidge* v. *Anderson* [1942] A.C. 206

[85] The *Wednesbury* case itself (p. 179, above) and the planning condition cases (pp. 176–177) illustrate this approach to "think fit" clauses. *Tameside* applies it authoritatively to "if satisfied" clauses. For "if it appears" clauses, see the *Norwich* case (note 91 below).

Otherwise a power (*e.g.*) to impose on licensees such conditions as an authority thinks fit would entitle the authority to impose conditions entirely unrelated to the purpose of the legislation; and a power to act "if satisfied" would be virtually a power to act at pleasure. On this level the *Tameside* approach to subjective wording merely reflects the purpose axiom itself. Equally, though, it reflects the courts' familiar[86] unwillingness to see their review jurisdiction ousted. Moreover, it is often (as we shall see it was in *Tameside*) a matter of delicate inference to say whether or not the authority did indeed have grounds for being satisfied or thinking fit. Here, if the court appears to carry inference too far, its apparent conversion of subjective into objective language can fuel accusations of interventionism.

Next, observe that in *Tameside* the statute required the minister to be satisfied that the authority was acting "unreasonably." The House of Lords held that this in effect required the minister, in exercising his default power, to apply to the actions of the education authority the *Wednesbury* test which the courts themselves apply in reviewing the exercise of discretionary power. As an elucidation of the statutory word "unreasonable" used in the context of a default power this surely has much to commend it. As Lord Diplock said:[87]

> ". . . in public law 'unreasonable' as decriptive of the way in which a public authority has purported to exercise a discretion vested in it by statute has become a term of legal art. To fall within this expression it must be conduct which no sensible authority acting with due appreciation of its responsibilities would have decided to adopt."[88]

[86] *cf.* Chap 2, p. 46 *et seq.*
[87] [1977] A.C. 1014 at 1064.
[88] In the council house rent cases (p. 175 above) the power was to make such "reasonable" charges as the authority might determine. As already observed, the courts eschewed any suggestion that this entitled them to review council policy which they considered unreasonable in the sense merely that they thought the policy misguided. It had to be unreasonable in the *Wednesbury* sense (see esp. *per* Diplock L.J. in *Luby* [1964] 2 Q.B. at 70). This is precisely the approach in *Tameside*, adopted also in *R.* v. *Kent County Council ex p. Bruce* [1986] *The Times* February 8: default power exercisable where minister "of opinion . . . that local authority have failed to discharge any of their functions." Held, authority would have "failed to discharge" functions only if it had acted unreasonably in the *Wednesbury* sense. But *cf.* Craig p. 365. And see Harlow and Rawlings above note 44 pp. 333–334.

It is to be observed, however, that recent statutes have cast aside the *Wednesbury* restraint by enacting default powers in far more draconian terms. For example, the council tenant's statutory "right to buy,[89] his house is buttressed by a provision that the Secretary of State may in effect act in the matter instead of a council where it appears to him that tenants are having difficulty in exercising their right.[90] In *Norwich City Council* v. *Secretary of State for the Environment*[91] the Court of Appeal upheld the Secretary's exercise of this power: there were grounds on which it could "appear" to the Secretary that tenants were having difficulty; and there was nothing in the wording of the power to indicate (as in *Tameside*) that the authority must be shown to have acted "unreasonably."[92]

Possibly the most controversial aspect of the *Tameside* case was the process of inference which led the House to rule that the minister was not entitled to issue his directive. The minister relied chiefly on the difficulty of satisfactory pupil reallocation in the few weeks available before the new school year. The majority of their lordships held in effect that there was no basis on which the minister could have been satisfied that the authority was acting unreasonably in the *Wednesbury* sense. This was largely a matter of inference from somewhat opaque correspondence issuing from the ministry. As in the *Bromley* case,[93] Lord Diplock was more cautious, resting his judgment on the ground that the minister had not applied the *Wednesbury* test but had, in effect, treated "unreasonably" in the statute as meaning "wrongly in my view." Accordingly he had not directed himself properly in law.

We began this section by asking whether the notions of statutory purpose and relevant consideration were sufficiently precise to enable parties to discern with certainty what actions fall within and what outside the legitimate field of official discretion. The cases considered in the previous sections suggest that the purpose axiom is capable, if used with circumspection, of leading to the imposition of justifiable limits on the exercise of official discretionary power while avoiding unjustifiable judicial intervention in policy making and execution. Judicial intervention is "justifiable" only where the purpose of an authority in exercising its statutory

[89] Housing Act 1980, Part I.
[90] *Ibid*. s.23.
[91] [1982] 1 All E.R. 737.
[92] *Ibid*. 749 (Kerr L.J) 754 (May L.J.); *cf*. p. 745 (Lord Denning M.R.).
[93] [1983] 1 A.C. 768.

powers and that of Parliament in conferring the powers are demonstrably at variance. Just as under the *Edwards* v. *Bairstow* doctrine[94] the courts should not endue statutory words of wide meaning with more precision than they can sustain, so under the purpose axiom the courts should not read into general statutory indications of purpose greater limitations on official discretion than such general words plainly warrant; nor should they lightly draw inferences upon which the lawfulness of a public authority's exercise of its discretion will turn.

As we observed when discussing the royal prerogative and review,[95] one way of characterising the boundary between law and policy is by reference to the notion of "justiciability." In the *G.C.H.Q.* case[96] the House of Lords indicated that the justiciability of a question arising from the exercise of a prerogative power would turn on the subject-matter of the power: compare, for example, the treaty-making power or the power to dispose of the armed forces with the power to employ and to fix conditions of crown service or the power of pardon in its various aspects. In the case of discretionary powers conferred by statute the question of justiciability may perhaps turn not only on the subject-matter of the power but also on the degree of precision with which Parliament has spelt out its limits. Take, for example, a statutory power to fix wages. It may be argued that in *Roberts* v. *Hopwood*[97] the House of Lords turned the question "what wages are lawful?" into a justiciable issue by reading the words of the statute too restrictively. But were a statute expressly to prescribe the considerations to which an authority must have regard in fixing wages, it would be difficult to criticise a court which reviewed a wage-fixing process which ignored the prescribed criteria.

The cases considered in this section are among those commonly cited to illustrate the imprecision and uncertainty inherent in the operation of the purpose axiom. It may be doubted whether cases of this ilk are either so numerous or such blatant exhibitions of unfettered judicial discretion as to justify the sweeping view "that the rules governing judicial review have no more substance at the

94 See Chap. 3, p. 114 *et seq.*
95 See Chap. 2, p. 77.
96 *Council of Civil Service Unions* v. *Minister for the Civil Service* [1985] A.C. 374. Note that a governmental claim of "security considerations" may stifle an application for judicial review of the exercise of statutory, just as much as of prerogative, power: see *e.g. R.* v. *Home Secretary ex p. McAvoy* [1984] 1 W.L.R. 1408.
97 [1925] A.C. 578.

core than a seedless grape."[98] Nevertheless it must be conceded that in such cases the courts have not always shown that degree of circumspection without which the purpose axiom would cease to be a viable tool of judicial review. In the *G.C.H.Q* case Lord Scarman said that "there is a common sense limitation recognised by the judges as to what is justiciable; and the limitation is entirely consistent with the general development of the modern case law of judicial review."[99] In the light of some of that case law, this might perhaps be regarded as a statement of an ideal to be striven for rather than as a description of perfection attained.

C. Irrelevant Considerations—Particular Issues

Our discussion of the purpose axiom started with Lord Reid's observation that Parliament is taken to have conferred discretion "with the intention that it should be used to promote the policy and objects of the Act."[1] We have seen how the courts may identify the policy and objects of an Act and how they use the notions of relevant and irrelevant consideration to establish that an authority has exercised a power for extraneous purposes. We now consider briefly certain particular applications of the notion of irrelevant consideration.

(1) Combination of relevant and irrelevant considerations

Suppose that a public authority has exercised a statutory discretion to resurface a particular road,[2] or to provide public lavatories at a particular place,[3] or to refuse to consider a particular complaint.[4] Suppose too that the considerations upon which the authority has acted include considerations which in themselves would have provided a proper basis for the action: *e.g.*, the road needed resurfacing; lavatories could be and were considered

[98] E. Gellhorn and G. O. Robinson in (1975) 75 Col.L.R. 771 at 780, cited in Harlow and Rawlings above note 44 p. 311, *passim*.
[99] [1985] A.C. at 407.
[1] See above, p. 171.
[2] See, *e.g. R.* v. *Brighton Corporation ex p. Shoosmith* (1907) 96 L.T. 762.
[3] See, *e.g. Westminster Corporation* v. *L.N.W. Rly*. [1905] A.C. 426. (*cf.* also *Biddulph* v. *Vestry of St George, Hanover Square* (1863) 33 L.J. (Eq) 411: an entertaining case).
[4] See, *e.g. R.* v. *Broadcasting Complaints Commission ex p. Owen* [1985] 2 W.L.R. 1025. (*cf.* also *Padfield*'s case, discussed above, p. 178).

necessary at the particular place; the complaint could be and was considered unsuitable for the procedure in question. What is the position if, in deciding to act as it did, the authority took into account not only the proper considerations but also improper ones?—*e.g.* that the road when resurfaced could be hired to a motor club for a club event[5]; that access to the lavatories would also provide a pedestrian subway linking two sides of a busy street[6]; that to consider the complaint would be burdensome.[7]

The approach currently adopted by the courts is to inquire whether the decision was "materially"[8] or "substantially"[9] affected by the irrelevant consideration. The action will be held unlawful if it appears that it would not have been taken in the absence of the irrelevant consideration. In the three cases referred to in the above examples, challenges failed on this basis—even though in the road-mending case "in truth and in fact the corporation would not have gone to the expense of [resurfacing] at the time when they did if it had not been for the fact that the Automobile Club made [an application to them to use the road for a motor racing event]."[10] It was enough that the council exercised their resurfacing power to make an improvement which, irrespective of the Club's application, was considered necessary. By contrast, where a rating authority's decision not to refund a payment made on the basis of an over-assessment had probably been substantially influenced by the erroneous advice of its treasurer, the decision was quashed even though there might have been other and good reasons for refusing the refund.[11] Similarly, the decision of a local education authority to retain an advertising agency, briefed both to inform the public of the effect of government "rate-capping" and to persuade the public that the government's plan to abolish the authority was misconceived, was declared invalid.[12] Statute empowered the authority to inform but not to persuade; and the decision to employ the agency was materially affected by the irrelevant consideration.

[5] As in *Shoosmith* (above, note 2).
[6] As in *Westminster Corporation* case (above, note 3).
[7] As in *Owen* (above, note 4).
[8] *R.* v. *Inner London Education Authority ex p. Westminster City Council* [1986] 1 All E.R. 19, 36.
[9] *R.* v. *Rochdale M.B.C. ex p. Cromer Ltd.* [1982] 3 All E.R. 761.
[10] *Ex p. Shoosmith* (see note 2), *per* Vaughan-Williams L.J. at p. 763.
[11] *Rochdale* case (see note 9).
[12] *Inner London Education Authority* case (above).

(2) Improper exercise of discretion; bad faith

The issue just considered may be seen as a particular manifestation of a general problem—the relationship between the purpose for which a statutory power has been conferred and the purpose which an authority has pursued in exercising the power. Often, of course, if the authority's purpose is improper, the action it takes will fail to achieve the statutory purpose—as, *e.g.* in *Padfield's* case.[13] But an exercise of discretionary power wholly or substantially based on considerations irrelevant to the attainment of the statutory purpose or without regard to relevant considerations, may nevertheless appear to achieve the statutory purpose. Suppose that in *Roberts* v. *Hopwood*[14] the authority, notwithstanding its failure to adopt criteria appropriate for the fixing of wages, had arrived at a figure similar to the "going rate." Should the court then have ruled that the power had been unlawfully exercised? Some dicta suggest not.[15] But in principle, surely, it should. Statute has conferred a power to fix and pay "wages"; not a power to fix and pay either an arbitrary sum or a sum fixed by reference to criteria other than those appropriate to the fixing of wages. That power has not been exercised even though the sum fixed (arbitrarily or by reference to the improper criteria) might well have been the sum arrived at by reference to proper criteria. Recall Lord Reid's reference[16] to the intention of Parliament that "discretion should be used" to promote the policy and objects of an Act. In the example just considered the policy of the Act may appear to have been promoted. But if it has, it is by chance and not by the proper use of discretion.[17]

It is axiomatic[18] that "bad faith" vitiates the exercise of a discretionary power.[19] "Bad faith . . . means dishonesty."[20] An authority is guilty of bad faith if it "intends to achieve an object

[13] [1968] A.C. 997. (see above, p. 178).
[14] [1925] A.C. 578.
[15] See Lord Sumner, *ibid* at 604; Ormrod L.J. in *Pickwell* v. *Camden L.B.C.* [1983] Q.B. 962 at 999. *cf.* also de Smith J.R.A.A., pp. 328–329.
[16] In *Padfield's* case [1968] A.C. at 1030.
[17] It might be appropriate for a review court in the exercise of its discretion as to the award of remedies (see Chap. 8) to decline to award a mandatory remedy in a case where the policy of the statute had palpably been achieved despite the abuse of discretion.
[18] See, *e.g. per* Lord Greene in *Wednesbury* [1948] 1 K.B. at 229.
[19] But even this vice may be immunised from challenge by an appropriately worded ouster clause: see the *East Elloe* and *Ostler* cases discussed in Chap. 2, pp. 55–56.
[20] *Per* Megaw L.J. in *Cannock Chase D.C.* v. *Kelly* [1978] 1 W.L.R. 1 at 6.

other than that for which [it] believes the power to have been conferred."[21] Instances of bad faith are rare,[22] but in most of the cases where it is present the object intended will actually be (as the authority believes) other than that for which the power has been conferred.[23] In such a case, while the existence of bad faith may establish civil liability,[24] the fact that the purpose is actually other than that contemplated by the Act will itself be a basis for judicial review, irrespective of the bad faith. Conceivably there might be a case where the authority intended to achieve an object which it wrongly believed to be other than that for which the power was conferred. An education authority with power to dismiss teachers on financial as well as educational grounds[25] might believe mistakenly that it could act only on educational grounds. If it dismissed a teacher on financial grounds disguised as educational grounds it would have acted in bad faith. Surely the teacher should be able to challenge the decision on that basis, notwithstanding that he might later be dismissed expressly on financial grounds. Indeed, it appears that the authority, if apprised of its power to dismiss on financial grounds before the challenge came before the court, might defeat the challenge by ratifying the dismissal on those grounds.[26] These possibilities, though, do not suggest that the original decision, involving as it did an abuse of the discretion conferred by Parliament upon the authority, should be immune from challenge. Had the authority initially been aware of its power to dismiss on financial grounds it might have acted differently.

(3) Surrender of discretion

The previous section suggests that any lawful exercise of discretionary power should involve a proper choice of action by the conferee of the power. "Proper choice" means a decision based substantially[27] on relevant considerations. But "proper choice" means also true choice. If a repository of discretionary power effectively leaves the choice to another he fails properly to exercise the power himself. He may have improperly delegated the decision to another; he may in effect have precluded himself from

[21] De Smith J.R.A.A., p. 335.

[22] Allegations of bad faith may be more frequent; but he who alleges must plead and prove: *Kelly's* case (above).

[23] As in *Roncarelli* v. *Duplessis* (1959) 16 D.L.R. (2d) 689; *Smith* v. *Skinner* [1986] *The Times*, March 6 (above, note 81): councillors "at the very least recklessly indifferent" to consequences of unlawful conduct.

[24] *Roncarelli* (previous note); and see Chap. 2, p. 89.

[25] *cf. Hanson* v. *Radcliffe U.D.C.* [1922] 2 Ch. 490 (see above, p. 174).

[26] *Stoke on Trent City Council* v. *B. & Q. (Retail) Ltd* [1984] Ch. 1.

[27] See p. 191 above.

making a decision on the merits of the case by a slavish adherence to a predetermined policy; or he may regard himself as bound to proceed in a particular way by contractual obligations previously undertaken. In each case he may be said to have acted on the basis of a particular variety of improper, or irrelevant, consideration.[28] Each is a variety of "surrender" of, or failure to exercise, discretion. In the following paragraphs we illustrate the varieties of surrender just referred to.[29]

(a) *Improper delegation*

Statute may expressly authorise delegation of discretion as, for example, in the case of local authorities. The number and extent of their powers necessitates that decisions should be able to be taken by committees, sub-committees or officers of the authority.[30] Of course, many other authorities have statutory powers so wide and so numerous that such delegation becomes a practical necessity. Central government ministers are the most obvious example: here the courts hold that Parliament must be taken to have authorised delegation by a minister to his departmental staff.[31] Currently there are indications of an increasing willingness in the courts to extend this principle of "delegation based on administrative necessity."[32]

Nevertheless the general principle remains that an authority upon which statute has conferred discretion must exercise that discretion itself.[33] So, a cinema licensing authority improperly delegated its power to decide which films should and should not be shown in a cinema when it adopted as a hard-and-fast criterion whether or not the film had been certified by the British Board of Film Censors.[34] And there was improper delegation when a minister treated as conclusive against the grant of planning permission for gravel extraction the refusal of another minister to withdraw

[28] See *per* Lord Greene in *Wednesbury*, [1948] 1 K.B. at 231.
[29] For more details of this highly complex area see De Smith J.R.A.A., pp. 298–322; Wade A.L., Ch. 11; Craig, pp. 371–383; Chaps. 16, 17.
[30] Local Government Act 1972, ss.101, 102. But *cf. R.* v. *Environment Secretary ex p. Hillingdon L.B.C.* [1986] 1 All E.R. 810 (aff'd. (C.A.) [1986] 2 All E.R. 273): no power to delegate decisions to committee chairman alone.
[31] *Carltona Ltd.* v. *Commrs. of Works* [1943] 2 All E.R. 560.
[32] See D. Lanham (1984) 100 L.Q.R. 587 at 611.
[33] See, *e.g. Vine* v. *National Dock Labour Board* [1957] A.C. 488.
[34] *Ellis* v. *Dubowski* [1921] 3 K.B. 621; *cf. Mills* v. *L.C.C.* [1925] 1 K.B. 213 (licensing authority did not treat B.B.F.C. certificate as absolute criterion but showed itself willing to consider films on their merits: no improper delegation). See too *R.* v. *G.L.C. ex p. Blackburn* [1976] 1 W.L.R. 550.

his objection based on probable long-term damage to the agricultural value of the land.[35] The crux of improper delegation appears from the words "hard-and-fast" and "conclusive" in the previous sentences. An authority may properly base its decision on expert opinion not only because of administrative necessity but also to ensure a high quality of decision. Indeed, failure to take account of expert opinion might well amount to failure to take account of a relevant consideration—as, for example, if a public authority were to authorise particular building works without taking architectural advice. But the authority must not simply act as a rubber stamp for that opinion. Although in most cases it will no doubt follow the advice proffered, it must be seen to be willing to reject the advice where, for good reasons, it might think fit to do so.[36]

(b) *Fettering by policy*

If it is sometimes a delicate matter to chart a course between too much and too little reliance on expert opinion, so too with reliance on "policy." Fairness and consistency in the exercise of discretionary power will commonly demand that an authority formulate a policy—a set of guidelines—as the basis upon which individual decisions will be made.[37] But just as an authority must not, by improper delegation, allow others to take its decisions for it, so it must not, as it were, allow its policy to take its decisions for it. It must not apply its policy so rigidly that general guidelines become unbreakable rules to the exclusion of the exercise of any real discretion in individual cases. In short, it must not fetter its discretion by policy.

In *British Oxygen Co. Ltd* v. *Board of Trade*[38] Lord Reid said:

> "What the authority must not do is to refuse to listen at all. But a Ministry or large authority may have had to deal already

[35] *Lavender & Son Ltd.* v. *Minister of Housing & Local Government* [1970] 1 W.L.R. 1231.

[36] As in *Mills* and *Blackburn* cases, above note 34. See also *Blackburn* cases cited above, p. 179. The line may, of course, be difficult to draw. In *R.* v. *Independent Broadcasting Authority ex p. Whitehouse* [1984] *The Times* April 14 (D.C.); [1985] *The Times* April 4 (C.A.) the question was essentially whether "the inevitable delegation of day-to-day duties by the IBA to its senior staff" was properly to be regarded as a means of exercising a statutory discretion or, on the contrary, a failure to exercise its discretion in regard to just those cases where that was required. The Court of Appeal (in holding the former) reversed the Divisional Court.

[37] Statute sometimes expressly authorises or requires this—see *e.g.* Local Government Planning and Land Act 1980, s.59(11A)—see *Nottinghamshire C.C.* v. *Environment Secretary* [1986] 1 All E.R. 199.

[38] [1971] A.C. 610.

> with a multitude of similar applications and then they will almost certainly have evolved a policy so precise that it could well be called a rule. There can be no objection to that, provided the authority is always willing to listen to anyone with something to say . . ."

In the case, the Board (empowered to make grants towards capital expenditure on new industrial plant) had refused the Company a grant towards the £4 million it had spent on gas cylinders costing £20 each. The Board's policy was not to give grants for items costing singly less than £25. The House of Lords found, however, that the Board was still willing to hear any arguments from a particular applicant as to why the policy should not apply to his case.[39] In *R* v. *Secretary of State for the Environment ex p. Brent L.B.C.*,[40] on the other hand, the Divisional Court quashed the minister's reduction of a local authority's rate support grant on the basis that he had unlawfully fettered his discretion by policy when he refused to hear representations from the authority before making his decision.[41]

A policy adopted by an authority must, of course, be consistent with the policy and objects of the Act in question. Otherwise the policy becomes itself an irrelevant consideration.[42] Action based upon it will be unlawful for this reason and irrespective of any question of fettering.

(c) *Fettering by contract*

Public authorities can, of course, make binding contracts which they can enforce and which can be enforced against them.[43] Any such contract made in the exercise of a discretionary power inevi-

[39] The House of Lords has endorsed the *British Oxygen* test in *Eastleigh B.C.* v. *Betts* [1983] 2 A.C. 613 (approving local authority association guidelines on "local connection" for purposes of Housing (Homeless Persons) Act 1977, s.18); and in *Re Findlay* [1985] A.C. 318 (approving Home Secretary's adoption of parole policy requiring exceptional circumstances or compelling reasons for departure from it). See also *R.* v. *Mansfield J.J. ex p. Sharkey* [1985] Q.B. 613 (magistrates did not fetter discretion as to bail conditions by policy where in 90 per cent. of cases they acceded to police application to prohibit miners accused of public order offences from returning to picket lines).

[40] [1982] Q.B. 593.

[41] See too *Lavender*'s case (above, note 35): minister's approach characterised by court as both improper delegation and fettering by policy. For discussion of the role of policy as a means of confining, structuring and checking discretion, see the writings of K. C. Davis and others considered in Craig., p. 380 *passim*.

[42] See, *e.g.* *Roberts* v. *Hopwood* and *Padfield* v. *Min. of Agriculture* (discussed in section B above).

[43] See Chap. 2., p. 84.

tably limits the freedom of choice which the authority enjoyed immediately before it made the contract. In that sense such a contract fetters, or limits, the future discretion of the authority: having accepted Smith's tender for building work, it must not then give the work to Jones.

If a contract can be seen as a mode of exercising discretion, the limit it imposes on future action under the power in question will be lawful. So, a contract by an electricity supply authority to keep its prices in line with those of a neighbouring authority was upheld by the House of Lords. The price limit was to be regarded as a legitimate exercise of commercial judgment, and so of the authority's power to fix prices, rather than as a fetter on its future discretion to fix prices.[44] Of course, an authority may have other statutory powers (either existing at the time the contract was made[45] or conferred later[46]) whose effect is to entitle the authority to breach a binding contract.[47] In such cases, however, the existence of the contract is a matter to which the authority must have regard in the exercise of the statutory power under which the contract may be breached.[48]

If, however, the performance of a contract would actually be inconsistent with the advancement of the purpose for which Parliament conferred the discretionary power under which the contract is purportedly made, the contract will be void. So, the House of Lords declared void a contract under which an authority, exercising a power to acquire land compulsorily for harbour purposes, purported to reduce the compensation payable to the erstwhile owner by granting him access to the harbour from his adjacent land.[49] The effect of the contract would have been to interfere

[44] *Birkdale District Electric Supply Co.* v. *Southport Corpn.* [1926] A.C. 355.

[45] *Dowty Boulton Paul Ltd.* v. *Wolverhampton Corpn. (No. 2)* [1976] Ch. 13 (local authority had covenanted to permit company to use local authority airfield for 99 years; authority empowered by statute to break covenant by exercising power to reappropriate land when it considered it "not required" any longer as airfield); *cf. Dowty Boulton Paul Ltd.* v. *Wolverhampton Corpn.* [1971] 1 W.L.R. 204: earlier interlocutory proceedings in the same case in which the court had taken a different view of the effect of the statutory provision and had applied the principle exemplified in the *Southport Corpn.* case (previous note).

[46] *R.* v. *Hillingdon Health Authority ex p. Goodwin* [1983] *The Times*, December 13 (below).

[47] Legislation may (as in the *Wolverhampton* case (above)) or may not provide for compensation. On whether there should be a general right to compensation, see Craig, p. 601.

[48] In *Goodwin's* case (above) the Divisional Court quashed a Health Authority's decision to close a hospital under statutory financial constraints: the authority had failed to consider terminations of contractual arrangements with staff.

[49] *Ayr Harbour Trustees* v. *Oswald* (1883) 8 App.Cas. 623.

with the authority's use of the land for the purpose for which it was authorised to acquire it.

Where a contract is void, neither party can, of course, enforce it. In particular the public authority cannot be prevented by the other party from exercising its powers in a manner inconsistent with the terms of the void contract.[50] It would seem also to follow that for an authority to exercise a discretionary power on the basis that the contract bound it, would amount to unlawful surrender of discretion. In this sense, then, "a public authority cannot by contract fetter the exercise of its discretion."[51] But a void contract (like a valid contract which the authority has power to break) may be a consideration which the authority should take into account in deciding whether or not to act inconsistently with it. So, for example, it appears that if the revenue agree to make no further inquiry into certain of a tax-payer's affairs in return for his withdrawal of claims to relief, they may be restrained from breaking the agreement (which is devoid of contractual force) if they purport to do so without considering the propriety of frustrating the expectations which they have created.[52] In these circumstances an agreement (like another's advice, and like a policy) must not be treated as compelling[53] but must be taken into consideration in the decision-making process.

Note on estoppel, revocability and res judicata

There are many circumstances in private law in which an individual may be held to what he has done or represented or promised even though he acted initially under no legal obligation. Students of contract and property law will be acquainted, for example, with the doctrines of promissory and proprietary estoppel. Litigants have on occasion invited the courts to impose on public authorities the restraints which such doctrines impose on

[50] See, *e.g. Windsor Borough Council* v. *Brandrose Ltd* [1983] 1 W.L.R. 509.

[51] *Per* Lord Parker C.J. in *Southend-on-sea Corpn.* v. *Hodgson Ltd* [1962] 1 Q.B. 416 at 424.

[52] So held by Woolf J. in *R.* v. *I.R.C. ex p. Preston* [1983] 2 All E.R. 300. The Court of Appeal [1984] 3 W.L.R. 945. reversed Woolf J. on the basis that it was not clear that the I.R.C. had not considered the agreement and that fresh material had emerged. The House of Lords [1985] 2 W.L.R. 836 upheld the Court of Appeal but endorsed the principle in Woolf J's judgment referred to in the text. See too *Att.-Gen. of Hong Kong* v. *Ng Yuen Shiu* [1983] 2 A.C. 629, Chap. 6, p. 219.

[53] But, *cf. Preston*'s case (above) where Woolf J. held that the I.R.C. had no material upon which to reopen the case and so were in effect bound by their undertaking. The judgments in the House of Lords are equivocal on whether in those circumstances the authority might actually renege on its agreement provided it considered the propriety of doing so.

private individuals. Take some examples. A dairy company budgeted on the basis that its most recent electricity bill was correct. In fact the electricity authority had mistakenly charged only one tenth of the correct amount. The company argued that the authority should be estopped from recovering the balance.[54] A builder bought land for a builder's yard on the strength of an assurance from a planning official that planning permission existed. In fact it did not. The builder attempted to resist enforcement proceedings by arguing that the authority was estopped by the assurance given on its behalf.[55] A parent acted in reliance on the local education authority's estimate that her home was more than three miles from her child's school, thus entitling the child to a free bus pass. The distance was in fact less than three miles; but the parent argued that the authority should be estopped from withdrawing the pass.[56]

In all these cases the courts applied the principle that "estoppel cannot operate to prevent or hinder the performance of a statutory duty or the exercise of a statutory discretion."[57] In the dairy and in the bus pass cases the courts similarly rejected arguments based on the notion that the act or decision was irrevocable—arguments based in effect on analogy with the principles of *res judicata*. Under those principles, parties to litigation are prevented from re-opening issues[58] between them which have been finally[59] disposed of by a competent court. In essence these attempts "to introduce into public administrative law concepts such as equitable estoppel which are essentially aids to the doing of justice in private law"[60]

[54] *Maritime Electric Co.* v. *General Dairies Ltd* [1937] A.C. 610.

[55] *Southend-on-Sea Corpn.* v. *Hodgson Ltd.* [1962] 1 Q.B. 416.

[56] *Rootkin* v. *Kent C.C.* [1981] 1 W.L.R. 1186, (in reliance on three mile rule, parent refrained from seeking re-allocation of child).

[57] *Per* Lord Parker C.J. in the *Southend* case, [1962] 1 Q.B. at 422.

[58] "Estoppel *per rem judicatam*" embodies the two notions of "issue estoppel" and "cause of action estoppel." See Wade A.L., pp. 239 *et seq*.

[59] *i.e.* any possibility of appeal having been exhausted.

[60] *Per* Lord Scarman, describing such attempts as "wrong" in *Newbury D.C.* v. *Sec. of State for the Environment* [1981] A.C. 578 at 617. We may note, however, the principle of "severance" as one private law notion which has been adapted to public law purposes. The principle is that where an administrative order or decision is partly valid and partly invalid (*e.g.* one of several conditions of a licence is *ultra vires*) then, unless the invalid part is inextricably interconnected with the valid, a court is entitled to set aside or disregard the invalid part, leaving the rest intact: *per* Ormrod L.J. in *Dunkley* v. *Evans* [1981] 1 W.L.R. 1522, 1524; *R.* v. *North Herts. D.C. ex p. Cobbold* [1985] 3 All E.R. 486; *R.* v. *Transport Secretary ex p. G.L.C.* [1985] 3 W.L.R. 574. See generally de Smith J.R.A.A., pp. 105–106.

failed on the principle we have seen exemplified in the cases on fettering discretion. As Lord Parker said in the builder's yard case[61]

> "[I]n a case of discretion there is a duty under the statute to exercise a free and unhindered discretion. There is a long line of cases . . . which lay down that a public authority cannot by contract fetter the exercise of its discretion. Similarly . . . an estoppel cannot be raised to prevent or hinder the exercise of the discretion.[62]"

Such is the approach which has been generally applied by the English courts. But complex issues may arise, particularly where it is alleged that a public authority has acted through a duly authorised agent.[63] Indeed the Court of Appeal has indicated that an estoppel may arise where an authority is empowered to delegate functions and there is evidence which would justify an individual's thinking that it had.[64] The area seems ripe for reform. Not only is the case law confused but there is insufficient recognition of the need to reconcile two sometimes opposed principles: that statutory duties and powers cannot be fettered; and that individuals should be able to rely on what appear to be final and authoritative determinations of public authorities.[65]

[61] [1962] 1 Q.B. at 424.

[62] "An estoppel cannot be raised to prevent or hinder the exercise of discretion." But note that once a discretion has been validly exercised so as to confer private rights on an individual, the authority may be restrained from revoking its decision: *Livingstone* v. *Westminster Corporation* [1904] 2 K.B. 109 (minor arithmetical error leading to over-assessment of compensation payable for loss of office: assessment valid and irrevocable). Consider also *Gowa* v. *Att.-Gen.* [1984] *The Times*, December 27 (citizenship granted under mistake of law, yet Court of Appeal held Crown estopped from denying grant since in reliance upon it applicant had refrained from taking further steps to obtain citizenship. House of Lords upheld Court of Appeal on different ground, observing that the estoppel solution did "involve difficulties" [1985] 1 W.L.R. 1003 at 1009. As to *res judicata*, the courts have not only refused to extend the doctrine by analogy into the area of public authority decision-making; they have also declined to apply it to proceedings by way of application for judicial review under R.S.C., Ord. 53: *R.* v. *Secretary of State for the Environment ex p. Hackney L.B.C.* [1983] 1 W.L.R. 524 at 539 *passim* (D.C.); [1984] 1 W.L.R. 592 at 602, 606 (C.A.). But *cf.* Chap. 8, p. 303 below.

[63] De Smith J.R.A.A., pp. 100–105.

[64] *Western Fish Products Ltd.* v. *Penwith D.C.* [1981] 2 All E.R. 204 (obiter: neither representation nor reliance established).

[65] See generally Craig, Chap. 16.

D. Supervisory and Appellate Review of Unlawful Exercise of Discretion

We have now seen how the extent of discretionary power may be defined by reference to the purpose for which it is conferred. And we have seen that the "purpose axiom," embodying that notion, requires not only that a lawful exercise of discretionary power should tend towards the attainment of the statutory purpose but also that it should reflect a proper exercise of choice by the authority concerned. Otherwise, according to the purpose axiom, the power has not been validly exercised. Such, essentially, are the legal limits of the freedom of public authorities to resolve policy issues according to criteria of their own choosing.

How may judicial review jurisdiction—supervisory and appellate—operate so as to give effect to these legal limits?

(1) Supervisory review

If an authority subject to supervisory review jurisdiction goes beyond the limits imposed by the operation of the purpose axiom, it acts *ultra vires*.[66] Subject to any statutory ouster of review jurisdiction, the superior courts may, as necessary, quash or prohibit an *ultra vires* decision or act, order the authority to exercise its discretion according to law, or make declarations. In appropriate circumstances also a party may rely upon the action being *ultra vires* as the basis of a collateral challenge.[67]

How far, if at all, can the exercise of the supervisory jurisdiction affect the substance of the action which, in the proper exercise of its discretion, an authority may ultimately take? If a particular act or decision is held *ultra vires* on the basis of improper purpose or irrelevant considerations, is the authority free thereafter to take the same action or make the same decision, ensuring that it does so for a proper purpose and with regard only to relevant considerations? In short, how far is it true in the context of supervisory review of the exercise of discretionary power to say that "judicial review is concerned not with the merits of a decision but with the

[66] Improper purpose, irrelevant considerations etc. may, alternatively, be characterised by a court exercising supervisory review jurisdiction as (jurisdictional) error of law: see p. 180 above.

[67] As, *e.g.* in *Ellis* v. *Dubowski* (above, note 34): cinema operator successfully resisted prosecution for breach of *ultra vires* licence condition; *Roncarelli* v. *Duplessis* (above, p. 175): Quebec Prime Minister liable in tort for *ultra vires* revocation of liquor licence.

manner in which the decision was made"[68]? Reference to some of the cases already discussed will show quickly that there is no short answer to this question.

In some cases an authority may be able to take the same action albeit on different grounds. Take for example the local authorities which sought injunctions against retailers for their breach of Sunday trading laws.[69] One action was dismissed because the authority's decision to seek the injunction was taken without regard to relevant considerations. But the authority was free to repeat the process if, meanwhile, it had decided on proper grounds to do so.[70] Again, the rating authority which declined on improper grounds to grant a refund[71] might still, when properly advised, reach the same decision. In the "Fares Fair" campaign The Greater London Council ultimately achieved a 25 per cent. fares reduction by adopting a policy held by the Divisional Court to be within the powers of the Act.[72] And the Environment Secretary who was held to have fettered his discretion by over-rigid application of his policy on rate support grant reduction[73] reached the same decision after he had considered representations by the local authorities concerned.[74] In all these cases the original act or decision was *ultra vires* not because it was in itself incapable of furthering the purpose for which the statutory power in question was conferred; but because the authority acted without considering whether or not it would in fact further that purpose.

In other cases an act or decision has been held to be in itself incapable of furthering the statutory purpose. In such cases the authority is constrained to make a substantive change in what it proposed but still retains a wide choice as to what it may do. The planning authority in *R.* v. *Hillingdon London Borough Council ex p. Royco Ltd*[75] could not impose a planning condition requiring the developer to make his flats available to persons on the council's housing waiting-list. But the authority remained free to impose such proper conditions as it chose. Similarly, the transport

[68] *Per* Lord Fraser in *R.* v. *Entry Clearance Officer ex p. Amin* [1983] 2 A.C. 818 at 829. See also Chap. 2, p. 58.
[69] *Stoke-on-Trent City Council* v. *B & Q (Retail) Ltd and other appeals* [1984] Ch. 1.
[70] And see p. 193 above.
[71] *R.* v. *Rochdale M.B.C. ex p. Cromer Ltd* [1982] 3 All E.R. 761.
[72] *R.* v. *L.T.E. ex p. G.L.C.* [1983] Q.B. 484.
[73] *R.* v. *Secretary of State for the Environment ex p. Brent L.B.C.* [1982] Q.B. 593.
[74] Challenged unsuccessfully in *R.* v. *Secretary of State for the Environment ex p. Hackney L.B.C.* [1984] 1 W.L.R. 592.
[75] [1974] Q.B. 720.

authority precluded from providing free transport for pensioners[76] would have remained able to take account of pensioners' means in fixing fare levels.

Many cases, however, sit awkwardly between these two categories. In *Padfield's* case,[77] for example, the court ordered the minister to consider the appellant's complaint according to law. He did in fact refer the complaint to the committee.[78] Could he, though, have declined to do so? It might have appeared at least disingenuous for the minister at that stage to reach on proper grounds the very decision to which he had previously been led by improper ones. In cases like the *Tameside* case[79] and *Roberts* v. *Hopwood*[80] it is difficult to say that the court is not concerned with the merits of a decision. In *Tameside*, as we saw, the majority of the House held in effect that there was no basis on which the minister could properly have exercised his default power; and *Roberts* v. *Hopwood* may be interpreted as a ruling that the amounts fixed as wages were too high according to some objective, yet undefined, standard of reasonableness. The propriety of these decisions has already been discussed.[81]

There is a third category of case where not only is the effect of review to rule out the action originally proposed but also, in the circumstances, to constrain the authority to follow a particular course of action. Recall, for example, the restaurateur deprived of his licence because he stood bail surety for Jehovah's Witnesses[82]; and the market stall holder whose licence was revoked because he urinated in a side-street.[83] Here the authority must continue to license the individuals concerned. And there are cases where the effect of review is to constrain the authority to take positive steps which it has declined to take. For example, a decision to exclude certain persons from an authority's deliberations may be *ultra vires* where proper consideration of the matter could lead only to the

[76] *Prescott* v. *Birmingham Corporation* [1955] Ch. 310.

[77] [1968] A.C. 997.

[78] The committee found for the complainant. But the minister (as he was empowered to do) decided not to implement the committee's findings. Harlow and Rawlings in *Law and Administration* consider the case a "waste of time and money" (p. 273). But the minister was prevented from using his statutory power for the improper purpose of escaping criticism in Parliament.

[79] [1977] A.C. 1014.

[80] [1925] A.C. 578.

[81] See above, pp. 183–190.

[82] *Roncarelli* v. *Duplessis* (1959) 16. D.L.R. (2d) 689.

[83] *R.* v. *Barnsley M.B.C. ex p. Hook* [1976] 1 W.L.R. 1052.

conclusion that the persons should be admitted: the effect of the ruling is, then, that they must be.[84]

The cases considered above show that the effect of supervisory review on an authority's future freedom to act in a matter depends largely on whether in the circumstances the substance of what the authority has done or proposed to do is something which, on the basis of proper considerations, might tend to the fulfilment of the statutory purpose for which a power has been conferred. In the light of these considerations, the unvarnished statement that supervisory review is not concerned with the merits of a decision may be thought misleading.

(2) Appellate review

In most cases of appeal against exercises of discretion by courts of first instance an appeal court has jurisdiction to rehear and dispose of the matter as it thinks fit.[85] Nevertheless, just as such a court will rarely differ from the first instance judge's assessment of the credibility and reliability of witnesses, so it will show some circumspection in reviewing the exercise of judicial discretion:

> ". . . appellate authorities ought not to reverse the order merely because they would themselves have exercised the original discretion, had it attached to them, in a different way. If, however, the appellate tribunal reaches the clear conclusion that there has been a wrongful exercise of discretion, in that no weight, or no sufficient weight, has been given to relevant considerations . . . then the reversal of the order on appeal may be justified."[86]

In most cases of appeal against exercises of discretion by public authorities other than courts, the appeal court's jurisdiction is

[84] *R.* v. *Hackney L.B.C. ex p. Gamper* [1985] 3 All E.R. 275 (Labour council's decision to exclude Liberal councillor from sub-committees quashed: *cf.* now, Local Government (Access to Information) Act 1985 s.1(1)); *R.* v. *Burnham Committee ex p. Professional Association of Teachers* [1985] *The Times*, March 30 (Burnham panel acted *ultra vires* in excluding Association's representatives from sub-committees).

[85] See Chap. 2, pp. 42–43.

[86] *Per* Viscount Simon L.C. in *Osenton & Co.* v. *Johnston* [1942] A.C. 130 at 138, citing *Evans* v. *Bartlam* [1937] A.C. 473. The test is thus stricter than the *Wednesbury* test, under which one would need to show a *total failure* to take account of a relevant consideration. It would not be enough (as it is under the *Osenton* test) to show a failure to give such consideration *sufficient weight*—see *G.* v. *G.* [1985] 1 W.L.R. 647 at 653 (apparently misunderstood in *R.* v. *Cardiff JJ. ex p. Salter* [1986] F.L.R. 162).

limited by statute to the correction of error of law.[87] Here, then, the task of an appellant is substantially the same as the task of one who invokes the supervisory jurisdiction under the *Wednesbury* principles. And the jurisdiction of the court to correct the error is likewise substantially the same. On the one hand, correction of the error (*e.g.* failure to take account of a relevant consideration) may settle the issue between the parties, and an appeal court will make an appropriate order.[88] On the other hand, correction of the error may merely establish the correct basis upon which the deciding authority should have proceeded. In that case the appeal court will remit the matter to the authority for decision on that basis.[89]

Finally, as already noted,[90] Parliament has remitted to administrative authorities many functions of a sort discharged in the past by justices of the peace. Notwithstanding that the discharge of these functions frequently involves a considerable element of discretion, statute commonly provides for an appeal on the merits from the authority to a local court, *e.g.* magistrates' or Crown Court. In these cases the appeal is by way of a complete rehearing in which the court (although it must pay due regard to the authority's decision) may consider all available evidence and come to its own conclusion.[91]

[87] See Chap. 2, pp. 44–45. De Smith J.R.A.A., pp. 281–283.

[88] *e.g. Pepys* v. *London Transport Executive* [1975] 1 W.L.R. 234 (in exercise of its discretion as to costs, tribunal awarded costs against successful party. Holding that tribunal had erred in law in that there was, in the circumstances of the case, no basis for the award, the Court of Appeal ruled that the successful party should pay none of his opponent's costs). See too *Priddle* v. *Fisher* [1968] 1 W.L.R. 1478.

[89] *e.g. Melwood Units Pty Ltd.* v. *Commissioner of Main Roads* [1979] A.C. 426 (P.C.) (tribunal erred in law by applying wrong principles in assessing compulsory purchase compensation: Privy Council remitted case to tribunal so that it could apply correct principles). Appeal court may settle issue itself if (a) it has the necessary material and (b) the parties agree—see *e.g. Wootton* v. *Central Land Board* [1957] 1 W.L.R. 424 at 437.

[90] See Chap. 2, p. 45.

[91] *Sagnata Investments Ltd.* v. *Norwich Corpn.* [1971] 2 Q.B. 614 (amusement arcade permit); *Investors in Industry Ltd.* v. *Norwich City Council* [1986] 2 All E.R. 193 (rating appeals to Crown Court).

Chapter 6

IRREGULAR OR UNFAIR PROCEDURE

In the last two chapters we have been concerned with challenges to the substance of official acts or decisions—with allegations that either the substance of what an authority has done or decided to do, or the considerations which it has taken into account, have carried the authority outside its remit. In this chapter we turn to challenges based on procedural irregularity or on unfairness. In these cases a public authority is alleged to have breached a statutory duty to observe particular requirements of form or procedure—*e.g.* that it should proceed within a certain time, with notice to particular persons, giving particular persons the opportunity to state their case before an unbiased tribunal and giving reasons for its decision. We begin (section A) with cases of failure to observe procedural requirements expressly prescribed by statute. In section B, under the heading "Natural Justice—the Duty to Act Fairly," we then consider circumstances in which the courts will infer that Parliament intends a statutory authority to observe certain minimum standards of procedural fairness even though the statute makes no express provision on the matter.

At the outset we should ask why it may be important for a public authority to observe procedural requirements. Essentially these requirements are geared to enabling persons to participate at a satisfactory level in the making of official decisions and the taking of official action which concerns them. One criterion of what will count as a "satisfactory" level of participation will be whether or not the procedure adopted will give persons concerned sufficient insight into the decision-making process to enable them to detect any substantive irregularities of the kind dealt with in the preceding chapters. Reviewable errors of law, whether misstatements or misapplications of legal rules or failures to exercise discretion on proper bases, are unlikely to be able to be detected unless the procedure adopted by an authority causes some light to be shed on its decision-making processes. Considering as we are the possibility of challenges to the legality of official action, the fulfilment of such procedural requirements as the giving of notice, a fair hearing and reasons for decisions may be seen as prerequisites to the detection of any substantive illegality.

A. Express Statutory Procedural Requirements[1]

Statutes, or rules and regulations made under statutory authority, frequently make detailed provision for procedures to be followed by a public authority in the course of discharging its duties or exercising its powers. Sometimes, too, Parliament makes general provision for a particular aspect of the procedure of a wide range of individual authorities—*e.g.* the duty imposed by the Tribunals and Inquiries Act 1971[2] on scheduled tribunals, and on ministers notifying decisions after the holding of a statutory inquiry, to give reasons for their decisions if asked.

If an authority fails to observe an express procedural requirement, what steps may be taken by a person affected to rectify the situation?

(1) Mandatory and directory requirements

In responding to challenges to the legality of official action based on failure to observe express procedural requirements, the courts have long tended to classify the requirements themselves as either "mandatory" or "directory." To say that a requirement is mandatory means that failure to observe it makes the authority's act or decision invalid, and the court will grant an appropriate remedy. If, on the other hand, a requirement is classified as "directory," failure to observe it will not render the act or decision invalid, although there may be means of securing compliance, or sanctions for failure to comply. The classification of procedural requirements as mandatory or directory[3] is used in the context of all the various modes and jurisdictions by which judicial review may be obtained—*i.e.* common law supervisory review, whether the challenge is direct[4] or collateral[5]; the statutory supervisory jur-

[1] Wade A.L., p. 218 *et seq.*; de Smith J.R.A.A., p. 142 *et seq.*
[2] Section 12(1)—subject to limitations in s.12(2), (3), (4) and (6).
[3] Terminology, particularly in the older cases, is not uniform (see Wade A.L., p. 219); but the distinction itself is constant. For two recent examples of unorthodox use of "mandatory," see cases cited in notes 24 and 26 below.
[4] *e.g. Bradbury* v. *Enfield L.B.C.* [1967] 1 W.L.R. 1311 (below).
[5] *e.g. Howard* v. *Bodington* (1877) 2 P.D. 203 (below).

isdiction[6]; and appellate review.[7] So, according to the circumstances, breach of a mandatory procedural requirement may take an authority *ultra vires* (or its statutory equivalent); or constitute a defence to, or be a ground for success in civil or criminal proceedings; or count as an appealable error of law. In short, the mandatory/directory distinction is a general device by which the courts in the exercise of their review jurisdictions acknowledge that the importance and effect of breaches of procedural requirements will vary greatly according to the nature of the requirements and the context in which they appear.

How do the courts make the distinction in particular cases? A statute may, of course, state expressly or imply clearly what is to be the consequence of a failure to comply with a particular procedural requirement. It may be apparent, for example, from statutory wording that to give public notice of proposals to restructure an area's schools[8] or to register publicly a planning application[9] is a condition precedent to the action concerned. But the truth is that in the vast majority of cases where Parliament imposes procedural requirements, it does so without considering or providing for the consequences of breach.[10] In the absence of statutory guidance in this matter the courts have taken a somewhat impressionistic approach, considering on a case to case basis "the importance of the provision that has been disregarded, and the relation of that provision to the general object intended to be secured by the Act."[11] The result is "an inextricable tangle of loose ends."[12]

[6] *i.e.* under time-limited ouster clauses (Chap. 2, p. 54). *e.g. Givaudan* v. *Minister of Housing & Local Government* [1967] 1 W.L.R. 250 (below). In its common form the statutory jurisdiction extends to breaches of procedural requirements only in so far as they substantially prejudice an applicant—see *per* Lord Scarman in *Westminster City Council* v. *Great Portland Estates plc* [1985] A.C. 661 at 666; and *cf.* sub-section (2) below.

[7] *Brayhead Ltd* v. *Berks C.C.* [1964] 2 Q.B. 303; *James* v. *Minister of Housing & Local Government* [1966] 1 W.L.R. 135 (below).

[8] *Bradbury* v. *Enfield L.B.C.* (above) (statute required public notice before proposals submitted to minister and provided that "authority shall not do anything" until proposals approved by him).

[9] *Steeples* v. *Derbyshire C.C.* [1984] 3 All E.R. 468 (authority empowered to act only after expiry of prescribed period following registration). See too *R.* v. *Lambeth L.B.C. ex p. Sharp* [1984] *The Times*, December 28.

[10] De Smith, J.R.A.A., p. 142.

[11] *Howard* v. *Bodington* (above), *per* Lord Penzance at p. 211.

[12] De Smith, *op cit.*; more bluntly, "a bit of a mess" *per* Templeman J. in *Coney* v. *Choyce* [1975] 1 W.L.R. 422 at 433.

Nevertheless, "some classes of procedural requirements are so important that they will nearly always be held to be mandatory."[13] Thus, where statute imposes on a public authority a duty to inform[14] or consult[15] or give a hearing to[16] persons likely to be affected by proposed action, the requirement will usually be treated as mandatory. This approach is reinforced where the effect of the action on the individual concerned may be in the nature of a penal sanction[17] or loss of property or privilege.[18] In these contexts, too, statutory time limits are likely to be held mandatory. In *Howard* v. *Bodington*,[19] for example, where a clergyman was informed only after eight weeks, instead of the statutory maximum of 21 days, of a complaint laid against him by his parishioners, the proceedings were held void. Similarly, in *Edwick* v. *Sunbury-on-Thames U.D.C.*[20] a refusal of planning permission was held void (and an enforcement notice thus ineffective) where it was communicated to the applicant more than two years outside the two month limit for response to an application.

On the other hand, where the consequence of invalidating acts done in neglect of a statutory requirement would be to "work serious inconvenience, or injustice to persons who have no control over those entrusted with the duty, and at the same time would not promote the main object of the Legislature, it has been the practice to hold such provisions to be directory only . . . "[21] So, delay in the issue of a General Election warrant in New Zealand was held not to invalidate either the election or the subsequent legisla-

[13] De Smith, J.R.A.A., p. 144.

[14] See notes 8 and 9 above.

[15] See, *e.g. Agricultural etc. Training Board* v. *Aylesbury Mushrooms Ltd* [1972] 1 W.L.R. 190 (Mushroom Growers' Association not bound by regulations made without consulting them); *R.* v. *Sec. of State for Social Services ex p. Association of Metropolitan Authorities* [1986] 1 All E.R. 164. (Minister breached mandatory duty to consult Association adequately before changing housing benefit regulations: declaration granted but certiorari refused in exercise of court's discretion as to remedy—see Chap. 8 below).

[16] *Ridge* v. *Baldwin* [1964] A.C. 40; and see *per* Lord Diplock in *O'Reilly* v. *Mackman* [1983] 2 A.C. 237 at 276.

[17] *Howard* v. *Bodington* (1877) 2 P.D. 203 at 213–214.

[18] See cases in note 16 above.

[19] (1877) 2 P.D. 203.

[20] [1962] 1 Q.B. 229.

[21] *Per* Sir Arthur Channell in *Montreal Street Rly Co.* v. *Normandin* [1917] A.C. 170 at 175, cited with approval by the Court of Appeal in *Re T* (*a minor*) [1986] 1 All E.R. 817 (adoption regulations requiring written notices to natural parents held directory on grounds considered in this paragraph; court also held that there had been substantial compliance and no substantial prejudice—see below—to natural parents).

tive output of the elected assembly[22]; and failure to revise jury lists annually as prescribed did not invalidate proceedings involving juries summoned from out-of-date lists.[23] Similarly, where "the extreme result [of holding action invalid] is not required for the effective achievement of the purposes of the statute,"[24] a procedural requirement may be treated as directory only. So, where failure to give reasons for a decision as required[25] or failure to give details, as required, of points of appeal[26] can be remedied by other means,[27] that failure will not be fatal to the validity of the proceedings.

(2) Substantial compliance/no substantial prejudice

There are increasing indications of the courts' willingness in appropriate cases to refrain from a rigid classification of a particular procedural requirement as in itself mandatory or directory and, instead, to consider the nature and consequences of breach in a particular case. In *Coney* v. *Choyce*,[28] for example, a trivial and partial failure to comply with the public notice requirements regarding school restructuring (held mandatory in the case referred to above[29]) was held not to invalidate the action taken. And in *James* v. *Minister of Housing and Local Government*[30] the Court of Appeal distinguished *Edwick*[31] and ruled that a shorter delay did not invalidate a planning permission granted out of time. In both these cases the court reclassified the requirement in question as "directory." Surely, though, the better approach would be to recognise a third category of procedural requirement—where failure to comply is capable of nullifying an act or decision but will not necessarily do so.[32] Whether it does or not would depend on

[22] *Simpson* v. *Att.-Gen.* [1955] N.Z.L.R. 271.
[23] *Montreal Street Rly Co.* case (above).
[24] *Per* Winn J. in *Brayhead Ltd* v. *Berks. C.C.* [1964] 2 Q.B. 303 at 314.
[25] As in *Brayhead's* case (note 24 above).
[26] As in *Howard* v. *Environment Secretary* [1975] Q.B. 235.
[27] For means of enforcing directory requirements, see sub-section (3) below.
[28] [1975] 1 W.L.R. 422.
[29] *Bradbury* v. *Enfield L.B.C.* (above, note 8).
[30] [1966] 1 W.L.R. 135 (point did not arise on appeal to H.L. [1968] A.C. 409).
[31] Above, note 20.
[32] Lord Denning in effect took this approach in *James*: he accepted that in an extreme case such as *Edwick* the breach of the time limit could lead to invalidity: [1966] 1 W.L.R. 135 at p. 142 and *cf. per* Webster J. in *R.* v. *Secretary of State ex p. Association of Metropolitan Authorities* [1986] 1 All E.R. at pp. 168–9.

such considerations as the extent of the failure and of the prejudice, if any, suffered by the parties concerned.[33]

This approach may be particularly helpful in time-limit cases.[34] It may perhaps be applied also in the context of a statutory duty to give reasons for decisions. Normally, no doubt, breach of such a duty would cause substantial prejudice and it would be proper for a review court to characterise the failure as an error of law[35] or failure to comply with the requirements of an Act.[36] It would be otherwise where no substantial prejudice had been suffered (*e.g.* because the reasons for a decision were already known to the individual concerned[37]). On the question of how detailed the reasons need to be, the courts in effect already take a "substantial compliance" approach. The reasons "must be reasons which . . . deal with the substantial points that have been raised."[38] And, although they can be brief,[39] mere recitation of the statutory words conferring the powers is not enough.[40] "The important

[33] See *Coney* v. *Choyce* (note 12 above) at pp. 433–434; *R.* v. *H.M. Inspector of Taxes ex p. Clarke* [1974] Q.B. 220; *Hughes* v. *Viner* [1985] 3 All E.R. 40 (time-limit provisions held directory where minor infringement would not prejudice party concerned); *R.* v. *Environment Secretary ex p. Leicester City Council* (1985) 25 R.V.R. 31 (local authorities given proper notice of government's "rate-capping" intentions even though Report, required to be laid before Parliament before notice given, contained printers' errors and had to be re-laid nine days after notice given).

[34] See Walton J. in *Viner* (note 33 above) at pp. 45, 47. *cf.* also effect of delay in conveyancing where time is not of the essence: J.T. Farrand, *Contract and Conveyance* (4th ed.), Chap. IX.

[35] As, *e.g.* in *Re Poyser and Mills Arbitration* [1964] 2 Q.B. 467; *R.* v. *Immigration Appeal Tribunal ex p. Khan* [1983] Q.B. 790.

[36] *i.e.* under a statutory review provision such as Town and Country Planning Act 1971, s.245—see, *e.g. Givaudan* v. *Min. of Housing & Loc. Govt.* [1967] 1 W.L.R. 250.

[37] As in *Brayhead Ltd.* v. *Berks C.C.* [1964] 2 Q.B. 303 (Divisional Court held in effect that statutory duty to give reasons for planning conditions was not mandatory; but it was plain that the applicants were well aware of the reason—see p. 310).

[38] *Re Poyser and Mills* (note 35 above) at p. 478.

[39] *Bradley & Sons* v. *Environment Secretary* [1983] J.P.L. 43, *per* Glidewell J. (*Poyser* and *Bradley* endorsed on this point by House of Lords in *Westminster City Council* v. *Great Portland Estates* [1985] A.C. 661 at 673.

[40] *Bone* v. *Mental Health Review Tribunal* [1985] 3 All E.R. 330 (mere statement that Tribunal 'not satisfied' that appellant not liable to be detained held inadequate as a statement of 'reasons for being satisfied'). *Cf. R.* v. *Home Secretary ex p. Swati* [1986] 1 All E.R. 717 (immigration officer's statement that she was not satisfied that applicant was genuinely seeking limited entry held sufficient statement of reasons for refusal of leave to enter). It is perhaps difficult to see why in *Swati* the applicant, although made aware *that* the officer doubted his credibility, was not entitled to know *why*; whereas in *Bone* the patient was held entitled to know why the tribunal took its view.

matter . . . is that it must be apparent from what [the authority] state by way of reasons first of all that they have considered the point which is at issue . . . and they should indicate the evidence on which they have come to their conclusions."[41]

(3) Failure to comply with directory requirements

The fact that failure to comply with a procedural requirement is held not to invalidate an act or decision does not mean, of course, that the requirement cannot be enforced. In the first place, "the person responsible for the failure to comply may in particular cases be punishable,"[42] *e.g.* by award of costs of an election petition against an officer guilty of "personal default"[43]; or by statutory penalty or prosecution.[44] And there are other direct means of enforcement: a failure to give reasons where required may be remedied by mandamus[45]; and it may be proper for an authority to waive exact compliance with detailed formal requirements where they can be sufficiently enforced by the exercise of its power to control its own procedure.[46] Indeed, the very availability of means of enforcement other than treating an act as invalid may be a reason for classifying a procedural requirement as directory only.[47] Only in the absence of alternative means of enforcement would it be true that an authority "has a discretion not to comply with [a directory requirement] if, in its opinion, the exceptional circumstances of a particular case justify departing from it."[48]

Finally, one encounters occasionally a provision such as that failure to comply with specified procedural requirements "shall not render the proceedings, or anything done in pursuance

[41] *Ex p. Khan* (note 35 above) at p. 794, *per* Lord Lane C.J. See too *R.* v. *Mental Health Review Tribunal ex p. Pickering* [1986] 1 All E.R. 99 (reasons not clearly directed to specific points at issue).

[42] *Simpson* v. *Att.-Gen.* [1955] N.Z.L.R. 271 at 281, *per* Court of Appeal, referring to *Montreal* case (note 21 above).

[43] *Woodward* v. *Sarsons* (1875) 10 L.R.C.P. 733 at 751 (officer not guilty).

[44] See, *e.g. Margate Pier Co* v. *Hannam* (1819) 3 B. & Ald. 266 (acting as justice where not qualified).

[45] *Per* Winn J. in *Brayhead* v. *Berks C.C.* (note 37 above) at p. 314.

[46] *cf.* per Roskill L.J. in *Howard* v. *Environment Secretary* (note 26 above) at p. 245.

[47] See previous two cases and also *Bradbury* v. *Enfield L.B.C.* [1967] 1 W.L.R. 1311 (public notice requirement held mandatory—note 8 above; but requirement that building plans be submitted to minister held directory since statute provided complaints machinery where failure to comply—see esp. *per* Diplock L.J. at p. 1326). *cf.* also Chap. 9, p. 313.

[48] *Per* Lord Diplock in *O'Reilly* v. *Mackman* [1983] 2 A.C. 237 at 276.

thereof, invalid unless the chairman or the tribunal so direct."[49] In the light of the courts' approach to ouster clauses generally[50] it may be doubted that such a provision would be construed as, in effect, making all the specified procedural requirements directory only.[51] Instead, the mandatory/directory distinction might be applied in the ordinary way, perhaps with the modification that the authority could, in appropriate circumstances, treat proceedings as invalid even though only a directory requirement had been breached.

B. Natural Justice—the Duty to Act Fairly[52]

(1) Introduction—nature and source of the duty

Suppose that a statute empowers a public authority to act in a fashion which impinges on some aspect of what a person might regard as his legitimate interests or expectations. In this vague phrase "interests" would no doubt include not only individual liberty and property rights protected by private law but also, for example, official licences or permissions of various sorts and, perhaps, the preservation of civic and rural amenity in its many aspects. One may have some, albeit imprecise, notion that one should at any rate be given a fair hearing before these interests are adversely affected by the exercise of official power. Similarly one may regard oneself as having a "legitimate expectation" to, albeit imprecisely defined, "fair treatment" in the official processing of one's claims, complaints and applications for official licences and permissions.

As we observed in the previous section, there is often express statutory provision relating to procedures to be followed by a public authority in the exercise of its powers and discharge of its duties. The remainder of this chapter is concerned with the position where there is no express provision for interested parties to be heard before action affecting them is taken. We shall see that there is a wide variety of circumstances in which, in the absence of such express provision, the courts infer that Parliament must have intended that certain elements of fair procedure should be

[49] As in Plant Variety Rights Tribunal Rules 1965 (S.I. 1965 No. 1623), r. 21.
[50] See Chap. 2, p. 46 *et seq*.
[51] Wade A.L., p. 224.
[52] De Smith J.R.A.A., Chaps. 4, 5; Wade A.L., Part V; Craig Chaps. 7, 8; P. Jackson, *Natural Justice* (2nd ed., 1979).

observed.[53] These elements of fair procedure have long been referred to as rules, or principles, of "natural justice." However, for reasons which will appear, that phrase is now becoming unfashionable: the current tendency is to speak instead of a duty to act fairly.

To avoid confusion we should observe here that the rules of natural justice are held to apply not only to statutory authorities (on the basis of judicial inference as to what Parliament must have intended) but also in certain circumstances to private individuals and organisations. In particular, the courts have implied a duty to act fairly into contracts of membership, *e.g.* of clubs,[54] trade unions,[55] and political parties,[56]—and on this basis members have been able to resist expulsion without a hearing. Our concern is with the application of the rules of natural justice to public authorities, but we refer, where appropriate, to cases in the contractual sphere.

Since the basis upon which the rules of natural justice are held to apply to a public authority is judicial inference as to what Parliament must have intended, it follows that the rules do not apply where the courts can detect a contrary statutory intention.[57] Furthermore, because of the wide variety of circumstances in which the duty to act fairly has been held to exist, the precise details of the duty will vary greatly from one kind of situation to another. We shall consider some aspects of the notion of fairness under the broad headings of "the right to a hearing" and "the rule against bias."[58]

Breach of the rules of natural justice when they apply, *i.e.* failure to act fairly when required to do so, is treated by the courts[59] in broadly the same way as breach of an express mandatory procedural requirement (which, as we saw, renders an act or decision invalid). It may, then, be helpful to think of the demands imposed by the implied duty to act fairly as "implied mandatory requirements."[60]

[53] See below pp. 215–221. For the application of the rules of natural justice in the exercise of prerogative power, see Chap. 2, p. 78.
[54] *e.g. Dawkins* v. *Antrobus* (1881) 17 Ch.D. 615 (members' club).
[55] *e.g. Lawlor* v. *Union of Post Office Workers* [1965] Ch. 712.
[56] *e.g. John* v. *Rees* [1970] 1 Ch. 345 (suspension of constituency Labour party by National Executive).
[57] See below, pp. 221–229.
[58] See below, pp. 231–236.
[59] See below, pp. 240–243.
[60] Wade A.L., p. 415.

(2) When is there a duty to act fairly?

(a) *"Property rights or privileges of persons"*
In 1963, in *Ridge* v. *Baldwin*,[61] Lord Reid said:

> "The older authorities clearly show how the courts engrafted the principles of natural justice on to a host of provisions authorising administrative interference with private rights. Parliament knew quite well that the courts had an inveterate habit of doing that and must therefore be held to have authorised them to do it unless a particular Act showed a contrary intention."[62]

In the case, a police authority had acted under a statutory power to dismiss a chief constable whom they thought negligent in the discharge of his duty. The authority had not heard the officer in his own defence but had proceeded on the basis of remarks made by a judge during the trial of the officer on corruption charges of which he was in the event acquitted. A majority of the House of Lords declared the dismissal void on the basis that the officer had not been given the fair hearing to which, under the rules of natural justice,[63] he was entitled.

Ridge v. *Baldwin* is of signal importance in that it re-established an approach to the question "when do the rules of natural justice apply?" from which, for reasons which are well documented elsewhere,[64] the courts had been diverted in the earlier part of this century. Essentially, the older authorities to which Lord Reid referred in the quotation above showed that, in general, where a public authority was empowered by statute, for cause shown, to act in derogation of "the property rights or privileges of persons,"[65] the courts would presume (subject to contrary indications) that Parliament intended that the persons concerned should be given an opportunity to state their case: *i.e.* that they should have the opportunity to consider and respond to the allegations or assertions on the basis of which the public authority proposed to act. The crucial consideration in deciding whether or not a person had the right to answer the case against him was "the nature of the

[61] [1964] A.C. 40.
[62] *Ibid*. p. 73.
[63] There were also, under statutory regulations, express requirements of a hearing (note 16 above).
[64] De Smith J.R.A.A., pp. 164–172; Wade A.L., pp. 458–461.
[65] *Per* Lord Reid in *Ridge* v. *Baldwin* (note 61 above) at p. 68.

thing [to be] done"[66] rather than whether the power under which it was to be done should be labelled "judicial" or otherwise. In the period before *Ridge* v. *Baldwin* some courts, emphasising the judicial overtones of the phrase "natural justice" had held that the rules applied only where a public authority could be said to be "acting judicially."[67] *Ridge* v. *Baldwin* eradicated this " 'judicial' fallacy."[68]

The emphasis, then, is upon the substance and effect of statutory power. This emphasis shows how the answer to the question "when do the rules of natural justice apply?" is linked to the bases upon which, as we have seen in Chapters 4 and 5, the courts will review decisions on issues of law, fact and degree and on matters of policy. Judicial review is widely available to correct errors of law in both these contexts. The substantive limits of statutory powers thus drawn are reflected in and buttressed by the procedural protection afforded by the rules of natural justice. The very existence of substantive limits (*i.e.* of a legal prescription of what counts as a proper basis for action) suggests that, in principle, a person whose "property rights or privileges" are likely to be affected is entitled to be informed of the basis upon which the authority proposes to proceed and to be heard in response.[69] So, for example, if a power to impose conditions on a discotheque licence may be exercised only to achieve certain limited purposes, fairness seems to require that the applicant be given an opportunity to argue that the purposes will not be served by, say, a total ban on Sunday opening.[70]

[66] *Per* Wills J. in *Hopkins* v. *Smethwick Local Board of Health* (1890) 24 Q.B.D. 712 at 715.

[67] See especially the Privy Council decision in *Nakkuda Ali* v. *Jayaratne* [1951] A.C. 66, disapproved in *Ridge* v. *Baldwin*.

[68] Wade A.L., p. 463. The essence of the fallacy was to make the applicability of the rules of natural justice turn on the question "is the power judicial or not?" As indicated in the text, this conceptualism has largely disappeared. However in many reported cases on the question of the precise content of natural justice in the widely different situations in which the rules do apply (see sub-section (3) below) the courts continue to emphasise that the procedure appropriate to a court of justice is unlikely to be appropriate for tribunals and authorities further away from the judicial archetype (see de Smith J.R.A.A., p. 180 *passim*). In this context, then, the distinction between judicial and non-judicial remains. Inevitably, in some reported cases the boundary between the fallacious and the legitimate uses of the distinction seems blurred: see, *e.g. R.* v. *Home Secretary ex p. Gunnell* [1984] Crim.L.R. 170 (D.C.) (parole board's revocation of parole); *cf.* [1985] Crim.L.R. 105 (C.A.).

[69] See de Smith J.R.A.A., pp. 175–178. For the position where statute confers "ostensibly unfettered discretion" on an authority, see below, p. 223.

[70] *cf.* Chaps. 1, p. 25 and 5, p. 173 and text below.

"Property rights or privileges" is a broad notion. "Property rights" includes not only the claims which a person has to his house[71] or land[72] but also his tenure of a public office[73] and his right to the stipend attached to it.[74] It includes too, statutory entitlement to sums of money—and the "person" entitled may be itself a public authority.[75] Again, it seems that where statute confers a default power[76] entitling one public authority to take over the functions of another, the deprived authority will *prima facie* be entitled to be heard in its defence.[77]

Public authority licences of various sorts may perhaps be regarded as "privileges" in that a person has no strict legal claim to them. It appears now that "the exercise of a licensing function . . . by any authority is one to which the rules of natural justice . . . would normally apply."[78] So, for example, a person is entitled to state his case before he is refused a public entertainments licence[79]; or before his market trader's licence is withdrawn[80]—even where the market is unofficial and the licence granted by the authority is merely contractual.[81]

[71] *Cooper* v. *Wandsworth Board of Works* (1863) 14 C.B.N.S. 180 (housebuilder entitled to be heard before local authority demolished house built in breach of requirement to give notice of intention to build).

[72] *Smith* v. *R.* (1878) 3 App.Cas. 614 (Crown lessee entitled to be heard before governor forfeited lease on basis that lessee had abandoned or ceased to reside on land). See too *De Verteuil* v. *Knaggs* [1918] A.C. 557.

[73] *Ridge* v. *Baldwin* itself and cases there cited.

[74] *Capel* v. *Child* (1832) 2 C. & J. 558 (parish incumbent entitled to be heard before bishop appointed curate to be paid out of incumbent's stipend where incumbent alleged to have performed duties inadequately).

[75] *R.* v. *Environment Secretary ex p. Brent L.B.C.* [1982] Q.B. 593: minister bound to hear anything new which might be said by local authority before he reduced its rate support grant—"a right to substantial sums of money," *per* Ackner L.J. at p. 643; *R.* v. *Transport Secretary ex p. G.L.C.* [1985] 3 W.L.R. 574 (G.L.C. entitled to be consulted by Secretary of State before he decided what sum (below a statutory maximum) he should require G.L.C. to pay in context of transfer of responsibility for London Regional Transport from G.L.C. to Secretary of State). But *cf.* London (Regional Transport) Amendment Act 1985.

[76] See Chap. 5, p. 185.

[77] See *Norwich City Council* v. *Environment Secretary* [1982] 1 All E.R. 737, *per* Lord Denning M.R. at p. 745, *per* Kerr L.J. at p. 751.

[78] *Per* Glidewell J. in *R.* v. *Huntingdon D.C. ex p. Cowan* [1984] 1 W.L.R. 501 at 508 (not referring to Megarry V.-C.'s suggestion in *McInnes* v. *Onslow Fane* [1978] 1 W.L.R. 1520 at 1529 that there is a substantial difference between cases of refusal and cases of revocation or withdrawal). See also *per* Lord Denning M.R. in *R.* v. *Gaming Board ex p. Benaim* [1970] 2 Q.B. 417 at 430. On natural justice and licensing, see generally de Smith J.R.A.A., pp. 221–225.

[79] *Cowan* (note 78 above).

[80] *R.* v. *Barnsley M.B.C. ex p. Hook* [1976] 1 W.L.R. 1052.

[81] *R.* v. *Wear Valley D.C. ex p. Binks* [1985] 2 All E.R. 699.

In an entirely different context, a person who was being denied permission—licence—to enter the United Kingdom on the basis that he was not (as he claimed) under 16 years of age was held entitled to a fair hearing.[82] Although the court held that, in the event, he had been treated fairly, the case is of importance in that it initiated what may be regarded as terminological confirmation of the repudiation in *Ridge* v. *Baldwin* of the "judicial" fallacy. Lord Parker observed[83] that

> "to the limited extent that the circumstances of any particular case allow, and within the legislative framework under which the administrator is working, only to that limited extent do the so-called rules of natural justice apply, which in a case such as this is merely a duty to act fairly."

The new nomenclature is now commonly adopted; and in the *G.C.H.Q.* case Lord Roskill went so far as to suggest[84] that the phrase "natural justice," though "hallowed by time and much judicial repetition," was "often widely misunderstood and therefore as often misused" and "perhaps might now be allowed to find a permanent resting-place and be better replaced by speaking of a duty to act fairly."[85]

(b) *Legitimate expectation*

In recent years the courts have tended to define the circumstances in which "privileges" are protected by the rules of natural justice by reference to the notion of "legitimate expectation." Legitimate expectation "may arise either from an express promise given on behalf of a public authority or from the existence of a regular practice which the claimant can reasonably expect to continue."[86] Taking first "express promise": an alien with permission to remain in this country for a certain period would have a legit-

[82] *Re H.K.* [1967] 2 Q.B. 617.
[83] *Ibid.* p. 630.
[84] *Council of Civil Service Unions* v. *Minister for the Civil Service* [1985] A.C. 374 at 414; see also *per* Lord Fraser at p. 399.
[85] See also *per* Lord Diplock in *Bushell* v. *Environment Secretary* [1981] A.C. 75 at 95. But for potential dangers in the new approach see de Smith J.R.A.A., pp. 238–240.
[86] *Per* Lord Fraser in the *G.C.H.Q.* case (note 84 above) at p. 401.

imate expectation of being heard before the period was curtailed[87]; an illegal immigrant to Hong Kong had a legitimate expectation that his case would be considered on its merits, as the governor had expressly promised[88]; and Liverpool taxi owners were entitled to be heard before their local authority increased the number of licences issued, the authority having promised full consultation before so acting.[89] As to "regular practice," the G.C.H.Q. civil servants had a legitimate expectation on that basis to consultation before being prohibited by their employer from union membership[90]; prisoners have a legitimate expectation to a fair hearing before loss of remission for disciplinary offences[91]; and parents have a legitimate expectation that they will be consulted before the closure of their children's schools.[92]

In all the cases just referred to, the legitimate expectation protected by the courts was an expectation of being heard or consulted. In the cases of the Hong Kong immigrant, the Liverpool taxi owners and the school parents, the "privilege" was identified as such—as an interest deserving some degree of legal protection—precisely because of the assurances as to hearing or consultation given by the authority. The "privilege" was in effect created by the promise or practice of hearing or consulting before the status quo was changed. The notion of legitimate expectation deriving from promise or practice therefore becomes a test by which the elusive notion of privilege, in the context of natural justice, may be to some extent defined. But will legitimate expectation play a more radical role in the development of judicial review?

The question is whether the courts' protection of legitimate expectation of fair procedure will extend beyond this to requiring that a certain state of affairs should continue or that a certain benefit (other than fair procedure) should be conferred. In the *Hong Kong* case Lord Fraser emphasised that

[87] *Per* Lord Denning M.R. in *Schmidt* v. *Home Secretary* [1969] 2 Ch. 149 at 171 (but no legitimate expectation, it appears, of being heard before a refusal to extend the period, even though that might be the usual practice. For criticism of the courts' general attitude to natural justice for aliens see Wade A.L., pp. 507–510; Craig, pp. 287–8).

[88] *Att.-Gen. (Hong Kong)* v. *Ng Yuen Shiu* [1983] 2 A.C. 629. See (1983) 99 L.Q.R. 499 (P. Jackson).

[89] *R.* v. *Liverpool Corporation ex p. Liverpool Taxi etc. Assocn.* [1972] 2 Q.B. 299.

[90] *Council of Civil Service Unions* v. *Minister for the Civil Service* [1985] A.C. 374—but judicial review refused on grounds of national security: see Chap. 2, p. 78.

[91] *R.* v. *Hull Prison Visitors ex p. St. Germain* [1979] Q.B. 425, approved by House of Lords in *O'Reilly* v. *Mackman* [1983] 2 A.C. 237.

[92] *R.* v. *Brent L.B.C. ex p. Gunning* [1985] *The Times*, April 30.

> "the court order [in the Liverpool taxi case] was limited to ensuring that the corporation followed a fair procedure by holding an inquiry before reaching a decision: provided such procedure was followed the decision was left with the corporation to whom it had been entrusted by Parliament."[93]

And in two recent cases[94] the House of Lords has refused to extend the notion of legitimate expectation to prevent ministers from changing existing policies. The effect of the change in each case was to deprive individuals of substantive benefits which they would otherwise have enjoyed; but their "legitimate expectations" were held not to extend beyond being treated fairly under whatever was the current policy.

It is nevertheless the case that the notion of legitimate expectation reflects a principle that express or implied assurances given by a public authority should be honoured. Now, were that principle to be applied quite generally to assurances that "such and such a thing will be done," there would be an obvious conflict with the principle (already considered[95]) against fettering discretion by contract or policy. This conflict may, of course, be avoided by treating such assurances as merely obliging the authority, before frustrating the expectations which have been created, to consider the propriety of so doing.[96] But in some cases a court ruling to this effect can come very close to a ruling that the authority must act as it promised. In *R.* v. *Home Secretary ex p. Khan*,[97] for example, the Home Secretary was held, by a majority of the Court of Appeal, to have raised, in a letter written to the applicants, the legitimate expectation that, if certain criteria were fulfilled, entry clearance would be given for a foreign child whom they hoped to adopt. The court quashed the Home Secretary's refusal of clearance because it was based on a criterion not previously announced. Parker L.J. remarked

> "The Secretary of State is, of course, at liberty to change the policy but in my view, *vis à vis* the recipient of such a letter, a new policy can only be implemented after such recipient has been given a full and serious consideration whether there is

[93] *Att.-Gen. (Hong Kong)* v. *Ng Yuen Shiu* (note 88 above) at p. 637.
[94] *Re Findlay* [1985] A.C. 318. (Home Secretary changed parole policy to detriment of applicants); *Hughes* v. *D.H.S.S.* [1985] A.C. 776 (D.H.S.S. lowered normal retiring age of employees). In neither case did the individuals concerned complain that they were not consulted.
[95] See Chap. 5, p. 196.
[96] *Ibid.*
[97] [1984] 1 W.L.R. 1337.

> some overriding public interest which justifies a departure from the procedures stated . . ."[98]

Dunn L.J. said that "what happened in this case was not only unfair but unreasonable."[99] Now, as we have seen, the principles governing judicial review of policy decisions do not yield any general proposition that it is unreasonable in the *Wednesbury* sense for a public authority to frustrate, by a change of policy, expectations which it may have created. It would surely be undesirable were the notion of legitimate expectation to be used not merely to ensure that expectations should not be frustrated without procedural safeguards but also to extend the courts' power to review the merits or substance of policy decisions.

(c) *Contrary intention in statute*

The notions of "property rights and privileges" and "legitimate expectation" are broad and flexible. It is impossible to list exhaustively the circumstances in which they will be used by the courts to impose a duty to act fairly. Yet it is in these broad terms that we must describe the circumstances in which the rules of natural justice prima facie apply. The "prima facie" is thus of crucial importance when answering in particular cases the question "is there a duty to act fairly?" It is evident that one's ability to answer this question with any confidence will depend in part on the precision with which one can predict what will be taken by the courts as indications of statutory intention that the rules of natural justice are not to apply. The question is then: in a case where prima facie (*i.e.* contrary intention apart) the rules would apply, what will count as contrary intention? The answer to this question will provide one indication[1] of the degree of circumspection with which the courts have used the considerable room for manoeuvre which they have created for themselves by their use of the broad and flexible notions just referred to.[2]

[98] *Ibid*. p. 1347.
[99] *Ibid*. p. 1352.
[1] Another indication is the degree of sensitivity with which the courts tailor the requirement of "fair hearing" to meet the needs of widely different situations—see sub-section (3) below.
[2] On the need for such circumspection, see de Smith J.R.A.A., pp. 178–182 and references.

(i) *Express provision.* Occasionally a statute will expressly relieve a public authority of any duty to secure for interested persons "a right to be heard"[3] or "to give public notice" of proposals.[4] Usually, however, contrary intention must be inferred.

(ii) *Inference from statute.* The inference may be drawn from the wording of the statute: as, for example, by the application of the *expressio unius* maxim ("the mention of one thing implies the exclusion of another")[5]. So, a bail surety was held not entitled to a hearing before the bail conditions were varied: there were several statutory provisions for notice to sureties but no provision for this case.[6] This is one of very many reported cases raising the contrary intention issue which turn on the interpretation of a particular statute. In the present brief account a few further examples of such cases must suffice.

If one part of a prescribed statutory procedure is *ex parte* (*i.e.* in the presence of one party only) and provision is made for an *inter partes* hearing at a later stage there will be no duty to hear any other party at the *ex parte* stage.[7] Even where it is not clear from a statute whether or not a hearing for interested parties is contemplated at an early stage in proceedings it may be that provision for such hearing at a later stage will obviate any earlier duty to hear. This may be true, for example, of a refusal of planning permission by a local authority from which refusal there is a right of appeal and public inquiry.[8] However, there is no general principle that the existence of a right of appeal will cure a denial of natural justice at an earlier hearing.[9] On the other hand, while there is no

[3] Town and Country Planning Act 1971, s.9(5).

[4] Charitable Trusts Act 1869, s.7: see *Re Berkhamstead Grammar School* [1908] 2 Ch. 25.

[5] Cross, *Statutory Interpretation*, p. 115.

[6] *R.* v. *Wells St. Magistrates' Court ex p. Albanese* [1981] 3 W.L.R. 694. See further de Smith, J.R.A.A., p. 187.

[7] *Aristides* v. *Minister of Housing and Local Government* [1970] 1 All E.R. 195 (minister's decision to grant local authority extension of time for submission to him of compulsory purchase order); *R.* v. *Raymond* [1981] 3 W.L.R. 3 (*ex parte* preferment of bill of indictment); *Pearlberg* v. *Varty* [1972] 1 W.L.R. 534 (tax commissioner entitled to grant *ex parte* leave to Revenue to raise late assessments on taxpayers. The case also illustrates the *expressio unius* rule: see text above).

[8] Wade A.L., p. 489; de Smith J.R.A.A., pp. 193–194.

[9] *Leary* v. *National Union of Vehicle Builders* [1971] Ch. 34 at 47–53: a trade union case. A fair appeal may cure an unfair hearing in some contractual (but query public law) contexts: *Calvin* v. *Carr* [1980] A.C. 574 at 591–596.

general rule that where a finding will be only provisional the rules of natural justice do not apply,[10] nevertheless:

> "it is very unusual for there to be a judicial determination of the question whether there is a *prima facie* case. Every public officer who has to decide whether to prosecute or raise proceedings ought first to decide whether there is a *prima facie* case but no one supposes that justice requires that he should first seek the comments of the accused or the defendant on the material before him,"[11]

(iii) *Inference from nature of power.* Contrary intention may be inferred from the nature of the power conferred. *Ridge* v. *Baldwin*,[12] as we saw, eradicated the "judicial" fallacy. But the judgments appear to perpetuate another conundrum. Essentially the proposition seems to be that if a public authority has a very wide, and so substantially unreviewable, discretion it follows that there is no duty to observe the rules of natural justice in its exercise.[13] So, *e.g.* "if a statute gives an unfettered power to dismiss at pleasure without more, that is an end of the matter."[14] This is said to be because "acting at pleasure means that there is no obligation to formulate reasons."[15] Surely, though, from the proposition that one need not have reasons it does not follow that one need not hear arguments. For an authority might well be swayed by hearing a person before acting: "indeed, the unreviewability of the substantive grounds for removal indicates that procedural protection may be all the more necessary."[16] In any event (a) since *Ridge* v.

[10] *Wiseman* v. *Borneman* [1971] A.C. 297 at 311, 316, 317–318. See generally de Smith J.R.A.A., pp. 233–237.

[11] *Per* Lord Reid, *ibid.* at p. 308. House of Lords held taxpayer not entitled to hearing before tribunal decided whether there was *prima facie* case against him of (redressable) tax avoidance. See too *Pearlberg* v. *Varty* (above); but *cf. Furnell* v. *Whangarei High Schools Board* [1973] A.C. 660: Privy Council decided by 3:2 that school teacher suspended without pay pending hearing of disciplinary charges not entitled to hearing before suspension. But Lords Dilhorne and Reid dissented pointing out the potentially serious consequences of the interim suspension.

[12] [1964] A.C. 40.

[13] See generally de Smith J.R.A.A., p. 186.

[14] *Per* Lord Hodson in *Ridge* v. *Baldwin* [1964] A.C. 40 at 129; Lord Reid at p. 65.

[15] *Per* Lord Reid in *Malloch* v. *Aberdeen Corporation* [1971] 1 W.L.R. 1578 at 1582; see too *per* Lord Morris at p. 1588; *per* Lord Wilberforce at p. 1596. (School teacher dismissible "at pleasure" but held entitled to hearing because of other express statutory provision).

[16] De Smith J.R.A.A., p. 228.

Baldwin the courts have been loth to interpret statutes as conferring unreviewable discretion[17]; and (b) there are indications that if an authority, though empowered to act at pleasure, actually does base a decision on alleged misconduct by the person concerned, the person will be entitled to be heard in his own defence.[18]

Note on natural justice and employment

We may note here in passing that there is abundant authority for the proposition that an employee, as distinct from one who holds an office (other than at pleasure), has no common law right to a fair hearing before dismissal.[19] Now, the line between office and employment appears sometimes, as Lord Wilberforce has said, "illogical and even bizarre."[20] But, even accepting that a person is an employee rather than an officer of a public authority it is hard to see the logic in denying him the protection of natural justice on that basis. The reason given is that a contract of service is not specifically enforceable "so no room exists for such remedies as administrative law may grant, such as a declaration that the dismissal is void."[21] But even where an officer is removed in breach of natural justice it may not be appropriate for a court to order reinstatement, and a declaration may be tailored accordingly.[22] In the case of an employee the specific enforceability point could be dealt with similarly.

[17] See, *e.g. Malloch* (note 15 above); also *Durayappah* v. *Fernando* [1967] 2 A.C. 337 and *R.* v. *Chief Constable (North Wales) ex p. Evans* [1982] 1 W.L.R. 1155—statutory powers empowering authority to act if satisfied on (respectively) "incompetence" or "unfitness" grounds: held, duty to act fairly. Contrary dicta in *Ridge* v. *Baldwin* not referred to.

[18] See *ex p. Evans* (above): probationary constable dismissed on allegations (undisclosed to him) of scandalous behaviour etc. House of Lords held power was "to be exercised only after due consideration of [allegations]." Accordingly "E did not have the fair hearing to which he was entitled" (see *per* Lord Brightman at pp. 1171, 1175). On whether *voluntary* hearing (*i.e.* where no duty to hear) can be challenged for unfairness, see de Smith J.R.A.A., p. 237.

[19] See *Ridge* v. *Baldwin* [1964] A.C. 40 at 65; *Malloch* [1971] 1 W.L.R. 1578 at 1595 where Lord Wilberforce gave as *indicia* of an office an "element of public employment or service," "support by statute" and "status capable of protection."

[20] *Malloch* (note 19 above) at p. 1595. So, *e.g.* there are reported cases in which a university professor (*Vidyodaya University of Ceylon* v. *Silva* [1965] 1 W.L.R. 77) and a consultant obstetrician (*Barber* v. *Manchester Regional Hospital Board* [1958] 1 W.L.R. 181) have been held mere employees; while a school teacher (*Malloch*) and a hospital houseman (*Palmer* v. *Inverness Hospitals Board* [1963] S.C. 311) have been protected as officers.

[21] *Per* Lord Wilberforce in *Malloch* (note 19 above).

[22] As in *ex p. Evans* (above): declaration that constable entitled to all rights and remedies for unfair dismissal except re-instatement.

Current indications are that the distinction between employee and officer may be largely obsolescent in this context.[23]

> "Employment protection legislation . . . now provides that an industrial tribunal can order the reinstatement of an employee. It is true that the order cannot be specifically enforced. However, the existence of that power does indicate that even the ordinary contract of master and servant now has many of the attributes of an office, and the distinction which previously existed between pure cases of master and servant and cases where a person holds an office is no longer clear."[24]

A public authority (like any other person) may thus be bound to act fairly in the dismissal of both officers and employees. But even though a public authority employee may be entitled to natural justice before dismissal, it does not follow that he may vindicate his right by the public law procedure of application for judicial review.[25]

(iv) *Policy issues*. We examined above the proposition that if an authority may act at pleasure there is no duty to consider counter-arguments. There, contrary intention obviating any duty of fairness is in effect inferred from the non-justiciable nature of the power: Parliament has chosen to confer the discretion in terms which do not provide sufficiently precise criteria by which the legality of its exercise may be impugned.[26] A kindred approach may be detected in the cases on natural justice in the context of official projects in the course of which a statutory public inquiry is held.[27] On the one hand, in *Errington* v. *Minister of Health*[28] a slum clearance order affecting E's property was quashed where, after the public inquiry, the minister had received from the local authority fresh representations on matters of fact and degree which had been in issue at the inquiry: E had had no opportunity to respond to these representations. The Court of Appeal held in effect that the statutory requirement of a public inquiry implied that "at such

[23] The distinction may remain vital in contexts other than the applicability of natural justice—see, *e.g. Miles* v. *Wakefield Metropolitan District Council* [1985] 1 W.L.R. 822. (Office-holder's right to full salary despite participating in industrial action).

[24] *Per* Woolf J. in *R.* v. *B.B.C. ex p. Lavelle* [1983] 1 W.L.R. 23 at 34.

[25] See *R.* v. *East Berks Health Authority ex p. Walsh* [1985] Q.B. 152, esp. *per* Purchas L.J. at p. 181: See Chap. 7, p. 268.

[26] On justiciability, see Chap. 5, p. 189.

[27] Wade A.L., pp. 452–458.

[28] [1935] 1 K.B. 249.

an inquiry the two sides may be heard."[29] But the minister had deprived the inquiry of its character as a fair hearing by later holding "a private inquiry of his own to which one party only [was] admitted."[30]

Contrast, however, *Bushell* v. *Secretary of State for the Environment*[31] where, after a public inquiry relating to motorway construction, the minister on departmental advice adopted a method of predicting future traffic density for the proposed road different from that which had been in issue at the inquiry. The House of Lords rejected the objectors' argument that they had been denied a fair hearing in being deprived of the opportunity to challenge the new method. Lord Diplock said that

> "No one could reasonably suggest that as part of the decision-making process after receipt of the [inspector's] report [on the inquiry] the minister ought not to consult with the officials of his department and obtain from them the best informed advice he can to enable him to form a balanced judgment on the strength of the objections and merits of the scheme in the interests of the public as a whole . . . "[32]

The implication seems to be that on issues of pure policy (non-justiciable) there is no duty to accord a hearing: *Bushell.* Whereas on (justiciable) issues of law, fact and degree the authority must confine its findings—as distinct from the weight it gives to them in the final decision—to material elicited in the context of the public inquiry: *Errington*. It is questionable, however, whether this rigid distinction[32a] is appropriate in the context of procedural fairness. Clearly many aspects of policy will fall outside the scope of legitimate objection to projected public works. But if an issue has been properly the subject of opposing representations at an inquiry it is difficult to see how, after the inquiry, it ceases to be

[29] *Ibid.* p. 272, *per* Maugham L.J.
[30] *Ibid.*
[31] [1981] A.C. 75.
[32] *Ibid.* p. 102. On the need in such contexts to tailor the rules of natural justice so as to contribute to the achievement of "decisions which strike a reasonable balance between the interests of the individual immediately concerned, the interests of other person and authorities in the area, and the national interest," see generally de Smith J.R.A.A., pp. 207–212.
[32a] *Cf.* the less rigid approach of Webster J. in *R.* v. *Transport Secretary ex p. Gwent C.C.* [1986] 2 All E.R. 18: Severn Bridge toll increase declared *ultra vires* because inquiry inspector refused to evaluate objections (see p. 23) on aspects of government policy which were, the judge held, appropriate subjects for full investigation at a local inquiry.

one on which objectors should be heard if new considerations emerge. Furthermore, as we have observed, it is difficult to see that it follows inexorably from the fact that a substantive issue is non-justiciable that Parliament intended that interested individuals should not be heard on the issue before a decision is taken.

(v) *Inference from context.* Contrary intention may be inferred from the context in which statutory powers are conferred or will operate. For example, it seemed to Lord Reid[33] "a reasonable and almost an inevitable inference from the circumstances in which Defence Regulations were made [in the war] and from their subject-matter that at least in many cases the intention must have been to exclude the principles of natural justice." There is room for such inference also in some peacetime contexts—*e.g.* public order and security, public health and safety. There is some case law[34] but "there will be disagreement . . . about the circumstances in which a deviation [from the duty to hear] ought to be permissible"[35] An example, perhaps, of a controversial ruling would be that of Taylor J.[36] that in the "statutory and factual context"[37] of the Local Government (Interim Provisions) Act 1984 the Secretary of State had no duty to hear the Greater London Council's objections before exercising his statutory power to defer consideration of the Council's proposed alterations to the Greater London Development Plan.

(vi) *Hearing a useless formality.* Parliament will not be taken to have imposed a duty to accord a hearing which, in the circumstances, would have been a useless formality. Of course, it is easy for an authority to argue that "to have afforded a hearing to [an individual] would have been a useless formality because whatever he might have said could have made no difference."[38] But the courts apply a strict test. The question is not "*would* the authority actually have changed its mind?" but "*could* it properly have done so?"—could the arguments advanced have provided a basis upon which a different decision could properly have been reached? So, in cases where an individual had an arguable point of law,[39] or

[33] In *Ridge* v. *Baldwin* [1964] A.C. at 73.

[34] De Smith J.R.A.A., pp. 189–192, 216–219; Wade A.L., p. 472.

[35] De Smith J.R.A.A., p. 191.

[36] *R.* v. *Environment Secretary ex p. G.L.C.* [1985] J.P.L. 543.

[37] *i.e.* "the impasse between the [council] and the Minister" (*ibid.* p. 548) no doubt generated substantially by government steps to abolish the G.L.C.

[38] *Per* Lord Reid summarising the authority's argument in *Malloch* v. *Aberdeen Corporation* [1971] 1 W.L.R. 1578 at 1582.

[39] As in *Malloch* (note 38 above) where the school teacher wished to argue that he was under no duty to register, for failure to do which the authority proposed to dismiss him.

wished to respond to allegations of misconduct,[40] or to test in the context of a public inquiry a view conflicting with the official line,[41] the "useless formality" argument has failed. But where there has been no arguable issue of law or policy,[42] or where misconduct has been flagrant, persistent and undeniable,[43] or where an authority had no discretion to act otherwise than in derogation of an individual's rights,[44] the argument has succeeded.

We may observe here in passing that where an authority comes to reconsider a decision after a court ruling that a party is entitled to a hearing, it may well reach the very conclusion that it had reached initially.[45] While this may cause the party to feel that the hearing was indeed a useless formality, the fact is that (as already observed) any substantive impropriety in the decision is likely to become apparent. And even if there is no such impropriety, the authority will have been forced to expose its decision-making process to political scrutiny.

(vii) *Delegated legislation.* Plainly, a public authority's exercise of statutory powers to make rules and regulations (delegated legislation)[46] is in principle as much subject to judicial review as the exercise of any other statutory power.[47] But particular questions as to the reviewability of delegated legislation arise both in the context of natural justice and elsewhere.[48] Since delegated legis-

[40] As in *Ridge* v. *Baldwin* (above). See also *John* v. *Rees* [1970] 1 Ch. 345 at 402 (a private law case concerning expulsion of a constituency Labour party from the national Party).

[41] As in *R.* v. *Environment Secretary ex p. Binney* [1983] *The Times*, October 8.

[42] As in *Cheall* v. *A.P.E.X.* [1983] 2 A.C. 180 (a private law case concerning expulsion from a trade union where, in the circumstances, to have given the individual a hearing would have been "a cruel deception" *per* Lord Diplock at p. 190).

[43] As in *Cinnamond* v. *British Airports Authority* [1980] 1 W.L.R. 582 (unlicensed minicab drivers persistently refused to comply with airport bye-laws or to pay fines for breach. Held not entitled to hearing before being prohibited from entering airport).

[44] As in *R.* v. *Chichester Justices ex p. Collins* [1982] 1 W.L.R. 334 (Divisional Court held that where justices had postponed individual's committal to prison for non-payment of fines to enable him to pay, they had no discretion to grant further postponement if he failed to pay. Thus no duty to hear individual before committal. *Collins* overruled by House of Lords on the discretion point in *Wilson* v. *Colchester Justices* [1985] 2 W.L.R. 694. But presumably the principle of "no hearing if no discretion" remains).

[45] As in the *Brent* and *Malloch* cases (above, notes 75 and 38 respectively). For the aftermath to *Brent*, see *R.* v. *Environment Secretary ex p. Hackney L.B.C.* [1984] 1 W.L.R. 592; to *Malloch*, Harlow and Rawlings, *Law and Administration*, pp. 274–283.

[46] See Chap. 1, p. 9.

[47] For case law, see Wade A.L., pp. 748–755.

[48] See generally de Smith J.R.A.A., pp. 467–469. See also Chap. 8, p. 289 below.

lation may affect a huge number of individuals it would be unrealistic for the courts to presume that (in the absence of express provision)[49] Parliament intends as a general rule that persons liable to be affected are entitled to be heard or consulted before such legislation is made. And the courts make no such presumption.[50] There may, of course, be circumstances where a particular statutory instrument (*e.g.* a price-fixing order) closely and specially affects only one or a few persons. Here, possibly, the courts might hold that the rules of natural justice do apply.[51]

In the preceding paragraphs we have placed under several broad categories cases where, although the rules of natural justice would appear prima facie to be applicable, the courts have detected a statutory intention that they should not apply. There are in addition to these broad categories a number of situations raising specific problems about the applicability of natural justice. The problems may be jurisdictional, as in the case of members of corporations, particularly universities, subject to visitatorial jurisdiction[52]; or they may be of public policy, as exemplified in the case law on the rights of aliens to natural justice.[53] Further details must be sought elsewhere.

(d) *Conclusion*

We conclude this section on when there is a duty to act fairly by observing a familiar tension in the case law between, on the one hand, the courts' wish to preserve a flexibility in the principles according to which natural justice is held to apply or not to apply and, on the other, a consciousness in the judges that "the principles on which this question is to be decided should be reasonably clear and definite."[54] The desire to combine satisfactorily flexibility and certainty is, of course, both perennial and unattainable. The cases abound with judicial caveats against attempting to for-

[49] For an example of such provision see *Aylesbury Mushrooms* case, above p. 209, n. 15.

[50] *Bates* v. *Lord Hailsham* [1972] 1 W.L.R. 1373; but *cf. R.* v. *Lord Chancellor (Hailsham) ex p. Alexander* [1986] *The Times*, March 21, 22, 27.

[51] *cf. Hoffman-La Roche & Co.* v. *Secretary of State for Trade and Industry* [1975] A.C. 295 where, in such circumstances, the company did allege breach of natural justice. But in the interlocutory proceedings the court found it unnecessary to express a view on the point.

[52] Wade A.L., p. 501; Craig, p. 283; see also Chap. 1, note 6, above.

[53] Wade A.L., p. 507; Craig, p. 287.

[54] *Per* Lord Guest in *Wiseman* v. *Borneman* [1971] A.C. 297 at 310.

mulate general principles as to when there is a duty to act fairly. The caveats are based on the infinite variety both of statutory provision[55] and of context in which the issue may arise.[56] Here, no doubt, as with negligence, categories are never closed. But the student may care to ponder the following extract from Lord Reid's speech in *Ridge* v. *Baldwin*[57]:

> "In modern times opinions have sometimes been expressed to the effect that natural justice is so vague as to be practically meaningless. But I would regard these as tainted by the perennial fallacy that because something cannot be cut and dried or nicely weighed or measured therefore it does not exist. The idea of negligence is equally insusceptible of exact definition but what a reasonable man would regard as fair procedure in particular circumstances and what he would regard as negligence in particular circumstances are equally capable of serving as tests in law, and natural justice as it has been interpreted in the courts is much more definite than that. It appears to me that one reason why the authorities on natural justice have been found difficult to reconcile is that insufficient attention has been paid to the great difference between various kinds of cases in which it has been sought to apply the principle."

(3) What counts as acting fairly?

We turn now to the content of natural justice: from the question "when is there a duty to act fairly?" to the question "what counts as acting fairly when there is a duty to do so?" Beginning this section in the same vein as we ended the last, "[i]t is not possible [as we have seen] to lay down rigid rules as to when the principles of natural justice are to apply; nor [as we are about to see] as to their scope and extent."[58] Much-cited in reported judgments is a dictum of Tucker L.J.[59] that "[t]he requirements of natural justice must depend on the circumstances of the case, the nature of the inquiry, the rules under which the tribunal is acting, the subject-matter that is being dealt with, and so forth." A moment's reflection will show that what might be a fair procedure for the disposal of a planning application would be unlikely to be so regarded if adopted in a

[55] See, *e.g.* Lord Hailsham in *Pearlberg* v. *Varty* [1972] 1 W.L.R. 534 at 540.
[56] See, *e.g.* Lord Upjohn in *Durayappah* v. *Fernando* [1967] 2 A.C. 337 at 349.
[57] [1964] A.C. 40 at 64–65.
[58] *Per* Lord Denning M.R. in *R.* v. *Gaming Board ex p. Benaim* [1970] 2 Q.B. 417 at 430.
[59] In *Russell* v. *Duke of Norfolk* [1949] 1 All E.R. 109 at 118.

criminal trial. Nevertheless, some general indication may be given of what, in particular circumstances, may count as acting fairly.

In *Ridge* v. *Baldwin* Lord Hodson observed[60] that

> " . . . three features of natural justice stand out—(1) the right to be heard by an unbiased tribunal, (2) the right to have notice of charges of misconduct, (3) the right to be heard in answer to those charges."

Clearly the duty to act fairly applies in many circumstances where no question of "misconduct" arises. So, a more generalised statement would refer to "the opposing case" rather than to "charges of misconduct." The rights to notice and to a hearing are features of the so-called *audi alteram partem* rule ("hear the other side"); and the rule against bias commonly appears as *nemo iudex in causa sua* ("no one a judge in his own case"). Before considering separately hearings and bias, we may recall that natural justice is generally called in aid only in circumstances where statute has not made detailed provision for a fair procedure.[61] Today, statutory rules of procedure for tribunals and inquiries (as well as courts) "are far more comprehensive than any body of judge-made rules stemming from a concept of natural justice or duty to act fairly."[62]

(a) *The right to a hearing*

(i) *Prior notice.* Generally speaking a right to a hearing "necessarily extends to a reasonable opportunity to prepare your case before you are called on to present it"[63]: *i.e.* to prior notice of the proceedings at which the matter is to be considered. But in the event of "obstructive conduct on the part of the person affected,"[64] or where in special circumstances the person will not be prejudiced,[65] prior notice may be unnecessary.[66]

[60] [1964] A.C. 40 at 132.

[61] But a court may take the view that particular statutory procedural provisions are not intended to be comprehensive and so do not entirely rule out considerations of natural justice: see Lord Wilberforce in *Wiseman* v. *Borneman* [1971] A.C. 297 at 317.

[62] See de Smith J.R.A.A., p. 198 *passim*.

[63] *Per* Lord Widgery C.J. in *R.* v. *Thames Magistrates' Court ex p. Polemis* [1974] 1 W.L.R. 1371 at 1375 (P's conviction of pollution offence quashed where case heard only hours after summons served).

[64] *Per* Lord Parmoor (*obiter*) in *De Verteuil* v. *Knaggs* [1918] A.C. 557 at 561.

[65] *Davis* v. *Carew-Pole* [1956] 1 W.L.R. 833 (Racehorse trainer not prejudiced where inquiry, of which he had notice, into alleged irregularities in training named horse extended also to another horse in same circumstances).

[66] For cases where reasonable attempt to serve notice (as distinct from actual service) may suffice, see de Smith J.R.A.A., p. 197.

(ii) *The opposing case.* Prior notice must obviously include such features of the opposing case as will fairly enable a person to marshal his own case.[67] Equally obviously, many details (of evidence, submissions etc) will appear only at the hearing itself. Moreover, in certain circumstances the courts have permitted considerations of public policy to justify concealment of certain aspects of the opposing case, *e.g.* details of a confidential medical report[68] or the identity of sources relied on by the other side.[69]

(iii) *Non-disclosure of relevant material.* An individual will have been deprived of a fair hearing before a court or tribunal where his opponent has failed to disclose information in his possession which would be of assistance to the individual.[70] This may appear at first sight to be merely an extension of the right to know the opposing case; but it seems that the principle goes beyond this. It may apply also where the fault is that of the individual's own legal advisers,[71] and possibly that of the individual himself.[72] In all these cases, of course, the tribunal itself is faultless—but [t]he real question is

[67] *R.* v. *Secretary of State for Transport ex p. Phillipine Airlines Inc* [1984] *The Times*, October 17: minister changed basis on which he purported to curtail airline flight permission without giving airline notice of his new approach or opportunity of answering allegations: variation quashed. See also *Mahon* v. *Air New Zealand* [1984] A.C. 808; *Fairmount Investments Ltd.* v. *Environment Secretary* [1976] 1 W.L.R. 1255.

[68] *R.* v. *Kent Police Authority ex p. Godden* [1971] 2 Q.B. 662: no duty on police authority to show officer psychiatrist's report on basis of which he was invalided out of force; but court ordered (mandamus) report to be available to any doctor employed by officer for purposes of challenging decision.

[69] *R.* v. *Gaming Board ex p. Benaim* [1970] 2 Q.B. 417: Board refused applicants gaming licence consent on basis of adverse reports from third parties—substance of reports disclosed to applicants but no duty to name sources; see similarly *Re Pergamon Press Ltd* [1971] Ch. 388.

[70] *R.* v. *Leyland Justices ex p. Hawthorn* [1979] Q.B. 283 (careless driving conviction quashed where prosecution had withheld names of two witnesses); *R.* v. *Blundeston Prison Visitors ex p. Fox-Taylor* [1982] 1 All E.R. 646 (prison authorities withheld name of witness of incident for which applicant punished by visitors: visitors' decision quashed); *R.* v. *Knightsbridge Crown Court ex p. Goonatilleke* [1985] 3 W.L.R. 553 (sole prosecution witness failed to disclose bad character: applicant's conviction of theft quashed).

[71] *R.* v. *Diggines ex p. Rahmani* [1985] 2 W.L.R. 611, C.A. (immigration adjudicator's dismissal of R's appeal against refusal of leave to remain in U.K. quashed where R's advisers had failed to notify R's wish for oral hearing). The adjudicator's appeal to the House of Lords was dismissed on another ground: [1986] 1 All E.R. 921. Lord Scarman observed (at p. 922) that the principle accepted by the courts below, if good law, was of very great importance. But the point was held not to arise in the case.

[72] *Per* Stephenson L.J. [1985] 2 W.L.R. 611, 622; but in such a case relief may be refused in the exercise of the court's discretion (*ibid.* p. 629).

whether there was, in truth, a breach of the rules of natural justice."[73] A hearing is not fair if there is relevant material available[74] which is not placed before the tribunal.

(iv) *Details of procedure.* The actual extent of a person's knowledge of and ability to answer an opposing case will turn very much on the details of the procedure adopted by the deciding authority—*e.g.* whether the hearing is oral or, on the contrary, by way of written submissions; if it is oral, whether or not there is a right to legal or other representation and a right to call and to cross-examine witnesses. As already observed, there is often detailed statutory provision on matters of procedure. But in cases where statute is silent the courts have refrained from any general statement beyond that "what [the] procedure is to be in detail must depend on the nature of the tribunal."[75] And, in order that tribunals may dispose of their business with due speed and efficiency, they have at common law a wide discretion in the matter of their own procedure.[76]

Hearings will commonly be oral; and failure to give an oral hearing may be a denial of natural justice where in all the circumstances of the case it seems "possible that if the applicant had had an oral hearing . . . further matters could have been advanced on his behalf."[77] But there are many situations where a case may be put adequately in writing and where, accordingly, the courts have refused to rule that an oral hearing is essential.[78] Many licensing authorities, for example, may decide on paper[79]; and there is com-

[73] *Ibid. per* Fox L.J. at p. 625.

[74] *cf.* where new material comes to light after the hearing. This will not detract from the fairness of the hearing itself and so will not attract supervisory review for want of natural justice: *R.* v. *West Sussex Quarter Sessions ex p. Albert and Maud Ltd.* [1974] Q.B. 24 (Lord Denning dissenting). Courts with appellate review jurisdiction are commonly empowered to consider fresh evidence.

[75] *Per* Viscount Haldane L.C. in *Local Government Board* v. *Arlidge* [1915] A.C. 120 at 132.

[76] See, *e.g. R.* v. *Judge Amphlett* [1915] 2 K.B. 223 at 239, 241; *Re Pergamon Press Ltd.* [1971] Ch. 388 at 400, 403; *R.* v. *Home Secretary ex p. Tarrant* [1985] Q.B. 251 at 273, 280.

[77] *Per* Slynn J. in *R.* v. *Immigration Appeal Tribunal ex p. Mehmet* [1977] 1 W.L.R. 795 at 804–805 (Tribunal's refusal of application for leave to appeal against adjudicator quashed because it failed to give applicant oral hearing).

[78] *e.g. R.* v. *Amphlett* (above): mandamus to minimum wage board chairman to hear workmen's case for variation of minimum wage; board to decide whether or not hearing should be oral.

[79] See, *e.g. Kavanagh* v. *Chief Constable of Devon* [1974] Q.B. 624 at 634 (firearms certificate); *R.* v. *Huntingdon D.C. ex p. Cowan* [1984] 1 W.L.R. 501 at 508 (entertainments licence); *R.* v. *Bristol City Council ex p. Pearce* [1984] *The Times*, December 7 (street trading).

monly provision for oral hearing later by way of appeal on the merits to a local court.

Again, whether or not (in the absence of statutory provision) to permit parties to be represented at an oral hearing will commonly fall within a deciding authority's procedural discretion.[80] But the seriousness or complexity of a particular case may be such that "no [authority], properly directing itself, could reasonably decide not to allow . . . legal representation."[81]

Finally, especially in penal and other cases where questions of fact are in issue, a fair hearing will normally include the right to call witnesses[82] and to cross-examine those called by the other side.[83] But a tribunal chairman may limit the number of witnesses, *e.g.* "on the basis that he has good reason for considering that the total number sought to be called is an attempt . . . to render the hearing of [a] charge virtually impracticable or where . . . it would be quite unnecessary to call so many witnesses to establish [a] point."[84]

(v) *Reasons for decisions.* It is plain that the value of a right to a hearing will be considerably diminished if it does not extend to a right to know the reasons upon which a decision is ultimately based. In particular, of course, it is difficult effectively to challenge a decision (by way of appeal or otherwise) if one is not apprised of the reasons for it. Statutory procedural rules very commonly require reasons to be given[85]; and we have already noted the

[80] See, *e.g. Ex p. Tarrant* [1985] Q.B. 251. Prison visitors' decision not to allow prisoners legal representation at disciplinary hearing quashed: although no invariable duty to allow representation (*Fraser* v. *Mudge* [1975] 1 W.L.R. 1132), visitors were in breach of their duty to consider (when asked or in exceptional circumstances, *R.* v. *Swansea Prison Visitors ex p. M'Grath* [1984] *The Times*, November 21) whether or not to allow it at discretion. *cf. Maynard* v. *Osmond* [1977] Q.B. 240: common law duty of chief constable to consider whether police constable on serious disciplinary charge should be allowed legal representation ousted by express provision in statutory instrument.

[81] *Per* Webster J. in *Tarrant* (note 80 above) at p. 287 (charges of mutiny).

[82] *R.* v. *Hull Prison Visitors ex p. St. Germain (No. 2)* [1979] 1 W.L.R. 1401 at 1406–1408 (prisoner's conviction on disciplinary charge quashed where request to call witness refused by visitors on ground of administrative inconvenience).

[83] *Osgood* v. *Nelson* (1872) 5 L.R.H.L. 636 at 646, 650 (removal from public office). The tension noted earlier (p. 226) between justiciable issues (*e.g.* of fact) and non-justiciable policy issues is reflected in the case law on cross-examination: see *Bushell* v. *Secretary of State* (discussed *ibid.*) where the inquiry inspector's refusal to permit objectors to cross-examine civil servants on their method of predicting traffic density was upheld by the House of Lords. *Bushell* applied in *R.* v. *London Regional Passenger Committee ex p. Brent L.B.C.* [1985] *The Times*, May 23.

[84] *Per* Geoffrey Lane L.J. in *St Germain* (note 82 above) at p. 1406.

[85] See above, p. 211.

requirement of the Tribunals and Inquiries Act that certain tribunals and ministers must give reasons for their decisions.[86] But in the absence of express statutory provision and where reliance must be placed on the rules of natural justice, it is said that there is not "any general principle of law which imposes on a decision-maker a duty to make known the reasons for his decisions."[87] This statement, however, must be taken with some reserve. For, "a professional judge should, as a rule, give reasons for his decision."[88] His failure to do so may be a basis for either appellate[89] or supervisory[90] review. However, "the particularity with which he is required to set [reasons] out must depend upon the circumstances of the case before him and the nature of the decision he is giving."[91] As for statutory tribunals: in a case where statute has expressly excluded the Tribunals and Inquiries Act provision, for example where a social security commissioner refuses leave to appeal against certain decisions of local tribunals, "there is no basic requirement of natural justice that reasons should always be given," although "commissioners are always free to give reasons if they see fit."[92] In a case where there is simply no statutory provision on the matter, a refusal to give reasons may possibly be challengeable by way of judicial review.[92a]

At present, however, the case law indicates that in general the existence of a duty to give reasons as a matter of natural justice will depend (as the extent of the right to a hearing depends gener-

86 Tribunals and Inquiries Act 1971, s.12.

87 *Per* Brightman L.J. in *Payne* v. *Lord Harris of Greenwich* [1981] 1 W.L.R. 754 at 765.

88 *Per* Griffiths L.J. in *Eagil Trust Co. Ltd.* v. *Pigott-Brown*, [1985] 3 All E.R. 119 at 122, referring also to certain 'well-established exceptions' to the general rule. See too *R.* v. *Knightsbridge Crown Court ex p. I.S.C. Ltd.* [1981] 3 W.L.R. 640 at 648.

89 *e.g. Lennard* v. *International Institute for Medical Science* [1985] *The Times*, April 29 (High Court judge failed to give reasons for setting aside default judgment); *Banaskiewicz* v. *Mulholland* [1985] *The Times*, April 19 (county court judge dismissed claim without giving reasons: new trial ordered).

90 See *ex p. I.S.C. Ltd.* (*loc. cit.* note 88 above); *R.* v. *Clerkenwell Green Met. Stip. Magistrate ex p. Ibrahim* [1983] *The Times*, December 7 (magistrate gave no reason for declining to rehear case in presence of an accused who had been convicted in her absence).

91 *Per* Griffiths L.J. [1985] 3 All E.R. 119 at 122.

92 *R.* v. *Social Services Secretary ex p. Connolly* [1986] 1 All E.R. 998 at 1006–1007, *per* Slade L.J.

92a The Court of Appeal in *Connolly* (note 92 above) confined its refusal to affirm a general principle that commissioners should give reasons to 'the class of case now under discussion' (p. 1007) and felt 'some sympathy' (p. 1006) with the more liberal views of Woolf J. at first instance.

ally) upon the circumstances of the case.[93] Whether this is satisfactory may be questioned. We have noticed the courts' wide insistence that official decisions should be based on proper grounds.[94] It would surely complement this approach if the courts were to state that the giving of reasons is in general a constituent of natural justice, although the extent of the duty will depend on the particular circumstances of a case.

(b) *The rule against bias*

(i) *General considerations.* Where the rule against bias applies, a person exercising official power breaks the rule if either (a) he has a pecuniary interest in (*i.e.* stands to gain financially from) a decision or (b) there is real likelihood that he is predisposed to decide in a particular way.[95] The case law establishes in effect that the very existence of pecuniary interest is taken without more to show a real likelihood of bias; and that, in the absence of pecuniary interest, it is sufficient to demonstrate a real likelihood of bias in the circumstances of the case. In either event it is unnecessary to show that a person was actually biased.[96]

Commonly the rule against bias will co-exist with a duty to give a hearing; but there are circumstances in which one of the two rules of natural justice will apply while the application of the other will be diluted or excluded.

On the one hand, contrary intention[97] in a statute may relieve

[93] See *Payne* v. *Lord Harris* (above): Court of Appeal held that character of parole board and nature and circumstances of its operation relieved it of any duty to give reasons for refusing parole to prisoner serving life sentence.

[94] Chaps. 4 and 5. Some commentators detected from the speech of Lord Upjohn in *Padfield* v. *Minister of Agriculture etc.* [1968] A.C. 997 at 1061–1062 a suggestion that where there was a duty to have good reasons (*i.e.* "proper grounds") for a decision, there was in effect a duty to make them known. For Lord Upjohn seemed to say that a failure to state good reasons for a decision might be taken to imply that there were no good reasons to state. But in *British Airways Board* v. *Laker Airways Ltd.* [1985] A.C. 58 at 92. Lord Diplock said that the dictum "add[ed] nothing to" the *Wednesbury* principle and meant only that on some occasions where no proper grounds are stated it may be possible to infer from all the circumstances of the case that no such grounds exist.

[95] For pecuniary interest, see para. (iii) below; for real likelihood of bias, see para. (iv).

[96] See, *e.g. Dimes* v. *Grand Junction Canal Proprietors* (1852) 3 H.L.C. 759 at 793; *R.* v. *Barnsley Licensing Justices ex p. Barnsley etc. Victuallers* [1960] 2 Q.B. 167 at 187.

[97] See above, p. 221 *et seq.*

an authority of any duty to give a hearing, but its proceedings may still be open to challenge for bias.[98] For example, while, as we saw, a planning authority may not need to hear parties before deciding a planning application, the decision may be vitiated if a voting member of the authority stands to gain financially from it[99]; or if the authority itself has such a financial interest in the decision as patently disables it from exercising its discretion.[1]

On the other hand, the further an authority is from the judicial archetype, the less appropriate it may be to impose on it the rule against bias in its full rigour, notwithstanding that the authority may be under a duty to give a hearing. So, *e.g.* a licensing authority may have created a legitimate expectation that it will not change its policy before hearing representations from certain persons.[2] In that the occasion to hear will, *ex hypothesi*, arise only when the authority is inclined to adopt a new policy, it would be absurd to require the authority to take a completely neutral—"unbiased"—stance.[3]

(ii) *Exclusion of rule.* It is plain, of course, that private individual interest, whether pecuniary or otherwise, would generally be unacceptable, even where "policy bias" might not. But Parliament may expressly or by necessary implication exclude the rule against bias in circumstances where it would otherwise plainly apply.

As to express exclusion, the courts have construed such provisions strictly. For example, a statute may disqualify an individual (perhaps under penalty) from participating in a decision in which he has a pecuniary interest but may go on to provide (presumably in the interest of dispatch of business) that no decision shall be

[98] See, *e.g. per* Lord Donovan in *Wiseman* v. *Borneman* [1971] A.C. 297 at 316.

[99] *R.* v. *Hendon R.D.C. ex p. Chorley* [1933] 2 K.B. 696: sale of property depended on grant of permission; estate agent, whose commission depended on sale, was voting member of granting authority.

[1] As in *Steeples* v. *Derbyshire C.C.* [1984] 3 All E.R. 468: permission granted by county planning authority which was contractually bound to pay damages to developer if permission not obtained; but *cf. R.* v. *Sevenoaks D.C. ex p. Terry* [1985] 3 All E.R. 226; *R.* v. *St. Edmundsbury B.C. ex p. Investors in Industry Ltd.* [1985] 1 W.L.R. 1168: contract to lease council land conditional on grant of planning permission to prospective lessee. Permission not vitiated by bias.

[2] See, *e.g. R.* v. *Liverpool Corpn. ex p. Liverpool Taxi etc. Assocn.* [1972] 2 Q.B. 299. See above, p. 219.

[3] For an example of legitimate "policy bias," see *R.* v. *Amber Valley D.C. ex p. Jackson* [1984] 3 All E.R. 501: The developer in *Steeples* (above) had sought permission from a district planning authority under the same political control as the county council in that case. Held: authority's political predisposition to grant permission did not disable it from making decision; and see generally, de Smith J.R.A.A., pp. 253, 254–257.

invalid by reason only of the disqualification.[4] The courts have interpreted such "by reason only" provisions as immunising a decision where a challenge is based on the mere existence of the pecuniary interest; but not where, in the circumstances of the case, a real likelihood of bias can actually be shown.[5]

As to implication, it seems that legal necessity may immunise from challenge a decision which can lawfully be made only by a person who is in breach of the rule against bias.[6] "The doctrine has been applied very sparingly in modern English Law,"[7] but a standard example is of a minister required to consider a compulsory purchase order affecting his own property. In such a case "it is generally supposed . . . that a minister must act as best he can."[8]

(iii) *Pecuniary interest.* Where it applies, the rule against bias is broken if the decision-maker has "any direct pecuniary interest, however small, in the subject of inquiry."[9] So, in a well-known case, Lord Chancellor Cottenham had decided a land title dispute in favour of a company in which, as it later appeared, he owned shares. The House of Lords allowed an appeal on the basis of Lord Cottenham's pecuniary interest.[10] But although even a very small pecuniary interest may vitiate a decision, a purely speculative or fanciful one will not. In one case[11] a solicitor member of a bench of magistrates was held not to have a pecuniary interest in convicting an accused of falsely pretending to be a solicitor: the ingenious and unsuccessful argument was that as a member of the prosecuting Law Society the magistrate would stand to lose if the prosecution

[4] See, *e.g.* Local Government Act 1972, ss.94, 82; Licensing Act 1964, s.193(6).

[5] *R.* v. *Barnsley Licensing Justices* [1960] 2 Q.B. 167: justices granting off-licence to Co-operative store were members of Co-operative Society and in receipt of dividends. Grant valid by reason of statutory provision and absence of any real likelihood of bias in fact.

[6] See, *e.g. Dimes* v. *Grand Junction Canal Proprietors* (1852) 3 H.L.C. 759 at 787–789.

[7] De Smith J.R.A.A., p. 276. For example in *Steeples* (above) Webster J. declined to apply the doctrine to exonerate the county council, pointing out (p. 495) that the developer might himself have applied (as he later did—see *Amber Valley* case, above) to the district council.

[8] Wade A.L., p. 427.

[9] *Per* Blackburn J. in *R.* v. *Rand* (1866) L.R. 1 Q.B. 230 at 232: local authority shares owned by justices stood to gain value when justices certified new corporation reservoir serviceable. Although court held no bias because shares held by justices as trustees, the judgment of Blackburn J. is regarded as containing the classic statement of the rule against bias.

[10] *Dimes* v. *Grand Junction Canal Proprietors* (above). For other cases of pecuniary interest, see notes 99, 1, 5 above.

[11] *R.* v. *Burton ex p. Young* [1897] 2 Q.B. 468.

failed and costs were awarded against the Society—for if the Society were wound up he would be entitled to a fractionally smaller share of its assets!

(iv) *"Real likelihood" of bias.* Pecuniary interest apart, the rule against bias is broken when it can be shown that in the circumstances of the case there is a "real likelihood"[12] of bias on the part of the deciding authority. After some judicial oscillation[13] it appears now settled that the test of the existence of "real likelihood" is whether a reasonable person in possession of such relevant information as he might readily have ascertained would have thought that bias was likely.[14] On this test it is immaterial whether or not the review court is, on the basis of the facts established before it, of the opinion that there was actually a real likelihood of bias.[15]

There is, of course, an infinite number of circumstances in which the "real likelihood" test may be satisfied. For example, a court or tribunal may include or be advised by a person who might reasonably be thought to have an interest in the outcome of proceedings. The interest may be personal.[16] Or it may be professional, as where a magistrate's clerk who retired with them to consider a dangerous driving charge was solicitor to a party who was suing the accused in respect of the same incident[17]; or where a magistrate trying a charge of acting as an unqualified Thames pilot was himself a qualified pilot—a member of "a small class of privileged persons for whose protection the proceedings were taken."[18] On the other hand, in the Law Society case referred to above,[19] there was held to be no probability of bias since it was plain that the solicitor-magistrate had taken no part in the institution of proceedings. And

[12] The now-hallowed phrase is that of Blackburn J. in *Rand* (above).

[13] Wade A.L., pp. 430–432; de Smith J.R.A.A., pp. 262–264.

[14] See *R.* v. *Camborne Justices ex p. Pearce* [1955] 1 Q.B. 41 at 51 (see below, text to note 20); *Metropolitan Properties* v. *Lannon* [1969] 1 Q.B. 577 (landlord successfully challenged London rent assessment committee's settlement of fair rent where committee chairman was assisting his father in contesting rent assessment with same landlords elsewhere in London). The *Sevenoaks* and *St Edmundsbury* cases (note 1 above) indicate that in cases far from the judicial archetype (*e.g.* local authority decisions relating to property in which authority has interest) the question is simply whether the authority properly exercised its discretion. For, as we saw, these are cases in which it is inappropriate to require the authority to take a completedly neutral or "unbiased" stance.

[15] But this appears to be material in a case arising under a statutory "by reason only" clause: see note 5 above.

[16] As in *Lannon* (note 14 above).

[17] *R.* v. *Sussex Justices ex p. McCarthy* [1924] 1 K.B. 256.

[18] *Per* Wills J. in *R.* v. *Huggins* [1895] 1 Q.B. 563 at 565.

[19] See note 11 above.

in another case[20] magistrates considering a food hygiene charge preferred by a local authority had retired with their clerk who was himself a member of the authority. But an allegation of bias failed on the basis that (as could easily have been discovered) the clerk had taken no part in the proceedings leading to the prosecution.

Among other obvious bases upon which a reasonable man might think bias likely are personal hostility to or friendship with a party. The substantial case law is treated substantially elsewhere.[21]

(4) Effect of breach of duty to act fairly

(a) *Bases of challenge*

The rules of natural justice are, as we have seen, implied statutory procedural requirements. On what bases may a victim of a breach of the rules challenge that breach in the courts?

It is clearly established by authority[22] that for purposes of supervisory review, breach of the rules is to be regarded as tantamount to jurisdictional error or acting *ultra vires*, thus rendering an act or decision void rather than voidable.[23] So, for example, a "no certiorari" clause[24] is no bar to supervisory review based on denial of natural justice.[25] And it is clear that a party may make such a denial the basis of a collateral challenge.[26]

What of appellate review? A denial of natural justice may be the basis for an appeal, whether the appeal is by way of rehearing[27] or confined to point of law.[28] It is true that in a number of reported cases[29] appeal courts have declined to entertain appeals based on

[20] *R.* v. *Camborne JJ. ex p. Pearce* [1955] 1 Q.B. 41.
[21] *e.g.* de Smith J.R.A.A., pp. 262–272.
[22] *Ridge* v. *Baldwin* [1964] A.C. 40 (a majority of the House of Lords); and see *Anisminic Ltd.* v. *Foreign Compensation Commission* [1969] 2 A.C. 147 at 171, 195, 207; *O'Reilly* v. *Mackman* [1983] 2 A.C. 237 at 276.
[23] On void/voidable, see further below. In *Durayappah* v. *Fernando* [1967] 2 A.C. 337 the Privy Council held that a decision reached in breach of natural justice was voidable rather than void. But it appears that the case is authority merely for the "unexceptionable proposition . . . that a person has no *locus standi* to challenge a decision on the ground that another was denied a hearing"—de Smith J.R.A.A., p. 241n.
[24] See Chap. 2, p. 48.
[25] *Att.-Gen.* v. *Ryan* [1980] A.C. 718.
[26] *e.g.* *Cooper* v. *Wandsworth Board of Works* (1863) 14 C.B.N.S. 180. *cf.* Wade A.L., p. 299.
[27] As in *Dimes* v. *Grand Junction Canal Proprietors* (See note 10 above).
[28] *e.g.* *Ottley* v. *Morris* [1979] 1 All E.R. 65. Appeal by case stated may be regarded as too cumbersome in case of denial of natural justice: *R.* v. *Wandsworth JJ. ex p. Read* [1942] 1 K.B. 281.
[29] See de Smith J.R.A.A., p. 152.

denial of natural justice because such denial renders a decision void and, accordingly, there is no decision to appeal against. But this, it is submitted, is simply one of the nonsensical consequences which, at one time or another, have been said to flow from the void/voidable distinction. Fortunately, as we saw earlier,[30] the highest courts have recently indicated that the distinction is in many respects unsatisfactory and that it will not be allowed to produce such bizarre results.[31]

On principle, surely, if an appeal court has jurisdiction either to rehear a case itself or to remit it for hearing to the first instance tribunal,[32] it should not decline to exercise that jurisdiction in the case of denial of natural justice. After all, it appears that today most errors of law are jurisdictional[33]—*i.e.* in terms of the void/voidable distinction, they render a decision "void." But it has not been suggested on that account that where the authority concerned is subject to supervisory review it is improper for a party to challenge its decision by appeal on point of law.[34]

It is, however, the case that the void/voidable distinction has raised other particular problems in the context of breach of the rules of natural justice. These must now be considered briefly.

(b) *The void/voidable distinction*

(i) *Substantial injustice.* There appears to be some difficulty in reconciling the proposition that breach of the rules of natural justice renders a decision void with the commonsense principle that only breaches likely to have caused a substantial miscarriage of justice should be remedied.[35] But the remedies of common law supervisory review are all discretionary[36] and the question of substantial miscarriage can properly be dealt with in the exercise of this discretion.[37] In its exercise of appellate jurisdiction, a court may have express statutory power to dismiss the appeal "if they

[30] See Chap. 2, p. 64.

[31] See especially *Calvin* v. *Carr* [1980] A.C. 574 (decision which is "void" for want of natural justice is nevertheless appealable).

[32] *cf. Campbell* v. *Rochdale General Commissioners* [1975] 2 All E.R. 385 (court empowered neither to rehear nor to remit but only to confirm or reverse first instance decision).

[33] See Chap. 4.

[34] Of course where more than one mode of challenge is available, a court may regard one of the modes as the more appropriate and require it to be employed; see Chap. 9.

[35] See especially the dissenting speech of Lord Evershed in *Ridge* v. *Baldwin* [1964] A.C. 40.

[36] See Chap. 8, p. 280 *et seq.*

[37] See, *e.g. ex p. Rahmani* (note 71 above) esp. at [1985] 2 W.L.R., pp. 625, 627–628; de Smith J.R.A.A., p. 244 and cases cited.

consider that no miscarriage of justice has actually occurred."[38] Failing this, a court may well take the view (albeit arguably inconsistently with the principle that any denial of natural justice renders a decision void) that the appeal should be allowed only in the event of a substantial miscarriage.[39] In cases of collateral challenge, *e.g.* a suit for damages, the court may indeed have no discretion as to remedy. But, again, in such a case one might expect that a court might decline to accede to the challenge where no substantial injustice had been done. Finally, under the "statutory supervisory review" jurisdiction, as we have seen, a party complaining of breach of a procedural requirement must show "substantial prejudice."[40]

(ii) *Waiver.* There is authority[41] for the proposition that a breach of the rule against bias may be waived (so precluding subsequent challenge); and it may be likewise where a fair hearing is denied.[42] At first sight this may appear inconsistent with the proposition that denial of natural justice renders a decision void because outside jurisdiction. For as a general rule jurisdictional defects cannot be waived[43] so as to confer a power where none exists, any more than estoppel can operate to curtail a power which has been conferred.[44] The courts' approach to waiver of denials of natural justice may be seen, however, as another example of their refusal to be hidebound by the unsatisfactory concept of voidness, or "nullity." We saw earlier[45] that to say that an act or decision is "void" presupposes the existence of a successful challenge by the right person in the right circumstances. Now, the rules of natural justice may be seen as conferring personal benefit on individuals who, accordingly, should be entitled to waive their observance.[46] In these circumstances it appears sensible to treat a person who has waived a breach of the rules of natural justice as

[38] As under Criminal Appeal Act 1968, s.2(1) proviso.

[39] *Ottley* v. *Morris* (above): court allowed taxpayer's appeal on point of law, but only because commissioners' failure to observe natural justice probably caused him substantial injustice; de Smith J.R.A.A., p. 245.

[40] See p. 208, n.6 above; de Smith J.R.A.A., 155.

[41] *e.g. ex p. Young* (note 11 above) at pp. 470, 473: throughout summary trial for falsely pretending to be solicitor, accused knew that one of the magistrates was himself a solicitor. Since he did not then suggest that magistrate was likely to be biased against him, he was held to have waived any right to do so later. On waiver of bias see de Smith J.R.A.A., p. 275.

[42] *cf.* de Smith J.R.A.A., p. 242.

[43] See Wade A.L., p. 234; Craig, pp. 410, 469.

[44] See Chap. 5, p. 198.

[45] See Chap. 2, p. 62.

[46] See Craig, p. 411; and *cf.* note 23 above.

not being, in the circumstances, any more entitled to challenge the decision in question than a person who has delayed his challenge inordinately or who has no sufficient interest in the matter.

(iii) *Double jeopardy*. Under the rule against double jeopardy "a man cannot be tried for a crime in respect of which he has previously been acquitted or convicted."[47] Suppose that a court, in acquitting a defendant, denies natural justice to the prosecution by, for example, refusing to hear a competent witness. It appears that the acquittal is not to be regarded as void so as to deny to the acquitted defendant the protection of the rule.[48] But if a court wrongly declines jurisdiction (*e.g.* by refusing to hear the prosecution's case at all) the prosecution may obtain mandamus requiring the court to proceed.[49] For, no trial having occurred, the defendant was never in jeopardy of conviction.

The courts' treatment of the notion of "voidness" in each of the above three contexts illustrates well a judicial tendency already noted.[50] For, while the words "void" and "voidable"

> "may be helpful in argument [they] may be misleading in effect if relied on to show that the courts, in deciding the consequences of a defect in the exercise of power are necessarily bound to fit the facts of a particular case . . . into rigid legal categories or to stretch or cramp them on a bed of Procrustes invented by lawyers for the purposes of convenient exposition."[51]

[47] *Per* Lord Morris in *Connelly* v. *D.P.P.* [1964] A.C. 1254 at 1305.
[48] See *per* Lord Roskill in *Re Harrington* [1984] A.C. 743 at 753.
[49] *Re Harrington* (above). See too *R.* v. *Bournemouth Crown Court ex p. Weight* [1984] 1 W.L.R. 980.
[50] See Chap. 2, p. 64.
[51] *Per* Lord Hailsham in *London & Clydeside Estates Ltd.* v. *Aberdeen District Council* [1980] 1 W.L.R. 182 at 189.

PART III

THE MACHINERY OF REVIEW

In Chapter 1 we observed that since the seventeenth century, public authorities have been subject to the "ordinary law of the land administered in the ordinary courts of justice." By this we meant that there is no *droit administratif* administered by a court such as the Conseil d'Etat in France.[1] We saw that, in general, public authorities enjoy no privileged status in English Law and that the ordinary civil and criminal law applies to them as it applies to everyone else. On the other hand, we saw that public authorities may be entrusted with specific additional legal duties and may have precisely defined legal powers which we described as their "remit." Judicial review is that body of law specifically concerned to ensure that public authorities discharge the special duties imposed and do not exceed the special powers conferred upon them; to ensure, in short, that public authorities remain within their remit. While the ordinary mechanisms of the civil and criminal law may serve this purpose in some cases, it is not their exclusive function and they cannot deal with every eventuality. To this extent, the law of judicial review may be seen as being in some way different from what is understood as the ordinary civil and criminal law—in some way "special." In Chapter 7 we consider what is special about the remedies and procedures of supervisory review. In Chapter 8 we examine those remedies and procedures.

The procedures of appellate review are prescribed in detail by particular statutes and statutory instruments. These details must be sought elsewhere.[2] However, in Chapter 9, we observe that there are many circumstances in which, in principle, a direct challenge[3] may be mounted by invoking either supervisory or appel-

[1] On the Conseil d'Etat, see Neville Brown and J. F. Garner, *French Administrative Law* (3rd ed.), Chaps. 3 and 4.
[2] See in particular The Supreme Court Practice 1985: R.S.C., Ords. 55–61, 93, 94.
[3] See Chap. 2, p. 29 *et seq.*, 37 *et seq.*

late review jurisdiction. We consider the principles upon which one approach or the other may be preferred. We consider also the general question of "exhaustion of remedies" prior to direct resort to the supervisory jurisdiction.

Chapter 7

SUPERVISORY REVIEW: ITS PLACE IN THE LEGAL SYSTEM

A. What is special about Supervisory Review?

Since the law relating to supervisory review is administered in the ordinary courts of justice, those same courts that administer the "ordinary" civil and criminal law, it might be supposed that the only things special about supervisory review are its remedies and procedures. It might also be supposed that the question "what is special about supervisory review?" could be exhaustively answered by a description and explanation of those remedies and procedures. While such a task must, of course, be undertaken,[1] it would be seriously defective unless some effort were made to place the law of supervisory review in its proper perspective, and to explain how this branch of law interacts with other branches of law. This task will not be easy, and will require us to consider new ways of classifying law which are still in the process of being developed. It would not have been necessary but for a relatively recent example of that all too common failing, a tendency to piecemeal law reform. In 1977, following a report of the Law Commission,[2] the Rules of the Supreme Court[3] were changed in an effort to remove procedural anomalies in relation to judicial review that had become all too apparent. As we shall see, these reforms have, in some ways, merely replaced old problems with new, and we must go back more than a hundred years to another piecemeal reform in order to comprehend the present difficulties.

(1) The prerogative remedies and relator actions

Prior to the procedural reforms of the nineteenth century, that part of English Law not concerned with the prosecution of offences consisted of innumerable separate "forms of action,"

[1] See Chap. 8.

[2] Report on Remedies in Administrative Law (Law Comm. 73) Cmnd. 6407 (1976).

[3] Order 53, substituted by S.I. 1977 No. 1955.

each with its own initiating writ and its own procedures.[4] In addition, there existed the prerogative writs by means of which public authorities were kept within their remit. For our purposes, we may concentrate upon the writs of mandamus (which ordered the performance of a legal duty), prohibition (which prevented a public authority from exceeding its jurisdiction) and certiorari (which quashed an invalid decision by a public authority).[5] All writs were royal commands but, unlike initiating writs which ordered a defendant to appear before the court, the prerogative writs were themselves remedies, orders issued by the Court of King's Bench at the culmination of proceedings. Nominally, the Crown was the plaintiff, as in a criminal trial on indictment. Any individual wishing to invoke the High Court's jurisdiction to issue a prerogative writ had first to apply for leave. But the leave required was that of the court, rather than that of the Crown itself. An alternative means by which public authorities, or private individuals, might be compelled to keep within the law was for the Attorney-General, as the legal representative of the Crown,[6] to apply for an injunction in the Court of Chancery.[7] Just as an individual could seek leave to invoke the High Court's authority to issue a prerogative writ, so too an individual might seek to persuade[8] the Attorney-General to permit an application for an

[4] On the "forms of action," see J. H. Baker, *Introduction to English Legal History*, (2nd ed.), Chap. 4.

[5] Although Habeas Corpus is perhaps the most famous of the prerogative remedies its application is rather too specialised to be considered here (see Wade A.L., p. 540). Neither will we be concerned with the special form of injunction which replaced an information in the nature of quo warranto in 1938 (see Chap. 8(B)). For a historical explanation of the prerogative remedies, see De Smith J.R.A.A., appendix 1, p. 548.

[6] It seems to be regarded as axiomatic that the Crown is the repository of all public rights, sometimes on the basis of a *jus publicum* (in the case of public highways and navigable rivers), but otherwise simply as *parens patriae*. The Attorney-General could also apply for certiorari but has rarely done so in modern times (*cf. R.* v. *Amendt* [1915] 2 K.B. 276).

[7] *e.g. Att.-Gen.* v. *Cockermouth Local Board* (1874) L.R. 18 Eq 172.

[8] The Attorney-General's exercise of his discretion to grant or refuse authority for the bringing of a relator action is not subject to challenge in any court (*Gouriet* v. *Union of Post Office Workers* [1978] A.C. 435. Although the Attorney-General will lend his name to proceedings against local authorities, it seems he will never give approval to a relator action against a minister or government department (see Wade A.L., p. 532).

injunction to be made in his name, by what is called a relator action.[9] We need not now concern ourselves with the details of the procedures of either alternative except to note that, in relation to the prerogative writs, if an inappropriate writ were sought, the cause would be lost, even though it might have been apparent that an application for a different writ would have been successful.[10]

(2) Procedural reform of the civil law and its consequences

By comparison with the generally unsystematic nature of the legal procedures prevailing at the time, the procedures for obtaining prerogative writs would not have seemed to be in need of urgent reform. It was in relation to the procedures of what, for convenience, we will call the "civil law" that reform was a pressing need. The process of simplification and standardisation begun by the Uniformity of Process Act 1832 culminated in the wholesale rationalisation of the Judicature Acts 1873–75 but the prerogative actions were expressly excluded from these reforms.[11] In the years that followed, the judges readily embraced the spirit behind the reforms, recognising that procedure should be the servant of the law and not its master, and that no good cause should be lost through a mistake in procedure. In these circumstances, it was perhaps inevitable that those concerned to impose legal control upon the abuse of official power should turn away from the prerogative actions which came to be regarded as archaic and defective when compared with ordinary civil actions. The two civil remedies utilized in this context were the injunction and the declaration. The former was, of course, the very remedy used in cases brought against public authorities by or at the relation of the Attorney-General. The latter, although having a long history in Exchequer,[12] owes its modern form to a Rule of the Supreme Court of 1883.[13] It is not necessary now to trace the way in which the courts extended the availability of these two remedies, although the

[9] *e.g. Att.-Gen* v. *Oglender* (1740) 1 Ves.Jun. 246. Today, relator actions are cited as, *e.g. Att.-Gen. ex rel McWhirter* v. *I.B.A.* [1973] Q.B. 629.
[10] See Wade A.L., p. 568.
[11] See Supreme Court of Judicature Act 1875, 1st Sched.: Rules of Court, Ord. 62.
[12] *e.g. Pawlett* v. *Att.-Gen.* (1668) Hard. 465.
[13] Ord. 25, r. 2. See also below Chap. 8, p. 296.

resultant distortion[14] of the civil law lies at the heart of the present difficulties and may need to be re-examined once the proper ambit of supervisory review has been established.[15] What is important for our purposes is that, in time, the remedies became so freely available to individual litigants suing in their own right that, in some circumstances, they were seen as straightforward alternatives to a relator action, or to an application for a prerogative remedy, as a means of preventing a public authority from stepping outside its remit.[16] Increasingly, the courts looked to the substance of whether a public authority had breached a statutory duty rather than to the form of the procedure by which the matter was brought to the attention of the court. Since the remedies were in any event discretionary,[17] and since the courts did have jurisdiction to exercise this type of control, albeit by different procedures, these developments were very much in the spirit of the nineteenth century reforms. Indeed, the availability of these remedies in ordinary civil proceedings proved to be invaluable when the erroneous belief that certiorari would lie only in respect of "judicial" and "quasi-judicial" decisions threatened to limit severely the role of the prerogative remedies in the control of purely "administrative" action.[18] However, a casualty of this disregard for procedural nice-

[14] For example, the case of *Boyce* v. *Paddington B.C.* [1903] 1 Ch. 109 has been repeatedly treated as an authority for the proposition that an individual may obtain an injunction to restrain a breach of a statutory duty by a public authority, without having to rely upon the Attorney-General to authorise a relator action, and despite having no cause of action sounding in damages, if he can show "special damage" peculiar to himself. The cases cited in support of this proposition by Buckley J. were in fact actions for damages which contradict rather than support the proposition. Furthermore, the authority of Buckley J.'s remarks is very much weakened by the facts that (a) in *Boyce* itself the Court of Appeal intimated that the Attorney-General should be added as plaintiff so that the matter could proceed (as it did) as a relator action: [1903] 2 Ch. 556 at 561; and (b) in a subsequent case Buckley J. himself directly denied the very proposition for which his judgment in *Boyce* is treated as authority. (See Buckley L.J. in *Guaranty Trust Co. of New York* v. *Hannay & Co.* [1915] 2 K.B. 536 at 548). Although the *Boyce* case was not, and cannot be, an authority for any such proposition, it was uncritically cited as such in the House of Lords in *Gouriet* v. *Union of Post Office Workers* [1978] A.C. 435. It seems that the Law Commission took a more realistic and sceptical view of the alleged authority (see Law Comm. 73, para. 22, note 41).

[15] In relation to the availability of these remedies against private individuals and non-public bodies, see *Gouriet* above.

[16] *e.g.* See *Lee* v. *Enfield L.B.C.* (1967) 66 L.G.R. 195; *Bradbury* v. *Enfield B.C.* [1967] 1 W.L.R. 1311; *Legg* v. *I.L.E.A* [1972] 1 W.L.R. 1245, in which the plaintiffs' ability to sue was readily assumed but by no means justified by the authorities cited.

[17] See Chap. 8, p. 280.

[18] See Wade A.L., p. 555.

ties was the historical distinction between the "public" actions brought in the name of the Crown or the Attorney-General, and the "private" actions by ordinary litigants.

In principle, there was no real need for the remedies of injunction and declaration to be added to those of mandamus, prohibition and certiorari as weapons in the armoury of judicial review. The only difference in substance was that a declaration could be made in a case involving the Crown[19] which, naturally, could not be compelled by its own prerogative orders and also could not be made subject to an injunction. Apart from this, there was nothing that could be commanded by an injunction, or confirmed by a declaration, that could not be commanded or confirmed by mandamus, prohibition and certiorari once the full scope of those remedies was restored to deal with purely administrative actions.[20] There were however, very considerable procedural advantages in seeking an injunction or declaration in an action commenced by writ. The exact form of the injunction or declaration might well be decided by the court at the very end of the proceedings but if the wrong prerogative remedy had been requested at the outset, the court had no alternative but to dismiss the application. In proceedings for an injunction, various forms of interim relief could be given, and in the case of both injunctions and declarations the civil law processes of discovery were available.[21] No leave[22] was needed before ordinary proceedings could be commenced and the only time limits were those of the rules of laches[23] and the ordinary limitation periods, where applicable. Conversely, much shorter time limits[24] had come to apply to the initiation of proceedings for a prerogative remedy.

[19] See *Pawlett* v. *Att.-Gen.* above, *Dyson* v. *Att.-Gen.* [1911] 1 K.B. 410 and Crown Proceedings Act 1947, s.21.

[20] See Wade A.L., p. 557.

[21] See *Barnard* v. *National Dock Labour Board* [1953] 2 Q.B 18 and *Anisminic* v. *Foreign Compensation Commission* [1969] 2 A.C. 147 as examples of cases in which material crucial to the success of the plaintiffs' actions became available only on discovery. The absence of this material, and the means of discovering it, would almost certainly have prevented the plaintiffs from succeeding had they sought orders of certiorari.

[22] By the Administration of Justice (Miscellaneous Provisions) Act 1933, s.5, a system was introduced requiring *ex p.* motions for leave to apply for certiorari, mandamus and prohibition.

[23] See Chap. 8, p. 307.

[24] Rules of court provided for a six month time limit in the case of certiorari although the court had discretion to extend the period. See Chap. 8, p. 307.

(3) Redrawing the boundaries

Eventually, the overlap between the prerogative remedies and the ordinary civil law remedies of injunction and declaration began to cause concern and the matter was referred to the Law Commission. Its report in 1976[25] was its third attempt to find an answer and, with hindsight, it must be doubted whether it was a case of third time lucky. Initially, the Law Commission had recommended[26] a Royal Commission to review the whole field of administrative law but this suggestion was rejected by the Lord Chancellor[27] who required the Law Commission to restrict itself to considering the problems of the existing remedies.[28] In a Working Paper[29] two years later, the Law Commission introduced for the first time a distinction between "public" and "private" law reflecting, in essence, the special nature of actions for the prerogative remedies, which were matters of public law, as against ordinary civil actions which were private law matters between the litigants. It was proposed that the two types of procedure and their associated remedies should be mutually exclusive and that the difference between them should be statutorily defined; but this proposal had been abandoned when the Law Commission produced its final report after a further five years.

Having considered and rejected the idea of one form of procedure for both types of remedy,[30] the Law Commission recommended that the remedies of injunction and declaration should be available as alternatives to the prerogative remedies in an improved form of procedure to be known as application for judicial review. While this solution had its attractions, there were some very obvious questions which the Law Commission did not answer. Nonetheless, the recommendations were acted upon with alacrity, if not indecent haste,[31] and in substance at least were later confirmed by statute.[32]

We shall look at the precise nature of the 1977 reforms in due

[25] See note 2 above.
[26] Law Comm. 20, Cmnd. 4059 (1969) (preceded by Working Paper No. 13).
[27] Lord Gardiner, see *Hansard* (1969), Vol. 306, cols. 189–90.
[28] The limited terms of reference were subsequently confirmed by Lord Chancellor Hailsham.
[29] Working Paper No. 40 (1971) Remedies in Administrative Law.
[30] Law Comm. 73, paras. 35, 36.
[31] A Draft Bill was appended to the report but, rather than waiting upon the pleasure of Parliament, the Rules Committee of the Supreme Court incorporated most of the recommendations in S.I. 1977/1955 and thereby substituted the existing Order 53.
[32] Section 31 of the Supreme Court Act 1981.

course but it is important to note certain factors at once. Perhaps the most important was that the new procedure was to apply only to cases in which, immediately before 1977, the prerogative orders of mandamus, prohibition and certiorari could have been granted.[33] In other words, the reforms were directed expressly and exclusively to the "special" law concerning judicial review of public authorities and did not purport to change what had previously been regarded as the ordinary civil law. Within this circumscribed jurisdiction there was to be a single form of procedure by which any of the remedies might be sought, either individually, together, or as alternatives.[34] In addition the court was to be able to award damages in any case in which damages could have been awarded in an ordinary civil action.[35] Provision was made for the new procedure to have the benefit of machinery for discovery and interim relief[36] and, on the other side of the coin, the existing restrictions applying to prerogative actions were to be retained so that the leave of the court would still be required,[37] and actions would still have to be initiated within a shorter time span than was the case for ordinary civil actions commenced by writ.[38] While the 1977 reforms certainly removed the defects that had caused litigants to prefer ordinary civil actions to applications for prerogative remedies, they had a very serious flaw. Although the Law Commission recognised that, over the years, ordinary civil actions had resulted in the grant of injunctions and declarations to those seeking to keep public authorities within their remit, they seemed to overlook the significance of this fact.

The Law Commission's report is ambiguous,[39] but it is difficult to believe that it could have been intended that applications for judicial review should be merely an alternative means of obtaining

[33] See Supreme Court Act 1981, s.31(2). In *I.R.C.* v. *Nat. Fed. of Self-Employed and Small Businesses Ltd* (hereafter the *Self-Employed* case) [1982] A.C. 617 at 647–648 Lord Scarman observed that the two "private law" remedies could be granted only in circumstances in which one or other of the prerogative remedies could issue. He considered that the amendment to Ord. 53 would be *ultra vires* if it purported to do any more. Although the vires of the rules had been placed beyond doubt by the 1981 Act, Lord Scarman's words were expressly approved by Lord Wilberforce in *Davy* v. *Spelthorne B.C.* [1984] A.C. 262. See however, Chap. 8, p. 270 and p. 296 below.

[34] Ord. 53, r. 2.

[35] Ord. 53, r. 7, provided damages are claimed in the application.

[36] Ord. 53, r. 8.

[37] Ord. 53, r. 3.

[38] Ord. 53, r. 4(1). See Chap. 8, p. 306 and p. 307 on the extent to which the Law Commission's recommendations were ignored or misunderstood in relation to both the question of leave and the time limits.

[39] Law Comm. 73, para. 34.

the remedies of injunction and declaration against a public authority in circumstances where it was alleged to have acted *ultra vires* or outside jurisdiction. If this was the intention, why should one procedure be hedged about with the need to obtain prior leave and to observe more restricted time limits while the other was not? If applications for judicial review and ordinary civil actions for injunctions and declarations were to cover precisely the same ground, there would be no point in the new procedure. The same results could be achieved by an ordinary civil action without the need to obtain leave or to act with more expedition. Conversely, if there were some circumstances in which an application for judicial review was to be the only proper means of proceeding, it would be necessary to do what had been proposed in Working Paper No. 40,[40] but rejected in the final report,[41] and draw a line between the availability of the two types of procedure. Whatever might have been the intention of the Law Commission, the failure clearly to state it placed the courts in a difficult, and perhaps even an impossible, position.[42] Eventually, in order to make some sense of the more stringent requirements of the new procedure, the House of Lords concluded in *O'Reilly* v. *Mackman*[43] that such a line did indeed have to be drawn.

The case concerned actions for declarations by certain prisoners who alleged that unfair procedures before the Board of Visitors of Hull Prison had deprived them of remission to which they would otherwise have been entitled. Most of the actions had been commenced by writ although one had been commenced by an originating summons. All were commenced outside the time permitted for applications for judicial review. In a judgment with which the other Law Lords concurred, Lord Diplock said[44]:

> "It is not, and could not be, contended that the decision of the board [of visitors] awarding him forfeiture of remission had infringed or threatened to infringe any right of the appellant derived from private law, whether a common law right or one created by a statute. . . . [N]one of the appellants had any remedy in private law.

[40] Paras. 76–82, 154(2).
[41] See note 39 above.
[42] *e.g.* see differences of view expressed by Megarry V.C. at first instance and Roskill L.J. on appeal in *Uppal* v. *Home Office* [1978] *The Times*, October 21 and November 11. See also *Din* v. *Wandsworth L.B.C.* [1983] 1 A.C. 657 and *Lambert* v. *Ealing L.B.C.* [1982] 1 W.L.R. 550.
[43] [1983] 2 A.C. 237.
[44] *Ibid.* p. 275.

In public law, as distinguished from private law, however, such legitimate expectation [of remission of sentence] gave to each appellant a sufficient interest to challenge the legality of the adverse disciplinary award . . ."

These words suggest a distinction between a "right" deriving from "private law" and a "sufficient interest" entitling an applicant to challenge the lawfulness of a "public law" act or decision. Later, Lord Diplock said[45]:

"So Order 53 since 1977 has provided a procedure by which every type of remedy for infringement of the *rights* of individuals that are entitled to protection in public law can be obtained . . . .If what should emerge is that [the applicant's] complaint is not an infringement of any of his rights that are entitled to protection in public law, but may be an infringement of his rights in private law and thus not a proper subject for judicial review, the court has power . . . to order the proceedings to continue as if they had begun by writ."

Here the terminology has changed and his Lordship is speaking of "rights" deriving from public law. Further, it seems to be implicit in the possibility of it emerging in the course of a hearing that the applicant's private, as opposed to public, law "rights" have been infringed, that it is not the "public" status of the defendant authority alone that governs whether the issue is a matter of public or private law. Indeed, in the very next case considered by the House[46] it was recognised[47] that a breach by a housing authority of its statutory duties under the Housing (Homeless Persons) Act 1977 would be a matter of public law if it occurred at an early[48] stage in the process of considering an applicant's claim for accommodation, but would be a breach of a private law right if it occurred at a later stage in the same process.[49] Here, as in the previous case, the House held that it was against public policy, as being an abuse of the process of the court, for a litigant to initiate proceedings by way of a writ or originating summons when the issue was one of public law which should have been pursued by

[45] *Ibid.* pp. 283–284 (emphasis added).
[46] *Cocks* v. *Thanet D.C.* [1983] 2 A.C. 286.
[47] By Lord Bridge at pp. 292–293.
[48] *i.e.* a breach of the statutory duty to inquire into the case under s.3.
[49] *i.e.* a breach of the duty to house under s.4(5) arising on the conclusion of the inquiry in favour of the claimant's entitlement to accommodation.

means of an application for judicial review. Unfortunately, in neither decision did the House provide clear guidelines as to when an issue was one of public as opposed to private law and it was anticipated that the problem would be resolved on a case to case basis.[50] It was taken for granted in both cases that whenever a plaintiff is entitled to damages, there must have been an infringement of a private law right and this fact provides us with a starting point for making the distinction between public and private law. However, since damages may now be claimed in applications for judicial review, the availability or otherwise of damages does not, of itself, explain why some claims for damages are not a proper subject for judicial review,[51] or what cases may be pursued only by the new procedure.

Part of the explanation we seek lies in the distinction made in Chapter 1 between "liability" on the one hand and "remit" on the other. Let us examine that question again.

B. Liability and Remit: Direct and Collateral Challenge

(1) Liability pure and simple

We have observed that, generally speaking, if a public authority commits a crime or a tort, or breaches a contract, or infringes a property right, it may be prosecuted or sued like any other wrongdoer. The commission of a legal wrong does not necessarily mean that a public authority has stepped outside its remit. It does not necessarily mean that it has acted *ultra vires*. As an artificial legal person, a public authority will have statutory powers and duties, perhaps peculiar to itself. But it also has the legal capacity to commit wrongs which would be actionable wrongs if committed by any other legal entity.[52]

For example, if a public authority fails to maintain its vehicles, or fails to pay suppliers for goods delivered, or fails to put adequate warnings around properly authorised road works, or erects a building on its own land in breach of a restrictive covenant, it will have committed all four wrongs without necessarily having acted *ultra vires*. In the case of the criminal offence the authority may be prosecuted, and in the case of the other wrongs it may be sued by the persons whose rights it has infringed. The fact

[50] *O'Reilly* v. *Mackman* p. 254 above, *per* Lord Diplock at p. 285.
[51] See Ord. 53, r. 9.
[52] See Chap. 2, p. 82.

that the defendant is a public authority is largely irrelevant.[53] These are cases of liability pure and simple and no question of remit arises. As such they can be dealt with by the ordinary processes of the ordinary courts.

At this stage, it will simplify matters if we use the term "liability" in a somewhat restricted sense, unless we are speaking of criminal liability which implies liability to any penal sanction. In all other cases, we will use the term to mean something more specific than simply being visited with the consequences of being an unsuccessful defendant in a civil action. In fact, we will use it to mean liability to make compensation to the plaintiff by the payment of damages. By adopting this limited meaning, we can postpone dealing with injunctions and declarations for the moment. Certain clear distinctions can be perceived if we restrict ourselves to the remedy of damages. Once these distinctions have been established we can reconsider their validity in relation to the other remedies available.

(2) Liability involving collateral challenge to remit[54]

We have also seen that there are cases in which questions of remit may be important. A public authority might be prosecuted for causing pollution and its defence might be that its statutory powers permit it to do that which, if done by others, would be offences. Here, the precise extent of the authority's special powers would be crucial to the question of whether or not it was liable. Similarly, it might be sued in trespass for demolishing a house, and its defence might be that its statutory powers, say in relation to slum clearance, made it lawful for it to do what it had done. Once again, the question of whether it had acted within its powers, or not, would govern whether or not it was liable. These would be cases of liability which involve remit issues collaterally. We say collaterally because the purpose of the litigation is to decide a question of liability. The same would be true of a case where, for example, someone was prosecuted by a public authority for failing to obtain a licence which the authority claimed was necessary, and the defendant alleged that the licensing scheme itself was outside

[53] *cf.* Chap. 2, p. 85 (Immunity from suit).

[54] As already explained, this chapter is concerned with the relationship between the remedies and procedures of supervisory review and the remedies and procedures of the ordinary "civil" and "criminal" law. Thus, references in this chapter to "questions of remit" or "remit issues" are confined to questions as to whether an authority has acted *ultra vires*, outside jurisdiction or patently wrongly and do not extend to questions of whether a particular act or decision is subject to statutory appeal. Aspects of the relationship between the machinery of supervisory review and that of appeals are considered in Chapter 9.

the authority's powers. Once again, this is a case concerned with liability, but here the public authority is the prosecutor. Cases of these types can also be dealt with by the ordinary processes of the ordinary courts. Further examples of collateral challenges to remit were provided in Chapter 2.

(3) Remit pure and simple (direct challenge to remit)

In addition to cases involving questions of liability pure and simple, and cases in which questions of remit arise collaterally to questions of liability, there are also cases solely concerned with remit and not involving questions of liability in the sense in which it has been used so far. Such would be the case if, to use an example already considered, someone wished to challenge the lawfulness of a bus company delivering parcels. The bus company has not committed any offences, it has not committed any torts, it has not breached any contracts and it has not infringed any property rights. It is alleged, quite simply, that its statutory powers enable it to do certain things and it has no power to do anything else. Similarly, it might be alleged that a public authority is failing to perform a duty placed upon it by statute, although in so failing it is not committing any crime or tort, it is not breaking any contracts, nor is it infringing any property rights. An example might be if a local authority ceased to enforce consumer protection legislation. We may say that in these circumstances it is a question of remit pure and simple in which no question of liability arises.

Deciding questions of liability is the primary function of the ordinary processes of the ordinary civil and criminal courts. It is therefore a statement of the obvious to say that questions of liability pure and simple can be dealt with by these ordinary processes. It is less obvious, but equally true, that the ordinary processes of the ordinary courts can deal with the questions of liability even when a question of remit arises collaterally and has to be decided first. On the other hand, the ordinary processes of the ordinary courts are primarily designed to answer questions of liability, and since there are other processes within the legal system designed to deal with issues in which liability as defined does not arise, we might be prepared to accept that the ordinary processes are not the most appropriate means of proceeding unless this form of liability is in issue. Since the primary function of the prerogative remedies was to deal with remit issues—questions of whether or not a public authority had stepped outside its jurisdiction, or had patently gone wrong—we might be prepared to accept at this stage that applications for judicial review are the most appropriate, if not the only, means of proceeding in such cases. We can express this as follows:

liability pure and simple liability involving remit issues collaterally	ordinary civil or criminal actions
remit pure and simple	applications for judicial review

This representation, however, obscures the degree of choice of procedure facing a potential plaintiff when the case raises both liability and remit issues. We must examine this question more closely.

(4) Choice of procedure

(a) *Liability pure and simple*

In these cases, where the plaintiff is seeking damages or the imposition of a penal sanction, whether or not there is any choice will depend upon whether or not the alleged wrong is both a crime and a civil wrong. If the wrong is (say) simply a breach of contract, the plaintiff's only option is a civil action for damages. Similarly, if the wrong is simply a criminal offence, the only option is to procure or initiate a prosecution with a view to the defendant being made subject to a penal sanction. On the other hand, if the wrong is both a crime and a civil wrong (*e.g.* "stealing"), the wrongdoer may be sued for damages, or prosecuted, or both.

(b) *Remit pure and simple*

We have defined these cases as those in which proof of the unlawfulness of a public authority's action would not expose that authority to liability to a penal sanction, or liability to pay damages by way of compensation. Plainly it would be fruitless in such a case to initiate a prosecution, or to initiate a civil action with a view to the recovery of damages. As between these types of action, and an application for judicial review, the latter is the only practical possibility.

(c) *Liability and remit mixed*

Here the choices are extremely wide. The only case in which there is but one way of proceeding is where the purpose of the action is to secure the imposition of a penal sanction which, of course, requires a prosecution. However, even in such a case, where criminal liability is dependent upon proof that the defendant has acted *ultra vires*,[55] it does not follow that the imposition of a penal sanction is the most effective means of enforcing the obligation. Rather than seeking to have the defendant punished, it might be preferable to ignore the liability issue and to treat the case as one of remit, using an application for judicial review to obtain a remedy which will force the defendant to obey the law.[56]

If the wrong generates liability to pay damages, as well as or instead of generating liability to a penal sanction, the action for damages may be brought by means of ordinary civil proceedings. In such a case, the remit issue involved would be a collateral question. Alternatively, the plaintiff may mount a direct challenge to the remit issue by means of an application for judicial review. Damages could be claimed in the same action but would, in a sense, be a collateral matter. In an ordinary civil action, the plaintiff could obtain an injunction or declaration in addition to damages, and in an application for judicial review the applicant could obtain damages in addition to any of the remedies of certiorari, prohibition, mandamus, injunction or declaration. The major constraint on the litigant's choice is whether he is in time to use an application for judicial review.[57]

When a collateral challenge to remit provides the basis of a defence, as in our licence case, the person affected may choose to make a direct challenge to the remit issue by means of an application for judicial review, or may prefer to wait and see whether or not he is prosecuted.[58] If a person believes that he will be made liable in damages unless he can show that an act of a public authority is *ultra vires*, he would seem to have a choice between raising the *vires* issues as a defence, or challenging it by judicial review, or seeking a declaration in ordinary civil proceedings.[59]

[55] *e.g.* where a public authority asserts a power to do that which would be an offence if done by anyone else.

[56] Where the penal sanction is an insignificant fine, a mandatory order to desist from the unlawful conduct would be more effective.

[57] See Chap. 8, p. 307.

[58] See *Att.-Gen.* v. *Dyson* [1911] 1 K.B. 410.

[59] See *Wandsworth L.B.C.* v. *Winder* [1985] A.C. 461 (discussed in Chap. 2, p. 31 and p. 66). Since it was not a missuse of process for the remit issue to be raised by way of a defence in civil proceedings for possession, it would seem to follow that the tenant might have sought a declaration in the county court to ascertain his legal position rather than being put to the expense of making an application for judicial review in the High Court. It might be otherwise if the time for making such an application had passed, or if it was considered that he was merely seeking to attack rather than defend (see comments of Farwell L.J. in *Dyson* above, p. 424). Such an objection would be unlikely on the facts of this case.

We may express these choices as follows:

liability pure and simple	} ordinary civil action for damages and/or criminal prosecution
remit pure and simple	} application for judicial review
liability and remit mixed	} any of the above, choice depends upon the consequences sought. plus defence.

(5) Limits of competence

Perhaps more important than the choices of procedure that an intending litigant has are the limitations of each means of proceeding. We have seen that a criminal prosecution *alone* can secure the imposition of a penal sanction. Since an application for judicial review can be made only in those cases in which, prior to 1977, the remedies of certiorari, prohibition and mandamus could have been awarded,[60] it follows that an ordinary civil action *alone* can deal with claims for damages in which no question of remit arises. Finally, and subject to the possibility of obtaining an injunction or declaration in ordinary civil proceedings,[61] we can say that an application for judicial review alone can deal with remit issues in which no question of liability to damages or a penal sanction arises.

At this point, our analysis of the distinction between remit and liability appears to enable us to "pencil in" the line which the House of Lords requires us to draw.[62] If we remind ourselves that we are concerned with an intending litigant's ability to challenge the lawfulness of acts or decisions by public authorities independently of the Attorney-General, we can say that:

(i) If unlawfulness by a public authority exposes that authority to liability to a penal sanction without carrying it outside remit, a *criminal prosecution* is the only means of proceeding.[63]

(ii) If unlawfulness by a public authority exposes that authority

[60] See note 33 above.
[61] See below, p. 263.
[62] In *O'Reilly* v. *Mackman*, p. 254 above.
[63] *i.e.* criminal liability pure and simple.

to liability in damages without carrying it outside remit, an ordinary *civil action* (commenced by writ or originating summons) is the only means of proceeding.[64]

(iii) If unlawfulness by a public authority is solely a matter of remit and does *not* expose that authority to liability in damages or to a penal sanction, an *application for judicial review* is the only means of proceeding.[65]

(iv) If unlawfulness by a public authority exposes that authority to a penal sanction *or* to liability in damages *and* also carries it outside remit, an intending litigant may choose between an *ordinary civil action* or *prosecution* and an *application for judicial review*.[66]

(v) An assertion that a public authority has gone outside its remit may be the basis of a defence. Here the person concerned may raise the defence in *ordinary proceedings* brought against him, or may prefer to mount a direct challenge to the authority's action or decision by making an application for judicial review.[67]

Of course, this analysis ignores the fact that, for many years, plaintiffs in ordinary civil actions, commenced by writ or originating summons, have been granted injunctions and declarations for the sole purpose of preventing public authorities from stepping outside their remit.[68] The Law Commission seemed to anticipate that this alternative might still be available[69] but the House of Lords has indicated[70] that actions which were once regarded as prefectly proper might now be regarded as an abuse of process.[71] It is not possible within the confines of this chapter to provide a detailed analysis of the relationship between the availability of injunctions and declaration and the availability of damages. However, it may be accepted for the purposes of argument that in some instances

[64] *i.e.* civil liability pure and simple.
[65] *i.e.* remit pure and simple.
[66] *i.e.* liability and remit mixed.
[67] It would be a collateral challenge in the former, and a direct challenge in the latter.
[68] See Wade A.L., p. 515.
[69] See Law Comm. 73, para. 34.
[70] *O'Reilly* v. *Mackman* p. 254 above.
[71] Given the prevailing uncertainty as to which form of proceedings is appropriate in any given case, the courts have wisely categorised the choice of the wrong procedure as a "misuse," rather than an "abuse" of process. See, *e.g. per* Donaldson M.R. in *R.* v. *East Berks Health Authority ex p. Walsh* [1985] Q.B. 152 at 162.

injunctions and declarations are available in lieu of or in addition to damages, while in other cases they have been made available to plaintiffs in ordinary civil actions in cases in which the plaintiff would not, in any circumstances, have been entitled to damages.[72] It will be helpful to say that in the former cases, the remedies are available because of an infringement or, at least a prospective threat to, a private law right.[73] In the latter cases they must be available on some other basis. This distinction will help us to see when a plaintiff seeking an injunction or declaration should make an application for judicial review, and when an ordinary civil action will be available as an alternative.

C. Injunctions and Declarations: Public or Private Law?

(1) Private law rights and public law duties

As we have seen, the House of Lords accepts that an award of damages is the hallmark of a private law right. Indeed, this would seem to be an inevitable conclusion since the common law itself can be regarded as a catalogue of private law rights established over the years by the award of damages to plaintiffs.[74] Equity too built up its own catalogue of rights[75] in a similar way and, although these rights were originally established by the award of injunctions, damages have been available as an alternative since Lord Cairns' Act[76] so that, for our purposes, we may regard the possibility of damages as being the hallmark of a private law right, be it legal or equitable. In both common law and equity, the award of a remedy established, or confirmed, the existence of a right. It also confirmed the existence, and breach, of a correlative private law duty lying on the defendant.

In criminal cases at common law, when a defendant was found liable to a penal sanction in circumstances in which no defendant

[72] *e.g.* see cases cited in note 16 above.

[73] It would seem to be axiomatic, and was so regarded by the House of Lords, that any right the infringement of which sounds in damages is a "private law right." See *O'Reilly* v. *Mackman, Cocks* v. *Thanet D.C.* above.

[74] This "catalogue" is too extensive to be itemised here but is discernible in works on tort, contract, real property etc., etc.

[75] Paramount amongst these are beneficiaries' rights against trustees. Rights under a restrictive covenant are another example of purely equitable rights.

[76] Chancery Amendment Act 1858.

had been found liable before, the finding established the existence, and breach, of a legal duty. Such a finding at the culmination of a criminal prosecution would not establish the existence of a private law right since that was not the purpose of the proceedings.[77] We may therefore categorise such a legal duty as a public law duty, being owed to society at large rather than to any particular individual.[78]

When the law was being developed through the cases, new legal duties were established but, inevitably, the nature of any duty was immediately apparent because it followed from the nature of the proceedings. The recognition of the duty was a *consequence* of the litigation. If the litigation was civil litigation for the vindication of a private right of the plaintiff's, the duty must have been a private law duty. Conversely, if the litigation was criminal, the duty must have been a criminal law, or public law, duty.

(2) Statutory duties

Of course, the common law and equity are not the only sources of legal rights and duties. These may also be created by statute. In practice statutes rarely declare rights as such and it is more usual for them to be cast in terms of powers or duties. Unlike common law duties, which are inevitably categorised as public law or private law duties by the nature of the litigation which establishes their existence, statutory duties are created by Parliament *de novo* and their nature as public or private law duties must be discerned by interpretation. Often, a statute will be so clearly addressed to a familiar problem in public or private law that there will be no difficulty in recognising the branch of law to which the statute

[77] At least not in the development law: *cf.* Baker, *loc. cit.* above Chap. 24.

[78] A criminal prosecution is a true example of an *actio popularis* which may be brought by anyone. A "private" prosecution is only private to the extent that it is not brought by an agency of the state and is therefore not "official". It is nonetheless a public law action. There is no need for the prosecutor to show that he, or anyone else, has been injured by the commission of the offence (save where that is an ingredient of a particular offence), and it is immaterial that he may be motivated by nothing more than personal antipathy towards the defendant. The Attorney-General may, in the public interest, take over and discontinue any prosecution by entering a *nolle prosequi* and it would seem that the Director of Public Prosecutions may achieve a similar result by taking over a prosecution and offering no evidence (see Prosecution of Offences Act 1985, s.3). A prosecutor makes no representations concerning the disposal of a case and the court has a wide discretion in the matter of sentencing. It may grant an absolute discharge if guilt is established but no punishment is considered necessary.

belongs.[79] Sometimes, however, the practice of expressing the law in terms of duties can give rise to very substantial problems. If the statutory duty is backed by a penal sanction, it will be plain that the statute has created a public law duty.[80] But it may be difficult to discern whether or not it has also created a private law right.[81] Indeed, it must be admitted that this question, whether or not a breach of a statutory duty sounds in damages, has proved to be one of the most intractable of legal problems.[82] Fortunately, our particular concern with public authorities enables us to progress without attempting to resolve this problem.

Let us suppose that a statute creates a duty. A breach of that duty may, or may not, give an individual a right to damages.[83] Whether or not it does may only be resolved by litigation and, if an individual injured by the breach seeks damages, an ordinary civil action would be a proper means of proceeding. If an individual is injured or threatened by the breach of the statutory duty he may wish to obtain a declaration that the proposed conduct is indeed a breach of the duty, or an injunction forbidding the defendant from committing or continuing the breach. In these circumstances, the important point for our purposes is not whether the breach does or does not sound in damages, but upon whom the duty is cast by the statute.

(3) Public defendants

Plainly, the defendant may, or may not, be a public authority.[84] If the defendant is *not* a public authority, the plaintiff has no alternative but to initiate ordinary civil proceedings by means of a writ or originating summons, or to persuade the Attorney-General to authorise a relator action. Whether or not a court will grant the plaintiff the remedies he requires in the absence of his being able

[79] *e.g.* the Unfair Contract Terms Act 1977, the Occupier's Liability Act 1984 or the Offences Against the Person Act 1861.

[80] *e.g.* s.193(4) of the Law of Property Act 1925 which creates an offence despite being essentially "private law" legislation. See *R.* v. *Horseferry Road J.J. ex p. I.B.A.* [1986] *The Times*, January 31 on when no penalty is provided.

[81] See Chap. 7 "Breach of Statutory Duty" in Winfield & Jolowicz, *Tort* (12th ed.).

[82] For a powerful and persuasive analysis of the current difficulties in relation to this question see R. A. Buckley "Liability in Tort for Breach of Statutory Duty" [1984] 100 L.Q.R. 204.

[83] See generally *Cutler* v. *Wandsworth Stadium* [1949] A.C. 398 and Buckley, *loc. cit.* above, note 82.

[84] See Chap. 1 and Chap. 8, pp. 3–9 and p. 271.

to show an infringement of, or prospective threat to, a private law right is a matter which does not concern us directly.[85] If, on the other hand, the defendant *is* a public authority, we know that the person affected may make an application for judicial review, irrespective of whether he is alleging the breach of a private law right, *provided* he can show that the public authority has acted *ultra vires*, outside its jurisdiction, or patently wrongly.[86] Of course, if the applicant does require damages as well, he will have to establish the breach of a private law right,[87] but may do so in his application for judicial review.[88] Given that it is necessary to show that the public authority defendant has acted outside its remit, it is not enough simply to show that a public authority has breached a statutory duty in order to be certain that an application for judicial review will lie. Some statutes, such as health and safety and road traffic legislation, impose duties upon public authorities and private individuals alike. Other statutes cast duties exclusively upon public authorities.[89] Where the statutory duty binds individuals and public authorities alike, a breach of the duty by a public authority will no more carry the authority outside its remit than will the

[85] It is arguable that the willingness of the courts to grant injunctions and declarations to litigants suing in their own right, rather than by relator actions, in cases in which there was no prospective threat to any private law right of the plaintiff, was legitimate only in relation to actions against defendants who were public authorities. If the wrong alleged was a remit issue, the same results could have been achieved by means of the prerogative remedies, but they were a less convenient means of proceeding. Of course, individuals and non-public bodies are not subject to the prerogative orders and are not perceived as having the same limited remit. (A non-public body may limit its sphere of operation by contract with its members and may therefore be subject to declaration or injunction). To grant a declaration against a defendant who could ignore it without exposing himself to some other legal action would seem to be a breach of the principle that the court will not act in vain. It appears that the availability of injunctions against public authorities threatening to exceed their remit has led to some confusion concerning the availability of this remedy against those with no limited "remit" as such (see *Gouriet* above). It may well be that the position of relator actions will be restored now that actions against public authorities fall under a separate procedure.

[86] See above, p. 259.

[87] See Chap. 8, p. 303.

[88] See Ord. 53, r. 7(1)(a).

[89] *e.g.* Housing (Homeless Persons) Act 1977.

commission of a crime, a tort or breach of contract.[90] Conversely, when a statutory duty is cast exclusively upon a public authority that duty would seem to be part of the authority's remit since it is one of the factors which distinguishes a public authority, in law, from other legal persons.[91]

(4) A working hypothesis

Whatever misgivings may be entertained about the emerging distinction between public and private law, and the difficulties it may present to litigants by apparently returning to a formalism that had all but disappeared,[92] it can be argued that, if such a distinction is to be made, and to be applied consistently, the following questions will help to reveal the choices available to an intending litigant:

(i) Is the proposed defendant a public authority?
If it is not, an ordinary civil action, a prosecution, or a relator action, are the only proceedings open to the plaintiff.

(ii) If the defendant is a public authority, is it alleged that it has breached a legal duty cast exclusively upon public authorities?
If it is not, it will not be possible to show that the public authority defendant has acted unlawfully in the unique

[90] At one time it seems to have been assumed that public authorities were to be regarded as trustees of their statutory powers and duties (see *Att.-Gen.* v. *Aspinall* (1837) 2 M. & C. 613) but this assumption would seem to have been strictly appropriate only in those instances in which local authorities took over the property, and responsibilities, of charitable trusts. There would seem to be no reason why a public authority should be treated any differently from any other legal entity in relation to a breach of a statutory duty of general application (see Chap. 2, p. 82 above). Note, however, that disregard of a "general" duty may count as an improper consideration, causing a purported exercise of a "special" power to be *ultra vires*. See, *e.g. R.* v. *Secretary of State for Education ex p. Keating* [1985] *The Times*, December 3: decision to close single-sex school quashed because authority failed to take account of Sex Discrimination Act 1975.

[91] The statutory duties of local authorities are considerably broader than the "purposes" for which such authorities were created in the nineteenth century. However, whenever a new statutory duty is cast exclusively upon a public authority, that duty must surely be regarded as reflecting one of the purposes which the authority exists to fulfil. If a statutory duty were cast upon charitable trustees as well as upon public authorities (*e.g.* in relation to education, medical services or the care of the aged) the fact that the duty is not exclusive to public authorities would not prevent it from being part of their remit since charitable trustees, like public authorities, do have a limited remit and are subject to "public law" actions by the Attorney-General.

[92] See H. W. R. Wade "Procedure & Prerogative in Public Law" [1985] 101 L.Q.R. 181.

manner which arises from the fact that public authorities, unlike private individuals, are perceived as having a limited remit. Once again, it would not be appropriate to seek judicial review in these circumstances.[93]

If both questions are answered in the affirmative, the matter *may* be dealt with by an application for judicial review, and this would be the *only* appropriate way of proceeding *unless* the breach of the statutory duty would also expose the public authority to liability to damages or a penal sanction. If the unlawfulness does expose the public authority to such liability, the choices indicated in section B(iv) will apply.[94]

It remains to be seen whether the courts will approach the problem in this way but, at the moment, the indications are that they will.[95] Having considered the relationship between applications for judicial review and other types of action, we can now consider the remedies and procedures of Order 53.

[93] It may sometimes be a question of whether a public authority is acting under its particular statutory remit or, rather, is acting outside the public domain in a purely contractual, managerial or business capacity, in which case its actions will not be subject to judicial review. See *R.* v. *East Berks Health Authority ex p. Walsh* [1985] Q.B. 152; *R.* v. *National Coal Board ex p. National Union of Mineworkers* [1986] *The Times*, March 8; *R.* v. *I.B.A. ex p. Rank Organisation plc* [1986] *The Times*, March 14. See also *R.* v. *Wear Valley D.C. ex p. Binks* [1985] 2 All E.R. 699 and P. Jackson [1986] 102 L.Q.R. 24.

[94] See Chap. 8, p. 305 and Chap. 9 below on factors influencing a litigant's choice.

[95] See especially *Cocks* v. *Thanet D.C.* [1983] 2 A.C. 286; *Davy* v. *Spelthorne B.C.* [1984] A.C. 262; *Wandsworth L.B.C.* v. *Winder* [1985] A.C. 461; *An Bord Bainne Co-operative Ltd. (Irish Dairy Board)* v. *Milk Marketing Board* [1984] 2 C.M.L.R. 584; *Ettridge* v. *Morrell* [1986] *The Times* May 5 (provided application for judicial review also available) *cf. Gillick* v. *West Norfolk Area Health Authority* [1985] 3 All E.R. 402 where Lords Bridge and Templeman indicated that the challenge should have been by way of application for judicial review. Surely, though, the view of Lords Scarman and Fraser is to be preferred. They held that since "Mrs Gillick's action [was] essentially to protect what she allege[d] to be her rights as a parent under private law" she was "fully entitled to proceed by ordinary action, even though she could also have proceeded by way of judicial review" (p. 416): but *cf.* Chap. 8, p. 300 below.

Chapter 8

APPLICATIONS FOR JUDICIAL REVIEW

A. General Considerations

(1) Introduction

The recommendations of the Law Commission in 1976,[1] now translated into Order 53 of the Rules of the Supreme Court[2] and given statutory form in section 31 of the Supreme Court Act 1981, were similar in purpose to the Judicature Acts.[3] Both may be seen as attempts to free the substantive law from the fetters of its procedural origins. In this respect the 1977 reforms are a hundred years late, and so much has happened in those hundred years that these reforms are likely to cause us more difficulties than were experienced by our predecessors after the Judicature Acts. For they were accustomed to catalogues of wrongs, while we expect to be able to identify underlying principles. At this stage we should not be too impatient with an apparent lack of principle. It is a stage through which most other areas of law have passed, and from which they have eventually emerged. It is plain that the courts themselves are searching for principles, and equally plain that neither the Law Commission nor Parliament conceived it to be possible to arrive at guiding principles otherwise than through the cases. The new procedure frees the courts from the need to allow litigants to obtain redress by whatever means could be bent to that purpose—or, perhaps, deprives them of the excuse for so doing. It does not provide many answers itself, but it creates the opportunity for answers to be found. With these reservations in mind, let us consider some of its more important features.

Section 31(1) of the Supreme Court Act 1981 provides, in effect, that all applications for orders of mandamus, prohibition and certiorari, for declarations and injunctions under subsection (2), and

[1] Report on Remedies in Administrative Law (Law Comm. 73) Cmnd. 6407 (1976), hereafter Law Comm. 73.
[2] As amended by R.S.C., (amendment No. 4) Ord. 1980 (S.I. 1980 No. 2000).
[3] Supreme Court of Judicature Acts 1873–1875.

for a special form of statutory injunction[4] *shall* be made by a procedure known as application for judicial review. Subsection (2) then provides:

> "A declaration *may* be made or an injunction granted under this subsection in any case where an application for judicial review, seeking that relief, has been made and the High Court considers that, having regard to
> (a) *the nature of* the *matters* in respect of which relief may be granted by orders of mandamus, prohibition or certiorari;
> (b) *the nature of* the *persons* and *bodies* against whom relief may be granted by such orders; and
> (c) all the circumstances of the case,
> it would be just and convenient for the declaration to be made or the injunction to be granted as the case may be.[5]"

From this it appears that the wrongs remediable by injunctions and declarations via applications for judicial review are the wrongs previously remediable by the prerogative orders. Similarly, the defendants against whom the remedies of injunction and declaration may be given are those against whom prerogative orders might previously have been made. In other words, the ambit or scope of applications for judicial review is governed by the ambit or scope of the three prerogative remedies, and this is how the section has been interpreted.[6]

However, it should be noted that the Law Commission used the words "the nature of" for the express purpose of indicating the "public law" nature of judicial review without having to define the scope of the prerogative remedies which task it considered to be beyond its terms of reference.[7] The inclusion of these words in the statute would seem to allow the courts a greater degree of latitude than is provided by the "just and convenient" formula which was also used in the Judicature Acts.[8] It would therefore seem to be open to the court to permit an application for judicial review in a case in which no prerogative order would have been available pre-

[4] Introduced in 1938 to replace the information in the nature of quo waranto. See below p. 286.
[5] Emphasis added. See similar wording in Ord. 53, r. 1.
[6] *I.R.C.* v. *Nat. Fed. of Self-Employed & Small Businesses Ltd* (hereafter *The Self-Employed Case*) [1982] A.C. 617 at 647.
[7] Law Comm. 73 (note 1 above), para. 45 and explanatory note to cl. 2 of the Draft Bill annexed to the report.
[8] See, for example, *Day* v. *Brownrigg* (1878) 10 Ch.D. 294 explaining the limited effect of these words.

viously, provided the issue is a matter of public law. So far, the courts have not asserted a jurisdiction to extend the scope of supervisory review[9] but we shall see later[10] that there are some circumstances in which to do so would seem sensible and reasonable. By basing the scope of applications for judicial review upon the availability of the prerogative remedies prior to 1977, the reforms seem to necessitate an historical examination of the earlier law. Such an examination may be found elsewhere[11] but, in the light of the approach currently being adopted by the House of Lords,[12] it would be both artificial and misleading to assume that a thorough understanding of past decisions is either necessary or sufficient. In fact, the confused state of the authorities in relation to most of the prerogative remedies is such that very few clear guidelines are available in any event. At this stage, and with some trepidation, it is therefore proposed to venture a general description of the nature of the persons and bodies against whom applications may be made, rather than to produce a mere catalogue based upon past decisions, or to try to identify one fundamental principle.

(2) Against whom may applications be made?

In Part I,[13] we described the "public authorities" subject to judicial review as persons or bodies endowed with (generally) statutory powers, and funded by the public purse for the purpose of conferring what are conceived to be benefits upon the community or a section thereof. We saw too that the exercise of the Crown prerogative powers of government may be subject to review.[14] But there are peculiar difficulties in applying for judicial review against the Crown.

[9] In *R.* v. *Bromley L.B.C. ex p. Lambeth L.B.C.* [1984] *The Times*, June 16 it seems to have been argued that a declaration could not be awarded on an application for judicial review unless one of the prerogative orders was also *claimed* in the application and would, apart from convenience, have been an appropriate remedy. In disposing of this bizarre suggestion, Hodgson J. is reported as saying that "it was not now necessary to consider whether one of the prerogative remedies would have been available . . . but whether the application was the sort of thing to which a prerogative order could apply." While this may appear to be an assertion of a wider jurisdiction, the facts, and arguments, as reported do not make this case a convincing authority. But see now *R.* v. *Secretary of State for the Environment ex p. G.L.C.* [1985] *The Times*, December 30, and p. 298 note 78(a), below.

[10] See below, p. 296.

[11] See De Smith J.R.A.A., Part III, Wade A.L., Part VI.

[12] See for example *Self-Employed Case* above; *O'Reilly* v. *Mackman*; [1983] 2 A.C. 237, *Davy* v. *Spelthorne B.C.* [1984] A.C. 262.

[13] See Chap. I, pp. 3–14.

[14] See Chap. 2, p. 74.

We saw in Chapter 7[15] that it is not possible to obtain an injunction or any prerogative remedy against the Crown, although no such restriction applies to declarations. The impossibility of getting the Crown to make a prerogative order against itself has been avoided in the past by applying for an order against the individual responsible for exercising the power concerned.[16] Most Crown powers have been incorporated into statutes or delegated to a particular person by Orders in Council.[17] In these circumstances it may be appropriate to use a prerogative order to ensure that the power is properly exercised by the person to whom it is entrusted. Sometimes, however, a Crown power may have no statutory framework and may not be expressly delegated. In these cases, prerogative orders would not be available. If, as section 31(2) of the Supreme Court Act 1981 suggests, declarations (and injunctions) are to be available by means of an application for judicial review only in those cases in which, prior to 1977, a prerogative remedy would lie, it would appear that a declaration against the Crown in any case in which a prerogative order would not lie would still need to be sought by means of an ordinary civil action, rather than by application for judicial review. In fact, although declarations may be made in matters affecting the Crown, the Crown itself is not the proper defendant. In these cases declarations should be sought against the appropriate Government Department or, if there is none, against the Attorney-General.[18]

It is difficult to predict exactly how the uncertainty as to the availability of declarations against the Crown by application for judicial review will be resolved and we shall return to this question when looking at the declaration itself.[19] However, despite clear dicta to the effect that the availability of applications for judicial review will continue to be governed by the availability of one or other of the prerogative remedies,[20] it seems inherently unlikely that a litigant seeking a declaration against the Crown would in fact be compelled to proceed by means of an ordinary civil action. If the issue is justiciable, and involves a duty owed to the public or

[15] See Chap. 7, p. 251.

[16] See, *e.g. R.* v. *Minister of Health ex p. Davis* [1929] 1 K.B. 619; *R.* v. *Minister of Health ex p. Yaffe* [1930] 2 K.B. 98. But see criticism of the artificiality of this approach in *Town Investments Ltd* v. *Department of the Environment* [1978] A.C. 359.

[17] See Chap. 1, p. 12.

[18] See Crown Proceedings Act 1947, s.17(3).

[19] See below, p. 296.

[20] See note 6 above.

a section thereof, it seems more likely that an application for judicial review would be permitted.

Returning to our description of those against whom an application for judicial review may be made, we must obviously include all statutory authorities[21] inferior courts[22] and tribunals. We must exclude the universities, but not their Visitors,[23] and we must exclude other bodies, such as Trades Unions, which derive their power from contracts with their members. Refinements to this general description may have to be made in relation to particular remedies, but we should not assume that the courts will decline to entertain applications for judicial review in relation to persons or bodies exercising statutory powers or duties of a public nature, even though, in the past, civil actions for injunctions or declarations might have been considered to be the appropriate way of proceeding[24]

Having considered against whom applications for judicial review may be made, we must now consider by whom such applications may be made. Once again, it may be more helpful to offer a general explanation rather than to concentrate upon past decisions or to seek to establish a fundamental principle.

(3) By whom may applications be made?

Application for judicial review represents a curious amalgam of two very different means by which prior to 1977 public authorities were kept within the law. On the one hand were the public law remedies of the prerogative orders, and on the other were the private law remedies of damages, injunction and declaration. Of course, to use the labels "public" and "private" is to make assumptions that may be difficult or impossible to justify. If, for the purposes of argument, an action for damages is taken to typify a private law action, and if the prerogative writs, in their original form of commands by the King, are taken to be matters of public law, a basic working distinction emerges. At the point when it became possible for private individuals to utilise the prerogative

[21] Judicial review is also available against the Board set up by administrative announcement to administer a non-statutory scheme of *ex gratia* payments to those injured by criminal activities. Although claimants have no "right" to payments, the scheme requires the Board to follow a form of judicial procedure and lays down clear criteria for assessing claims. See *R* v. *Criminal Injuries Compensation Board ex p. Lain* [1967] 2 Q.B. 864.

[22] On supervisory review of the decisions of courts, see Chap. 4, p. 152.

[23] See *Patel* v. *University of Bradford Senate* [1978] 1 W.L.R. 1488; also *Herring* v. *Templeman* [1973] 3 All E.R. 569.

[24] See, *e.g. R.* v. *General Medical Council ex p. Gee* [1985] *The Times*, November 5. *Cf. R.* v. *Deputy Governor of Camphill Prison, ex. p. King* [1985] Q.B. 735.

writs for their own purposes, one may detect a shift away from the purely public, towards the private. However, the use of these remedies by public-spirited citizens might be seen[25] as a constructive collaboration between the citizen and the Crown in matters of mutual interest since the Crown clearly has an interest to see that the law is obeyed.

A very similar collaboration existed, and still exists, in relation to the prosecution of offences under the criminal law. It might reasonably be supposed that a private citizen would not seek a prerogative order, and would not initiate a prosecution, unless some purpose of his own were served by so doing. Nonetheless, in the case of the criminal law, a prosecutor does not have to establish any particular "interest" in the case and, indeed, is not debarred from prosecuting even when activated by nothing but antipathy towards the defendant. This we may describe as the closest thing in English law to an *actio popularis*.[26] In the light of the position in relation to prosecutions, it is not immediately apparent why an applicant for a prerogative order should need to establish any particular interest, other than that of a public-spirited citizen who has become aware of an unlawful abuse of official power and wishes to draw it to the attention of the court. However, it has long been accepted that some degree of interest, or *locus standi,*[27] is required and that "the court would not listen, of course, to a mere busybody who was interfering in things which did not concern him."[28]

Actions for damages, injunctions and declarations may on some occasions serve to keep public authorities within their remit but, until relatively recently, this was merely a fortuitous side-effect of actions brought by private individuals to vindicate their private law rights. This remains the case in relation to actions for damages but increasingly the remedies of injunction and declaration have come to be used against public authorities by plaintiffs with no private law rights sounding in damages, but who were not mere busybodies interfering with things that did not concern them. Indeed, in some cases, the degree of "interest" required of a plaintiff seek-

[25] See Wade A.L., p. 583.

[26] In Roman law any citizen could bring an *actio popularis* in respect of any public wrong without having to establish that he was in any way personally or particularly affected by the commission of the wrong.

[27] This term is sometimes taken to mean "standing to sue" but it is better regarded as meaning being entitled to claim the particular remedy sought.

[28] *Per* Lord Denning M.R. in *R.* v. *Paddington Valuation Officer ex p. Peachey Property Corpn. Ltd.* [1966] 1 Q.B. 380 at 401.

ing an injunction was less than that required of an applicant for one of the prerogative remedies.

With the merger of these two types of remedy in one procedure it was plainly necessary for some guidance to be given on the issue of what sort of interest in the matter in question an applicant would need to establish if the procedure was not to be a pure *actio popularis*. Having attempted to state the confused, anomalous and uncertain tests apparently being applied in relation to the different remedies,[29] the Law Commission declined to recommend any uniform test under the new procedure for fear of imposing undesirable rigidity. Instead, it merely indicated that the question of the interest of the applicant should be an element of the court's discretion to grant or withhold a remedy by recommending that[30]:

> "The court [should] not grant any relief sought on an application for judicial review unless it considers that the applicant has a sufficient interest in the matter to which the application relates."

Unfortunately, when this recommendation was translated into the new Order 53[31] it appears that the draftsman misunderstood the nature of the issue, as it was included in Rule 3 which deals not with the grant of remedies but with leave to apply.[32] Inevitably, this created a misleading impression that establishing a sufficient interest, or *locus standi*, was essentially a "threshold" question to be determined before the application itself may commence.[33] In every application for judicial review certain questions are bound to arise. These include:

(i) Is the defendant subject to supervisory review?[34];
(ii) If so, has the defendant acted unlawfully in the sense of going outside its remit?[35]

[29] See Law Comm. 73 above, paras. 13, 22, 27 and 31(b).
[30] *Ibid.* para. 48 and Cl. 1(3) of Draft Bill.
[31] By S.I. 1977 No. 1955.
[32] Order 53, r. 3(5) provided: "The Court shall not grant leave unless it considers that the applicant has a sufficient interest in the matter to which the application relates." Identical words are now contained in Rule 3(7). Similar words were also used in s.31(3) of the Supreme Court Act 1981.
[33] See *R.* v. *I.R.C. ex p. Nat. Fed. of Self-Employed & Small Businesses Ltd.* [1980] 2 All E.R. 378 at 382 *per* Lord Widgery C.J.: "Before we embark on the case itself, we have to decide whether the Federation has power to bring it at all."
[34] See above, p. 271.
[35] See Chap. 2 and Part II.

(iii) If so, should the court exercise its discretion in favour of granting the remedy sought?[36]

This third question may itself have several components:

(a) Is it in the public interest that the public authority concerned should be subjected to the order sought?[37]
(b) If so, it is appropriate to grant the order at the suit of someone in this applicant's position?
(c) If so, has the particular applicant done anything to disqualify himself from obtaining a remedy?[38]

Of these questions, (iii)(b) is the only true and objective *locus standi* question. Although a court might be expected to refuse leave if it is plain at the outset that the case is bound to fail because any of the questions can be answered in the negative without further inquiry, [39] there seems to be no reason to single out question (iii)(b) as being more relevant to the question of whether or not leave should be granted than any of the other questions. In the *Self-Employed Case* the House of Lords recognised this fact and, with a somewhat bold piece of statutory interpretation, made it clear that whether or not leave should be granted will be determined by reference to the strength of the applicant's case in all respects, rather than in relation to his particular interest in the issue in dispute. This will enable the question of standing to be dealt with as part and parcel of the court's general discretion and should prevent the emergence of any rigid test of *locus standi* unconnected with the precise facts of each case.

While the House was unanimous in regarding the sufficiency of the applicant's interest as a matter inextricably bound up with the discretion to grant or refuse the remedy sought once the case had been fully examined, it is much more difficult to discern any clear agreement on a "test" of sufficiency. Lord Diplock's approach was the most radical and, in terms of an intelligible distinction between public and private law, the most coherent. He suggested that the choice of the term "sufficient interest" rather than a reference to the more commonly used statutory expression giving rights of

[36] See below, pp. 280–286.
[37] See below, pp. 282–286.
[38] See below, p. 281.
[39] This view affirmed in *The Self-Employed Case,* see Lord Diplock at pp. 642–643. See also *R.* v. *Monopolies & Mergers Commission ex p. Argyll Group plc* [1986] *The Times*, March 6.

action to any "person aggrieved," indicated a less restrictive approach which gave the court an "unfettered discretion."[40] He concluded[41]

> "It would in my view be a grave lacuna in our system of public law if a pressure group . . . or even a single public-spirited taxpayer, were prevented by outdated technical rules of *locus standi* from bringing the matter to the attention of the court to vindicate the rule of law and get the unlawful conduct stopped."

Lords Fraser and Scarman both adopted a more "rights" orientated approach. Both agreed that it was necessary to examine the statute in question: in Lord Fraser's view to see whether it gave the applicant any express or implied right to complain[42] and in Lord Scarman's to see whether the duty owed to the applicant was recognised by law.[43] Lord Wilberforce considered that to ask whether or not the would-be applicant was within the scope of the statutory duty was a good working rule but was not an exhaustive test,[44] while Lord Roskill plainly regarded the nature of the statutory duty as of paramount importance.[45]

Despite these differences, there was general acceptance of the proposition that if there were a grievous or flagrant violation of the law, *anyone at all* might be treated as having a sufficient interest to bring the matter to the attention of the court. Such a concession must be on the basis of the public interest in what Lord Diplock described as the vindication of the rule of law. If this is possible in any case, however unlikely or extreme, it must follow that, in a case solely concerned with a remit question, the difference between an *actio popularis* that could be brought by any one at all, and applications that could be made only by those with a particular interest in the issue in question, must ultimately be a question of degree.

Whatever conclusions may be drawn from this case, the underlying difficulty is that statutes create duties of widely differing types.

40 [1982] A.C. at 642.
41 *Ibid.* p. 644.
42 *Ibid.* p. 646.
43 *Ibid.* p. 650.
44 *Ibid.* p. 631.
45 *Ibid.* p. 662.

At one extreme, a duty may be so general[46] that the question of whether or not it has been breached is simply not justiciable and the statutory words must be taken as statements of political intent rather than as words creating a legally enforceable duty. At the other extreme, a statute may create a private law right, sounding in damages in the event of a breach of the statutory duty.[47] In cases of the latter type, the relationship between the public authority under the duty, and the person to whom that duty is owed, is effectively a private law relationship, very similar to that between contracting parties. In private law, no one other than the contracting parties may sue on the contract. No one but a contracting party may obtain damages in the event of a breach, or obtain an injunction to restrain a breach, or obtain a declaration concerning the contract, unless they can show that their legal interests are materially affected and that the declaration would serve some purpose.

In the case of what we might regard as a "statutory contract," we would not expect anyone other than the party directly affected to obtain the remedy of mandamus, which would have the effect of an order of specific performance. We might expect that someone in the same position as the person directly affected by the breach of the statutory duty might seek one of the other remedies if it were clear that unless the public authority's wrongdoing were condemned, he would suffer the same wrong. However, save in exceptional circumstances, a court might well prefer to wait and see whether or not the wrong actually materialised, rather than facilitate a pre-emptive strike by the applicant. Conversely, it is conceivable that the breach of the duty owed to a particular individual might constitute such a flagrant disregard for the law that the court would entertain an application from any public-spirited citizen who was moved to bring the matter to its attention even if the individual most immediately affected chose not to do so.

In these circumstances, and the more so in those cases in which the duty owed is more general, it would seem to be futile to postulate a general test of sufficiency of interest in isolation from the exact facts, and the remedy sought, in any given case. Clearly the sufficient interest test, now given statutory form, enables the

[46] *e.g.* see examples cited by Wade A.L., p. 625 such as the opening words of section 1 of the National Health Service Act 1977: "It is the Secretary of State's duty to continue the promotion in England and Wales of a comprehensive health service . . . ."

[47] *e.g.* the "full housing duty" under s.4(5) of the Housing (Homeless Persons) Act 1977 referred to in *Cocks* v. *Thanet D.C.* [1983] 2 A.C. 286.

courts to disregard the outdated and often contradictory technical rules of standing that had grown up around the prerogative orders. Similarly, it frees the courts from the need to regard applications for injunctions and declarations as actions for the resolution of *inter partes* disputes in the strict civil law sense that applies to actions for damages.[48] It gives the court a discretion, but one which must be exercised in accordance with principle as it is established from case to case.[49] In some instances it may permit a virtual *actio popularis* and in others it may mean that a particular remedy is available only to one particular category of applicant. However, it would be prejudicial to the credibility of supervisory review if any substantial relaxation of the rules of standing were not matched by a recognition that those with a sufficient motive to seek a remedy do not necessarily represent the true public interest.[49a]

In some cases an application for judicial review may be made by a public authority.[50] It is inherently unlikely that public authorities will commonly seek judicial review in circumstances in which they do not have a sufficient interest, but it is not unknown[51] and it would seem that they enjoy no special privileges in this respect. Local authorities now have a limited power to obtain injunctions in some circumstances in which previously an Attorney-General's

[48] See comments of Ackner L.J. in *R.* v. *Stratford-on-Avon D.C. ex p. Jackson* [1985] 1 W.L.R. 1319 at 1323. Rules applicable in ordinary civil litigation do not apply to "judicial review, which involves public law proceedings [where] there is no true *lis inter partes* or suit by one person against another." See also *R.* v. *Hallstrom ex p. W* [1985] 3 All E.R. 775 (C.A.). Application for judicial review not "civil proceedings" within s.139, Mental Health Act 1983.

[49] See note 6 above *Self-Employed Case, Per* Lord Wilberforce at p. 631.

[49a] In *R.* v. *Oxford ex p. Levey The Times*, December 18, 1985 the applicant failed to establish any breach of duty in relation to the policing of Toxteth. In these circumstances it was perhaps unfortunate that the court should have concluded that he did not in any event have a "sufficient interest" when he had apparently suffered "special damage." Indeed, if the case is properly reported it suggests a stricter test than that in *Gouriet* (see Chap. 7, p. 250, note 14).

[50] *e.g. R.* v. *London Transport Executive ex p. Greater London Council* [1983] Q.B. 484; *R.* v. *Nat. Ins. Commissioners ex p. Secretary of State for Social Services* [1974] 1 W.L.R. 1290.

[51] See for example *R.* v. *Secretary of State for Social Services ex p. Child Poverty Action Group* [1985] *The Times*, August 8 in which the C.P.A.G., but not the co-applicant, the G.L.C., were held to have a sufficient interest to seek a declaration that the D.H.S.S. was obliged to search its "dead" files for claimants who had been underpaid. In the event the application was unsuccessful. For comment on this case see Wikeley, [1985] New L.J. 1123.

relator action was necessary.[52] Even when the defendant in such an action is itself a public authority, it does not follow that the application for an injunction should necessarily be made by application for judicial review.[53] If the wrong alleged is a breach of the criminal law, or of planning law, there is no reason why the public authority defendant should be treated any differently from any other defendant. Conversely, if the alleged wrong is the breach of a duty cast exclusively upon the defendant authority, an application for judicial review would seem to be the appropriate way of proceeding. It remains to be seen whether or not, in applications for judicial review, the court will equate the sufficiency of the applicant authority's interest with the statutory requirements relating to the availability of an injunction by the other form of proceedings.[54]

(4) The court's discretion

With the exception of damages, the remedies available by means of applications for judicial review are all discretionary. This does not mean that they may be granted or refused at the whim of the court. It means in fact that, in addition to the question of whether or not the applicant has succeeded in establishing that the defendant has acted unlawfully, the court must have regard to other factors. But it must reach its conclusions in relation to those other factors according to established and settled principles. Before examining these factors, we should note one difficulty.

Prior to the 1977 reforms, an applicant might seek more than one prerogative remedy (such as certiorari and prohibition or certiorari and mandamus) but if he sought an inappropriate remedy his application would be refused even if it was plain that a different remedy would lie. Further, it was not possible for an applicant to

[52] See Local Government Act 1972, s.222. A local authority may seek an injunction in its own name when it is expedient for the promotion or protection of the interests of the inhabitants of its area. See, *e.g. Stoke on Trent City Council* v. *B. & Q. (Retail) Ltd.* [1984] A.C. 754 (injunction against unlawful Sunday trading). But see *Bradford Metropolitan City Council* v. *Brown* [1986] *The Times*, March 18.

[53] See *Bedfordshire C.C.* v. *C.E.G.B.* [1985] J.P.L. 43.

[54] In the light of the *C.P.A.G. case* (note 51 above) it would appear that the test of a sufficient interest for the purposes of an application for judicial review was regarded as at least requiring that the application should be "for the protection of the interest of the inhabitants of their area." This seems to suggest that a local authority may only properly act, even in relation to applications for judicial review, when the action is "in the interests of the inhabitants of the local authority's area." Further elucidation of this question is plainly necessary if the courts are to avoid the danger of making policy decisions on behalf of local authorities.

seek damages, or one of the equitable remedies of injunction or declaration, at the same time as a prerogative remedy. Now, of course, an applicant may seek any of the remedies in the armoury of judicial review, either together or as alternatives.[55] To varying degrees, each of the five principal discretionary remedies had developed factors relating to its availability that were peculiar to itself. It remains to be seen how far these factors will be preserved to limit the availability of particular remedies when an applicant has established that the defendant has acted unlawfully and has requested several alternative remedies, some of which are plainly appropriate. Indeed, it is arguable that the preservation of five separate remedies, several of which may duplicate each other in some circumstances, is an unnecessary complication and that the law would be improved if they were assimilated into one flexible order. Be this as it may, it would certainly be regrettable if archaic technicalities were perpetuated simply to preserve the distinctions between the various remedies. The particular factors affecting the availability of the different remedies will be considered when we examine each remedy in turn. First, however, we should see what factors will influence the court's exercise of its discretion irrespective of the particular remedy requested.

(a) *Conduct of the applicant*

The maxim that "he who seeks equity must come with clean hands"[56] seems to be equally applicable in relation to the prerogative remedies.[57] Thus an applicant may be refused the remedy sought, despite having established that the defendant public authority has gone outside its remit, if the applicant's conduct has been unmeritorious[58] or unreasonable.[59] Further, a party appearing before a tribunal which he knows to be improperly constituted may be refused a remedy on the grounds of having failed to object to the impropriety at the time.[60] In equity, the doctrine of laches enables the court to refuse a discretionary remedy in the event of undue delay[61] and Order 53, rule 4(1) requires application to be made "promptly and in any event within three months . . . unless

[55] Ord. 53, r. 2.
[56] Snell, *Equity* (28th ed.), p. 32.
[57] See *R.* v. *Kensington General Commissioners of Income Tax ex p. Polignac* [1917] 1 K.B. 486.
[58] See *R.* v. *Chief Nat. Ins. Commissioner ex p. Connor* [1981] Q.B. 758; *R.* v. *Home Secretary ex p. Puttick* [1981] 1 Q.B. 767; *R.* v. *Secretary of State for Education & Science ex p. Birmingham D.C.*. [1984] *The Times*, July 18.
[59] *Fullbrook* v. *Berkshire Mags. Ct. Committee* (1971) 69 L.G.R. 75.
[60] *London Corpn.* v. *Cox* (1867) L.R. 2 H.L. 239.
[61] Snell, *op. cit.* note 56, p. 36.

the court considers there is good reason for extending the period within which the application shall be made."[62] In a recent decision, for example, the Court of Appeal accepted that delay occasioned by difficulties in obtaining a legal aid certificate justified granting leave to apply long after the three month period had elapsed but made it plain that a "good reason" in this respect would not prevent the court which was hearing the actual application from refusing the remedy sought on the grounds of undue delay.[63]

(b) *Applicant insufficiently interested*

Although Order 53, rule 3(7) appears to treat the degree of interest of the applicant as a "threshold" matter, it has been held[64] that, provided the applicant has an arguable case, the question whether the remedy sought should be awarded to someone in the applicant's position is a matter to be considered at the hearing itself and in relation to the exercise of the discretion.[65]

(c) *Remedy futile*

Just as "equity will not act in vain"[66] neither will the common law.[67] Thus the court will exercise its discretion against the grant of any remedy if it would be pointless or futile to do otherwise. There would be no point in quashing a decision, or ordering the reconsideration of an issue which was no longer relevant. For example, even if it could be shown that a housing authority had wrongly determined that an applicant under the Housing (Homeless Persons) Act 1977 was intentionally homeless, there would be no point in quashing the decision and requiring the authority to investigate the matter afresh if the person concerned was no longer homeless. Whether or not the award of a remedy would be futile might depend upon the particular remedy sought and the interest of the applicant. In some cases the remedy may have become otiose in respect of the person most closely affected by the unlawful conduct concerned, and yet a declaration might still be sought

[62] See p. 307 below for further comment on time limits.
[63] *R.* v. *Stratford-on-Avon D.C. ex p. Jackson* (note 48 above).
[64] *Self-Employed Case* note 6 & 39 above.
[65] See p. 273 above and further comment below in relation to specific remedies.
[66] Snell, *op. cit.* note 56, p. 576.
[67] *R.* v. *Commonwealth Public Service Commissioner ex p. Killeen* (1914) 18 C.L.R. 586 (Aust.).

by someone less immediately affected so as to prevent a wrongful practice from becoming established.[68]

(d) *Remedy unnecessary*

One of the least questioned but, perhaps, most questionable maxims of equity is that its remedies are not available unless damages would not provide an adequate remedy.[69] Given the original role of equity in mitigating the shortcomings of the common law, the approach is understandable, but not necessarily still defensible. A similarly restrictive approach can be seen in relation to mandamus. The remedy was once described as one which "ought to be used upon all occasions where the law has established no specific remedy and where in justice and good government there ought to be one."[70] Subsequent courts have fastened upon part of a statement that was probably intended to liberalise the availability of the remedy, and have treated it as a restriction so that mandamus would be denied if any other remedy were available.[71] Fortunately, this willingness to send applications away empty-handed on the grounds that, although deserving redress, there was some other means of achieving it, had already begun to disappear before the introduction of applications for judicial review,[72] although some writers seem unwilling to acknowledge this fact.[73] Since there is nothing that can be commanded by mandamus that could not be commanded by injunction,[74] the perpetuation of the "no other remedy" rule after 1977 would simply achieve the abolition of mandamus, something patently not intended by the Law Commission or, we may assume, by Parliament. In any event, it is hardly credible that this archaic and obstructive approach will continue to apply to applications for judicial review, either in relation to mandamus, or in relation to the adequacy of damages as against the equitable and other rem-

[68] See *R.* v. *Secretary of State for Social Services ex p. Association of Metropolitan Authorities* (1985) 17 H.L.R. 487, in which the court refused to quash delegated legislation made without proper consultation on the grounds, *inter alia*, that the resultant confusion would not be justified in terms of any benefits conferred. However, a declaration relating to the need for consultation was granted.

[69] Snell, *op. cit.* note 56, pp. 569, 625.

[70] *Per* Lord Mansfield in *R.* v. *Barker* (1762) 3 Burr. 1265 at 1267.

[71] *R.* v. *I.R.C. re Nathan* (1884) 12 Q.B.D. 461.

[72] See Wade, A.L., p. 644.

[73] See De Smith J.R.A.A., p. 561.

[74] In practice mandatory injunctions seem to have played no part in public law issues but Order 53 is not expressly restricted to prohibitory injunctions. In *R.* v. *Kent C.C. ex p. Bruce The Times*, February 8, 1986 for no apparent reason, mandatory injunctions were sought instead of mandamus. The applications failed but no comment on the choice of remedy was reported.

edies now available. In a given case, an applicant might be adequately compensated by an award of damages but the "public law" aspects of the case could well justify the grant of a declaration, or perhaps mandamus, in the public interest.

It is to be hoped that in deciding which of the alternative remedies is the most appropriate, the courts will adopt the approach of balancing the benefit conferred upon the applicant against the detriment imposed upon the defendant.[75] If some other remedy is equally effective so far as the applicant is concerned, but less damaging to the defendant,[76] then there is some sense in denying an unnecessarily injurious remedy. However, even in these circumstances, it is to be hoped that the court would encourage the applicant to amend his application in time,[77] rather than send him away empty-handed.

Another aspect of the question of "unnecessary remedies" is the extent to which the courts recognise that when dealing with responsible public authorities it will often be unnecessary in a factual, as opposed to a legal, sense to grant a "coercive" remedy such as an injunction, prohibition or mandamus, when a mere declaration would be scrupulously observed.[78] In one recent private law action, Megarry V.-C. implied that where there was a justifiable expectation that a declaration would be observed this might provide grounds for the refusal of an injunction in support, but there seems to be little direct authority on the question.[79] When one remedy is granted while another is refused, the reasoning seems to be either that one is technically, rather than factually, unnecessary,[80] or that the applicant is entitled to a declaration that

[75] This approach is adopted in private law (see, *e.g. Redland Bricks Ltd.* v. *Morris* [1970] A.C. 652) and may therefore be appropriate when the applicant is seeking the private law remedies of injunction, declaration or damages. However, it is difficult to envisage circumstances in which a choice between the available prerogative remedies will be influenced by such considerations except where it is desirable to spare an authority the embarrassment of an unnecessarily peremptory order.

[76] The introduction of a new remedy in damages for unlawful administrative action might actually be advantageous to public authorities if an increased use of applications for judicial review has the effect of compelling them to undo the wrongs they have done rather than to make compensation. It would certainly facilitate the court's task of giving effective relief to the applicant with the minimum of detriment to the defendant.

[77] Under Ord. 53, r. 6(2).

[78] *e.g. R.* v. *Boundary Commission for England ex p. Foot* [1983] Q.B. 600.

[79] *Clarke* v. *Chadburn* [1985] 1 W.L.R. 78.

[80] See *Re Harrington* [1984] A.C. 743; but see also *R.* v. *Devon and Cornwall Chief Constable ex p. C.E.G.B.* [1982] Q.B. 458.

the authority's acts were unlawful although circumstances prevent the grant of a mandatory remedy.[81] In some circumstances the choice is not between the various remedies but between an application for judical review and some statutory redress in the form of an appeal. We shall consider this question in Chapter 9.

(e) *Discretion—general comments*

We shall consider particular factors relevant to the exercise of the discretion in relation to the particular remedies when we look at the remedies themselves but it would not be inappropriate here to expand briefly on an issue raised earlier.[82] If, as appears to be the case, applications for judicial review are to be identified more plainly as "public law" matters, rather than as disputes *inter partes*,[83] it would seem to be wholly desirable that the courts should adopt a different approach to the exercise of their discretion from that once prevalent in actions for injunctions in ordinary civil proceedings. It should be recognised that it is not necessarily in the public interest that public authorities should be compelled in every case to keep within the precise letter of the law merely because one litigant is able to establish a technical infringement of some statutory requirement. It is to be hoped that the courts no longer believe that "Even if chaos should result, still the law must be obeyed"[84] is an appropriate maxim in cases in which no private law rights are infringed. There are indications that the courts are prepared to adopt a more realistic attitude and to refuse a remedy where, for example, only one of two alterative grounds for a decision is open to criticism,[85] or where a failure to take relevant factors into consideration could not have affected an inevitable decision.[86] Both of these cases concerned inferior courts but in a case involving a health authority[87] Forbes J. concluded that even if the authority had not had power to exclude the public from its meetings, he would not have granted certiorari to a person excluded if the result would have been to nullify all the many

[81] See note 68 above.
[82] See p. 273 above.
[83] See *R.* v. *Secretary of State for the Environment ex p. Hackney L.B.C.* [1983] 1 W.L.R. 524 at 537–539 and note 48 above.
[84] *Per* Lord Denning in *Bradbury* v. *Enfield L.B.C.* [1967] 1 W.L.R. 1311 at 1324.
[85] See *R.* v. *Knightsbridge Crown Court ex p. Marcrest* [1983] 1 W.L.R. 300.
[86] *R.* v. *Mansfield JJ ex p. Sharkey* [1985] Q.B. 613.
[87] *R.* v. *Brent Health Authority ex p. Francis* [1985] Q.B. 869.

decisions taken at the impugned meeting which, apart from the absence of a public audience, was otherwise perfectly lawful.[88]

Some years ago, certiorari was refused in a case in which, although it was established that a supplementary benefits appeals tribunal was wrong in point of law, it was held that the tribunal had acted reasonably and, since the dispute was about an allowance of only £50, the High Court should not have been troubled with the matter, being one of "small importance."[89] It is difficult to explain or justify an exercise of the discretion which effectively denies the jurisdiction, and this case must be regarded with serious misgivings.

Where it is impossible for a defendant to comply with the court's judgment immediately, the discretion may be exercised by refusing the remedy sought but giving the applicant leave to re-apply if the matter complained of has not been put right within a specified time.[90]

Let us now consider the remedies themselves.

B. The Remedies of Judicial Review

The remedies with which this section is primarily concerned are those of certiorari, prohibition, mandamus, injunction and declaration. It will be necessary to examine the remedy of damages in relation to applications for judicial review but a full treatment of that remedy must be sought elsewhere.[91] In 1938,[92] informations in the nature of quo warranto were replaced by a distinct form of injunction to restrain a person from holding a public office to which he was not lawfully entitled.[93] This special form of injunction is preserved by section 30 of the Supreme Court Act 1981[94] and must now be sought by means of application for judicial

[88] The statement was *obiter* since it was held that the authority did have power to exclude the public in the circumstances. In *R.* v. *Monopolies & Mergers Commission ex p. Argyll Group plc* (see note 39 above) the Court of Appeal refused an application for judicial review of a decision by the Chairman of the Commission on the grounds that, even if he had no power to make the decision on his own, the Commission itself would have been certain to have made the same decision.

[89] *Per* Lord Denning in *R.* v. *Sheffield Supplementary Benefits Appeal Tribunal ex p. Shine* [1975] 1 W.L.R. 624 at 632.

[90] *R.* v. *G.L.C. ex p. Blackburn* [1976] 1 W.L.R. 550.

[91] F. H. Lawson *Remedies of English Law* (2nd. ed.), Chap. 4.

[92] Administration of Justice (Miscellaneous Provisions) Act 1938, s.9.

[93] See also Local Government Act 1972, s.92.

[94] For an account of this special form of injunction, see De Smith J.R.A.A., p. 463.

review[95] but no such application seems to have been made since 1977, or indeed for many years previously.[96] Reference to injunctions in this chapter will therefore be restricted to those injunctions which, prior to 1977 were available in ordinary civil proceedings.

(1) Certiorari and prohibition

It is convenient to deal with certiorari and prohibition together as their similarities are greater than their differences. The former lies to "quash" a decision so as to make it, or declare[97] it to be, a nullity which may be ignored and treated as having no effect.[98] Prohibition is primarily concerned with preventing the making of *ultra vires* decisions but it may also be used where such a decision has already been made, to restrain its execution.[99] In the past, it was common for both remedies to be sought in relation to one decision but this involves a degree of duplication since a court prohibiting the execution of an existing decision must, *ex hypothesi*, have found the decision itself to have been invalid. Although Order 53 may seem to encourage applications for alternative remedies, the court's freedom to select the more appropriate of the remedies requested may prevent the unnecessary use of both remedies when one will serve.[1] Disobedience to prohibition is punishable as a contempt of court but it is not necessarily a contempt for a tribunal or public authority to treat as still valid a decision quashed by certiorari. In some cases such action would expose the authority to liability,[2] but if it would not, it would be prudent for an application for prohibition or mandamus to be made as well, or instead.[3]

Both remedies lie against inferior courts and tribunals and against public authorities acting in excess of jurisdiction or patently wrongly.[4] Certiorari, by its very nature, requires a

[95] s.31(1)(*c*).

[96] The most notable use of this remedy this century was *R.* v. *Speyer, R* v. *Cassel* [1916] 1 K.B. 595.

[97] At one time it was thought that certiorari would not lie to quash a nullity but "that fallacy has died a natural death"—Wade A.L., pp. 563–564.

[98] But *cf.* Chap. 2, p. 61 on the void/voidable distinction.

[99] See *R.* v. *Electricity Commissioners ex p. London Electricity Joint Comm. Co. (1920) Ltd.* [1924] 1 K.B. 171.

[1] See *Re Harrington* [1984] A.C. 743 at 753–754 where Lord Roskill held that certiorari, unlike mandamus, would have been inappropriate.

[2] *e.g.* where the implementation of the decision would be tortious or would be a breach of a statutory duty sounding in damages.

[3] *e.g.* where the decision impugned was purely negative so that the authority might continue to "do nothing" for, or to, the applicant.

[4] See Chap. 4.

decision or determination[5] which, while not necessarily infringing any legal rights of the applicant, does at least have some legal effect and does "affect subjects."[6] There may be difficulty in some cases in drawing a distinction between a mere recommendation and a preliminary decision. Certiorari will lie in relation to the latter[7] but not the former.[8] The test would seem to be related to the position of the "decision" on a spectrum between "mere evidence" which might be rebutted before a final decision is made,[9] and a step in a statutory procedure which, while not necessarily being final,[10] may at least serve as an impediment to the question being reconsidered.[11] Certiorari will go to quash the decisions of magistrates whether acting as courts of summary jurisdiction[12] or as administrative authorities[13]; of Crown courts[14]; of statutory tribunals and authorities[15]; of ministers of state[16] of local authorities[17] and against at least one non-statutory body.[18] Prohibition will go to as wide a range of authorities as certiorari and, although historically it was first used to supervise the proceedings of inferior courts,[19] it will now go to prevent any statutory authority from acting outside its powers.[20]

[5] See *R.* v. *St. Lawrence's Hospital Statutory Visitors ex p. Pritchard* [1953] 1 W.L.R. 1158 at 1166.

[6] See *R.* v. *Criminal Injuries Compensation Board ex p. Lain* [1967] 2 Q.B. 864 at 888 and 892.

[7] See *R.* v. *Postmaster General ex p. Carmichael* [1928] 1 K.B. 291.

[8] See note 5 above.

[9] See *R.* v. *Macfarlane ex p. O'Flanagan* (1923) 32 C.L.R. 518 (Aust.).

[10] If the decision is final, certiorari and prohibition will clearly lie.

[11] See note 7 above. In *R.* v. *Secretary of State for the Environment ex p. G.L.C.* (see p. 271, note 9 above) Woolf J. held, *obiter*, that a declaration might be granted when it was desirable as a matter of general public importance to challenge the reasoning behind a decision, even though the decision itself may not be open to challenge. The use of the declaration instead of certiorari might avoid the difficulty of establishing whether or not a reviewable 'decision' had been made, a matter apparently not without difficulty, see *R.* v. *Oxford Regional Mental Health Review Tribunal ex p. Secretary of State for the Home Department*, and *R.* v. *Yorkshire M.H.R.T. ex p. the same The Times*, April 28, 1986.

[12] See *R.* v. *Sussex J.J. ex p. McCarthy* [1924] 1 K.B. 256.

[13] *R.* v. *Bradford* [1908] 1 K.B. 365.

[14] *R.* v. *Knightsbridge Crown Ct. ex p. I.S.C. Ltd.* [1981] 3 W.L.R. 640.

[15] *R.* v. *Northumberland Comp. Appeals Tribunal ex p. Shaw* [1952] 1 K.B. 338, *R.* v. *Chief Immigration Officer ex p. Kharrazi* [1980] 1 W.L.R. 1396.

[16] *R.* v. *Secretary of State for the Environment ex p. Brent L.B.C.* [1982] Q.B. 593.

[17] *Shah* v. *Barnet L.B.C.* [1983] 2 A.C. 309.

[18] The Criminal Injuries Compensation Board, see note 21 above.

[19] See Holdsworth, *History of English Law*, Vol. 1 pp. 228, 464.

[20] See *R.* v. *G.L.C. ex p. Blackburn* [1976] 1 W.L.R. 550; *R.* v. *Newcastle J.J. ex p. Hindle* [1984] 1 All E.R. 770, *R.* v. *Liverpool Corporation ex p. Liverpool Taxi etc. Assocn.* [1972] 2 Q.B. 299.

The prerogative remedies generally do not seem to have been regarded as being appropriate for challenging delegated legislation,[21] the enactment of which may be seen as an exercise of power rather than as a series of decisions. Similarly, certiorari may not be appropriate to deal with such "decisions" as the decision to prosecute, or to indict a defendant rather than proceed summarily. Although such decisions plainly affect the person concerned, and may be influenced by improper considerations, it may be that whatever "rights" an individual has in such matters are capable of being protected at any trial which results from such decisions.[22] Although the prerogative remedies do not lie against the Crown itself, the practice of proceeding against the person or body exercising the relevant power on behalf of the Crown has rendered this limitation more theoretical than real.[23] Of course, the remedies will not lie, even against public authorities, when the powers they are exercising are contractual rather than statutory.[24] Neither will the remedies go against any court that is not an inferior court,[25] and there are some limitations in relation to special jurisdictions.[26]

(2) Mandamus

The purpose of mandamus today[27] is to compel the performance of a public duty, whether it be the duty of an inferior court or tri-

[21] See Wade A.L., pp. 560–561. A declaratory judgment was effective for this purpose. See, *e.g. Brownsea Haven Properties* v. *Poole Corporation* [1958] Ch. 574. But *cf. R.* v. *Social Services Secretary ex p. Assocn. of Metropolitan Authorities* (1985) 17 H.L.R. 487 (certiorari refused solely as a matter of discretion). On the difficulty of obtaining a judicial order *restraining the making* of delegated legislation, see de Smith J.R.A.A., pp. 468–469; and *R.* v. *Boundary Commn. for England ex p. Foot* [1983] Q.B. 600. See also *Nottinghamshire C.C.* v. *Secretary of State for the Environment* [1986] 1 All E.R. 199.

[22] See *Estate & Trust Agencies (1927) Ltd.* v. *Singapore Improvement Trust* [1937] A.C. 898. But see *R.* v. *Newcastle J.J. ex p. Hindle* [1984] 1 All E.R. 770 where prohibition was granted to prevent magistrates from proceeding on a summons that was an abuse of process, and see also *R.* v. *Horseferry Road J.J. ex p. I.B.A. The Times*, January 31, 1986 committal summons quashed as showing no offence known to law.

[23] See above p. 271.

[24] See *R.* v. *East Berkshire Health Authority ex p. Walsh* [1985] Q.B. 152; but *cf. R.* v. *Home Secretary ex p. Benwell* [1985] Q.B. 554.

[25] See Chap. 4, p. 152.

[26] See Wade A.L., p. 565.

[27] In the past mandamus was also used to enforce purely private law duties such as the admission of copyhold tenants (see *R.* v. *Garland* (1870) L.R. 5 Q.B. 269). Indeed, a mandatory order of the Court of Chancery was also called "mandamus" and although the prerogative and equitable remedies were distinct, it appears that the former was sometimes used when the latter would have been more appropriate. The purely public law role of mandamus was re-established early this century (see *Davies* v. *Gas Light & Coke Co.* [1909] 1 Ch. 708).

bunal to exercise its jurisdiction, or that of an administrative authority to fulfil the obligations cast upon in by statute.[28] Unlike the negative order of prohibition, mandamus is a positive order although it may be couched in general rather than specific terms. Where the obligation is to reach a decision, the standard form of mandamus is to "hear and determine according to law."[29] In Chapter 2[30] we noted the distinction between appellate and supervisory review and, in particular, that a supervisory court may not substitute its decision for that of the body having jurisdiction to decide the question in issue. While this distinction has little impact upon certiorari and prohibition, it can be of crucial importance in relation to mandamus and it would clearly be wrong for an order of mandamus to be worded so as to amount to a substitution of the reviewing court's decision for that of the defendant authority unless the correction of an error of law means that only one decision is possible.[31]

In principle, there is no public law duty which cannot be enforced by mandamus but, perhaps because its scope is so wide, the courts have shown a certain reluctance to grant the remedy too readily. Some statutory duties are so vague[32] that whether or not they have been breached can hardly be regarded as a justiciable issue. Clearly, it would be inappropriate for mandamus to be granted in relation to duties of this sort which would seem to be more political than legal.

In private law, the equitable remedies of an injunction against the breach of a negative term in a contract and an order of specific performance may be available to a person to whom a contractual obligation is owed. Both remedies are discretionary but the court will exercise its discretion in favour of granting the remedy much more readily in the case of the former than the latter.[33] In relation

[28] Mandamus may also be available to enforce non-statutory duties such as those of a university visitor to adjudicate upon disputes (see *R.* v. *Chancellor of Cambridge University* (1723) 1 Str. 557). It also lies to enforce the non-statutory duties of the Criminal Injuries Compensation Board (see *R.* v. *Criminal Injuries Comp. Bd. ex p. Clowes* [1977] 1 W.L.R. 1353) and "rules or practice" adopted in the exercise of statutory duties (see *R.* v. *Derby JJ. ex p. Kooner* [1971] 1 Q.B. 147).

[29] Perhaps an oddly inappropriate order in relation to the activities of the Criminal Injuries Compensation Board.

[30] See Chap. 2, p. 56.

[31] *Ibid.*

[32] See p. 278 above note 46.

[33] See *Doherty* v. *Allman* (1878) 3 App.Cas. 709 (injunction); for grounds on which specific performance may be refused, see Snell *op. cit.* note 56 especially at pp. 571, 577, 595.

to statutory obligations of public authorities, one remedy, mandamus, compels observance of statutory duties both at very general and at very specific levels. Inevitably, this makes it more difficult to state precisely the grounds upon which the discretion to award the remedy will be exercised than to state the position with regard to either of the two private law remedies. The position is further complicated by the fact that, as a public law remedy, mandamus may be sought by a wider range of applicants than would be the case in relation to the two equitable remedies in private law. Clearly, while the court might, in an appropriate case, grant mandamus so as to order, effectively, the specific performance of a statutory duty, it would do so only on the application of the person most immediately and directly affected by the breach or neglect of the duty in question.[34] Conversely, where the duty sought to be enforced is very general[35] the same remedy might be granted to an applicant with only a general personal interest in seeing that the law is obeyed.

Another rather curious feature of the remedy is that, although it is no longer regarded as being exclusively a remedy of last resort, it still seems to be seen as particularly peremptory and, consequently, will not usually be granted unless it is absolutely necessary. Thus, although an applicant might seem to be entitled to certiorari to quash a wrongful decision, and mandamus to require the question to be reconsidered, the court may well grant certiorari alone on the assumption that the quashing of the original decision will inevitably lead to the question being reconsidered.[36] However, where jurisdiction has been declined in circumstances which make it difficult to point to a "decision" which may be quashed, mandamus may be awarded even though there is no suggestion that the defendant authority is being intransigent or is anything but anxious to act in accordance with the law.[37]

During the long history of the remedy, many "restrictions and contradictions" have emerged.[38] At one time it was regarded as

[34] *e.g.* in relation to the "full housing duty" under s.4(5) of the Housing (Homeless Persons) Act 1977.

[35] As in the example given in Chap. 7 of a local authority refusing or neglecting to enforce consumer protection legislation.

[36] See *R.* v. *West Yorks Coroner ex p. Smith* [1982] 3 W.L.R. 920, but *cf. R.* v. *Croydon Crown Court ex p. Smith* (1983) 77 Cr.App.R. 277. See also *R.* v. *Devon & Cornwall Chief Constable ex p. C.E.G.B.* [1982] Q.B. 458, no need for mandamus.

[37] See *R.* v. *Notts County Ct. ex p. Byers* [1985] 1 W.L.R. 403.

[38] See Wade A.L., p. 640.

essential for an applicant to have made an express demand that the duty in question be fulfilled, and that this demand had been refused.[39] Obviously, it would be inappropriate for a court to grant leave to apply for mandamus following an *ex parte* application[40] unless there were some grounds for believing that the defendant authority was unwilling to perform the duty in question, but it is hardly necessary to require more, or to elevate the requirement into a principle.[41] It is also said that mandamus will not lie for the purpose of undoing what has already been done in contravention of a statute.[42] In *R.* v. *Paddington Valuation Officer ex p. Peachey Property Corporation*,[43] the Court of Appeal found itself in some difficulty as to whether mandamus would lie to compel the authority to prepare a new rating list where administrative convenience made it desirable to refuse certiorari so that the impugned list could be used until a proper replacement had been drawn up.[44] However, now that the remedies of injunction and declaration may be sought in the same proceedings, difficulties of this sought may be avoided but, so far as they still exist, they cast some doubt upon the wisdom of preserving the separate remedies obtainable by application for judicial review.

A similar difficulty arises in relation to mandamus and the Crown. As is the case with the other prerogative remedies and the injunction, mandamus will not lie against the Crown. We have seen[45] that in most cases it is possible to avoid any difficulty since most statutes cast duties upon particular ministers and they can be named as defendants, rather than the Crown itself. However, the breadth of the apparent scope of mandamus may create special problems. The Crown has some "duties" which are not statutory and the breach of which may not be justiciable.[46] In other cases, although a duty may be cast upon a specified servant of the Crown,

[39] See Tapping, *on Mandamus* p. 282.

[40] *i.e.* when only the applicant's side of the dispute is being considered.

[41] See *R.* v. *Hanley Revising Barrister* [1912] 3 K.B. 518. *cf.* De Smith J.R.A.A., p. 540. However, in *R.* v. *Kent C.C. ex p. Bruce* (see note 74 above), in which an applicant sought mandatory injunctions to enforce alleged duties under the Chronically Sick and Disabled Persons Act 1970, it was held that for such a claim to succeed the applicant would have to establish precisely the needs for which provision should have been made, and would need to prove a clear failure to satisfy an express request.

[42] See De Smith J.R.A.A., p. 542 and cases there cited.

[43] [1966] 1 Q.B. 380.

[44] Compare the comments of Lord Denning M.R. at p. 402 and Salmon L.J. at p. 419.

[45] See p. 271 above.

[46] See Chap. 2, p. 74.

the duty may be owed to the Crown, rather than to the public or to an individual affected.[47] Once again, the availability of declaratory relief in applications for judicial review should enable uncertainties in this area to be resolved on the basis of the nature of the duty and the justiciability of the issue, rather than on the less satisfactory basis of the appropriateness of the particular remedy sought.

Finally, it now seems clear that the inextricable confusions of the past in relation to the degree of interest which an applicant needed to establish in order to obtain mandamus may be consigned to history. In one of the major decisions on the effect of the 1977 reforms[48] the House of Lords has made it clear that the question of standing, however it is eventually resolved, will not vary from remedy to remedy on purely technical grounds. Of course, as has been noted,[49] it would be perfectly reasonable for the courts to require a higher degree of interest from an applicant seeking, in effect, the specific performance of a statutory duty owed to him personally. But this arises from what the applicant is seeking to achieve, rather than from the particular means by which those ends are pursued.

(3) Injunctions

Although in their heyday the remedies of injunction and declaration threatened to eclipse the prerogative remedies,[50] it is difficult now[51] to see exactly what role it will play in applications for judicial review. We saw in Chapter 7[52] that its popularity arose from the procedural advantages inherent in a private law action. We also saw that what had previously been regarded as a condition precedent to the availability of the remedy, a threat to or infringement of a private law right,[53] had gradually been replaced by a far more liberal test requiring only a more substantial interest in the issue in question than the generality of citizens.[54] Although *O'Reilly* v. *Mackman*[55] was specifically concerned with the other private law remedy, the declaration, it can hardly be suggested that the approach adopted in that case will not apply with equal

[47] See *R.* v. *Secretary of State for War* [1891] 2 Q.B. 326. However it is doubtful whether a court would adopt this reasoning in relation to the duties of an officer of the Crown today.
[48] The *Self-Employed Case* [1982] A.C. 617.
[49] See notes 34 and 35 above.
[50] See Wade A.L., p. 570.
[51] Since *O'Reilly* v. *Mackman* [1983] 2 A.C. 237.
[52] See p. 249.
[53] *Ibid.* and part C(i).
[54] See, *e.g.* *Mead* v. *Haringey L.B.C.* [1979] 1 W.L.R. 637.
[55] Above note 51.

force to injunctions and that they too will now be available against public authorities in ordinary civil actions only in those cases in which there is a threat to, or infringement of, a private law right or by means of a relator action or an action by a local authority under section 222.[56] Of course, there will be many cases in which unlawful action by a public authority will infringe or threaten private law rights[57] and here the full range of injunctions[58] will be available. These will be cases of liability pure and simple, or of liability and remit mixed.[59] In cases of liability and remit mixed, applications for judicial review are available as an alternative to ordinary civil proceedings but it is difficult to see what role injunctions could play in cases of remit pure and simple where applications for judicial review are the only means of proceeding.[60]

Prior to 1977, mandatory injunctions do not seem to have been sought to enforce public law duties[61] and, so far, there seems to have been only one reported decision concerning an application for judicial review in which mandatory injunctions were sought.[61a] Order 53 makes no distinction between mandatory and prohibitory injunctions and it remains to be seen whether mandatory injunctions will be awarded to applicants for judicial review. If the court considers that it can grant mandatory injunctions, the remedy could be used in those cases in which narrow and questionable restrictions were placed upon the availability of mandamus in the past.[62] However, this possibility aside, it would seem that the remedy of injunction merely duplicates the remedies of mandamus and prohibition.

It is certainly not clear that the Law Commission envisaged mandatory injunctions being available in applications for judicial review in cases of remit pure and simple. In its report, the Law Commission mentioned mandatory as well as prohibitory

[56] *i.e.* of the Local Government Act 1972, see above p. 280, note 52.
[57] See Chap. 7, p. 256.
[58] Mandatory (commanding something to be done), prohibitory (forbidding the doing of something) and *quia timet* (prohibiting the commission of an anticipated wrong). Injunctions may also be perpetual (final) or interlocutory (effective until the case is tried out). Further, an interim injunction (effective until the question is further considered) or an *ex parte* injunction (a temporary injunction granted without hearing the other side) may be available to deal with matters of greater urgency.
[59] See Chap. 7, pp. 256, 257.
[60] See Chap. 7, pp. 259, 267.
[61] See Wade A.L., p. 515.
[61a] *R.* v. *Kent C.C. ex p. Bruce* (see note 74 above) where the application was unsuccessful.
[62] See above p. 289.

injunctions and gave examples of what it described as the "limited availability" of the injunction generally against public authorities.[63] The first two examples concerned threats to or infringements of private law rights. In the first case the rights were those arising at common law and, in the second, rights arising from statute. Both of these instances we would describe as cases involving liability.[64] The third example was of the relator action.[65] The Commission then observed that, in addition to these "clear" cases, there was a further category "of doubtful scope" and referred to the *Boyce* case.[66] We have seen that the *Boyce* case has been used as authority for the grant of an injunction in cases of remit pure and simple but we have suggested that it provides no such authority.[67] However, even if, as seems doubtful, the Law Commission anticipated the availability of injunctions in such cases in future, it was a *prohibitory* injunction that was sought in *Boyce*, and in every other case in which it has been used as an authority.

In these circumstances, it would appear that the reason for making injunctions available in applications for judicial review when there were no longer any procedural advantages in seeking an injunction by means of ordinary civil actions, was the same as the reason for making damages available: so that the new procedure could provide a range of private law remedies for those using applications for judicial review to deal with issues of liability and remit mixed. In other words, it may never have been contemplated that injunctions, whether mandatory or prohibitory, would have been available in applications for judicial review unless there was a liability issue as well as a remit issue. This is certainly the case with the other private law remedy, damages.[68]

Another factor supports this conjecture. While it has always been clear that neither injunctions nor prerogative remedies will lie against the Crown, it has been recognised that a prerogative order will lie against a servant of the Crown as *persona designata*.[69] This rather contrived means of circumventing Crown immunity was not possible in relation to the injunction since section 21(2) of the Crown Proceedings Act 1947 provides that no injunction may be granted against an officer of the Crown if the effect of granting

[63] Law Comm. 73, para. 22.
[64] See Chap. 7, pp. 256, 257.
[65] See Chap. 7, p. 247.
[66] [1903] 1 Ch. 109.
[67] See Chap. 7, p. 250, note 14.
[68] See p. 303 below.
[69] See p. 272 above, note 17.

it would be to grant relief against the Crown which might not have been obtained against the Crown directly. This restriction applies only to "civil proceedings" since, of course, in 1947 injunctions were not available by any other proceedings. Section 38(2) of the 1947 Act defines civil proceedings so as to exclude "proceedings on the Crown side of the [Queen's] Bench Division" unless the context otherwise requires. Now that injunctions are available by applications for judicial review, which would seem to be "proceedings on the Crown side of the Queen's Bench Division," a question of interpretation arises. It could be said that the statutory prohibition against injunctions against officers of the Crown in section 21(2) does not apply to applications for judicial review.[69a] Alternatively, it could be said that applications for injunctions in cases of liability and remit mixed are indeed civil proceedings, even when brought by applications for judicial review, or at least that the context requires them to be so regarded.[69b] It would be difficult to say otherwise when a claim for damages is added to an application for an injunction in such cases. It is plain from the proposed amendments to section 21(1) of the Crown Proceeding Act contained in Clause 3(2) of the Draft Bill that the Law Commission did not contemplate the repeal of section 21(2). To the extent that the 1977 Order 53 was in conflict with the 1947 Act, the order would have been *ultra vires*. Now, of course, injunctions are available in applications for judicial review by virtue of section 31 of the Supreme Court Act 1981 which could be taken as impliedly repealing section 21(2). Even if this is the case, so that injunctions would be available against officers of the Crown, it still remains the case that the remedy merely duplicates the prerogative remedies except in cases involving liability and this suggests that the true role of injunctions in the new procedure is indeed, like that of damages, to give full relief to those who might have chosen to bring ordinary civil actions in cases of liability and remit mixed.

(4) Declarations

With the exception of damages, which are available only in the event of an infringement of a private law right,[70] the declaration is

[69a] This approach seems to have been adopted by Hodgson J. in *R.* v. *Governor of Pentonville Prison ex. p. Herbage The Times*, May 21, 1986, in which the issues were exclusively matters of public law.

[69b] This is not inconsistent with the conclusion in *R.* v. *Hallstrom, ex p. W.* [1985] 3 All E.R. 775 that an application by way of judicial review for certiorari and a declaration did not constitute 'civil proceedings' within s.139 of the Mental Health Act 1983. It would have been otherwise had damages been claimed in the same proceedings.

[70] See p. 303 below.

the only remedy in the armoury of judicial review that is unarguably available against the Crown.[71] As noted earlier[72] this creates a difficulty in relation to the interpretation of section 31(2) of the Supreme Court Act 1981 which seems to limit the availability of injunctions, declarations and, by implication, damages, to those circumstances in which one or other of the prerogative remedies were previously available. Indeed, this impression has been confirmed in the House of Lords[73] when Lord Scarman said[74]:

> "Rule 1(2) enables the court to grant a declaration or injunction instead of, or in addition to, a prerogative order where to do so would be just and convenient. This is a procedural innovation of great consequence, but it neither extends nor diminishes the substantive law. For the two remedies (borrowed from the private law) are put in harness with the prerogative remedies. They may be granted only in circumstances in which one or other of the prerogative orders can issue. I so interpret Order 53, r. 1(2) because to do otherwise would be to condemn the rule as *ultra vires*."

This statement was made before the Supreme Court Act 1981 gave statutory authority to Order 53 but Lord Scarman's words were cited with approval by Lord Wilberforce in a House of Lords' decision after section 31 of the Supreme Court Act 1981 had placed the *vires* of Order 53 beyond doubt.[75]

Since the prerogative remedies were never available against the Crown, and were not considered appropriate as a means of challenging the validity of delegated legislation[76] this interpretation appears to preclude the use of an application for judicial review whenever a declaration is required for either of these two purposes. However, subject to observance of section 17(3) of the Crown Proceedings Act 1947[77] is there any reason in principle why

[71] See *Dyson* v. *Att.-Gen.* [1911] 1 K.B. 410.
[72] See p. 271 above.
[73] *Self-Employed Case* [1982] A.C. 617.
[74] *Ibid.* p. 647.
[75] *Davy* v. *Spelthorne B.C.* [1984] A.C. 262. *R.* v. *Bromley L.B.C. ex p. Lambeth L.B.C.* (See p. 271 note 9 above) cannot be taken as affecting this issue although it seems to favour a liberal interpretation of s.31.
[76] See Wade A.L., pp. 560–561.
[77] Requiring actions for declarations to be brought against the relevant government department or, if none, the Attorney-General, as opposed to the practice of making applications for prerogative orders against the relevant minister as *persona designata*.

a declaration against the Crown, or to challenge the validity of delegated legislation, should not be sought by means of an application for judicial review after 1981? Since the procedural requirements of Order 53 are intended to protect public authorities, it is difficult to see why this protection should be denied to the Crown, or to any other public authority when it is enacting delegated legislation. If it could be shown that the standing requirements of ordinary civil actions for declarations were more onerous than those under Order 53, there might be some basis for arguing that Order 53 should not be used in these cases. But it does not appear to have been suggested that a litigant seeking a declaration against the Crown had to establish any higher degree of standing than a litigant against any other public authority. A litigant seeking to challenge the validity of delegated legislation had to show that his personal interests had been, or were likely to be, directly and prejudicially affected by the operation of the regulation, order, or bye-law concerned.[78] While this may be a higher degree of standing than is required, say, for certiorari in some cases, Order 53, rule 3(7) merely requires a sufficient interest "in the matter to which the application relates" so that it would not be inconsistent for a higher degree of interest to be required in this case, just as it might be when an applicant seeks mandamus in circumstances which make it an order specifically to perform a statutory duty owed to only one person.

It would therefore appear that there is no reason in principle why Order 53 should not be interpreted as permitting declarations to be sought against the Crown, or to challenge the validity of delegated legislation, by means of applications for judicial review. The words "the nature of" in section 31(2)(a) and (b) would seem to give sufficient flexibility and, since the matter was not before the House of Lords in either of the two cases mentioned, it would be misleading to regard them as being even *sub silentio* authorities against such an interpretation.[78a]

In private law, the declaration is the remedy with the least direct and immediate connection with an infringement of a private law right of the plaintiff. As Lord Denning once said[79]:

[78] See De Smith J.R.A.A., p. 485 and cases there cited.

[78a] Conversely, Woolf J. in *R.* v. *Secretary of State for the Environment ex p. G.L.C.* (see p. 271, note 9 above) provides persuasive support for the view that s.31(2)(*a*) and (*b*) does allow declarations to be made in some circumstances in which no prerogative order would lie.

[79] *Pyx Granite Co.* v. *Ministry of Housing & Local Government* [1958] 1 Q.B. 554 at 571.

> "... if a substantial question exists which one person has an interest to raise, and the other to oppose, then the court has a discretion to resolve it by a declaration, which it will exercise if there is good reason for so doing."

In its modern form, the declaration derives from Order 25, rule 5 of the Rules of the Supreme Court 1888 which provided:

> "No action or proceedings shall be open to objection on the ground that a merely declaratory judgment or order is sought thereby, and the court may make a declaration of right whether any consequential relief is or could be claimed or not."

This wording was apparently intended to remove the self-imposed limitations adopted by the Court of Chancery which would make a declaration only when some other relief was claimed.[80] Initially, the order was regarded as enabling the court to declare the "rights" of the parties when an infringement of the plaintiff's rights was in prospect but had yet to become a sufficiently immediate threat to justify the award of a *quia timet* injunction.[81] However, this cautious approach was rejected[82] and in *Dyson* v. *Attorney-General*[83] the range and constitutional significance of the remedy emerged in an action in which a landowner successfully challenged the legality of a demand for information, with a penalty for non-compliance, from the Commissioners of Inland Revenue.

Although it is not necessary for a plaintiff to show a prospective threat to an interest which, if carried through, would give him a remedy in damages, the courts, ever fearful of a flood of litigation, have insisted that there must be a real issue between the parties, and that a declaration of their respective legal positions would serve some purpose. Thus, in private law, the court might grant a declaration at the request of one party to a contract that proposed

[80] See *Rooke* v. *Lord Kensington* (1856) 2 K. & J. 753.

[81] See *London Association of Shipowners & Brokers* v. *London & India Docks Joint Committee* [1892] 3 Ch.D. 242 and Buckley L.J's dissenting judgment in *Guaranty Trust Co. of New York* v. *Hannay & Co.* [1915] 2 K.B. 536 at 548.

[82] See the majority judgments of Bankes & Pickford L.JJ. in *Hannay*'s case (above).

[83] [1912] 1 Ch. 158.

action by the other party would amount to a breach of the contract. But it would not grant such a declaration at the request of a non-contracting party, however adversely affected by the proposed conduct, unless that person would be able to show that, if the conduct were carried through, he would be able to sue. There would be no point in telling the defendant that his proposed conduct was unlawful if making the declaration would have no legal significance for the plaintiff. In relation to actions for declarations against public authorities, this limitation was less inhibiting. Even though proceeding with the proposed unlawfulness might not make the defendant liable to the plaintiff in private law, it might nonetheless expose the defendant to an action for a prerogative remedy initiated by the plaintiff. There would therefore be some point in making the declaration in these circumstances since the defendant could not ignore it with impunity.

Unless the character of the declaration can be said to have changed now that it has been incorporated in Order 53, it would seem to follow that the remedy ought not to be granted unless two points can be established. First, that the defendant authority's acts will carry it outside its remit. Second, that if the defendant acts in contravention of the law as declared by the judgment, the declaration will serve some purpose by enabling the applicant to establish:

(i) that he would have a cause of action in damages or for an injunction[84] or
(ii) that his legal status would be affected[85] or
(iii) that he would have a defence in any proceedings based upon the impugned act or decision[86] or
(iv) that he would have a sufficient interest to seek one of the prerogative orders[87] and that such an order would lie.[88]

[84] *e.g.* If a housing authority determined that an applicant was entitled to accommodation under the Housing (Homeless Persons) Act 1977 but refused or neglected to fulfil its statutory obligations. (See *Cocks* v. *Thanet D.C.* [1983] 2 A.C. 286).

[85] *e.g. Att.-Gen.* v. *Prince Ernest Augustus of Hanover* [1957] A.C. 436; *Royal College of Nursing* v. *D.H.S.S.* [1981] 1 All E.R. 545 at 551 (Woolf J.).

[86] *Dyson* v. *Att.-Gen.* above.

[87] It is difficult to imagine any circumstances in which an applicant for a declaration by way of application for judicial review would not have sufficient standing for at least one of the prerogative remedies.

[88] *e.g.* as on the facts of *Anisminic* v. *Foreign Compensation Commission* [1969] 2 A.C. 147. Of course an applicant challenging the validity of delegated legislation would not be embarrassed by the fact that no prerogative order would lie if he could rely on (ii) or (iii).

It remains to be seen whether the courts will apply this rather restricted approach or whether the willingness of the Crown, and of responsible public authorities, to act in accordance with the law as declared by the courts, has come to be regarded as preventing declarations from being "in vain" even when there might be no legal consequences in ignoring them.

The question of the scope of declarations in applications for judicial review arose obliquely in *Gillick* v. *West Norfolk Area Health Authority*.[89]

The plaintiff brought ordinary civil proceedings for a declaration that advice contained in a DHSS circular, and the provision by an area health authority of contraceptives to girls under 16, were both unlawful as amounting to the criminal offence of causing or encouraging unlawful sexual intercourse, and also as an interference with the plaintiff's "parental rights." It is doubtful whether the plaintiff could have been given a declaration that the matters complained of amounted to a crime unless she could have shown that she was entitled to an injunction under the principles explained in *Gouriet* v. *Union of Post Office Workers*[90] as being a person suffering special damage. However, she might well have been entitled to such a remedy by virtue of the alleged interference with her "parental rights." In the event, it was held that no criminal offence had been committed and that the plaintiff's parental rights had not been infringed.

Doubts were expressed as to whether under the *O'Reilly* v. *Mackman* principle, the case should not have been brought by application for judicial review. Plainly, whatever may be the extent of "parental rights" they must in any event be private law rights so that an application for judicial review would be appropriate only if a remit issue were involved. Lord Bridge recognised[91] that it would be difficult for a court to regard the production of a circular containing "unlawful" advice as something which carried the authority *ultra vires*. However, he concluded that an application for judicial review would have been an appropriate means of proceeding in the case of *Royal College of Nursing* v. *DHSS*[92] and that "therefore" the ambit of judicial review had been

[89] [1985] 3 All E.R. 402.

[90] [1978] A.C. 435, *i.e.* assuming that it is accepted that injunctions are available to those suffering "special damage." A statement to this effect in *Gouriet* seems to have been based on an uncritical acceptance of the *Boyce* case criticised on p. 250 above.

[91] *Ibid.* p. 427.

[92] [1981] A.C. 800, concerning advice given on the legality of nurses' participation in a certain novel means of terminating pregnancies.

extended to include challenges to advice given by a public authority that was "wrong in law." It is submitted, with respect, that no such extension is warranted on authority or principle. Both cases were clearly appropriately brought as ordinary civil actions. The mere fact that the defendant is a public authority, and that the plaintiff (as in the *Gillick* case) turns out to have no private law right, does not mean that a declaration could be obtained by means of an application for judicial review. That would be the case only if the authority had acted *ultra vires* or otherwise outside its remit; but to give advice that is wrong in law is surely no more to go outside remit than to give advice that is negligent, or defamatory.

To the extent that a decision impugned for mere error on the face of the record may be characterised as invalid but nevertheless *intra vires*[93] a declaration would be a less effective remedy than certiorari for dealing with such a decision since declaring it to be invalid does not prevent it from being operative.[94] Similarly, it would be prudent to add a claim for an injunction or prerogative order in any case in which there was doubt as to whether the declaration would be observed.[95] On the other hand, the non-peremptory nature of the declaration makes it particularly appropriate when even the appearance of compulsion is undesirable or unnecessary.[96] It also has a useful role to play when a court wishes to condemn as unlawful the actions of a public authority although the particular circumstances make it impossible or inappropriate to give effective redress by awarding one of the mandatory remedies.[97]

Although it is not a contempt of court to ignore a declaration, in an ordinary civil action at least, the judgment of the court is *res judicata* and cannot be re-opened in any subsequent proceedings. Whether or not the doctrine of *res judicata*, or issue estoppel, applies in applications for judicial review is less certain. In *R.* v. *Secretary of State for the Environment ex p. Brent London Borough Council*[98] certiorari was granted to quash a decision of

[93] See Chap. 4, p. 164.

[94] See *Punton* v. *Minister of Pensions (No. 2)* [1964] 1 W.L.R. 226.

[95] Although it is inherently unlikely that a public authority would act in breach of the law as declared by the court, recent tensions between certain local authorities and the central government suggest that this possibility cannot be ignored.

[96] *e.g. R.* v. *Boundary Commissioners for England ex p. Foot* [1983] Q.B. 600 at 634.

[97] See *R.* v. *Chief Constable of North Wales Police ex p. Evans* [1982] 1 W.L.R. 1155.

[98] [1982] Q.B. 593.

the Secretary of State to withold rate support grant because his refusal to hear representations before making the decision was a breach of natural justice. Subsequently the Secretary of State, after hearing representations, again decided to withold the grant. In *R.* v. *Secretary of State ex p. Hackney L.B.C.*[99] it was argued that a finding in the first case to the effect that the council had a legal right to the sums improperly withheld could not be re-opened. The court did not consider that any such finding had been made in the first case or, even if it had, that this prevented the Secretary of State from deciding to withhold the sums having heard representations. However, the court went on to say that the doctrine of issue estoppel, or *res judicata*, was inappropriate in applications for judicial review which were more like criminal cases, in which the doctrine does not apply, than civil actions *inter partes* in which it does. While this may be correct, it could hardly be suggested that the "core" of a declaratory judgment, that an act or decision, or delegated legislation, was "invalid" or "unlawful" could be open to challenge in subsequent proceedings (other than an appeal) between the same parties. If this were not so, then declarations would always be "in vain" and would never be made. Issue estoppel aside, it is obviously important that, although the court may declare a decision to be *ultra vires*, it should not declare what the decision should have been unless the correction of the error of law makes only one decision possible.[1]

(5) Damages

It is not within the compass of this book to provide a detailed treatment of the remedy of damages[2] nor indeed to attempt to unravel the mystery of when a breach of a statutory duty gives rise to an action in damages.[3] However, certain observations concerning the remedy are necessary. The first is that the Law Commission did not consider it to be within its terms of reference to recommend a new remedy of damages for loss arising from illegal administrative acts or omissions independent of the existing law of tort and contract.[4] It was clear, however, that when the possibility of such a remedy was canvassed in the earlier report and subsequent Working Paper[5] there was substantial support for a separate

[99] [1983] 1 W.L.R. 524 (affirmed: [1984] 1 W.L.R. 592).
[1] As, *e.g.* in *Anisminic* note 88 above.
[2] See Lawson, *op.cit.* Chap. 4.
[3] See R. A. Buckley "Liability in Tort for Breach of Statutory Duty" (1984) 100 L.Q.R. 204.
[4] See Law Comm. 73, para. 9.
[5] Law Comm. 20 (Cmnd. 4059 (1969)) and Working Paper 40.

inquiry into this issue.[6] In the absence of such a new remedy, damages are available in applications for judicial review only in those cases which we have described as being cases of liability and remit mixed.[7] Unless there is a remit issue, application for judicial review is not an appropriate way of proceeding[8] and unless there is liability in the conventional sense, damages cannot be awarded.[9]

While it is not yet possible to identify any established and convincing principle governing the question of whether or not a breach of a statutory duty will sound in damages, it is beginning to emerge that there is a significant difference between cases in which the acts of a public authority deprive an individual of an "asset currently enjoyed," and those in which the authority fails to confer an asset. In the former case there seems to be almost a presumption in favour of a remedy in damages.[10] It does not seem to matter that the "asset currently enjoyed" is itself conferred by statute, provided no further positive action is required in order for it to vest.[11]

Conversely, a statutory duty to confer a benefit or asset does not seem to be regarded as vesting in the plaintiff "a right arising under private law" unless and until the question of the individual's entitlement has been settled affirmatively. If the authority decides that a plaintiff is not entitled, the correctness of the decision may be challenged only by an application for judicial review.[12] However, once a decision has been made in favour of an individual, any subsequent failure or refusal to confer the benefit seems to be regarded as the infringement of a right deriving from private law and therefore as sounding in damages.[13] It will not always be easy to make the distinction between an "asset currently enjoyed" and an "asset to be conferred"[14] but it seems to be a more rational test

[6] The absence of such a remedy was criticised by Lord Wilberforce in *Hoffman-La Roche (F) & Co A.G.* v. *Secretary of State for Trade & Industry* [1975] A.C. 295 at 358–359.

[7] See Chap. 7, p. 257.

[8] Supreme Court Act 1981, s.31 and *Self-Employed Case* note 48 above.

[9] *Ibid.* s.31(4) and ord. 53, r. 7(b). This must be implied from the tenor of s.31(4) and the substance of the report on which it is based, as well as the use of the term "action" rather than "application" in s.31(4)(b).

[10] See *Garden Cottage Foods Ltd.* v. *Milk Marketing Board* [1984] A.C. 130; but *cf. Bourgoin S.A.* v. *Ministry of Ag. Fish. and Food* [1985] 3 All E.R. 585.

[11] *An Bord Bainne Co-operative Ltd (Irish Dairy Board)* v. *Milk Marketing Board* [1984] 2 C.M.L.R. 584.

[12] See *Cocks* v. *Thanet D.C.* [1983] 2 A.C. 286.

[13] *Cocks* v. *Thanet D.C.* and *O'Reilly* v. *Mackman* note 51 above.

[14] See *Freeman* v. *Wansbeck B.C.* [1984] 2 All E.R. 746 on "right" to buy council house which did not vest in the tenant if the house was one of those excepted from general provisions, a matter requiring a decision by the local authority.

than others used in this area in the past[15] and it is to be hoped that it will be developed further so as to alleviate some of the present difficulties.

C. Procedural Matters

It is also beyond the scope of this book to consider in detail the procedural requirements of applications for judicial review.[16] However, since the courts regard it as an abuse[17] or misuse[18] of process for a litigant to proceed otherwise than by an application for judicial review in cases of remit pure and simple[19], we should at least see what particular features of the procedure are considered to be so important.

In essence, the procedural peculiarities of applications for judicial review may be seen as serving two primary purposes. First, it is important that citizens aggrieved by abuses of official power should have a reasonably straightforward means of invoking the law. But the more straightforward the means provided, the more danger there will be of public authorities being continually harrassed by irresponsible applications. Public authorities are particularly at risk in this respect because of the vast range of individuals affected by their acts and decisions, and because, in addition to being liable for any breaches of the ordinary law, they are also liable to be challenged for exceeding their remit.[20] Clearly, it is in the interest of public authorities themselves, of the public at large which ultimately bears the cost of public authorities' activities, and of genuine and responsible applications for judicial review, that the procedures should be as straightforward and as inexpensive as possible, but that there should be some quick and simple filter for excluding worthless applications. These interests are served by the requirement of leave to apply.

Second, there will be some circumstances in which doubts concerning the legality of a public authority's acts or decisions will cause widespread inconvenience if they are not resolved as quickly as possible.[21] Equally, there will be cases in which the applicant

[15] See Buckley *loc. cit.* above, note 3.
[16] See R. J. F. Gordon, *Judicial Review: Law & Procedure* (1985).
[17] *O'Reilly* v. *Mackman* note 51 above.
[18] This less pejorative term was preferred by Donaldson M.R. in *R.* v. *East Berks Health Authority ex p. Walsh* [1985] Q.B. 152 at 162.
[19] See Chap. 7, pp. 258, 261.
[20] See Chap. 7.
[21] *e.g.* where the legal position of hundreds if not thousands is affected or where delay in implementing a decision may occasion great expense.

requires relief as a matter of great urgency.[22] However, there will be many cases in which there is no particular urgency, or at least no greater urgency than that felt by litigants in ordinary civil actions. A finance company would be just as inconvenienced by a challenge to the legality of its hire purchase or loan contracts as would a public authority which had made, or refused, benefit payments on the basis of an erroneous application of the law. If the consequence of illegality is an obligation to make money payments, whether in the form of damages, or in the form of refunds or additional benefit payments, it is difficult to see why public authorities should be freed from the obligation by the running of time more quickly than private companies or individuals. On the other hand, where a possible consequence of illegality is an obligation to put matters right, otherwise than by the payment of money, a delay in seeking redress might well have caused it to have become much more difficult for the defendant to undo what has been done. In private law, a mandatory injunction may be refused in such a case[23] and it is plain that public authorities should be similarly protected against late applications for judicial review. Clearly, in some cases it is desirable that if any application is to be made, it should be made very quickly, but it does not follow that all applications for judicial review need to be made more promptly than ordinary civil actions.

(1) Leave to apply for judicial review

Applications for leave to apply for judicial review are made by filing a notice of motion in the Crown Office, together with affidavits[24] purporting to verify the facts relied upon. Such applications are made *ex parte* and the defendant is not involved at this stage. However, the court may adjourn the application so as to give the intended defendant an opportunity to oppose the grant of leave. Unless the applicant requests a hearing, the matter can be dealt with by a judge in private purely on the basis of the docu-

[22] *e.g.* where an applicant wishes to challenge the legality of a refusal of leave to enter the country. But see now *R.* v. *Secretary of State for the Home Department, ex p. Swati* [1986] 1 All E.R. 717 discussed in Chap. 9.

[23] See for example *Wrotham Park Estate Co. Ltd.* v. *Parkside Homes* [1974] 1 W.L.R. 798 where the court refused to grant a mandatory injunction for the removal of a house built in breach of a restrictive covenant.

[24] Sworn statements. In addition to liability to perjury for deliberate falsehood, the applicant might be refused a remedy for being less than candid in disclosing all relevant facts in his application for leave. Exceptionally, certiorari might be granted summarily if the error is admitted in an affidavit. See *R.* v. *Newcastle-under-Lyme JJ. ex p. Whitehouse* [1952] 2 All E.R. 531 in which an affidavit by the Clerk to the Justices was treated as an admission.

ments. If the judge grants leave, the matter may proceed but, if leave is refused, the applicant may renew the application by requiring a hearing before a single judge in open court. Once there has been a hearing, either initially or on a renewed application, the applicant may no longer renew the application before another judge.[25]

We noted earlier[26] that the availability of discovery in ordinary civil actions enabled some cases to be won which would have been lost had they been applications for prerogative remedies in which the vital information would not have been discoverable. Even now, discovery is not available until leave is granted but it seems that courts will grant leave if the applicant is able to make out a prima facie case ("even if it is somewhat flimsy") that unless some explanation is forthcoming, there are grounds for reasonable suspicion of illegality.[27] This would seem to be entirely appropriate since the purpose of the requirement of leave to apply is to filter out only hopeless and irresponsible applications.

(2) Time limits

When the Law Commission considered the question of time limits, applications for the prerogative order of certiorari had to be made within six months and rules of court imposed a limit of two months in relation to certain applications for mandamus.[28] There were no specific time limits for actions for injunctions and declarations other than the general law of limitation but, as we have seen, undue delay can result in the refusal of an equitable remedy.[29] There had been considerable criticism of the fixed time limit for certiorari[30] and, although it had been suggested that limits of three or even six years would be more appropriate, the Law Commission recognised that any fixed period was bound to be somewhat arbitrary.[31] Very sensibly, it concentrated upon the reason for a provision against delay and recommended that, unless there was a specific statutory requirement to the contrary, no court should refuse either leave to apply, or any remedy, on the grounds of delay unless it considered that granting the remedy would cause

[25] An application may be renewed before the Court of Appeal, a rare example of the court's original jurisdiction, see *Re Poh* [1983] 1 W.L.R. 2, and Gordon *op. cit.* (note 16), 7–25.

[26] See *Barnard* v. *National Dock Labour Board* and the *Anisminic* case in note 21, Chap. 7.

[27] See the *Self-Employed Case* above.

[28] *i.e.* requiring a Crown Court to hear an appeal.

[29] See above p. 281.

[30] By those responding to the Law Commission's Working Paper.

[31] See Law Comm. 73, para. 50.

substantial hardship to, or substantially prejudice the rights of, any person, or would be detrimental to good administration.[32]

When Order 53 was substituted[33] following the Law Commission report, the provisions regarding delay[34] did not entirely reflect the cogent reasoning contained in the report in that an arbitrary three month time limit was imposed in respect of applications for certiorari. Subsequently, the delay provisions of Order 53 were amended again[35] to provide a much simpler formulation which required, in effect, that any application for judicial review, regardless of the remedy sought, should be made promptly and in any event within three months unless the court considered that there were good reasons for extending the period.[36] Finally, section 31(6) of the Supreme Court Act 1981 restored the wording of the 1977 amendment which permitted the court to refuse leave to apply, or to refuse a remedy, if the relief sought would be likely to cause substantial hardship to, or substantially prejudice the rights of, any person, or would be detrimental to good administration. However this provision is without prejudice to an enactment, or rule of court, which has the effect of limiting the time within which an application may be made.

Thus, contrary to the Law Commission's recommendations, a fixed time limit of three months now applies to all applications for judicial review unless some shorter period is prescribed by statute, and the court has a discretion to refuse leave or relief on the grounds of delay, even when an application is made within this period.[37] True, the period may be extended if there is good reason[38] but it would seem that permitting an application to be made after three months will now be regarded as exceptional rather than that, as the Law Commission intended, a refusal on the grounds of delay would itself be regarded as exceptional.[39] We have seen that there are many cases in which there is no reason at all why public authorities should be placed in such a favourable position compared with that of ordinary defendants and it remains

[32] Draft Bill, Clause 6.
[33] By S.I. 1977 No. 1955.
[34] Rule 4.
[35] By S.I. 1980 No. 2000.
[36] This amendment was without prejudice to any statutory provision providing a different time limit in any particular case.
[37] See *R.* v. *Greenwich L.B.C. ex p. Cedar Transport Group* [1983] R.A. 173.
[38] See *R.* v. *Stratford-on-Avon D.C. ex p. Jackson* above, p. 282, note 63.
[39] See, *e.g. per* Lord Diplock in *O'Reilly* v. *Mackman* [1983] 2 A.C. at 280–281; but *cf. per* Lawton L.J. in *Rootkin* v. *Kent C.C.* [1981] 1 W.L.R. 1186 at 1192 (a case under the original 1977 Ord. 53, r. 4).

to be seen whether the court will be astute to recognise this fact and to extend the period when delay in seeking redress causes no greater prejudice to "good administration" in the public sector than it would to "commercial convenience" in the case of ordinary defendants.

(3) Other procedural considerations

To the extent that the procedures of application for judicial review have been assimilated with those of ordinary civil actions,[40] we need not consider them further. However, one substantial difference does remain. In general, applications for judicial review are dealt with on the basis of evidence by affidavit rather than by the hearing of witnesses. The court has power to order witnesses to appear and to be cross-examined but the nature of the review jurisdiction is such that disputed issues of fact very rarely arise.[41] It has been suggested[42] that to permit the cross-examination of witnesses might lead the court to step outside its limited supervisory review jurisdiction and to substitute its own view of the facts for that of a decision making body. However, it is clear that cross-examination will be permitted "whenever the justice of the particular case so requires."[43]

The possibility of a substantial dispute on questions of fact could be the explanation for the provisions[44] which enable the court, when dealing with an application for judicial review requesting damages, an injunction or a declaration, to order the proceedings to be continued as if commenced by writ or originating summons, rather than simply refusing the application. Alternatively, the provision may be intended to mitigate the effect of a mistake by the applicant as to the existence of a remit issue which would enable the case to be dealt with by an application for judicial review.[45] In

[40] *e.g.* in relation to discovery, interlocutory relief, amendment etc.

[41] In 1928, Lord Hewart C.J. could not recall an application for cross-examination for some 50 or 60 years (see *R.* v. *Kent J.J. ex p. Smith* [1928] W.N. 137 at 138) and in 1956 Lord Goddard C.J. had never previously experienced such an application (see *R* v. *Stokesley J.J. ex p. Bartram* [1956] 1 W.L.R. 254 at 258.).

[42] By Lord Denning M.R. in *George* v. *Secretary of State for the Environment (1979)* 38 P & C.R. 609 at 615.

[43] *Per* Lord Diplock in *O'Reilly* v. *Mackman* [1983] 2 A.C. at 283.

[44] In Ord. 53, r. 9(5).

[45] The power to transfer applies only when the remedies of injunction, declaration or damages are sought by way of an application for judicial review. See *R.* v. *East Berkshire Health Authority ex p. Walsh* above: applicant who applied for certiorari in error not permitted to continue the action as though it had been begun by writ.

fact it is doubtful whether this express power was strictly necessary, given the very wide prohibition contained in Order 2, rule 1(3) against setting aside proceedings on the grounds that the wrong originating process has been used.[46] Curiously, the provision was not referred to by Lord Denning in *O'Reilly* v. *Mackman* when he asserted that the court had sufficient control over its own procedures to transfer an action commenced by writ to a hearing by way of application for judicial review or, if it did not, that the rules of court should be amended to permit such a transfer.[47] Neither was the rule mentioned by Lord Diplock who denied any inherent power and did not see any need to amend the rules so as to give such a power.[48]

Of course, since 1981, it is required by statute, rather than by rules of court, that actions for the prerogative remedies shall be commenced by way of judicial review,[49] and in *O'Reilly* the issue was one of remit pure and simple. Nonetheless, since the statute was itself enacted to remove any doubts concerning the *vires* of the rules of court, it would be unfortunate if the statute prevented Order 2 from being used to mitigate the effects of a mistake by a litigant in choosing the wrong form of procedure. In Chapter 7[50] we attempted to explain the choices open to a litigant and we return to that question in Chapter 9. However, the matter is by no means straightforward and, so far, the courts have been unable to lay down clear guidelines. In these circumstances, it seems quite wrong that the court should expect a litigant who has mistakenly chosen to proceed by writ or originating summons to bear the consequences of such an understandable error.

[46] "The court shall not wholly set aside any proceedings or the writ or other originating process by which they were begun on the ground that the proceedings were required *by any of these Rules* to be begun by an originating process other than the one employed." (emphasis added)

[47] [1983] 2 A.C. at 258 (C.A.).

[48] *Ibid.* p. 284.

[49] Supreme Court Act 1981, s.31(1). Ord. 2, r. 1(3) (see note 46 above) refers only to requirements of the rules of court.

[50] See pp. 259, 267.

Chapter 9

CHOICE OF MACHINERY

In chapter 7 we saw that a person affected by an unlawful exercise of official power may have a choice as to how to proceed to obtain redress. If the wrong alleged exposes the authority to civil or criminal liability, but does not carry it outside its remit, then an ordinary civil action or prosecution, as the case may be, will be the only means of proceeding. If, on the other hand, the unlawfulness carries the authority outside its remit but does not expose it to either civil or criminal liability, then an application for judicial review is the sole means by which redress may be sought. When the act does expose the authority to liability and also carries it outside its remit, then an intending litigant may choose between an application for judicial review and an ordinary action or prosecution.[1] Further, a challenge to remit may be used as the basis of a defence in either civil or criminal proceedings, or may be raised directly by an application for judicial review. So far we have excluded from our analysis the possibility that a statutory right of appeal may lie in relation to the act or decision impugned.

We must now consider the relationship between appeals and applications for judicial review or, to return to our earlier terminology, between appellate and supervisory review.

A. Appeal "on the Merits" or "on Point of Law"

We saw in Chapter 2 that while supervisory review is available unless excluded, appellate review is not available unless expressly provided by statute.[2] Different statutes give different types of rights to appeal and what the right of appeal will be in any case will depend upon the wording of the statute in question. For our purposes the important distinction is whether the statute provides an appeal "on the merits" or merely on "a point of law."[3] As was explained in Chapter 2, an appeal "on the merits" broadly enables the appellate court to make whatever decision it considers the

[1] Respectively, cases of liability pure & simple, remit pure & simple, and liability and remit mixed.

[2] Chap. 2, p. 57.

[3] Including the procedure by way of "case stated" of which perhaps the most familiar example is in the context of criminal appeals from magistrates' or Crown courts.

lower body ought to have made. Conversely, an appeal restricted to points of law enables the appellate body to correct errors of law but not to substitute its conclusions for those of the lower body unless the removal of the error can itself be said to "decide" the issue.[4]

Generally speaking, appeals "on the merits" are usually available only to the parties to a dispute, particularly when the tribunal is a court. On the other hand, statutes commonly give a right to appeal on a point of law to "any person aggrieved" by a decision. The meaning of this statutory phrase has varied from time to time[5] but the indications are that the courts are now beginning to recognise the desirability of assimilating it to the test of a "sufficient interest" required for applications for judicial review.[6]

B. Supervisory or Appellate Review?

In those cases in which it appears that a person wishing to challenge an act or decision by a public authority may do so either via appellate or via supervisory review a further question of choice arises but in these circumstances the choice is not simply a matter of the preference of the person concerned. In fact, the extent of the freedom of choice between these modes of redress has been obscured in the past by statements made in particular cases which, although appearing to be statements of principle, are not entirely consistent with each other. In particular, it has been asserted on many occasions that there is no rule that a litigant must have exhausted all other avenues of redress before seeking to invoke the court's supervisory jurisdiction.[7] Conversely, it is sometimes said to be a cardinal principle that, save in the most exceptional cases, the court's supervisory jurisdiction will not be exercised where other remedies are available and have not been used.[8]

[4] See Chap. 2, p. 57.

[5] See Wade A.L., pp. 619–622.

[6] See *Arsenal Football Club Ltd.* v. *Ende* [1979] A.C. 1. In the *Self-Employed Case*, [1982] A.C. 617 at 642 Lord Diplock suggested that the "sufficient interest" test might be more liberal. This might well be so in the postulated cases of grievous and flagrant disregard for the law in which "any one at all" might be treated as having a sufficient interest. Although "any one at all" might be aggrieved in such a case they might be aggrieved not so much by the decision as by the manner in which it was arrived at; and it would in any event seem more suitable to deal with such cases by supervisory rather than appellate review: see, *e.g. Greater London Council* v. *Secretary of State for the Environment* [1985] *The Times*, July 18.

[7] See Wade A.L., p. 593.

[8] See, *e.g. R.* v. *Epping & Harlow General Commissioners ex p. Goldstraw* [1983] 3 All E.R. 257 at 262.

Indeed, it has been said that in some circumstances the existence of a statutory remedy will operate as an implied exclusion of the review jurisdiction.[9] Recent decisions[10] have indicated that a principle is emerging, but its exact scope will not become entirely clear until further cases are decided.

It would seem that now that supervisory jurisdiction has been fully restored and placed upon a firm statutory foundation, there is a growing recognition that it would be undesirable, both practically and politically, to allow respect for the jurisdiction to be undermined by its excessive and unnecessary use.[11] In any event, it is clear that while there is no inflexible rule that any available statutory appeal must be pursued before an application for judicial review will lie, it is equally clear that recourse to supervisory review instead of appellate review will be regarded as exceptional rather than normal.[12] At this stage, the courts appear to be reluctant to be too dogmatic in stating what factors will justify regarding a case as exceptional and the Court of Appeal has warned against treating statements in cases like statutory provisions.[13]

It seems that even though applications for judicial review may

[9] See Wade A.L., p. 595, *Barraclough* v. *Brown* [1897] A.C. 615 distinguished in *Pyx Granite Co* v. *Ministry of Housing & Loc. Govt.* [1960] A.C. 260 and 626. On *express* exclusion, see Chap. 2, p. 46.

[10] See notes 12 and 13 below.

[11] In the light of the decisions of the Court of Appeal and House of Lords (see notes 12 and 13 below) it is not necessary to examine the plethora of first instance decisions reported during 1983 and 1984 when this issue assumed a surprising importance. However, it should be noted that in *Ellis & Sons Fourth Amalgamated Properties* v. *Southern Rent Assessment Panel* [1984] *The Times*, February 8, Mann J. suggested that application for judicial review should have been used in preference to the statutory appeal procedures in that case as it would have enabled the rent assessment committee to be represented, avoided delay in the appointment of an *amicus curiae*, and permitted an appeal if the application succeeded.

[12] *R.* v. *I.R.C. ex p. Preston* [1985] A.C. 835 at 862. (Lord Templeman) and 852 where Lord Scarman, contrasting supervisory review and appeal, described the former as a "collateral challenge." It is collateral in the sense that it amounts to an intervention by the supervisory court, as it were, "from the sidelines": *cf.* Ch. 1(D).

[13] See *R.* v. *Chief Constable of Merseyside Police ex p. Calveley* [1986] 1 All E.R. 257, in which the court expanded upon the general principle enunciated by the House of Lords in *Preston*. However, in *R.* v. *Secretary of State for the Home Department ex p. Swati* [1986] 1 All E.R. 717, the Court of Appeal appears to lay down a principle against the use of supervisory review to challenge refusals of temporary leave to enter the U.K. save in exceptional circumstances, even though a person refused leave at the point of entry must leave the country in order to pursue the statutory appeal. For criticism of this decision see M. Sunkin, New L.J. (1986), Vol. 136, p. 304.

be quicker, less expensive and more convenient for an applicant, and more effective, it will still be necessary for a litigant to establish particular reasons why these advantages should be made available to him as an exception to the general rule. Although it has not been stated in the recent decisions, it would be reasonable to suppose that when an application for judicial review would be cheaper and more convenient to both parties, and no more expensive in terms of the administration of justice, these reasons would suffice to justify not requiring a statutory appeal to be pursued first.[14] Indeed, such considerations may lead Parliament itself to provide that in certain circumstances application for judicial review shall be the sole means of challenge.[15] Conversely, where a statutory appeal procedure is tailored to cater for a particular type of challenge, the court may refuse to give leave for an application for judicial review.[16] In cases in which it is necessary for a review court to know the precise facts found by the court below in order to discern whether an error of law has occurred,[17] it would seem preferable to require the court below to state a case, rather than proceeding by way of application for judicial review in which only affidavit evidence is available.[18]

Another factor which has not so far been referred to in terms but which seems to be implicit in some recent instances in which application for judicial review has been allowed[19] is the "disciplinary role" of the jurisdiction. It is, above all, a public law jurisdic-

[14] See the *Ellis* case above and *R.* v. *Wandsworth J.J. ex p. Read* [1942] 1 K.B. 281 in which it was said that it would be "ludicrous" to initiate a formal appeal in order to rectify a glaring and admitted error by magistrates.

[15] See, *e.g.* Local Government Finance Act 1982, s.4(1): validity of rates and precepts not to be questioned except by an application for judicial review. Note that, under s.4(2), s.4(1) does not apply to challenges to rates "based on facts relating to a particular hereditament or to the inclusion or exclusion of any particular person in or from the rate." Such challenges may still be made by way of appeal to the Crown Court under General Rate Act 1967, s.7. For the limitations of appeal under s.7, see *R.* v. *Rochdale M.B.C. ex p. Cromer* [1982] 3 All E.R. 761 at 764.

[16] *Re Herbage* [1985] *The Times*, October 25 (inferior court's refusal of bail should be challenged in High Court by procedure in Criminal Justice Act 1967, s.22 and not by application for judicial review). See also *R.* v. *Guildhall J.J. ex p. Prushinowski* [1985] *The Times*, December 14 in which Watkins L.J. expressed the tentative view that, in the absence of bias, the court had no power to review the exercise of justices' discretion under the Bail Act 1976.

[17] Under the *Edwards* v. *Bairstow* doctrine described in Chap. 3 above.

[18] See *R.* v. *Ipswich Crown Court ex p. Baldwin* [1981] 1 All E.R. 596.

[19] See, *e.g. R.* v. *Hillingdon L.B.C. ex p. Royco Homes Ltd.* [1974] Q.B. 720 and the *Merseyside Police* case above note 13.

tion, as much concerned to ensure the legality of public authority action as to provide redress *inter partes*. Particularly in cases where appeal lies to a higher echelon of the same bureaucracy,[20] it would be unfortunate if the salutary effect of the possibility of a challenge before the courts were to be diminished by an unnecessarily restrictive approach.

The possibility that the supervisory jurisdiction might be excluded entirely because of the availability of a statutory means of redress[21] now appears to be extremely remote. It arose in relation to the enforcement of positive statutory duties where, for example, the statute in question gave a right to complain to a minister or some other body with "default powers"[22] over the public authority concerned. In these circumstances it might be held[23] that complaint to the relevant person under the statute was the only means of redress. Occasionally, the court distinguished between non-feasance and malfeasance[24] but a proper appreciation of the context of these cases suggests that they are no longer relevant on this point. They were in fact ordinary civil actions for injunctions and declarations and in this context may be seen as attempts to press too far the remedies available for the protection of private law rights. If such cases were brought today, they would not fail on this ground but would be declared an abuse of process under the *O'Reilly* v *Mackman*[25] principle. There is no reason to suppose that mandamus would not be available to enforce such duties at the suit of some person sufficiently interested, nor that the existence of a statutory right of complaint to a minister or other administrative body would be regarded in the same light as a statutory right of appeal that might have to be pursued first.

C. Relevant Considerations

The variety and scope of statutory appeals makes it difficult to formulate general guidelines as to when proceeding by way of appli-

[20] See *Healey* v. *Minister of Health* [1955] 1 Q.B. 221.
[21] See Wade A.L. p. 626, and cases there cited.
[22] See above, Chap. 5, p. 183 *et seq*.
[23] See, *e.g. Pasmore* v. *Oswaldtwistle U.D.C.* [1898] A.C. 387.
[24] See *Wilford* v. *West Riding of Yorkshire C.C.* [1908] 1 K.B. 685, *Bradbury* v. *Enfield L.B.C.* [1967] 1 W.L.R. 1311.
[25] See Chap. 7 above. See also *R.* v. *Secretary of State for the Environment ex p. Ward* [1984] 1 W.L.R. 834 on default powers and applications for judicial review.

cation for judicial review may or may not be permitted. It seems probable that if the appeal is to a court, rather than to some other administrative body, application for judicial review is less likely to be permitted except where that procedure would be more expeditious and there are reasons why the matter should be treated as urgent.[26] If the decision is plainly wrong, application for judicial review may be permitted so that the matter can be corrected summarily.[27] It is difficult to conceive of the "disciplinary role" of the supervisory jurisdiction being of significance in relation to an inferior court whose judgments are in any event subject to appeal. This would seem to apply whether or not the appeal is on the merits or on point of law.

In relation to appeals to other bodies, it might be pointless to insist upon the complainant pursuing an appeal on the merits when the appellate body may have no greater legal expertise than the first instance tribunal, or when a decision by the court would be helpful to appellate tribunals.[28] Similarly, it may be desirable for the unlawfulness of the first instance tribunal to be publicly exposed in the courts rather than merely reversed, but the courts are unlikely to be willing to provide an applicant with the unnecessary luxury of certiorari when the wrong alleged would be bound to be corrected on appeal. Once again, the need to put matters right as a matter of urgency may override other considerations.[29]

In some cases where a statutory appeal is provided, it may be possible for a complainant to show that it is not a true "alternative" remedy. Although it is unlikely that the courts would permit a significant difference to develop between "persons aggrieved" and those with a "sufficient interest," there may well be cases in which a person will have a sufficient interest to apply for supervisory review although not being entitled to an appeal on the merits. Further, the jurisdiction of an appellate tribunal may be limited in such a way that it cannot deal appropriately with matters giving

[26] See *R.* v. *Huntingdon D.C. ex p. Cowan* [1984] 1 W.L.R. 501, but see also the *Ellis* case above.

[27] See Chap. 8, p. 306, note 24.

[28] See *Cowan* above in which Glidewell J. observed that the question of which was the more convenient and effective remedy should be judged in terms of the public interest, as well as the interests of the applicant.

[29] See the *Merseyside Police* case note 13 above. It remains to be seen whether this will ever be of assistance to those refused temporary leave to enter the U.K. especially since *Swati* (see note 13 above) allows a mere statement of the issue on which the immigration officer was "not satisfied" to be regarded as the 'reason' for the refusal of leave. *Cf. R.* v. *Mental Health Review Tribunal ex p. Pickering* [1986] 1 All E.R. 99 on the adequacy of "reasons."

grounds for judicial review. This may be by reason of its power being limited either to confirming or reversing a decision when the proper course would be to remit it to the first instance tribunal,[30] or where the "decision" of the first instance tribunal does not fall within the statutory definition of matters which may be made the subject of an appeal.[31] In such cases, there is no alternative to application for judicial review which may thus be pursued. It should be noted that recourse to an administrative or other appeal does not amount to a waiver of the right to have recourse to supervisory review.[32]

Finally, it would seem that some confusion is now arising in the Family Division between application for judicial review[33] and wardship, which is itself a prerogative jurisdiction. In *Re M. (minors)*[34] Sheldon J. concluded that where it was desired to challenge a local authority's decision in relation to children in its care on the basis of "*Wednesbury* unreasonableness,"[35] application for judicial review is the only means of proceeding. Such a view seems inconsistent with *Re T. (AJJ) (an infant)*[36] and does not seem to be wholly justified by the authorities relied upon.[37] Given the proce-

[30] See *Campbell* v. *Rochdale General Commissioners* [1975] 2 All E.R. 385; and *cf. Bone* v. *Mental Health Review Tribunal* [1985] 3 All E.R. 330 (appellate jurisdiction not designed to correct tribunal's failure to give reasons as required. Nolan J.'s suggestion that challenge should be by way of application for judicial review followed in *R.* v. *Mental Health Review Tribunal ex p. Clatworthy* [1985] 3 All E.R. 699).

[31] See, *e.g. Streames* v. *Copping* [1985] 2 W.L.R. 993 (no appeal by case stated under Magistrates' Courts Act 1980, s.111(1) unless justices have reached final determination on matter. But application for judicial review may be appropriate to raise jurisdictional points where no final determination reached); *R.* v. *Special Commissioner ex p. Stipplechoice Ltd.* [1985] 2 All E.R. 465 (no appeal against grant of leave by commissioner to issue assessment out of time: leave to apply for judicial review granted). See also *R.* v. *Hallstrom ex p. W.* [1985] 3 All E.R. 775 in which the point of law arising from the decision of a mental health review tribunal which could have been the subject of appeal was not the jurisdictional issue raised on an application for judicial review.

[32] Suggested in *Ridge* v. *Baldwin* [1964] A.C. 40 and rejected by the House of Lords. See also Ord. 53, r. 3(8), power to adjourn application where issue subject to appeal to be brought within a prescribed time.

[33] See *R.* v. *Dover Magistrates' Court ex p. Kidner* [1983] 1 All E.R. 475 where it was recommended that applications for judicial review concerning matrimonial and family matters should be dealt with by a judge of the Family Division.

[34] (1986) 130 Sol. Jnl. 203. See also New L.J. (1986) Vol. 136, p. 393.

[35] *Associated Provincial Picture Houses* v. *Wednesbury Corporation* [1948] 1 K.B. 223. See Chap. 5 above.

[36] [1970] Ch. 668.

[37] *A.* v. *Liverpool City Council* [1982] A.C. 363 and *Re W.* (*a minor*) [1985] A.C. 791.

dural advantages of wardship[38] it is questionable whether it is appropriate for the wardship jurisdiction to be so circumscribed. This was not a development anticipated by the Law Commission.[39]

[38] See S. M. Cretney, Principles of Family Law (4th ed.), p. 570.
[39] Report on Remedies in Adminstrative Law (Law Comm. 73), Cmnd. 6407 (1976).

INDEX

ADMINISTRATIVE LAW,
  judicial review as part of, 3 n1, 15–17, 22–23
ADMINISTRATIVE TRIBUNALS,
  jurisdictional error by, 144–152.
  See also STATUTORY TRIBUNALS.
ADOPTION, 209 n21, 220
APPEAL,
  case stated, by, 42 n41
    supervisory review, contrasted with, 311 n3, 312
  courts, to
    courts, from, 42–44
    other public authorities, from, 44–45
    statutory tribunals, from, 44
  merits, on, 57–58
  ouster of, 47–48
  point of law, on, 44, 45, 46, 58–60
  procedure, choice of, 311–312
  rehearing, by, 42
  statutory tribunals, to, 11, 125–127
  void decision, against, 240–241.
  See also APPELLATE REVIEW.
APPELLATE REVIEW, 41–45
  collateral challenge, and, 68
  discretionary power, and, 45, 170–171, 204–205
  error of law, fact and degree, of, 130–131
  inferior courts, and, 155–157
  irregular or unfair procedure, of, 208, 240–241, 242
  royal prerogative, and, 80–81
  superior courts, and, 152–153
  supervisory review and,
    choice between, 311–318
    distinguished, 56–65, 311
    standing to initiate, 312
  supervisory review impliedly excluded by, 315.
  See also APPEAL.
APPLICATION FOR JUDICIAL REVIEW,
  appeal and, 311–318
  breaches of duty remediable only by, 259, 262 n65
  civil action, when available as alternative to, 259–261, 262 n66
APPLICATION FOR JUDICIAL REVIEW—*cont.*
  civil proceedings, whether including, 296
  Crown and, 272, 289, 292
  default powers, whether impliedly ousted by, 315
  direct challenge, as, 38, 45–46
  evidence in, 309
  Law Commission recommendations as to. *See* LAW COMMISSION.
  leave to make, requirement for, 253, 306
  originating summons, power to treat as if commenced by, 309
  prosecution, when available as alternative to, 259–260, 262 n66
  remedies available in. *See* CERTIORARI; DAMAGES; DECLARATION; DISCRETIONARY REMEDIES; INJUNCTION; MANDAMUS; PREROGATIVE REMEDIES; PROHIBITION.
  res judicata applicable in? 302
  scope of, 253, 270, 297
  standing to make. *See* LOCUS STANDI.
  time limits in. *See* TIME LIMITS.
  wardship and, 317
  writ, power to treat as if commenced by, 309
  wrongs not remediable by, 259, 261
ARMED FORCES, 12, 75–76
ATTORNEY-GENERAL,
  Charitable Trusts, supervision of, 267 n91
  Crown, legally representing, 248 n6, 272 n18
  relator actions, 13, 132 n18, 248, 249
    discretion in, 248 n8
AUDI ALTERAM PARTEM. *See* FAIR HEARING; NATURAL JUSTICE.

BAD FAITH, 53 n93e, 55, 71, 79, 89–90, 192–193. *See also* MISFEASANCE IN PUBLIC OFFICE.
BIAS, RULE AGAINST, 214, 236–240
  actual bias, 236, 238, 239
  exclusion of challenge, 237–238

BIAS, RULE AGAINST—*cont.*
legal necessity, 238
nemo iudex in causa sua, 231
pecuniary bias, 236, 238–239
"policy bias", 237
"real likelihood" of bias, 236, 239–240
separate head of natural justice? 236
waiver, 242–243
BREACH OF STATUTORY DUTY,
public authority, duty cast exclusively upon, 266–268
public or private law, whether, 264
sounding in damages, whether, 264–265
BRITISH BROADCASTING CORPORATION, 7, 13, 225 n24

CAPACITY, LEGAL. *See* LEGAL CAPACITY OF PUBLIC AUTHORITIES.
CASE STATED. *See* APPEAL.
CENTRAL CRIMINAL COURT, 153
CENTRAL GOVERNMENT. *See* GOVERNMENT, CENTRAL.
CERTIORARI, 38, 248, 253, 287–289. *See also* DISCRETIONARY REMEDIES.
CHANCERY, COURT OF, 248
CHARITABLE TRUSTS,
Attorney-General, supervision of by, 267 n91
public authorities, compared to, 4, 172, 267 n91
CHOICE OF MACHINERY. *See* APPELLATE REVIEW; SUPERVISORY REVIEW.
CIRCULARS, DEPARTMENTAL,
whether errors in carry *ultra vires*, 91, 301
CIVIL PROCEEDINGS. *See* PRIVATE LAW.
COLLATERAL CHALLENGE,
availability of, 65–69, 201
effect of, 73–74
forms of, 30–32
irregular or unfair procedure, to, 207, 240, 242
meaning of, 29–30, 257
not available, 65–67, 69–73
void and voidable decisions, to, 63, 65–69
COLLATERAL ISSUE,
meaning of, 138
tests for, 138–139
COMPULSORY PURCHASE,
challenge, statutory basis of, 56
error of law and, 108–109

COMPULSORY PURCHASE—*cont.*
exclusion of challenge, 54–55
inquiries, public, 11, 225–226
jurisdictional error and, 149–150
statutory purpose, 174
CONDITIONS ATTACHED TO LICENCES,
planning, 176–177, 202–203
"remit", and, 25–27, 168
severability of, 199 n60
validity of, 173 n21, 176–177, 180
CONSEIL D'ETAT, 245 n1
CONTEMPT OF COURT,
collateral challenge, and, 70
declaration, not contempt to disregard, 302
national security, and, 79–80
prohibition, contempt to disregard, 287
CONTRACT,
discretionary remedies, availability of, 290–291
fettering by. *See* FETTERING BY CONTRACT.
government, 13, 78
public authority,
breach by, 84–85, 86, 196–198, 256
capacity of, 84–85
service, of, 118–119, 125–126
void,
when relevant consideration, 198, 220
CORONER'S COURT, 157–158
COUNTY COURT,
appeal from, 42
inferior court, as, 153–154
review of, 33–35, 156–157
superior court, as, 154
COURT OF APPEAL,
appeal from, 42–43
appeal to,
Civil Division, 42
Criminal Division, 43
original jurisdiction of, 152 n18
statutory tribunals, appeal from, 44, 125–126
supervisory review, and, 37, 43, 152–153
COURTS,
appeals to and from. *See* APPEAL.
constitutional position of, 14, 15–17, 158–164, 169–171, 172, 183–90
linesmen, as, 23–27

COURTS—*cont.*
official power, as wielding, 9.
See also INFERIOR COURTS; SUPERIOR COURTS; *courts by name*.
COURTS-MARTIAL APPEAL COURT, 153
CRIMINAL LIABILITY OF PUBLIC AUTHORITIES, 14, 83–84, 256
CROWN,
application for judicial review in matter affecting, 272, 289, 292
declaration in matter affecting, 272, 296–298
immunity of, 85
injunction in matter affecting, 272, 296
legal capacity of, 12, 78
liability of, 12
prerogative powers of. *See* ROYAL PREROGATIVE.
public law rights reposing in, 248 n6
CROWN COURT,
appeal from, 42–43
jurisdiction of,
administrative, 45, 205
criminal, 42–43
superior court, as, 153
supervisory review, subject to, 153

DAMAGES,
application for judicial review, available in, 253 n35, 303
breach of statutory duty sounding in? 265
Crown, available in action against, 296
inferior court judges, against, 71–73
magistrates, against, 72 n79
maladministration not sounding in, 284 n76, 303
misfeasance in public office, for, 89
negligent failure to exercise power, for, 87–88
private law right established by award of, 256, 263, 304 n13
superior court judges, against, 71
ultra vires contracts, breach of, for, 84–85
DECLARATION,
application for judicial review, available in, 38–39, 252, 269, 296
Crown, against, 251, 272, 296–298
origins of, 249, 299
DE FACTO OFFICERS AND JUDGES, 70–71
DEFAULT POWERS, 19, 185–188
supervisory review, whether ousting, 315
DEGREE, QUESTION OF. *See* ERROR OF LAW.
DELEGATED LEGISLATION,
collateral challenge to, 66
natural justice, and, 228–229
Order in Council,
prerogative, 13, 75–76
statutory, 13
reviewability of, 9, 228
remedies, availability of, 289 n21, 297
statutory instrument, 9
DELEGATION OF DISCRETION, 194–195
DIRECT CHALLENGE,
appellate review, by way of, 41–46
Crown action, to, 80–81
discretionary action, to, 201, 204–205
forms of, 32–37
irregular or unfair procedure, to, 207–208, 240, 241–242
meaning of, 30, 32. *See also* REMIT ISSUE.
ouster of, 46–56
remedies available by way of, 38–39, 45–46, 57–60
supervisory review, by way of, 37–41
DIRECTORY. *See* MANDATORY AND DIRECTORY REQUIREMENTS.
DISCRETIONARY POWERS,
courts, of. *See* DISCRETIONARY REMEDIES; JUDICIAL DISCRETION.
duties, and. *See* POWERS AND DUTIES.
failure to exercise, liability for, 87–89
misuse of, liability for, 71–73, 87–90
"remit", and, 25–27
review of exercise of,
prerogative powers. *See* ROYAL PREROGATIVE.
statutory powers. *See* DELEGATION OF DISCRETION; FETTERING BY CONTRACT; FETTERING BY POLICY; RELEVANT AND IRRELEVANT CONSIDERATIONS; STATUTORY PURPOSE.
DISCRETIONARY REMEDIES,
factors affecting availability of,
conduct of applicant, 281
general considerations, 285
remedy futile, 282

DISCRETIONARY REMEDIES—*cont.*
factors affecting availability of—*cont.*
remedy unnecessary, 283
sufficiency of applicant's interest, 273–278, 282
natural justice, and, 241
private law, in, 249, 290.
See also CERTIORARI; DECLARATION; INJUNCTION; MANDAMUS; PROHIBITION.
DISMISSAL,
natural justice and, 224–225
DISPROPORTIONALITY, 181
DISTRICT AUDITOR, 186
DIVISIONAL COURT. *See* HIGH COURT.
DOUBLE JEOPARDY, 243

EDUCATION,
authorities, 6–7
Burnham Committee, membership of, 204 n84
grant purposes, ordinary residence for, 105, 146
pupil's home, distance of school from, 31 n7, 199 n56
schools,
closure of, 219
restructuring of, 186–188, 208, 210
study, full time course of, 146
teachers, dismissal of, 174, 193, 223 n15
universities, 4, 273
ELECTION COURTS, 154
EMPLOYMENT APPEAL TRIBUNAL, 11, 118–119, 124–126
ERROR OF LAW,
appeal against. *See* APPEAL; APPELLATE REVIEW.
basis of judicial review, as, 46
correction, methods of, 58–60
degree, and question of, 95–96, 108–109, 115, 122, 148–149
discretion, in exercise of, 128, 179–180, 181–182, 204–205
error of application as, 108–127, 147–150
Edwards v. *Bairstow* doctrine, 114–127, 130, 131, 147–149, 162–164, 181–182, 189
"open-texture" of words, 103–104, 108–109
error of fact as, 97–100, 150–152.
See also "NO EVIDENCE" RULE.
ERROR OF LAW—*cont.*
jurisdictional. *See* JURISDICTIONAL ERROR.
meaning of (summary), 127–128
misstatement of law as, 100–108, 144–147
"legal terms of art", 102–103
"ordinary words", 103–108
natural justice, and, 240
procedural irregularity as, 208
ERROR ON THE FACE OF THE RECORD,
contemporary obsolescence of, 41, 166–167
decision invalid but *intra vires*,
declaration ineffective remedy, 302
history of, 41, 164
law or fact? 165
ouster of jurisdiction to correct, 48–49
record, meaning of, 164–165
void or voidable? 61
ESTOPPEL, 198–200. *See also* DOUBLE JEOPARDY; RES JUDICATA.
EVIDENCE,
application for judicial review, in, 309, 314
EXCHEQUER, COURT OF, 249

FACT, QUESTION OF,
meaning of statutory words as, 103–108
primary facts, 93–94, 110 n76, 148
supervisory review not suitable to resolve? 152
threshold jurisdictional issues, in, 135 n27.
See also ERROR OF LAW.
FAIR HEARING,
audi alteram partem, 231
cross-examination, 234
material not disclosed, 232–233
oral? 233–234
prior notice of opposing case, 231–232
private consultations and, 225–226
reasons for decisions,
adequacy of, 211–212, 316 n29
duty to give, 211, 234–236
representation, 234
when required? *See* NATURAL JUSTICE.
witnesses, right to call, 234.
See also BIAS, RULE AGAINST.
FETTERING BY CONTRACT, 84, 196–198, 200, 220
FETTERING BY POLICY, 195–196, 220

FOREIGN COMPENSATION COMMISSION, 49, 51, 102, 140–141, 144
FRAUD. *See* BAD FAITH.

GOVERNMENT, CENTRAL,
Crown, and, 12. *See also* ROYAL PREROGATIVE.
functions, 5–6
judicial review, use of, 19
local authorities, relations with, 7, 19
Parliament, and, 5, 15–16, 18
police, and, 8
public corporations, relations with, 8. *See also* DEFAULT POWERS.
GOVERNMENT, LOCAL. *See* LOCAL AUTHORITIES.

HABEAS CORPUS, 38 n21, 248 n5
HEARINGS. *See* FAIR HEARING.
HIGH COURT,
appeal from, 42–43
appeal to, 42–43, 44, 45
creation of, 37 n16
Divisional Court of, 37 n16
King's Bench, Court of, 37, 38, 248
Queen's (King's) Bench Division, "Crown side", 296
superior court, as, 152
supervisory jurisdiction, historical basis of, 37, 38, 41, 164
HOUSE OF LORDS,
appellate jurisdiction of, 43, 152
controversial decisions of, 183–190
no judicial review of decisions of, 9, 37–38
HOUSING,
authorities, 6, 7
council houses,
management, 132–133
rents, 30–31, 65–66, 175–176
tenant's "right to buy", 188
homeless persons, 145, 149, 182 n62, 255, 266 n89, 278 n47, 282, 291 n34, 300 n84

IMMIGRATION,
adjudicators, 10
illegal, 151–152, 219
Immigration Appeal Tribunal, 11, 126 nn58, 59
leave, refusal of,
extension, refusal of, 179 n46, 219 n87, 232 n71
fair hearing before, 218, 233 n77
IMMIGRATION—*cont.*
leave, refusal of—*cont.*
reasons for, 211 nn35, 40, 316 n29
supervisory or appellate review, challenge by, 313 n13
study, for, 146
"INCIDENTAL OR CONSEQUENTIAL", 131–133
INDEPENDENT BROADCASTING AUTHORITY, 195 n36,
INDUSTRIAL TRIBUNALS, 10, 11, 118, 125–126
INFERIOR COURTS,
application for judicial review against decisions of, 273, 285, 289
contempt of, 70 n62
judicial immunity and, 71–73
meaning of, 34 n11, 152–154
record, of, 70 n62
supervisory review of, 154–158, 159. *See also courts by name*.
INJUNCTION,
application for judicial review,
availability by way of, 252, 269–270
Crown, availability of injunction against, 81, 251, 295
role of injunction in, 293–296
Attorney-General,
injunction at suit of, or at relation of, 248
direct challenge, as remedy by way of, 38–39
local authority,
application for injunction in own right, 173–174, 202, 294
standing in application for injunction, 279–280
private law,
availability of injunction in, 249, 262–265, 290
procedural advantages of, 251
quo warranto, statutory form of replacing, 248 n5, 270 n4, 286
types of, 249 n58.
See also DISCRETIONARY REMEDIES.
INLAND REVENUE,
commissioners of income tax, 10, 126–127, 241 n32
informal agreements by, enforceability of, 198, 220
preliminary hearings by, 223 n11
tax concessions, extra-statutory, 13–14, 78

Inland Revenue—*cont.*
tax cases, error of law in, 114–115, 119–121
V.A.T. tribunals, 120
Inquiries, Statutory, 11
fair hearing at, 225–227
reasons for ministerial decisions taken after, 207, 211–212
Invalidity. *See* Void and Voidable.
Irregular Procedure, 207–213
consequence of. *See* Mandatory and Directory Requirements.
judicial review of, 207–208
penal context, in, 209
reasons,
duty to give, 207
failure to give, 211–212
Irrelevant Considerations. *See* Relevant and Irrelevant Considerations.
Irrevocable Action. *See* Revocability.

Judicature Acts, 37 n16, 249, 269
Judicial Discretion,
appeal against exercise of, 204
remedies, as to grant of. *See* Discretionary Remedies.
Judicial Function,
distinguished from non-judicial,
difficulty of distinction, 40
significance of distinction, 40, 215–216, 218, 237
Judicial Immunity, 67, 71–73
Judicial Notice, 103
Judicial Review,
constitutional propriety of, 15–17, 158–164, 169–171, 172–173, 183–190, 229–230
meaning of, 3, 9, 14–15
need for, 15–23.
See also Appellate Review; Application for Judicial Review; Remedies; Supervisory Review.
Jurisdiction,
decide, to, 136–137, 142–143
err, to, 33–34, 137
pure theory of, 137 n34
want or excess of, 39–40, 71–73.
See also Jurisdictional Error.
Jurisdictional Error,
administrative tribunals and authorities, by, 144–152
Jurisdictional Error—*cont.*
"*Anisminic* presumption", 158 *et passim*
courts, by, 152–158
error of fact not commonly, 40–41, 135 n27, 140, 151–152
error of law as, 40, 46, 140–144 *et seq.*, 180, 181–182
meaning of, 40, 136–137
"substantive", 130, 136–164
"threshold", 130, 134–136
Justices of the Peace. *See* Magistrates.
Justiciability, 76–79, 189–190, 272, 290

"King Can Do No Wrong", 12 n30
King's Bench, Court of. *See* High Court.

Law Commission,
recommendations of, 247, 252–254, 269, 275, 295, 303, 307
statutory reforms not following, 275, 308
Law, Error of. *See* Error of Law.
Legal Capacity of Public Authorities,
Crown, 12, 78, 85
statutory authorities,
contract, 84–85, 196–198
crime, 83–84
tort, 82–83, 86
wrongs, to commit, 14, 256
Legal Representation, 234
Legitimate Expectation,
express promise, 218–219
only to hearing? 219–221
public law, in, 255
regular practice, 219
"Liability Issue",
collateral challenge and, 30–32, 257, 259
defined, 15
liability pure and simple,
meaning of, 256–257
procedures for resolving, choice of, 259–261
remit pure and simple, contrasted with, 258
Licensing,
amusement arcade permit, 205 n91
appeals, 45, 59–60, 205
aviation, 173

LICENSING—*cont.*
cinemas and films, 180, 194, 201 n67
conditions. *See* CONDITIONS ATTACHED TO LICENCES.
firearms certificate, 44, 233 n79
food, sale of, 45 n60
import, 89
liquor, 174–175, 238 n5
market trading, 176, 217
natural justice, and, 217–219, 222, 233–234, 237
offensive trades, 45 n60
planning permission. *See* PLANNING.
public entertainment, 25–26, 45, 217
revocation of licences, 174–175, 176, 203, 217
street trading, 45
television, 176
LOCAL AUTHORITIES,
application for judicial review of decisions of, 273
audit. *See* DISTRICT AUDITOR.
Central Government, and, 7, 19, 186–188, 191
compulsory purchase powers. *See* COMPULSORY PUCHASE.
default powers, and. *See* DEFAULT POWERS.
delegation by, 194
education. *See* EDUCATION.
functions of, 6–7, 45
housing. *See* HOUSING.
injunctions,
application for in own right, 294
standing, requirement of, 279–280
liability. *See* CONTRACT; CRIMINAL LIABILITY OF PUBLIC AUTHORITIES; TORT.
licensing powers. *See* LICENSING.
planning. *See* PLANNING.
rates. *See* RATES.
LOCUS STANDI,
application for judicial review,
discretion of court, 275, 290–291, 298
Law Commission recommendations, 275
not exclusively a threshold issue, 275–276
person aggrieved, sufficient interest and, 276–277, 312, 316
sufficient interest, 22, 61, 275–279, 282
LOCUS STANDI—*cont.*
injunction, private law,
Attorney-General and, 132 n18, 248
private individual and, 250 n14, 273

MAGISTRATES,
administrative functions of, 45, 205
courts,
appeal from, 42–43
appeal to, 45, 205
supervisory review of, 154, 158 n53
judicial immunity of, 71–73
MALICE. *See* BAD FAITH.
MANDAMUS, 38–39, 59, 248, 253, 289–293. *See also* DISCRETIONARY REMEDIES.
MANDATORY AND DIRECTORY REQUIREMENTS,
consequences of breach of,
directory, 212–213
mandatory, 207–208
definition of, 207
distinction between, 208–210
"implied mandatory requirements", 214
"no substantial prejudice", 210–212, 242
"substantial compliance", 210–212
MENTAL HEALTH REVIEW TRIBUNALS,
judicial immunity of, 67 n51
judicial review of, procedure for, 317 n30
reasons, failure to give, 211–212, 316 n29
MINISTERS, 5–6
default powers of. *See* DEFAULT POWERS.
delegation by, 194
discretionary powers of. *See* DISCRETIONARY POWERS.
MISFEASANCE IN PUBLIC OFFICE, 89–90. *See also* BAD FAITH.

NATIONALISED INDUSTRIES. *See* PUBLIC CORPORATIONS.
NATIONAL SECURITY,
judicial review, as bar to,
royal prerogative, 76, 78–80
statutory powers, 189 n96
justiciable issue, as, 79–80
NATIONAL TRUST, 4

NATURAL JUSTICE,
bias, rule against. *See* BIAS, RULE AGAINST.
contrary intention in statute, 221–229
delegated legislation, and, 228–229
denial of,
bases of challenge, 240–241
effect: void or voidable? 240–241, 241–243
waiver, 242–243
employment, and, 224–225
fair hearing,
when required? 215–230.
See generally FAIR HEARING.
fairness, as, 214, 218
legitimate expectation. *See* LEGITIMATE EXPECTATION.
presumption of statutory interpretation, as, 214
"property rights or privileges of persons", 215–218
public inquiries, and, 225–227
royal prerogative, and, 78
NEMO IUDEX IN CAUSA SUA. *See* BIAS, RULE AGAINST.
"NO EVIDENCE" RULE, 97–100, 150–152

OFFICE, PUBLIC, 224
OFFICIAL POWER,
legal limits of, 14–15, 23–27
meaning of, 3
sketch of, 5–14.
See also DISCRETIONARY POWERS; JURISDICTION; POWERS AND DUTIES.
ORIGINATING SUMMONS,
abuse or misuse of process, when, 255, 262 n71
action commenced by, 254
application for judicial review continuing as if commenced by, 309
OUSTER CLAUSES,
"anything which purports to be a determination", 52
bad faith, and, 53 n93e, 55
"conclusive", 52–54
"decisions as to jurisdiction", 51 n83
finality clauses, 47–48
"no certiorari", 48–49
"no other procedure", 51 n81
"shall not be questioned", 49–52
time-limited, 54–56, 69
Tribunal and Inquiries Acts and, 51

OUSTER CLAUSES—*cont.*
void decisions, and, 50, 55–56, 62, 69

PARLIAMENT,
Central Government, and, 5, 15–16, 18–19
judicial review jurisdiction, as source of, 29, 41–46, 170–171
legislative intent, courts and, 159–161, 170, 183–190, 214, 215, 221–230.
See also STATUTORY INTERPRETATION; STATUTORY PURPOSE.
sovereignty of, 5
PASSPORTS, 13, 78
PATENT ERROR. *See* ERROR ON THE FACE OF THE RECORD.
PERSON AGGRIEVED. *See* LOCUS STANDI.
PLANNING,
authorities, 7
conditions, 176–177, 202
decisions, legal challenge to,
appeal on point of law, 59–60
"statutory ultra vires", 56
supervisory review, 55 n94
natural justice, and, 222, 237
permission, refusal of, 195, 199, 209, 210, 222, 237
"planning purpose", 171 n10, 176–177
POLICE,
arming of, 20
authorities, 8
dismissal procedures, 215–216, 224 n18
"POLICY ISSUES",
justiciability. *See* JUSTICIABILITY.
See also DISCRETIONARY POWERS.
law and policy, boundary between, 25–27, 183–190
meaning of, 168
natural justice, and, 225–227, 237
POWERS AND DUTIES,
fiduciary nature of, 14–15, 87, 172, 185.
See also DISCRETIONARY POWERS.
PREROGATIVE REMEDIES, 38. *See also* CERTIORARI; HABEAS CORPUS; MANDAMUS; PROHIBITION; QUO WARRANTO.

PREROGATIVE REMEDIES—*cont.*
application for judicial review, influencing scope of, 253, 270, 297
Judicature Acts, excluded from, 249 n11
writs, in form of, 248
PREROGATIVE, ROYAL. *See* ROYAL PREROGATIVE.
PRISONS,
death in custody, 157 n52, 158 n53
parole, natural justice and, 216 n68, 220 n94, 236 n93
prison discipline, natural justice and, 232 n70, 234 nn80–82
prisoner's right of access to courts, 133
prison officer, dismissal of, 179 n46
prison rules, misconstruction of, 147 n80
security considerations, 189 n96
PRIVATE LAW,
civil proceedings,
abuse of process to initiate, 255, 262
application for judicial review classifiable as? 296
nineteenth century reforms of, 249
procedural advantages of, 251
remedies available in, 249–250
public law, distinguished from, 252, 254–256
rights in, 254, 255, 264–265
damages, availability of, as hallmark, 256, 263
"PROCEDURAL IMPROPRIETY", 91. *See also* IRREGULAR PROCEDURE; NATURAL JUSTICE.
PROCEEDINGS, FORM OF. *See* APPELLATE REVIEW; APPLICATION FOR JUDICIAL REVIEW; ORIGINATING SUMMONS; SUPERVISORY REVIEW; WRIT.
PROHIBITION, 38–39, 248, 253, 287–289. *See also* DISCRETIONARY REMEDIES.
PUBLIC AUTHORITY,
characteristics of, 3–5
fiduciary duty of, 14–15, 87, 172. *See also public authorities by name*.
PUBLIC CORPORATIONS,
area health authorities, 197 n48, 225 n25, 268 n95, 301
PUBLIC CORPORATIONS—*cont.*
British Broadcasting Corporation. *See* BRITISH BROADCASTING CORPORATION.
Civil Aviation Authority, 8, 173
generally, 7–8
Independent Broadcasting Authority. *See* INDEPENDENT BROADCASTING AUTHORITY.
Milk Marketing Board, 8, 178
National Coal Board, 268 n93
Post Office, 7, 86 n55
PUBLIC INQUIRIES. *See* INQUIRIES, STATUTORY.
PUBLIC INTEREST IMMUNITY, 79
PUBLIC LAW,
actio popularis as purest form of, 274
application for judicial review as a branch of, 270, 298
criminal law as creating duties in, 264
private law, distinguished from, 252, 254–255, 256
rights in, 254
statutory duties, breach of, remediable only in? 265
PURPOSE, STATUTORY. *See* STATUTORY PURPOSE.

QUEEN'S BENCH DIVISION. *See* HIGH COURT.
QUO WARRANTO,
statutory injunction replacing information in form of, 270 n4, 284 n5, 286

RATES,
failure to set, 186 n81. *See also* DISTRICT AUDITOR.
local authority housing, and, 175–176
"rate capping", 7, 191
ratepayers,
fiduciary duty of rating authority to, 172, 185
rate support grant, 196, 217 n75
rating appeals, 45 n61, 110–111, 205 n91
refund of, 191
REASONS FOR DECISIONS. *See* FAIR HEARING.
RECORD. *See* ERROR ON THE FACE OF THE RECORD.
RELATOR ACTIONS. *See* ATTORNEY-GENERAL.

RELEVANT AND IRRELEVANT CONSIDERATIONS,
combination of, 190–191
effect of irrelevant considerations, 192–193, 201–205
particular varieties of irrelevant consideration. *See* DELEGATION OF DISCRETION; FETTERING BY CONTRACT; FETTERING BY POLICY.
relevant to what? 178
statute, relevant considerations prescribed by, 179
"*Wednesbury* unreasonableness" as irrelevant consideration, 179–183, 185–188
REMEDIES. *See* CERTIORARI; DAMAGES; DECLARATION; DISCRETIONARY REMEDIES; INJUNCTION; MANDAMUS; PREROGATIVE REMEDIES; PROHIBITION.
"REMIT",
appeal, and, 33–34, 43, 45–46, 130–131, 204–205
error of law, and, 46
irregular or unfair procedure, and, 207–208, 240–241
meaning of, 14–15, 23–27, 33–35, 245, 257–258, 266
patent error, and, 41, 129
ultra vires/want of jurisdiction, and, 39–40, 129, 201
"REMIT ISSUE",
direct and collateral challenges,
choice of procedure, 259–262, 267–268
distinction between, 29–37, 256–259.
See also COLLATERAL CHALLENGE; DIRECT CHALLENGE.
meaning of, 15, 245, 257–258, 266
RENT,
council house. *See* HOUSING.
rent assessment committees, 10, 239 n14
RES JUDICATA,
application for judicial review and, 200 n62, 302
decisions of public authorities other than courts, whether applicable to, 199
RESTRICTIVE PRACTICES COURT, 153
REVENUE. *See* INLAND REVENUE.
REVIEW. *See* APPELLATE REVIEW; JUDICIAL REVIEW; SUPERVISORY REVIEW.
REVOCABILITY,
decisions following review for misuse of discretion, and, 201–204
decisions following review of unfairness, and, 228
legitimate expectation, and, 219–221
private rights, and, 200 n62
ROYAL PREROGATIVE,
appellate review, and, 80–81. *See also* WARDSHIP.
courts' role in defining extent of, 74–75
Crown's legal capacity, contrasted with, 12, 13–14, 78
definition of, 12
extent of, 12–13, 74–75
judicial review of exercise of, 74–80
national security, and, 78–80
Order in Council, 13
supervisory review, and, 81

SEVERANCE, 199 n60
SOCIAL SECURITY COMMISSIONERS,
appeals from, 44, 117, 126
appeals to, 11, 125, 126
reasons, duty to give? 235
SPECIFIC PERFORMANCE, 290
STANDING. *See* LOCUS STANDI.
STATUTORY INTERPRETATION,
courts or specialist tribunals, for? 163–164, 170
"legal terms of art", 102–103
"ordinary words", 103–108
ouster clauses, restrictive construction of, 46–52
presumptions of legislative intent,
duty to act fairly, 214, 215, 221–230
errors of law jurisdictional ("*Anisminic* presumption"), 143–144, 159–161
expressio unius est exclusio alterius, 222
no taxation without clear Parliamentary authority, 176
"purpose axiom", 171–173.
See also STATUTORY PURPOSE.
STATUTORY PURPOSE,
"purpose axiom", 171–173
purpose expressed in statute, 173–174, 184–185

STATUTORY PURPOSE—*cont.*
purpose to be inferred, 174–177, 185–190
Renton Committee recommendations, 177 n44
STATUTORY TRIBUNALS,
appeals from and to. *See* APPEAL.
generally, 9–11, 44
members,
lay element, 113
specialised knowledge of, 125–126, 163–164
tortious liability of, 67 n51
procedural rules, 207–212, 231
reasons, duty to give, 207, 211–212, 234–236
supervisory review of. *See* SUPERVISORY REVIEW.
See also tribunals by name; INLAND REVENUE; RENT.
SUBJECTIVE LANGUAGE, 186–187
SUPERIOR COURTS,
contempt of, 70
judicial immunity and, 71
meaning of, 34 n11, 152–154
record, of, 70 n62
supervisory review, not subject to, 152–153.
See also courts by name.
SUPERVISORY REVIEW,
alternative remedy impliedly excluding, 315
appellate review and,
choice between, 312–317
compared, 56–65, 312
standing to initiate, 312, 316
bases of,
jurisdictional error/*ultra vires*, 39–40. *See also* JURISDICTIONAL ERROR; ULTRA VIRES.
patent error, 41.
See also ERROR ON THE FACE OF THE RECORD.
constitutional propriety of, 15–23, 158–164, 169–171, 183–190
courts, of, 152–158
discretionary power, and, 201–204
error of law as ground for, 46.
See also ERROR ON THE FACE OF THE RECORD; JURISDICTIONAL ERROR.
irregular procedure, of, 207–208
SUPERVISORY REVIEW—*cont.*
meaning of, 37–39
Royal Prerogative and. *See* ROYAL PREROGATIVE.
statutory tribunals and administrative authorities, of, 144–152
unfair procedure, of, 240–243
wardship and, 317–318
SUPPLEMENTARY BENEFIT APPEAL TRIBUNALS, 10, 125 n54, 147 n80

TAX. *See* INLAND REVENUE.
"THRESHOLD" JURISDICTIONAL ISSUES, 134–136
TIME LIMITS,
application for judicial review, in, 251, 253, 254, 307–309
breach of by public authorities in performance of statutory duties, 209, 211
civil proceedings, in, 251, 253, 254
collateral challenge, and, 69
ouster clauses, in, 54–56
TORT,
breach of statutory duty remediable in? 264–265
capacity of public authorities to commit, 82–83, 256
"inevitable injury", 86
judicial liability in, 71–72
negligent failure to exercise power as, 87–89.
See also MISFEASANCE IN PUBLIC OFFICE.
TOWN AND COUNTRY PLANNING. *See* PLANNING.
TRANSPORT,
authorities, transfer of responsibility between, 217 n75
fares policy, 184–185
incidental and consequential powers, 24, 132
school children, of, 31 n7, 199 n56
Transport Tribunal, 126 n58

ULTRA VIRES,
discretionary powers, and, 201–204
incidental and consequential, acts beyond, 129–130, 131–133
irregular procedure as, 208
statutory formula, 56, 150, 208, 211, 242
unfair procedure as, 240

ULTRA VIRES—*cont.*
want of jurisdiction, compared with, 39–40.
See also JURISDICTIONAL ERROR; "REMIT"; "REMIT ISSUE".
UNFAIRNESS. *See* NATURAL JUSTICE.
UNIVERSITIES,
public authorities, as, 4
supervisory review not available in relation to, 273
UNREASONABLENESS. *See* RELEVANT AND IRRELEVANT CONSIDERATIONS.

VISITOR,
meaning of, 4 n6
supervisory review of decisions of, 273, 290 n28
VOID AND VOIDABLE,
appeal against void decision, 240–241
collateral challenge, and, 63, 65–68
generally, 61–65
natural justice, and, 240–243

VOID AND VOIDABLE—*cont.*
ouster clauses and nullity, 50, 62

WAIVER, 242–243
WARDSHIP,
appeal, and, 80–81
application for judicial review, and, 317–318
WITNESSES,
absence of witness statement, error of law and, 98–99
primary facts and, 94
right to call as constituent of fair hearing, 234
WONDERLAND,
Alice in, 24
WRIT,
abuse or misuse of process to initiate action by, when, 255, 262 n71
action commenced by, 254
application for judicial review continuing as if commenced by, 309
procedural advantages of, 251